Socio-Legal Studies

Edited by
PHILIP A. THOMAS

Dartmouth

Aldershot • Brookfield USA • Singapore • Sydney

Published by
Dartmouth Publishing Company Limited
Gower House
Croft Road
Aldershot
Hants GU11 3HR
England

Dartmouth Publishing Company
Old Post Road
Brookfield
Vermont 05036
USA

British Library Cataloguing in Publication Data
Socio-legal studies
    1.Sociological jurisprudence 2.Law - Social aspects - Great
    Britain
    I.Thomas, Philip A. (Philip Aneurin), 1940-
    340.1'15

Library of Congress Cataloging-in-Publication Data
Socio-legal studies / [edited by] Philip A. Thomas.
        p.   cm.
    Includes bibliographical references.
    ISBN 1-85521-717-1 (hb) 1-85521-968 9 (pb)
    1. Sociological jurisprudence. 2. Sociological jurisprudence-
-Research. I. Thomas, Philip A. (Philip Aneurin)
    K370.S65   1997
    340'.115--dc21   96-52819
                                                                     CIP

ISBN 1 85521 717 1 (hbk)
ISBN 1 85521 968 9 (pbk)

Printed and bound in Great Britain by
Biddles Limited, Guildford and King's Lynn

Contents

List of Contributors

ANNE BOTTOMLEY teaches land law and trusts at the University of Kent. She has published in the areas of feminist theory, family law and land law and is the editor of the first collection of papers giving feminist perspectives on (or 'in'!) to all of the 'core subjects' of the law degree. 'Feminist Perspectives on the Foundational Subjects of Law" was published by Cavendish in 1996.

ALAN BRADSHAW studied modern languages at Cambridge University and sociology at the University of Oxford. He worked as the staff development officer at the Law School, University of Wales, Cardiff, and is a guest lecturer at the International Institute for the Sociology of Law, Onati, Spain. He is currently in the employ of the University of Wales, Cardiff, as a field research officer working in France.

DAVID CAMPBELL, Bsc (Econ), LLM, PhD, FCI (Arb), was educated at University College Cardiff, the University of Michigan School of Law and the University of Edinburgh. He is Professor of Law at Sheffield Hallam University and a Member of the Centre for Socio-Legal Studies, University of Sheffield. His principal research interests are the law and economics of commercial transactions and the law and economics of corporate governance.

PETER FITZPATRICK is professor of Law at Queen Mary and Westfield College and has taught at universities in Europe, North America and Papua New Guinea. He has published works on law and social theory, law and racism and imperialism, a recent one being *The Mythology of Modern Law*.

DENIS GALLIGAN is the professor of Socio-Legal Studies at the University of Oxford, director of the Centre for Socio-Legal Studies and Fellow of Wolfson College, Oxford. He was formerly a professor at the Universities of Sydney and of Southampton. He specialises in the areas of public law, jurisprudence, civil and criminal justice.

PADDY HILLYARD is a Senior Lecturer in the Department of Social Administration at the University of Bristol. His academic work involves the study of Northern Ireland, the police and liberation movements. He has been involved for for many years with reform groups including Liberty.

SIMON JOLLY is a lecturer in law at the University of Nottingham. He has published articles in the area of family law, and is currently completing a doctoral thesis examining the production of legal ideology in the context of the jury system.

ROBERT LEE is Professor of Law and Head of Cardiff Law School. He has worked in legal practice as Development Director for Hammond Suddards and Research Director for Wilde Sapte. He is a member of the Executive Committee of the Socio-Legal Studies Association.

WADE MANSELL teaches law at the University of Kent. He is co-author (with Joanne Conaghan) of "The Wrongs of Tort" and of "A Critical Introduction to Law". His current interests oscillate and vacillate between tort and public international law.

KATHERINE O'DONOVAN is Professor of Law at Queen Mary and Westfield College. She works on feminist jurisprudence and in the general area of socio-legal studies. Her current work is a comparative study of children and identity, particularly referring to genetic parentage.

MARTIN PARTINGTON is Professor of Law and Pro-Vice-Chancellor at the University of Bristol. He is also director of the Bristol Centre for the Study of Administrative Justice. He played an active part in the creation of SLSA, having chaired the steering committee that led to its creation in 1990, and having been elected its second chair. He has written extensively on housing law and social security law, as well as legal services and legal education. His present research interests are primarily in the areas of administrative justice.

ANDREW SANDERS was educated at the universities of Warwick and Sheffield. He was a fellow at Pembroke College, Oxford, and currently holds a chair at the University of Bristol. His special interests are criminal law, criminal justice and criminology.

JO SHAW, BA (Cantab), LenDr (Brussels). Professor of European law at the University of Leeds. Director of the Centre for the Study of Law in Europe, and convenor of the Leeds MA in European Legal Studies. Holder of a Jean Monnet Chair in European Law and Integration. Specialist in the field of EU institutional law, internal market law, competition law and social law.

JOE SIM is a Professor of Criminology at the John Moores University, Liverpool. He was formerly at the Open University. His expertise covers prison institutions and he is currently working on closed circuit television and its impact on civil liberties.

PHILIP THOMAS is Professor of Socio-Legal Studies at Cardiff Law School, University of Wales, Cardiff. He is the founding and current editor of the *Journal of Law and Society* and is the general editor of the Socio-Legal Studies Series published by Dartmouth. He is an Executive Committee member of the Socio-Legal Studies Association.

SALLY WHEELER is Professor of Law Business and Society at Leeds University. She is the Chair of the Socio-Legal Studies Association. She is interested in socio-legal aspects of company law, insolvency law, contract law and legal history.

The Royalties from this book have been donated by the authors to the Socio-Legal Studies Association.

1 Socio-Legal Studies: The Case Of Disappearing Fleas And Bustards

PHILIP THOMAS

This book is the product of a group of papers commissioned by the editor for first presentation at the Socio-Legal Studies Association 1995 annual conference at Leeds University. However, the motivation for that conference stream was the publication and reception of the Economic and Social Research Council's "Review of Socio-Legal Studies". The review was initiated in April 1991 and published in May 1994. The 46 page report received a mixed response within the academic community.[1] Thereafter the ESRC commissioned Professor Martin Partington to prepare a paper which would constitute the b̶ NOT WHAT LAW WAS ESRC's Research Programmes Board for a res̶ TRADITIONALLY SO IT RAISED QUESTIONS ABOUT legal studies. In turn, his findings and conclusio̶ ITS UNCERTAINTY AND socio-legal, academic constituency with varyi̶ṉ VALIDITY. criticism, as indicated in his contribution to this book. But more generally and substantively these responses reflect the uncertain and disputed nature and direction of socio-legal studies. In addition, the undeclared persona of socio-legal studies is complicated by dramatic changes within tertiary level education and the diverse, changing but increasingly limited sources of funding. Thus, with a view to carrying the issue forward I invited a number of scholars to prepare papers for presentation and discussion at Leeds. The papers were later rewritten and edited for publication.[2]

Common lawyers by training have been disinterested in theoretical definitions. Essentially they deal with problems as presented by individual clients: through issues and cases. The inductive reasoning associated with BASIS OF LAW SLIDE 3 traditional English jurisprudence appears to have left its mark on socio-legal studies for we remain without a generally accepted definition of the subject area although it was recognised by the Review as having been in existence since the 1960s. For example the uncertainty of the defining subject matter is illustrated by Donald Harris, former director of the Socio-Legal Centre at Oxford university, who wrote in 1983:

> There is no agreed definition of socio-legal studies: some use the term broadly to cover the study of law in its social context, but I prefer to use it to refer to the study of the law and legal institutions from the perspectives of the social sciences.[3]

Harris was following the path blazed by Colin Campbell and Paul Wiles, who, in their important paper in 1976, pointed out the absence of law and society scholarship and its definition in the United Kingdom.[4] Subsequently, Hazel Genn and Martin Partington defined socio-legal studies as 'an approach' but continued:

> There may always be a problem in defining the essential nature of socio-legal scholarship... Thus the question of 'what in practice is socio-legal?' cannot be answered on the basis of any 'personal' definition used by individual scholars nor simply by reference to the work located within institutions of socio-legal research.[5]

More recently, the ESRC Review stated:

> 'Socio-legal studies' is an umbrella for what is now an exciting, wide-ranging and varied area of research activity. In all its forms, the approaches of socio-legal scholars to the contextual study of law and legal processes are very different from the pure doctrinal research which has been the staple of traditional legal scholarship. However, the diversity of activity that is subsumed under the label socio-legal studies makes the simple definition difficult to achieve..... it is arguable that the attempt to impose rigid boundaries is likely to inhibit the development of the field. For the purposes of this Report, and in order to reduce confusion and to assist the growth of socio-legal knowledge

2

and theory, we feel that the term 'socio-legal studies' should be given the broadest possible definition, as it is in other countries.[6]

Given the undoubted difficulty in obtaining an agreed definition it might cross our minds to ask the question, why bother? Does it matter if it is a new discipline, a sub-discipline and if so of what, an approach, a methodology, a political position or paradigm.[7] My response must be that it does matter if I am to be successful in encouraging you to read on.

Paradoxically, the very success of socio-legal studies demands that there be a review of the enterprise. For so long as it remained in unthreatening opposition to doctrinal legal scholarship its otherness, offered as a minority alternative, was acceptable. Its apparently unchallenging marginality ensured its untroubled existence from external scrutiny. But the growing plurality of law school recruitment and teaching which occurred during the periods of expansion in tertiary education and consequent faculty growth resulted in the appointment of non-doctrinal staff albeit dispersed throughout several institutions. Their positions were defined by their 'not-being' rather than in a positive and clearly defined alternative to traditional, doctrinal lawyers. Mark Twain stated 'a few fleas are good for every dog' in order to keep the beast awake and active. In turn, those who esposed socio-legal scholarship fulfilled a similarly useful but non-threatening function within educational institutions claiming the credentials of academic pluralism.

Nevertheless, the status of opposition, as politicians well know, is one of liberation providing licence to endorse the undoable as well as the doable. It was a status much prized by E.P.Thompson who allied himself with the extinct mythological species, the great bustard, in that he could never be gagged by opposition alone: "For the great bustard, by a well know law of aeronautics, can rise into the air against a strong headwind. It is only by facing into opposition that I am able to define my thought at all".[8] It may have come as a surprise to some within the loosely associated, socio-legal community who were working against the weight of dominant orthodoxies that the apparently seamless web of doctrinal law had broken apart.

However, the time and opportunity has arrived for the socio-legal community to claim the position of centre stage: state its research and teaching goals and lay out its agenda. The tasks of opposition are different from those of government as pointed out by Roger Cotterrell: "Socio-legal scholarship in the broadest sense is the most important scholarship presently being undertaken in the legal world. Its importance is not only in what it has achieved, which is considerable, but also in what it promises".[9] A similar, though less fulsome review, was offered by William Twining in the course of his Hamlyn Lectures: "Socio-legal studies is coming of age and achieving critical mass and has enormous potential, but it is approaching a critical point when it could either continue to develop or it could decline".[10] Nicola Lacey described the present status as follows: "The importance of socio-legal research is now so widely acknowledged and its contribution to legal education so firmly established that it is almost inconceivable that anyone could emerge from a reputable law faculty as ignorant of socio-legal scholarship as I was when I graduated in 1979".[11]

A New Discipline: A New Profession?

One important reason for focusing on the definition of socio-legal studies involves establishing the disciplinary boundaries of law and the possible place of socio-legal scholars within those boundaries.[12] There are some who would call for the title of 'discipline' to be placed around socio-legal studies. Yet, as I state elsewhere[13] the very term 'discipline' is problematic. Berns has suggested that "traditional disciplines tend to resist innovation, sometimes merely because of an attachment to what is old [and] therefore familiar".[14] But disciplines are neither fixed nor constant. Plato's academy offered philosophy, mathematics and gymnastics whilst medieval universities taught the *trivium quadrivium*, the seven liberal arts: grammar, logic and rhetoric [the *trevium*] along with arithmetic, geometry, astrology and music theory [the *quadrivium*]. The roots of many courses and modules can be traced to these subjects but many have subsequently

4

emerged and others submerged. Today for example, women's studies in law is claimed as a discipline. Tove Stang-Dahl states in the preface to her book, *Women's Law: an Introduction to Feminist Jurisprudence*[15] that the Faculty of Law at the University of Oslo commenced teaching 'women's law' as an 'autonomous legal discipline' in 1975 and went on to establish an Institute of Women's Law in 1978. A subject which has come, and possibly gone, is the sociology of deviance. Colin Sumner suggested that it was given a name by American sociologists in the late 1930s but only after 1951 did people agree to call it the sociology of deviance. However, by 1975 European sociologists and historians were writing about crime, law and social regulation as if the sociology of deviance were no longer recognised.[16] The twists and turns, developments and divisions within a discipline are well documented by Cardelli and Hicks in relation to criminology.[17] More recently Pavarini has taken the question of whether criminology is worth saving and thereafter even further by asking which criminology might be saved?[18] Sir Leon Radzinowicz, the first Wolfson Professor of Criminology and doyen of British criminology, stated that the growth of criminology as a discipline was slow within the United Kingdom. It was not rewarded with its first tenured and permanent chair until 1959.[19] Indeed, the very future of ordered disciplines is in question as was declared by the Dutch criminologist, Jaco Vos, who wrote "scholars are in doubt or even in despair whether their own little sub-discipline will survive into the second millenium".[20] The burgeoning of 'academic' subjects, if not disciplines, is well illustrated by courses currently offered within the tertiary level. For example, these include Band Studies; Business of Perfumery; Building Maintenance Management; Cosmetic Science; Energy Studies; Environmental Leisure and Heritage Management; Equitation and Horse Management; Film and TV Studies; Gamekeeping and Groundsmanship; Hotel and Catering; Popular Jazz and Commercial Music; Media Practices; Podiatry; Three D Studies; Turf Studies; and Yacht Manufacturing and Management.[21]

To be in charge of the august title of 'discipline' results in further ennoblement and enhances the claim to the title of profession. For as Adam Smith stated:

We trust our health to the physician; our fortune and sometimes our life and reputation to the lawyer and attorney. Such confidence could not safely be reposed in people of a very mean or low condition. Their reward must be such, therefore, as may give them that rank in society which so important a trust requires. The long time and great expense which must be laid out in their education, when combined with this circumstance, necessarily enhance still further the price of their labour.[22]

Functional analysis of the professions would suggest that socio-legal scholars could legitimately claim the status of professionals as in turn they could declare themselves to be the keepers of disciplines. For example, Millerson in *The Qualifying Associations*[23] took the work of twenty two scholars of the professions, including Carr-Saunders, Marshall, Parsons, the Webbs, Tawney and Whitehead. He extracted the constant characteristics of their work to see which were considered essential to a profession. The common features were found to be skill based upon theoretical knowledge; training and education; demonstration of competence by passing a test; integrity maintained by the adherence to a code of conduct; a professional organisation and service for the public good. Whereas this list of traits has been challenged by scholars such as Johnson,[24] and Larson,[25] it continued to be used, albeit in a refined manner, by scholars such as Etzioni[26] and Hickson and Thomas.[27]

Formalising Socio-Legal Studies

Another approach to defining socio-legal studies was developed by the Economic and Social Research Council. Its bureaucratic classification has been documented through correspondence between the author and Glyn Davies, Director of Resources, ESRC, who wrote:

6

When the then Social Science Research Council was established in 1965 the area of law and legal studies was seen as essentially outside its remit. At a very early stage, however, a number of developments reflected that the impact of law on society and on economic development was one which could not ignored by the social sciences. In the late 1960s the Council decided to give priority to the establishment of two research units in the areas of race (now ethnic) relations, and industrial relations. These were two examples of areas where the impact of law was very significant. This led to an agreement to review the position of legal studies in relation to the social sciences. A panel was established under the chairmanship of Council member Mrs Jean Floud.

As a result of the panel's deliberations it was agreed that this area should be within the Council's remit. This also led to the establishment of a new subject committee on social sciences and the law, initially chaired by Mrs Floud, and then by Lord Kilbrandon and Professor Geoffrey Wilson of the University of Warwick. It was also agreed to establish a Research Centre in socio-legal sudies, which was then located at the University of Oxford.

The 1970s saw significant expansion of support in this area, both as a committee set to its task of encouraging new research and training, and as the centre established both its own research programme, and itself as the hub of the network of a new community of socio-legal scholars in a number of institutions. The committee encouraged the establishment of new taught masters courses, such as that at the University of Sheffield. It also funded summer schools for the training of existing legal academics who are increasingly interested in the social context and social science dimension of their work. By the end of the 1970s the ESRC was funding 30 postgraduate studentships annually in the field of socio-legal studies. In addition 11 other research awards amounting to a total value of £320,000 were being funded, and the budget of the centre for socio-legal studies was running at over £200,000 annually.

In the early 1980s the structure of the SSRC was reviewed, and the Council itself changed into the ESRC. Responsibility for the social sciences and law area was invested in the new government and law committee. This committee, however, developed a significant number of new research developments in relevant areas, including those concerned in the police and criminal evidence act, procedures for citizen's grievance, and then a research programme on crime and criminal justice.

In 1987 the ESRC further refined its structure, and the broad subject committees were reorganised into three research development groups. The primary responsibility for the socio-legal studies area then rested with the Research Development Group on society and politics, which also took over the management of the programmes of citizen's grievance and crime and criminal justice. The prior existence of these programmes to some extent determined that the focus of the RDGs new developments were in areas other than socio-legal studies, but it has also been argued that the wider remit of these groups meant that it was more difficult for newer and small areas such as socio-legal studies to obtain sufficient attention.

As a result of this there were various discussions between the ESRC and the research community about the needs of the socio-legal studies field, and the priority for research in this area. This was particularly taken forward following the formation of the socio-legal studies association in 1991 *[sic]*.

In 1992 the Council further restructured, with the elimination of all subject based groups, which were replaced by five generic Boards concerned with Research Centres, Research Grants, Research Programmes, Research Resources, and Postgraduate Training. It was

8

also at this time that the 20 year support which ESRC had afforded to the Oxford Centre for Socio-Legal Studies, running latterly at £500,000 annually, came to a close. This, along with the completion of the programmes initiated by the government and law committee, represented a significant dis-investment by ESRC in the socio-legal studies area. A new programme on crime and social order was initiated, but the Council also agreed, in association with the Socio-Legal Studies Association, to initiate a review of the current state of development in the socio-legal field.[28]

By way of sharp contrast, my personal account derives from involvement beginning with the first meeting of the Socio-Legal Group in 1972. It met on an annual and nomadic basis. Its members were a loose knit group of scholars, mainly male lawyers, who gathered occasionally and informally to play football, to support and be supported by the bar, gossip, argue, exchange ideas, offer and even sometimes deliver papers. Communication was spasmodic, often ascerbic as we debated the merits and demerits of sociology of law v. socio-legal studies. The socio-legal camp stood accused of naked empiricism based upon the internalisation and reproduction of existing legal norms and institutions. 'Social policy' was at that time a pejorative term and it was firmly anchored to this work. Membership of the socio-legal camp was reputedly comprised of law lovers who practiced hermaphroditical reproduction. The sociologists of law claimed to be the true scholars and theorists who were able, usually through their Marxist spectacles, to apply a critical perspective to law. For them law was seen as part of the problem rather than part of the solution.[29] Probably an annual gathering was a tolerable frequency which ensured mutual tolerance! My own position, was and remains Fabian in character. It was recorded in the first and only editorial published in the *Journal of Law and Society* in 1974.

The study of the action of law in society has an old tradition. In the nineteenth century such scholars as Dicey, Durkheim, Maine, Marx and Weber established this as crucially important to those who wished to understand society. The aim is to transcend disciplinary boundaries by taking as the focus the subject areas of law in society. We do not not subscribe to the view that the social scientist is to be cast in the role of handmaiden to the lawyer, the lawyer being in the dominant position.... We reject the notion that socio-legal studies is to be an arena in which the lawyer solves problems of social policy on his own terms.[30]

At the Edinburgh conference in 1990 the Group's activities and goals were reviewed and placed within a formal structure. The Socio-Legal Studies Association was established with Hazel Genn, then a researcher based at the Socio-Legal Centre, Oxford, as its first chair. By 1996 it has developed into a self-styled 'learned society'. An executive committee made up of academics and practitioners meets on a frequent and regular basis at different university sites. Its first Newsletter was published in the spring of 1989 under the paid editorship of Nancy Drucker. Currently, it appears three times a year out of the Cardiff Law School under the paid editorship of Penny Smith. In 1993 a code of ethics was prepared by Kim Economides and adopted at Fingle's Bridge during the annual conference held at Exeter University. In 1993 the first list of members and their research interests was produced by myself, Lois Bibbings and Ruth Costigan. The next year saw the production of the second directory. However, in 1995 the annual Research Directory received the financial and publishing support of Butterworths. In the same year the Association published a national list of post-graduate courses and research programmes in socio-legal studies. A Scottish branch of the SLSA is established which runs its own annual conference. In addition, an annual SLSA post-graduate conference which attracts around 70 participants is well established alongside ad hoc meetings for specialist interest groups. The annual SLSA conference is accepted as the premier conference in the UK where academic papers of a socio-legal nature can be presented. For example, approximately 200 papers were given at the 1996 conference at Southampton University and over 300 people attended the three day meeting. The Association itself defines and rewards scholarship through the introduction in 1995 of its annual prizes for the best socio-legal book and academic article. The SLSA has been recognised by the ESRC, the Lord Chancellor's Department and by a number of external bodies which liaise with the Association through a 'users' forum'. Publishers, including Oxford University Press, Longmans, Butterworths, and Dartmouth have established, or are seeking to develop, links with the Association in order both to commission and sell books and journals. Finally, journals such as the *Journal of Family and Social Welfare Law* are identifying with the Association, alongside the *Journal of Law and Society* which continues to support the Association financially, with a view both to helping the Association and obtaining quality articles for publication through such support.

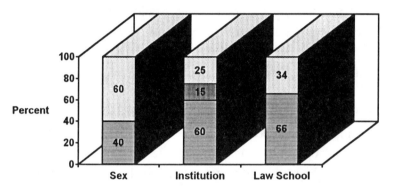

Sex - 40% female, 60% male

Institution - 60% old university, 15% new university, 25% other

Law school - 66% university law school, 34% other

Fig. 1 Composition of SLSA membership mid-1995

Membership of the Association in 1996 stands in excess of 500 [Figure 1]. The data informs us 66 per cent of the members are based in Law Schools and 60 per cent of members are in 'old' universities with 15 per cent in 'new' universities. Approximately, 40 per cent of members are female.[31] New members tend to be recruited from within existing clusters thereby seeing greater growth in identifiable 'old' law schools. Within the

Association there are significant numbers of law professors from 'old' universities. Indeed, the current chair, Sally Wheeler, is a professor at Leeds University. The previous chair, Martin Partington, is a Pro-Vice Chancellor at the University of Bristol and the first chair, Hazel Genn, is a professor of law at University College, London. The Association's membership, and executive, is dominated by academic lawyers from 'old' law schools which contrasts with the USA experience where the Law and Society Association is dominated numerically by non-lawyers from non-ivy league universities. Thus, size, growth, activity, internal cohesion and external recognition contribute to a functional argument for disciplinary status.

I am unattracted both personally and intellectually by this structural and functional account which would allow the SLSA to claim professional and thereby disciplinary status. For me socio-legal studies remains within the discipline of law but that begs the question of where does it sit within the discipline? There has been a major shift of socio-legal research and publishing interests in the past 20 years and it is within this movement that an answer to my question is found. But before addressing this question it is first necessary to look at the issue of the frontiers of the discipline and those elements considered to be central to the discipline. This provides the arena and focus within which socio-legal research and teaching occurs.

BLACK LETTER LAW

The socio-legal scholars of the 1970s argued that law was failing. Some thought it could be saved and others saw law itself as problematic, or indeed, as the problem. Sociology of law and socio-legal studies disagreed over this point. Energy was expended on this debate with a view to establishing new territory to be controlled by the new lawyers/social scientists. Colonisation on behalf of law continued. However, what was not fully appreciated was that even within established disciplines the potential for the dialectic of change exists. This point is ably illustrated by the papers in this book which show the new and changing challenges that socio-legal researchers face. The boundaries of disciplines are constantly moving and subject to renegotiation. In law not only are new areas being developed such as state regulation, discretion and judicial review in administrative law, but old areas such as Roman law have been replaced by politically defined subjects such as European Community law. Territory was also lost as illustrated by aspects of tax to the emerging accountancy profession. The tidal state of disciplines meant that the apparent homogeneity and stability of the discipline, thereby reflecting a major premise within law itself, was simply that: apparent.

Not only are the frontiers of law in flux but so is the content. In particular, the attempts to categorise 'importance' within the law school curriculum as previously undertaken by 'core' subjects and now by 'foundation' subjects reflect no more than the functional, self-defining activity of the Law Society. What makes European law central whilst conveyancing is not? A financial account reflecting work undertaken by provincial, rural or sole legal practitioners would prioritise the latter over the former. Surely, social welfare law should command the status of 'foundation' in a low waged economy where structural unemployment is supported by the government. Why is legal ethics not considered a foundation course given the self-styled altruistic character that the professi   ce of a 'core' of legal subjects is accepte   change as is illustrated by the introdu   adation course requirement by the Law So

[handwritten marginal note: WHERE MIGHT SOCIO-LEGAL STUDIES FIT INTO THE LAW SCHOOL CURRICULUM?]

[handwritten note over text: THE VIEW OF THE LAW MAY FLUCTUATE AND CHANGE DEPENDING ON WHICH OTHER DISCIPLINE IT IS CONSIDERED WITH.]

Thus, disciplines are not absolutes but territories. They are capable of being created, negotiated, conquered, exploited, developed and lost. Like nation states they are in constant danger, flux and territorial uncertainty. Similarly, the belief of disciplinary centrality is a construct inviting re-evaluation and change. The fluidity of boundaries and the opportunity to restructure the hicrachy of content provide opportunity to those who would seek to challenge dominant legal ideology: the socio-legal academy.

By returning to the question of socio-legal research priorities we can see how over two decades scholars have dramatically repositioned themselves. During the 1970s, undoubtedly affected by changes in the delivery of legal services in the USA, scholars in this country focused on the marginal, least academically patrolled areas of legal activity. Our

research and teaching activity was "down and out"! By this I mean the
research eye was directed away from doctrinal law, House of Lords

judgements, and the case reports. |Instead, law as practiced and
experienced became the areas of attention.| Tribunals and magistrates
courts, previously ignored as being 'khadi' justice and not courts of record,
were visited to observe and record the experiences of people as they
rubbed up against the justice system and its personnel. For example,
Doreen McBarnet's work on magistrates courts has become a socio-legal
classic.[32] Not only was the scholastic eye cast "down" but also outwards.
For the objects and subjects of research were not those normally examined
by lawyers. Indeed, legal research had traditionally been restricted to the

confines and contents of the law library. The new researchers spent time
observing and interviewing in the lower courts, in the new legal services
delivery centres such as neighbourhood law centres and duty solicitors
schemes. |Researchers got "out" of the libraries and examined legal culture
as made and practised. Whilst the outward gaze extended beyond the
"black letter" it also examined previously under-researched areas.| The
researcher as colonial explorer is illustrated by the work undertaken by
Maureen Cain in 1974.[33] I present a brief account of this in graphic form
in Figure 2.

Core subjects - 1974

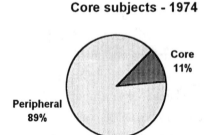

Fig. 2 Proportion of core research

The 'core' areas of study, as defined by the Law Society in order to gain
exemption from Part I of the Law Society Finals, attracted a mere 11 per

14

cent of the attention of the new researchers. Family commanded 5 per cent whilst land and commercial projects represented 3 per cent each. In 1994 I analysed the SLSA research directory and established that socio-legal researchers had changed the direction of their research activities.

As Figure 3 illustrates twenty years later 26 per cent of research projects were focused on 'core' or traditional 'black letter' areas.

Core subjects - 1994

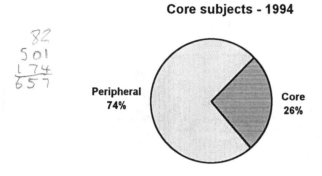

Fig. 3 Proportion of core research

Figure 4 shows that family research continued to dominate research activity within 'core' research.

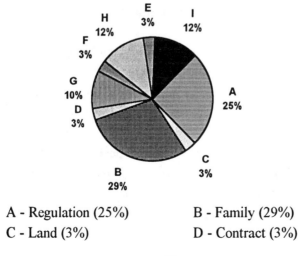

A - Regulation (25%)   B - Family (29%)
C - Land (3%)   D - Contract (3%)

15

E - Tort(3%)   F - Intellectual property (3%)
G - Planning (10%)   H - Administrative (12%)
I - Corporate / commercial / real property.(12%)

Fig. 4 Distribution of core research

The evaluation exercise was repeated in 1995 using the SLSA Directory of Members, published by Butterworths, as shown in Figure 5.

Core and peripheral research - 1995

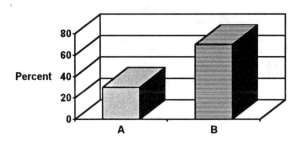

A - Total number of members researching in core areas - 228 (30.12%)
B - Total number of members researching in peripheral areas - 529 (69.88%)

Fig. 5 Proportion of core and peripheral research

The total number of members researching in 'core' areas had risen to 228 and they represented 30 per cent of research activity. Thus, both in absolute numbers and percentage terms the community of socio-legal scholars continues to redirect its research interests towards the 'core' of legal scholarship. In 1975 Dr Cain wrote: "By far the most disturbing finding of the survey, however, was that both academic staff and graduate students, most often members of the socio-legal group, were concentrating their research efforts disproportionately in the area of poor man's law".[34] Today, those concerns have less currency especially if the current trend to research inwards continues.

Further examination of the 1995 Directory indicates that there is a significant link between areas of research and teaching. 87 per cent of returns indicate that members are researching in at least one of the areas in which they have a teaching interest. Another survey I undertook in 1994 at a SLSA day school in London[35] also linked research with teaching interests. The 50 university staff attending the day school declared a strong relationship between research and teaching. 75 per cent of those researching in core areas stated that socio-legal materials affected the content of their teaching whilst the figure rose to 88 per cent of those teaching in non-core areas.

The description of ever developing numerical growth, status, influence and changing research and teaching patterns and directions must, however, be placed alongside a series of shortfalls which include the quality, quantity and spread of research activity and its publication. This distribution is reviewed briefly here and is based upon gender, institutional affiliation and the methodological ability to undertake sophisticated research tasks.

For example, scholars from the 'new' universities continue to be under-represented in the SLSA Research Directory of 1996.[36] There were 98 research projects related to the English Legal System from members of 'old' universities whilst the number from the new schools totalled 26. For civil liberties research projects the numbers totalled 38 'old' and 12 'new' respectively; for family law 55 'old' and 9 'new'; for medical law 38 'old' and 7 'new'; for women and the law 41 'old' and 7 'new'; for jurisprudence 51 'old' and 3 'new' and for criminal law 91 'old' and 20 'new'. More generally, it would appear that scholars from new university law schools may still find difficulty in being accepted for publication in the top-rated academic law journals. For example, between 1981 and 1990 the Modern Law Review published 4 per cent of its articles from new university scholars and this increased to 5 per cent between 1991 and 1994. Perhaps more disappointing for the socio-legal community is the evidence that the Journal of Law and Society between 1989 and 1994 carried only 12 per cent of its articles and reviews from new university authors.

The general publication breakdown based on gender shows that 15 per cent of articles published between 1981 and 1990 in the Modern Law Review were written by women and this figure rose to 26 per cent between 1991 and 1994. Between 1989 and 1994 some 28 per cent of articles in the Journal of Law and Society were written by women as were 40 per cent of the reviews. However, Social and Legal Studies leads this gender table with 70 per cent female authorship since its launch in 1992.[37]

Conclusion

The following words conclude this chapter but are not in themselves conclusive. The debates surrounding socio-legal studies continue. These discussions are not internalised within academia but reflect the real and growing pressures produced by changing but constantly inadequate funding sources for the late-twentieth century 'businessversities'. The restructuring of the intellectual workplace has little to do with efficient processing and application of knowledge and more to do with changes in funding, auditing and control by politicians, external and internal bureaucracies. It is the business management model that runs universities.[38] Paradoxically, the increasing academic status of socio-legal studies may be based upon its ability to attract new, external research and consultancy funding. Any discipline that can bring its institution closer to actual and potential funders and those with political power are to be praised and promoted. Cash starved universities are anxious to recognise any individual or department capable of injecting new money or acquiring influence for the benefit of the institution.

The temptation to sectorise socio-legal studies and ennoble it with the title of discipline is supported by the functional analysis I have presented above. But would such a step serve the cause of the socio-legal community? Stepping outside the legal world constructed by lawyers provides distance but it also produces isolation. The empirical evidence displays that the research is being reorientated towards foundation courses and elite activities and more socio-legal research is being undertaken by more scholars who identify themselves as part of this academy. By hiving off into a new discipline my concern is the growing challenges to orthodox legal pedagogy, traditional research areas and methods will be dismissed or undervalued by those who currently control the academic legal highground: the traditionalists. The struggle for that space is best undertaken through proximity not distance.

The work of Kuhn provides an 'alternative and helful analysis'.[39] He argued that established disciplines operate within a framework that created standards of its researchers for appropriate research, sets objectives, co-ordinates the acceptable standards of its researchers and teachers and provides for the reproduction of the paradigm through student initiation. But new paradigms appear when the accepted is replaced by the revolutionary new. The changeover from Newtonian mechanics to Einsteinian physics is a case in point.

What we may be experiencing is the emergence of a new legal paradigm: that of socio-legal studies. This will affect and alter the world of all academic lawyers. It does not appear as an alternative and should not be taken as a new or competing discipline. Rather it reviews the values, standards, commitments, teaching and research areas of the old paradigm and reshapes. The old is reworked by the new, out of which something different emerges. Kuhn argues there are no independent rational criteria for distinguishing between the old and new paradigms. The rational explanation is found within the paradigm itself. The implications are that socio-legal studies might not be that soft, cuddly toy that some once thought it to be. Certainly, there have been major personal and career successes as a result of an association with socio-legal studies. But to date these have not resulted in major institutional changes. Indeed, we should ask whether the legal edifice, as presently constructed, could be toppled by the socio-legal movement. If it challenges the sanctity of words, and the integrity of system, then, for example, the Rule of Law might be interpreted as nothing but a compilation of 'rules'. Thus, even if socio-legal studies were seen as simply a methodology does it constitute a dangerous instrument? On the other hand, are we merely experiencing a continuing beauty parade of intellectual dynasties? The dominance of legal positivism was challenged and replaced by other schools such as pre-war

American realism, which in turn were subject to the popular growth of sociology in the 1960s, economics in the 1980s, critical theory in the 1980s and post-modernists in the 1990s. Perhaps when all are self-proclaimed socio-legalists there awaits in the next century a new school of pretenders.

Finally, some of the dramatic changes in the tertiary sector and legal education have been noted in this chapter. The growth and direction of socio-legal studies is part of this process of change. It affects and is affected. The responsive, changeable core of law is increasingly being opened to investigation and this is being done by ever greater numbers of socio-legal scholars who in turn use the findings for teaching purposes. The contributors to this book identify discrete areas of study that have and require further investigation by the socio-legal community. They identify areas of neglect and failure in order that we may profit by this knowledge and, in addition, pick out issues that could constitute a new research agenda. However, as some of the authors argue, this is not a totally good news book. For example, the danger of failing to distinguish between policy-led and policy-relevant research should be borne in mind by all and especially those who rely on external funding to undertake their work. Also, given the narrow disciplinary basis of socio-legal scholarship, we should remember that what is lawful may also be that which is problematic! The development of socio-legal studies over two decades has been impressive but this growth may still be interpreted as the emergence rather than the arrival of a new legal paradigm. The authors of this book may no longer be classified as fleas and bustards but their new entomological and ornithological titles are no less challenging!

Notes

1   For example, see, A.Hunt, "Governing the Socio-Legal Project: or, What do Research Councils do?" [1994] *Journal of Law and Society* 520. The SLSA published a special issue of its Newsletter dedicated to the Review, No.13, August 1994.

2   All but one of the commissioned papers were received and for this support I thank the authors.

3   "The Development of Socio-Legal Studies in the United Kingdom" (1983) 2 *Legal Studies* 315.

4   'The Study of Law and Society in Britain"(1976) 11 *Law and Society Review* 547.

5   This quote comes from an unpublished paper presented at the ESRC conference held in London in April 1993. In essence, this line was maintained in the Review itself which is perhaps unsurprising given that both scholars were members of the Review panel.

6   'Review of Socio-Legal Studies" 1. The Review states that in the US the term is often used as a generic label to encompass sociology of law, law and society research, and critical legal studies.

7   See the debate between I.D.Willock 'Getting on with Sociologists' (1974) 1 *British Journal of Law and Society* 3 and C.M.Campbell 'Legal Thought and Juristic Values" (1974) 1 *British Journal of Law and Society* 13, where Campbell comes close to offering up socio-legal studies as a new paradigm.

8   B.D.Palmer, *E.P.Thompson: Objectives and Oppositions* (1994) xii.

9   R.Cotterrell, *Law's Community* (1995) 314.

10   W.Twining, *Blackstone's Tower: The English Law School* (1994) 145.

11   *Socio-Legal Newsletter* 12 (1994) 2.

12   I have pursued this issue in the Introduction of *Legal Frontiers*, ed. P.A.Thomas (1996) 1-10.

13   Ibid.

14   W.Berns, "Law and Behavioural Science" 28 *Law and Contemporary Problems* [1963] 185.

15   Norwegian University Press, 1987.

16   C.Sumner, *The Sociology of Deviance:An Obituary* [Open University Press, 1994] 5.

17   "Radicalism in Law and Criminology: A Retrospective View of Critical Legal Studies and Radical Criminology" 84 *Journal of Criminal and Criminology* [1993] 502.

18   "Is Criminology Worth Saving?" in ed. D.Nelken, *The Futures of Criminology* (1994).

19   "Reflections on the State of Criminology" 34 *British Journal of Criminology* [1994] 99.

20   *Journal of Law and Society* 3 [1996] 446.

21   These courses were selected from the UCAS clearing system list published in August 1996.

22   Adam Smith, *Wealth of Nations* BK 1,ch.10.

23   (1964) 3.

24   T.Johnson, *Professions and Power* (1972) and his subsequent writing.

25   M.S.Larson, *The Rise of Professionalism:A Sociological Analysis* (1977) and her subsequent writing.

26   A.Etzioni, *The Semi-Professionals and their Organisation: Teachers, Nurses and Social Workers* (1969).

27   D.J.Hickson and M.W.Thomas 'Professionalisation in Britain' (1969) 3 *Sociology* 37.

28   I am grateful to Glyn Davies for making time to discuss with me the issues addressed in the chapter and in particular for writing up his account of the development of socio-legal studies as appreciated by the ESRC. I have

reproduced his letter of June 1994 to me in full as I consider it an important historical document.

29   Professor Paul Wiles, Sheffield University, who was an active member of the Socio-Legal Group questions this account. "I am not sure that I would agree with you that early sociology of law in this country should necessarily be identified with Marxism. This is for two reasons. First, there were people who clearly espoused sociology of law who followed intellectual traditions that were clearly not Marxist. Second, I think that quite a lot of the sociology of law in the early days in Britain fitted into that general critical perspective which occasionally used Marxism but was not particularly wedded to Marxist theory. I think, in this sense, that what happened in Britain is even closer to the critical legal studies movement in the USA than you suggest". Personal correspondence between the author and Paul Wiles concerning a draft of this paper.

30   *British Journal of Law and Society* 1 (1974) 1. The term 'British' was dropped from the title in 1982. It has been suggested by J. Schlegel that the attempts of American Realists to engage in empirical social science between the late 1920s and the second World War was failure. "The twentieth century notion of science as an empirical activity could be brought into law and nothing really upset only if it was to be kept at its proper Japanese wife distance: law and ...." J.H.Schlegel, *American Realism and Empirical Social Science*, University of North Carolina Press, [1995] 255. See also, N.Duxbury, *Patterns of American Jurisprudence* [1994].

31   The membership secretary has informed me that the gender division cannot be established with total accuracy as some members identify themselves with initials.

32   D.McBarnet, *Conviction: Law, The State and the Construction of Justice*, [1981].

33   "Rich Man's Law or Poor Man's Law" [1975] Journal of Law and Society 61. There are methodological problems involved in the following figures which include the recognition that throughout the figures depend on self-reporting and self-evaluation as well as the difficulty of comparing Dr Cain's findings with a different data base some twenty years later. Therefore, whilst these figures must be treated with caution they do appear to present trends and changes in research activity.

34   Ibid. 63.

35   Socio-legal Newsletter, Number 17, [1995] 1.

36   Socio-legal Newsletter, Number 18, [1996] 1.

37   These percentage figures must be treated with some caution as it was not always obvious from the author's name to establish his or her sex.

38   See, for example, W. Readings, *The University in Ruins*, (Harvard UP, 1996): R.R.Davies"What is Happening to British Universities?" *The Welsh Journal of Education* (1995) 1.

39   T.S.Kuhn, The Structure of Scientific Revolution (1962).

2 Socio-Legal Research In Britain: Shaping The Funding Environment

MARTIN PARTINGTON

Introduction

This book offers a range of views about the future development of socio-legal research and scholarship in Britain. But the ambitions expressed will not be realised without additional funding. Acquiring additional funding, never easy at the best of times, is now even harder. There are at least two reasons for this.

First, the levels of resource provided for research by government through both the research councils and the university funding bodies have been severely constrained for a number of years. (The research charities face similar constraints.) In addition, the impact of Research Assessment Exercises on universities has resulted in increased demand for research funding. Those who are given the task of making funding decisions have to make increasingly hard choices. Thus cases for research funding - whether made by individuals or on a collective basis - have to be argued with increasing care and sophistication.

Secondly, and in many people's minds, more sinisterly, the terms on which the resource for research is provided have become more focused and market driven. Statements that research funding must give "value for money", or provide work of value to research users are regarded by some as attempts by government to direct the research agenda, and thus attack academic freedom.

These factors present researchers with a dilemma: do they forsake opportunities to seek additional funding, on the basis that the sources of that funding have become totally compromised, or do they seek research funding on the terms set down by the paymasters? The view developed in this chapter is that neither position is sensible. While the present environment is undoubtedly difficult, an understanding of that environment may reveal opportunities to influence the ways in which decisions are reached that will continue to allow fundamental and valuable research to be undertaken.

This argument is developed in the context of an account of the consultancy I was asked to undertake during the academic year 1994-1995 by the Economic and Social Research Council (ESRC). The objective was to prepare a paper which could be used as the basis for a formal bid to the ESRC's Research Programmes Board[1] for a research programme in socio-legal studies. This chapter falls into three unequal parts: after a brief section setting the background, the heart of the essay gives an account of the work associated with the consultancy; finally, some observations are offered as to how the research community should endeavour to address the challenges facing it.

Background

The consultancy was established in the light of two specific events.[2] First, in 1992, core funding from the ESRC to the Oxford Centre for Socio-Legal Studies was ended. An obvious consequence of this was that the funding formerly available to the Centre would not be available for general socio-legal research, unless the research community argued successfully for it. Second, and more directly, in 1993 the ESRC had established a panel to conduct a review of socio-legal studies. The report, initially submitted to the Council of the ESRC in January 1994, was published in a revised version in May 1994.[3]

While such reports are usually received by their sponsors more or less politely, they often lead nowhere. On this occasion, however, it was decided that there should be a further response. In June 1994, officials from the ESRC convened an informal meeting of potential users of socio-legal research to consider the report and what further developments might be encouraged in the light of it. Participants at the meeting were extremely enthusiastic and anxious to assist with further action.

This in turn led to two further steps being taken: first, the initial informal user's meeting established itself as a "Socio-Legal Research Users' Forum" with representatives from commerce, government and the professions[4]; and, second, the ESRC decided to establish my consultancy.

The terms of reference of the consultancy required me, in consultation with the research community, and with the participation of the Socio-Legal Research Users' Forum, to draft the paper mentioned above. The initial intention was that the whole process should be completed during the 1994-95 academic year. As events developed, however, it was decided that no bid could be submitted to the Programmes Board before 1996. This allowed the process of discussion and consultation to take somewhat longer, and be somewhat more detailed than had been originally envisaged.

The immediate objective of the consultancy was achieved. In October 1995, the Programmes Board considered a number of outline proposals for funding. The socio-legal studies proposal was included in a shortlist of proposals invited to be worked into a formal bid for consideration in March 1996. Unfortunately, the bid was unsuccessful.

The Programme Of Work

The programme of work associated with the consultancy fell into three distinct stages. First came an initial consultation exercise, which lasted from October to December 1994; secondly, there was a period of evaluation of responses and preparation of early drafts of the report (January-February, 1995); finally, there was a series of consultative meetings held throughout the country, during which successive drafts of the report were discussed and revised, leading to final drafting and completion (March - July 1995).

Stage (i): The Initial Consultation

Because of the limitations of time available to carry out the consultancy, it was essential to stimulate discussion within the research community and elsewhere as quickly as possible in the year. It seemed that the best way to achieve this was to draft and circulate a preliminary consultation paper as soon as practicable. In preparing the paper, I took as my starting point the report of the ERSC *Review*.

Although much of that review was a survey of past achievement, it also looked to the future, sketching out ideas for further research. In particular it suggested that new research should be promoted in areas including: the environment; business and the economy; historical studies; and civil justice. It also suggested that the strengthening of intellectual alliances should be encouraged, in particular between economists and lawyers, and psychologists and lawyers. More generally, the *Review* argued that continuing attention needed to be paid to the intellectual and scientific framework within which socio-legal research was conducted; the balance between policy related research and more fundamental theoretical research needed development. And it was indicated that there were training needs which required attention, both for staff in post, and for younger people contemplating a career in research who needed adequate training in research methods.

A preliminary draft, written in September 1994, was considered by a number of people, including the members of the Socio-Legal Research Users' Forum. In the light of comments received, a revised version was published and widely distributed - to over 500 addressees, in the United Kingdom and abroad - at the end of October 1994.

After a brief introductory section, the paper[5] raised a number of issues on which comments were particularly sought: (a) the implications of establishing a Socio-Legal Research Users' Forum; (b) the parameters within which the ESRC itself was operating; (c) the possible theme and contents of any research programme focused in the area of civil justice might be; and (d) the extent of problems with the capacity of the research community to carry out such a programme, if funded.

Stage (ii): Evaluation

The paper generated a substantial response. Over 80 written responses were received by the initial deadline of 31 December 1994.[6] Some represented the collective views of departmental and other meetings which had been held to discuss it; others merely reflected the opinions of individuals. The responses to the paper were, predictably, both critical (mainly constructively) and generous in the willingness to share ideas. It is not possible here to give a detailed account of the range of responses received, though all were fully considered and made a fundamental contribution to the shaping of the final report. The following summary gives a flavour of the range of ideas existing within the research community.[7]

The Role of the Socio-Legal Research Users' Forum

Inevitably, the very fact that the forum had established itself generated considerable comment. Many were extremely positive about its creation: "The Research Users Forum might have a very valuable role to play in increasing awareness of socio-legal research", wrote one respondent. Another, more specifically, noted: "[T]he Users' Forum ought to provide an opportunity once again to talk about the hindrance to research that the inability to audio or video tape [court] proceedings represents. We cannot evaluate hearings or produce realistic training materials until we have much better data and analyses of the face-to-face interaction in courts, tribunals, chambers hearings etc and the way in which it functions as a vehicle for doing legal business".

More generally, another respondent observed: "We very much support the need for meetings of the Research Users' Forum to consider interests in the area of socio-legal studies". "The Research Users' Forum might be an organisation which could be used to raise the profile of [socio-legal] work by demonstrating its value to users" and thus gain more resource for such research was the view of another.

Other respondents hedged their bets: "In general terms, consultation with a Research Users' Forum can be valuable. Care has to be taken not to allow the Forum to set the agenda". Or more candidly: "Research with such origins [i.e. the policy-maker audience] runs the twin dangers of narrowness and too ready acceptance of the economic and political status quo. I do very much like the point about using users to get access".

For a minority of respondents, however, the creation of the Forum was a matter to be strongly resisted. Amongst this group, there was a widespread assumption - or at least fear - that the members of the Users' Forum would, in fact, be determining the socio-legal research agenda; that the forum would only have limited and rather short-term research interests; that it would prevent the academic community from asking the "hard questions" and thus be a restriction on academic freedom. "I do feel that socio-legal research is at its most useful when it is looking at law in action and the practice of law without being so tightly limited by the needs of policymakers," wrote one.

The sharpest attack came from Michael King who circulated an open letter[8] in which he argued:

> It is perhaps inappropriate in a response to a consultation document to question the very idea that socio-legal research should aim to meet the requirement of 'users' and that these users should be identified as 'commerce, government and the professions'. Clearly this fits snugly with the consumerist and corporate model of society so strongly favoured by the present Government. Independent researchers may wish to question, however, whether they wish to see themselves in the role of servicing (or at least being responsive to the needs of) particular sections of society which the Government through

the medium of the ESRC has selected as being the constituency for research.

The ESRC's Parameters

Of course, the decision to establish the Forum is just one aspect of the wider context within which the ESRC (in common with the other research councils) has to operate. The consultation paper offered a summary of that context and suggested that any successful proposal would have to accept the ESRC's own mission.[9] This was stated to be:

> the promotion and support of high-quality basic, strategic and applied social science research; the promotion and support of related postgraduate training; both designed to increase understanding of social and economic change. In addition, there would be special emphasis on meeting the needs of users and beneficiaries of research and training designed to enhance the competitiveness of the UK economy; promote the effectiveness of public services and public policy; and improve the quality of life.

The problem with such statements is that they are not static. As the consultancy progressed, it was clear that official views relating to the research funding environment were being changed, for example as a result of the publication of the technology foresight reports.[10] And the ESRC's own programmes will be further influenced by the outcome of its new thematic approach.[11]

Most respondents who commented on this aspect of the consultation paper appeared to accept the practical reality of the ESRC's position. There was however a general warning against trying artificially to shape any research programme by utilizing a set of concepts or terminology defined by Government for the ESRC. This would be perceived as narrowly opportunistic; the case for any programme bid in the area of socio-legal research had to stand and be defended on its own terms.

29

As with the discussion of the Forum, a small number of respondents took strong exception to the linkage of the consultation paper to these corporate goals. Indeed, one faculty response took that view that the whole Consultation Paper was "shaped by political concerns which have no place in academic research...It carries with it the danger, whose gravity can scarcely be overstated, that young people who should be attracted to the field will instead see it as tainted by ideological considerations". They therefore suggested that the consultation process begin afresh (though what purpose this would have served was not made clear).

One or two others appeared to despair of any involvement by the ESRC regarding it as too intellectually conservative to sponsor the kind of socio-legal research currently required. One respondent had "little confidence that the ESRC will support the kind of research infrastructure which is required to support the field. I know no-one who has confidence in their abilities to pick formative research". He therefore boldly concluded that the "ESRC's socio-legal budget [should be] directly allocated to Law Schools and the ESRC disbanded".

Focus, Themes and Contents

The Consultation Paper proposed - indeed the terms of reference of the consultancy had effectively required this - that the *focus* of any socio-legal research programme should be restricted to civil justice. In making this suggestion, it was not intended that "civil law" or "civil justice" should be interpreted in any narrow technical fashion but broadly, to distinguish this proposal from those in the general areas of criminal justice and family justice on which much work had already been undertaken.

Nevertheless, a number of respondents complained of the failure of the exercise to embrace criminal law and criminal justice issues or family law issues. A sub-group of respondents adopted a slightly different point - that "civil law" or "civil justice" is itself a lawyer's construct, which if applied rigidly might have the effect of ruling out potentially valuable research even within the framework suggested. (For example, work on the impact of law in the context of, say, the regulation of environmental pollution would have to assess the impact not only of the civil law but also criminal law.) In addition, some argued that the focus on civil law would lead to the exclusion from consideration of, for example, alternative modes of dispute resolution falling outside formal court structures.

Notwithstanding the force of these arguments, the focus of the proposed programme on civil justice was, in general, welcomed. One respondent wrote, in somewhat apocalyptic vein:

> Put quite crudely, the justice system as at present constituted has hit the buffers. It evolved in a more prosperous age without regard to social and economic factors. Those administering the justice system are left with a series of processes whose cost is becoming unsupportable and whose effectiveness is in doubt. They are faced with a stark choice between maintaining a millenary rite masquerading as a law and order system (polishing the system if you like) and addressing the question of how to restore the justice system...If they opt for the latter they must address the design defects that stem from the failure to address social and economic factors as the system evolved. To do this they need the sort of "advice and assistance" that can be provided by socio-legal research, but the means of providing them in a structured way do not exist.

The agenda for socio-legal research must be settled in the context of a strategic overview of the justice system: the conceptual framework in which the research that needs to be done can be set in a way that is meaningful to policy makers.

As regards the overall *theme* of the programme, the Consultation Paper suggested that two specific themes might be considered: "the modernisation of civil justice" or "innovation in the civil justice system". There was some strong support for the former, though none for the latter. Respondents, however, provided a number of other suggestions: "the internationalisation of civil justice" was one; "Civil Justice in the Changing state: redefining the public and the private" another.

Another respondent approached the question of the theme from a rather broader angle, arguing that socio-legal work in the UK had, to date, been dominated by lawyers. Any new programme should therefore be attractive to those working in other social science disciplines. He argued that the consultation paper perpetuated the problem of legal dominance. He therefore suggested that the main theme should be: "Law, State and Civil Society" - thus including theoretical questions relating to the division between the public and the private; between the criminal and the civil. Paddy Hillyard, in an article published in the *SLSA Newsletter*, developed this idea of a broader thematic approach, suggesting: "the meaning of civil justice", to embrace issues around the notion of social justice and citizenship; and "civil law and social polarization", focusing on key structural questions such as race, gender, age and generational inequality.

There was more debate about the *contents* of any programme. The consultation paper had listed a small number of specific issues that might be included within a research programme, including: analysis of the impact of the Courts and Legal Services Act 1990, alternative dispute resolution, and the scope and effectiveness of judicial training and judicial performance. These were introduced into the paper to provoke a response. In this, they were undoubtedly successful.

There was a widespread feeling that the initial list was far too narrowly linked to the work of courts and legal process. A number of commentators felt that it represented precisely the matters which the ESRC should *not* be funding, as it would be far too policy dominated and short-term, and were indeed the sorts of project which should be the responsibility of the Lord Chancellor's Department or other government departments such as the Home Office or the Department for Trade and Industry.

One or two respondents offered a more fundamental critique, reflecting concern about the underlying basis of the whole proposal: "The very way in which the draft proposal is conceived effectively sets the research outside the current theoretical concerns of academic sociology,

32

legal theory, and social theory. There is a real danger that the Programme... will be cut off completely from any theoretical and scholastic roots" asserted one. Another urged, somewhat mysteriously, the creation of "something that is theoretically remarkable".

There was much support for a programme giving a new impetus to the further development of interdisciplinary research. Law and economics, law and psychology, new links between law and linguistics, were all mentioned, as were law and anthropology, and law and social work. (Surprisingly there was no mention of the possibilities of links between law and political science; nor was there any suggestion of strengthening links between law and geography.)

Many respondents urged that there should be a strong comparative dimension to the programme, not ignoring the opportunities for comparative research offered in Scotland as well as other jurisdictions in Europe and elsewhere. Others argued specifically for the expansion of feminist research agendas.

There were many detailed suggestions for topics which might fall within a research programme. They included: the operation of commercial law and financial and other forms of regulation and their impact on economic life; legal aid and the delivery of legal services; problems with adjudication/enforcement in cases of low economic value, such as housing disputes; the economics of the legal system, and the impact of the civil justice system on social and economic behaviour; Alternative Dispute Resolution and the comparative examination of the efficiency of civil justice procedures; the role of non-court bodies in the establishment, monitoring and enforcement of commercial law norms such as private trade standard-setting bodies; the relationship between law and competitiveness during the third industrial (information) revolution; the competitiveness of London as a centre of commercial arbitration and the desirability of private enterprise courts; the economics of intellectual property and the valuation of intellectual property rights and the relationship of this to the law on intellectual property.

More generally, it was argued that the collapse of communism in Europe had highlighted the fact that, within the general framework of capitalism, Western countries actually employed a different model of capitalism - the highly individualistic framework of the US, or Britain, contrasted with the more relational model in Germany or Scandinavian countries or Japan; this raised the question of the extent to which these different political economies are linked to differences in economic performance, and what the relation of legal form to these issues might be. Markets sustained by the underpinning of the common law might be found to work in ways different to those sustained by another legal tradition.

Others proposed close study of litigation strategies and the potential development of concepts of "a market for dispute resolution". One respondent suggested this should extend to research into the use of non-legal sanctions in the ordering of commercial relations. Yet others suggested studies of the efficiency of civil justice institutions, or, as another put it, the "preposterous inefficiencies" of the adversarial system. Some argued strongly that research involving economic analysis of the civil justice system had also to pay attention to questions of the quality of justice provided.

One respondent argued for a closer integration of work done on the criminal justice system to see what the lessons for the civil justice system might be. A major study of the work of the county court study was strongly supported by another group. Yet another supported the proposal for a study of the Court of Appeal.

One interesting response suggested a focus on "the changing need for social justice" resulting from rising living standards, and increased reliance on markets for services formerly provided by the state [pensions, health care, dentistry], which might lead to increasing scope for litigation. Finally, one respondent asked why the concept of "rights" appeared to be so popular, and wondered if the powerful were abandoning law by moving away from law and litigation just as the powerless were discovering it? A modern research programme should also have room for questions on the relationship between law, protest and social movements.

There was, in short, a rich set of research ideas which went far beyond the scope of what was contained in the initial consultation paper.

A final issue on which respondents were asked to comment, was the question of research capacity in socio-legal studies. This could have caused difficulties: if there was evidence that there was wholly inadequate research capacity, this of itself would undermine the case for the funding of a research programme. Those who did comment were unanimous in their view that there was a problem, though no one attempted to quantify its extent.

The question of research capacity relates to a more fundamental issue about the nature of socio-legal research. There is widespread agreement that socio-legal research is, or should be, at its base, interdisciplinary. This view led one respondent to the uncompromising view that the research community did not presently have the skills to do the job:

> The majority of researchers are lawyers and many of them lack basic research skills. But I don't think this is merely a matter of training: it concerns how individual disciplines value interdisciplinary work. Unfortunately, socio-legal work is marginal to both law and social science....Therefore both setting the agenda and training have to be attractive to the various university departments. Research must not only be of the highest quality, but the training must match. Currently, I suspect research students are better off than staff in post. I think it is important that staff are seen to be *formally* qualified to do the research...A danger is that lawyers might think they can "bolt on" the necessary skills as and when they need them without understanding the theoretical and methodological aspects of what they are dealing with. One method of dealing with this is for staff to undertake research training on a part-time basis...

Although this may not be what the respondent intended, this might lead to the view that socio-legal research can only be undertaken by individuals who have been trained both in law and in at least one other social science discipline.

A number of respondents thought that lawyers working in law schools did not have sufficient social science research skills; a smaller number noted the reverse problem, that social scientists did not have adequate legal research skills. One respondent - a lecturer in social work specifically observed that "the idea of providing legal training for social scientists sounds attractive". However, there was a view that the answer to these difficulties was not to educate large numbers of individuals in new disciplines. A more cost-effective approach was suggested: undertake sufficient training to ensure that those from specific disciplines understand the language and concepts of other disciplines; and then try to promote the virtues of collaborative work to ensure that research is undertaken on a genuinely interdisciplinary basis. It was noted that a number of universities had made a specific investment in this direction, for example by recruiting into law departments colleagues from other disciplines.

In terms of the present generation of research students, a number of respondents noted that many more masters courses and Ph.D courses now include instruction in research methods. The optimistic view was expressed that "the problem of skills may become increasingly historical".

A different problem also emerged which was that, once the period of research training was over, those who had recently finished Ph.D's, or indeed were still writing up, felt that they had to obtain lecturing posts. In many institutions this meant that instead of capitalising on their research training, they were instantly diverted into teaching, with heavy demands in terms of course preparation and classroom contact. The suggestion was therefore made that a programme of post-doctoral fellowships - analogous to those widely available in the sciences - would be extremely desirable to address this issue.

One difficulty noted was that "in the absence of a well-developed and active research programme, with funding to create research posts, there will be few incentives to draw people into this area". Again this suggests that the creation of a number of post-doctoral fellowships would be desirable.

Where centres for interdisciplinary research had been developed, those involved felt confident that they had "a growing body of teaching and research staff with interest and expertise in this area and our existing research programmes provide a base for future expansion". This view may reinforce that of another respondent that resources should perhaps be concentrated in centres with an established track-record.

A respondent from Scotland noted that there there was a very small research community. "One aspect of the problem might be to specify the need to build in linked post-graduate studentships to the projects which are ultimately commissioned". More ear-marked research studentships was advocated by another. The re-introduction of linked awards was also urged.

Stage (iii): Drafting and further consultation

In the light of this response, the third stage involved developing the case, using an interactive process of meetings and further consultation, both with the Users' Forum and the research community.

One of the major criticisms of the initial consultation paper, noted above, was that the list of research projects that had been suggested for possible inclusion in a programme bid was too narrowly focused. In addition, it emerged in discussion that the "art form" of a Research Programme Bid is not to prescribe a detailed set of research topics. Rather it is to devise a coherent but less prescriptive framework within which members of the research community can themselves submit particular research proposals.

With these points in mind, the first tentative draft of the report attempted to make a major shift from the very specific approach outlined in the consultation paper - which had attracted so much criticism - to a much more general and theoretical approach. Under the headline theme "Modernising Law: Civil Rights and Civil Justice in the Modern World", it was suggested that the programme might look at issues such as: the relationship between different models of capitalism, legal structure, and economic performance; the changing need for social justice; the changing nature of the state and alternative models of regulation; and the development of theory and models relating to access to justice.

There was an immediate reaction amongst those consulted - both researchers and users - that this alternative approach destabilised the balance between the particular and the general. There was concern that it might be difficult to argue that, within such an approach, there was a distinct socio-*legal* core.

Thus a second draft sought to develop a middle approach. First the headline theme was changed from modernisation to: "Reconstructing Justice: Rights and Citizenship in the Modern State - a research programme in socio-legal studies". The adoption of this theme, which built on a number of proposals from respondents to the initial consultation paper, was designed to signal an expansion of the scope of the proposed programme from that contained in the consultation paper - to make it clear that broader issues of the relationship between justice, citizenship and law were properly within the frame, not just a narrow focus on law and process.

Within this framework, it was suggested that a number of projects might be developed under a series of broader headings, such as: the aims and purpose of the civil justice system; economic progress and social justice; and changing models of regulation. While there was agreement that the broader focus was more desirable, there remained concern that the general headings lacked coherence.

The third and subsequent drafts retained the overarching theme of "reconstructing justice" but sought to present a more structured approach. Thus it was suggested that the central objective of any research programme should be a critical examination of the role of law in society; and that within this broad objective, the following themes should be encouraged: the creation of law; the europeanisation of law; the impact of law; the experience and use of law; the economics and management of law; and the practice of law. This seemed to provide the basis for the coherence that had been lacking in the second draft, while retaining considerable scope for scholars to advance a wide range of interesting, specific research proposals. It also seemed to reflect much better what the research community had itself been proposing in its responses, as well as be attractive to the users of this body of research.

At the same time a number of additional principles which should underpin any programme were developed: that it must be interdisciplinary; that it should encourage comparative study; and that there should be an element of additional investment in the research infrastructure. These too reflected much of the response from the research community. This general structure emerged by the end of April 1995; the document was subject to further refinement and editing, which was completed by July 1995.[12]

Conclusions

Although, ultimately the exercise was not adopted, some observations are appropriate.

First: the participative and consultative nature of the exercise was, if not unique, at least unusual. (The provision of resource from the ESRC to enable the exercise to be undertaken was also unusual.) Major developments in research policy often occur as the result of the relatively private machinations and limited consultations undertaken by the leaders of particular research areas - what might be described as the "top-down" or "robber-baron" approach. (A number of the responses to the consultation paper clearly assumed, despite assurances to the contrary - that this exercise was yet another example of the "robber-baron" model. I can only assert that this was not my intention, nor was it how the exercise developed in practice.)

An argument can of course be mounted that in many policy development exercises, a process of consultation is cynically designed to create a pretence of participation, which will in reality be ignored by the decision-takers.[13] Again I can only assert that this was not my intention. To the contrary, my judgement is that the process provided an opportunity for the socio-legal research community at large, in association with its user group, to make a major contribution to the shaping of a research programme over which, if funded, they might justifiably feel some sense of ownership. This might be described as the "bottom-up" or "participative" approach. Given the rapidly changing nature of the research funding environment, it gave people an opportunity both to understand the "realpolitik" of the present position, and at the same time make a personal contribution to its shape.

Despite this, not everyone in the research community will be happy with the outcome - in particular those with primary research interests in criminal justice and family justice. The only defence to this criticism is that any realistic level of research funding could not cover the entire field; it was necessary for the focus to be on areas which were relatively under-developed and where, as a consequence, the best opportunities for original research lay. A claim to originality should be an attraction for the final decision takers.

However, I was required to work under one overbearing constraint; bids for research programmes can be no more than six A4 pages in length. The process of distilling the vast array of good ideas advanced by respondents to six sides of coherent prose inevitably meant that some were lost; thus individual respondents will feel ignored. However, my perspective on the exercise is that all the responses - even the most critical - had an impact on the final shape of the report. It could not have been written without the input from the research community. Given the general scarcity of resources for research funding, it may be suggested that this participative model for the development of research programmes should be used much more often in future, in other areas of research activity.

Second, the exercise was relatively (though by no means wholly) unusual, at least in the social sciences, for the direct involvement of research users. The creation of the semi-formal Research Users' Forum and the general context within which the ESRC was having to operate were seen as a very profound threat by a small number of respondents. Bob Lee's chapter in this book reminds us forcibly that there are dangers if the academic research enterprise is being driven too vigorously by a narrow user/policy perspective.

However, my judgement is that this argument can be overstated. Although the political agenda of the Conservative government in relation to research may be put more strongly than was the case some years ago, there have in practice always been political constraints in the provision of public funding for research.

In fact, working with the Users' Forum felt rather different. There was a recognition by many, particularly those working in government, that their research needs and those of their political masters often had to be fitted into a short-term time scale and were directed to a very specific political agenda. However, they themselves were anxious to encourage the provision of funding for the more fundamental research which they would not be able to promote themselves out of departmental budgets. Furthermore, users do themselves have a number of extremely interesting ideas for research which they would wish to facilitate.

My judgement of the tenor of the responses from the research community, taken as a whole, was that, notwithstanding the possible dangers, on balance, most were in favour of closer links with the user community. (In any event, many saw it as inevitable, if not desirable.)

My view is that this is both realistic and the more interesting response. It reinforces the point made at the outset that the research community should not set its back to new factors, but face them and attempt to mould them to their advantage.

Third, throughout the process it was stressed that, although the ESRC had sponsored the consultancy, this did not imply any commitment to funding the final programme bid. I thus sought to encourage all groups with whom I had contact to themselves think of ways to take matters forward on their own account. There is now evidence that the very existence of exercise has itself stimulated further research-related activity. For example, it has become clear that, after much criticism, the Lord Chancellor's Department is making a renewed commitment to the development of a respectably funded research strategy.[14]

In addition, the department has convened a separate Law and Economists group, to explore interdisciplinary research ideas. It has also agreed to host, though not run, the Research Users' Forum.

In addition, a number of other government departments, which initially appeared unable to see the relevance of a socio-legal approach to their research interests, are now involved in the exercise, including the Department of Trade and Industry, the Department of the Environment, and the Home Office. Within the research community itself, the process of the consultation - together with other factors, in particular the existence of the Woolf inquiry into access to justice, and the White Paper on the Reform of Legal Aid - have helped to bring together a number of scholars. The formation of the SLSA Civil Justice Research Group is a notable development.

Fourth, on the question of research capacity, an American commentator observed: "The shortage in numbers of adequately trained socio-legal researchers goes, it seems to me, without saying. With our very much larger research capability in the US, we are seriously short-handed. If the question is, on the other hand, *are there enough people to spend the ESRC's money rather than do the work that ought to be done* (emphasis added), then the shortage may not be acute". I conclude that whatever the theoretical extent of the problem, in practice it is not a substantial one.

However, there is an investment problem. If socio-legal scholarship is to achieve the critical mass necessary for it to be taken as seriously as it should be in both social science and law departments, then there does seem to be a need for an additional programme of research training required. Thus any research programme proposal should contain an element for research training and development: the creation of a number of linked or targeted research studentships, offering research training; the establishment of a junior fellowship/post-doctoral programme; and the provision of new opportunities for relevant research training for staff in post, possibly by the provision of specialist summer schools.

Whatever the final outcome, further resources - for training as well as research projects - will be needed. There will have to be continuous argument of the case. The experience of this exercise suggests that a collective exercise, developing a research agenda on the basis of wide consultation and participation, can result in the production of a much stronger case than can be achieved by small groups working in isolation.

For some, this changing environment is - inevitably - hostile and threatening; however, simply to complain that things are not as one would wish is not productive. Rather, scholars must attempt to understand (even if they do not approve) the nature of this research funding environment, so that they can attempt to shape it and find ways in which they can take advantage of it. *[I am grateful to Professor Phil Thomas for his comments on an earlier draft of this paper. I am, of course, responsible for the final version.]*

Notes

1   The Research Programmes Board is responsible for deciding that part of the ESRC's budget attributable in advance to particular topics/subject areas. There are a number of such programme running at any one time, representing in total about a third of the total ESRC spend.

2   For a further essay, see Partington, M "Implementing the socio-legal: development in socio-legal scholarship and the curriculum" in Wilson G (ed), *Frontiers of Legal Scholarship* (1995).

3   The executive summary of the review was reprinted in a special summer number of the *Socio-Legal Studies Association (SLSA) Newsletter*, No 13, 1994. For a critique of the review, see, Hunt A, "Governing The Socio-Legal Project: or, What do Research Councils do?"(1994) J. Law and Society 520.

4   The membership, which changes quite regularly, is published from time to time in the *SLSA Newsletter*.

5   *Developing the socio-legal research agenda: A Consultation Paper.* I still have copies should anyone wish to see how the proposal developed, available from Faculty of Law, University of Bristol, BS8 1RJ.

6   Many more colleagues added their oral comments at the meetings held around the country during the spring of 1995. See also *SLSA Newsletter* No 15, Spring 1995.

7   In what follows, I have not attributed specific remarks to those who made them since the consultation paper itself did not indicate that submissions would be given publicity, though I have attributed names to comments which were published more widely.

8   Inserted in the Winter 1994 edition of the *SLSA Newsletter* No 14. See also the articles by Hillyard, P "Definitions and Directions for socio-legal studies: The Social Dimension" and Wheeler, S. "Definitions and Directions for socio-legal studies: A Lawyer's Perspective" in the Spring 1995 edition of the *SLSA Newsletter* No 15.

9   The following is derived from the *ESRC's Corporate Plan, 1994-1995* (ESRC, 1994).

10   *Progress through Partnership*, Report from the Steering Group of the Technology Foresight Programme, 1995 (HMSO, London).

11   ESRC (1995) *Thematic Priorities* (ESRC, Swindon).

12   The final draft, *Reconstructing Justice: Rights and Citizenship in the Modern State: A Research Programme in Socio-Legal Studies* (July 1995) is also available from me at the University of Bristol: for address, see above, note 5.

13   See, e.g. the argument developed by Thomas, P in "Royal Commissions" (1982) *Statute Law Review* pp.40-50.

14   LCD (1995) *Research Conference January 1995: Report and Papers* (Lord Chancellor's Department, London).

3   The Political Economy Of Socio-Legal Research

PADDY HILLYARD AND JOE SIM

Introduction

We are living in an age of rampant reform. This reform, however, has little in common with the discourses of benevolent development associated with liberal social change and progressive modernity but has everything to do with the cauterizing discourses of discipline, normalisation and individualism which have been central to the rise and consolidation of the new right in North America and Western Europe. In the UK any consideration and analysis of the politics of reform and its relationship to social research needs to confront this uncomfortable sociological fact. It is the new right under the banner of reform, with its hegemonic appeal to popular consciousness which has made the political running by launching a series of material and ideological attacks on the institutions of education, health, welfare and criminal justice. universities, as all of us who work in them are very much aware, have also been subject to the radical reforms which have affected other key institutions in our society.

The aim of this chapter is to focus both on these broader social and political changes as well as those which are radically affecting universities and to assess the impact that they have had, and continue to have, on socio-legal research. This is not the place to enter into a long discussion of what meant by socio-legal research. This is available elsewhere.[1] It is sufficient for the purposes of this chapter to define it as research which takes all forms of law and legal institutions, broadly defined, and attempts to further our understanding of how they are constructed, organised and operate in their social, cultural, political and economic contexts. As both authors have a principal interest in criminology a number of illustrations will be taken from this area of socio-legal studies. Throughout the chapter we are concerned with attempting to chart the impact to the changes not so much on socio-legal scholarship in general but more specifically on the prospects for critical socio-legal scholarship.

The chapter is structured into a number of sections. In the first we use Hall's notion of 'regressive modernisation' to capture some of the more important socio-legal developments in British society over the last two decades. It is argued that there has been a pincer movement on the interface of law and society. On the one hand the law, particularly the criminal and civil law, has been mobilised to impose more order and control on those who have been dispossessed and disenfranchised over the last 20 years while at the same time laws and legal regulation have been either abolished or extensively relaxed for those with capital resources and power who operate in a range of macro and micro social institutions. We want to capture not only the relaxations in the regulation of capital but also the non-control of the powerful in more economic situations. Within this context we look in the second section at the prospects for constructing a critical socio-legal agenda against two political and economic forces: the continuing centralisation of management of the mass media and the extent of political control which the government now exerts in virtually all walks of life, from health trusts to research councils. The third section considers the changing research context in British universities brought about by the rapid expansion in student numbers, the allocation of more research money for competitive tendering, the Research Assessment Exercises (RAEs), and the changes in the Economic and Social Research and other Councils' funding strategies. The fourth section examines the impact of the changes on socio-legal research in general and critical social-legal research in particular. The final section suggests what might be done.

Regressive Modernisation

Stuart Hall remains one of the sharpest commentators on the broader social changes that have been taking place in the United Kingdom over the last twenty years. He argues that at the theoretical level the transformation of the discourses underpinning the delivery of policy in and across the institutions of education, health, welfare and criminal justice can be understood as part of what he calls 'regressive modernisation', that is 'the attempt to 'educate' and discipline the society into a particularly regressive version of modernity by, paradoxically, dragging it backwards through an equally regressive version of the past".[2]

The 1980s and 1990s are littered with examples of reforms which confirm the trajectory of Hall's analysis at the interface of law and society. Within criminal justice there have been Bills passed, laws enacted and policies implemented which have strengthened the power and authority of the local and national state in a range of areas relating to crime, its punishment and the maintenance of moral and social order.[3] Recent proposals to reform the legal aid system, alter the divorce laws (with the subsequent impact on the ability of women to escape from abusive partners) and introduce military corrective training centres for young offenders are the latest in a long line of changes generated by successive Conservative Home Secretaries and their Cabinet colleagues under the banner of reform whose ramifications both individually and socially will be anything but benevolent.

One of the clearest illustrations of Hall's 'regressive modernisation' thesis has been in the area of public order legislation. The most recent reform which has come under the guise of the Criminal Justice and Public Order Act 1994 has added an iron stiffness to the already draconian powers contained in the Public Order Act 1986. Sections 52 and 53 of the 1994 Act criminalise the right to protest to the point where obstructing a bulldozer can result in three months' imprisonment and/or £2,500 fine. The same penalty applies if individuals fail to leave a piece of land and if the police 'believe' they "are about to commit aggravated trespass".[4]

The full implications of these reforms were seen in April 1995 at Brightingsea in Essex where every household in the town received a letter from the Assistant Chief Constable warning residents that they would be liable to arrest if they participated in demonstrations against the export of live animals. A number of those who did demonstrate utilised sticking plaster in order to seal their lips to avoid being arrested for inciting an unlawful assembly. A senior police officer was shown on nationwide television effectively enacting a modern version of the reading of the Riot Act spelling out to the protesters the inevitability of arrest should they pursue their protest. This was a searing and powerful moment that cut across the 250 years separating the utilisation of the original Riot Act in 1714 and its contemporary descendent and provides a vivid illustration of Hall's argument concerning the material and ideological link between a mythical past and mystical present embedded in the hegemony of the new right. Utilising silence as a disciplinary strategy in the management of dissent is thus no longer the prerogative of courtroom judges. In England and Wales, at this historical moment, horses have more rights on the roads than human beings, a point that those who believe in the natural unfolding of progressive development should bear in mind.[5]

One dominant characteristic of these myriad reforms has been the differential use of the law to criminalise, impoverish or disenfranchise the weak while further empowering the strong and the powerful. This perhaps is most visible in the state's concern with conventional crime and the maintenance of public order while paying little attention or actually increasing the risk from often far more devastating potential threats, such as 'accidents' at work or from pollution. For example, reforms to health and safety at work legislation have deregulated and undermined the state's already limited ability to police and prosecute powerful institutions and individuals responsible for deaths at work. The fact that more than 18,000 people died in industrial accidents in England and Wales between 1965 and 1992, many of them avoidable, provides a chilling reminder, still largely ignored by academics and legal agents, that crime in the suites can be as pernicious and dangerous as crime in the streets. And while, as Frank Pearce and Steve Tombs have noted, there may be some evidence that the activities of those involved in "occupational safety and environmental degradation" have been criminalised[6] the balance of legal and criminal justice reform has overwhelmingly been tilted towards dealing with crime and disorder as defined by law, particularly those activities which pose a threat to public as opposed to private order. As Susan Edwards has pointed out:

> both current legislation and policing priorities in public order reflect the view of the present government and the police that the maintenance and regulation of public order are of quintessential importance. By contrast the law in theory and in practice reflects the relegation of private or domestic 'crime' to that of the lowest priority.[7]

Closing rape crisis centres and hostels for abused women and restricting the funding for those which remain in operation provides further support for Edward's position that, seen through the lens of gender, reform has a specific meaning in relation to the mobilisation of law and the maintenance of order. These reforms to the criminal justice system are themselves taking place in the context of a broader set of economic reforms in which the power of capital has continued to enhance the fiscal strength of a small cadre of individuals and institutions while simultaneously laying waste the prospects and personal lives of many more millions.

The deregulation of the city in the early 1980s with the abolition of exchange controls and various restrictions over bank lending coupled with the decision to allow banks to enter the mortgage market in 1981 led to an orgy of borrowing which increased the stock of mortgage debt sixfold and led to a doubling of house prices between 1980 and 1990. The consequences for many have been devastating. Over one million people are still in negative equity and over 300,000 homes have been repossessed - a level of involuntary evictions which exceeds the numbers evicted in the 'great clearances' of 1849-53 in Ireland where more than one quarter of a million people lost their homes.[8] The consequence for others, of course, has been considerable personal enrichment. While it is impossible to be precise about the impact of deregulation on the redistribution of income and wealth within British society, there is little doubt that it played a significant part together with the fiscal changes, in reducing the disposable income of the bottom 20 per cent from 10 to 6 per cent and increasing the disposable income of the top 20 per cent from 34 to 45 per cent in the period 1979 to 1990.[9]

Another social and economic policy which is likely to have a similar or even more devastating impact is in the field of pensions. In the years ahead poverty and insecurity will revisit hundred of thousands of retired people as the government encourages the use of private pensions while allowing the value of the basic state pension to be eroded by inflation and quietly reducing the value of SERPS. By 2020 the basic pension and SERPS, as Hutton has pointed out, will be worth less than 20 per cent of average earnings, a third of what they would have been had the old consensus held. He suggests that it will be "one of the greatest frauds perpetuated by a democratic government against its people in modern times".[10] Alongside the withering of state pensions we have witnessed the enrichment of the pensions of the captains of the privatised industries through legal methods of acquisition, namely share options.

In all these areas law and legal agents have played a crucial role in the regressive modernisation of social and state institutions and the accompanying social polarisation and marginalisation which has taken place. In spite of a range of contradictions and key points of resistance, legal categories, legal ideology, legal discourses and legal forms as well as a range of legal institutions, including, of course, the legal profession, have been at the heart of this restructuring of modern Britain. This is the broad structural context in which social/legal research is taking place. In the next part of this paper we turn to the more specific issue of the changing research context itself.

The Changing Research Context

There have been five major changes in the last decade which have had a profound and long-lasting impact on research. To begin with there has been a 53 per cent increase in full and part-time student numbers since 1988/89 with only a marginal increase in resources. Second, and perhaps most important, there have been a series of Research Assessment Exercises (RAEs) beginning in 1986. The aim of these exercises is to develop a more selective and systematic approach in the allocation of research monies while at the same time removing funds from the Funding Councils which had previously been allocated to universities in the form of a block grant and handing them to the Research Councils for competitive distribution. In 1992/93 some £87 million or nearly 16 per cent of funds earmarked for research, was given to the Councils. Third, the main funding body, the ESRC, has also developed important new strategies for distributing research monies. Fourth, the government has increased the volume of research allocated on the basis of competitive tendering. Finally there has been an intensification in the control and governance of research, a process which began well before the present Conservative administration but which is now affecting the allocation of research funds and the dissemination of results and findings.

Expansion of Universities

In 1987 the government published its plans for the growth of full-time higher education.[11] It noted that the proportion of the 18-19 olds entering higher education should rise from 14 per cent in 1985 to 18.5 per cent in the year 2000. This meant an increase in home full-time equivalent students from 693,000 to 722,000. In 1991 these home full-time equivalent student figures were revised upwards to just under 1,200,000, a projected increase of 35 per cent in the period.[12] Both projections have been exceeded. This can be seen by taking the total number of home students studying in higher education. In 1988/89 there were 563,000 full-time students and by 1993/94 this had grown to 930,000, a 65 per cent increase. At the same time the number of part-time students increased from 377,000 to 511,000 - a 35 per cent increase.[13]

These extra students have been absorbed into the system with only a modest increase in the number of full-time academic staff from 46,300 to

53,900 - an increase of less than 17 per cent.[14] In addition it cannot be assumed that this extra resource has gone into teaching. Given the importance which universities have placed on the RAEs, many of these appointments will be to research dedicated posts. What is remarkable is the expansion in student and staff numbers has not been resourced by the Government. The Block Grant to universities was increased by a modest 5.8 per cent during the same period.[15]

The impact of this rapid increase in student numbers in a context of declining resources in real terms coupled with new administrative demands does not appear to have been studied systematically. But there can be little doubt from common experience that the workload of many teachers has increased significantly at the very same time as the RAEs created new pressures on academics' time either in terms of demanding that they become research active or that their research output be increased. These demands have certainly led to a lessening in morale and created an atmosphere which is neither conducive to good teaching, because teachers are always trying to find space for research, nor good research because there are too many pressures, particularly the constant pressure to publish, to mark increasing numbers of essays and exam scripts and to administrate.

Research Assessment Exercises

From the outset the RAEs have been subject to considerable criticism. The first exercise was criticised for the failure to make the criteria clear, for applying obviously very different standards across subject areas and for generally favouring larger departments. Although there have been a number of changes in subsequent RAEs and there has been some attempt to produce clearer criteria, there is the fundamental criticism that the whole assessment exercise is impossible because the tools for measurement do not exist. As Griffith has cogently pointed out:

> Whatever reforms were introduced however, much money was spent, however high the quality of the panellists, however comprehensive the

reading of the submitted papers, however many meetings were held to seek to reconcile differences and remove anomalies, at the end of the day there would be differences in gradings which were unacceptable because the system would be known to lack the necessary degree of precision and, on the margins, to be necessarily insecure because based on subjective judgments. You cannot make a silk purse out of a sow's ear. The solution is to abandon the pretence that valid assessments of the work of thousands of university teachers can be made by anything like the present system or that that system can result in fair treatment of the mass of less well-endowed institutions. As is inevitable in competitive exercises, the losers go to the wall. For education at any level, this is unacceptable.[16]

Alan Warde has also raised a number of issues in relation to the 1992 exercise. In particular he points to a survey conducted by *Network: The Newsletter of the British Sociological Association* in which respondents noted that while the exercise had encouraged greater emphasise on research in departments, this had led to a tendency to make appointments and promote individuals "on the basis of their research rather than their teaching performance". Furthermore, the appointment of research professors together with reduced teaching loads for those research active staff 'had resulted in more hours teaching for some full-time staff". Warde provides a pointed summary of the survey:

Most people noted an intensification of work; even if teaching loads were not increasing, administrative tasks or research time were instead. Most remarkable, probably, was the sense of declining morale, loss of job satisfaction and a decline of collegiality. Several people observed that they no longer had time to talk to their colleagues and that levels of personal interaction had reduced. Collegiality and senses of democratic control had been eroded, partly through greater competitiveness among colleagues, and more often because of changed, more centralised and more directive management practices. More than half said that heads of department had begun to extend forms of either commercial or bureaucratic practice on some, or all, members of staff. The effects were sometimes seen as unjust, sometimes as highly provocative, sometimes as a form of bullying, and sometimes as threatening the health and well-being of lecturers. As one put it, 'the levels of stress that I witness (and experience) can only result in illness and premature death'. Perhaps most significant was the fact that no-one reported any positive effects of the RAE. Most thought it detrimental to quality, of both teaching and research. This stands in stark, if predictable contrast, to the self-assurance of the people responsible for the exercise who, without making explicit the grounds for their beliefs, proclaim its unquestionable success.[17]

Changes In The ESRC

At the same time as the move towards greater selectivity in the allocation of research monies to universities by the Funding Councils, major changes have taken place in the Economic and Social Research Council (ESRC). Under the direction of Howard Newby the ESRC made a commitment to adopting a more developmental role in British Social Science Research with a greater emphasis on Research Centres where academics from all countries and disciplines could exchange views and work together. In 1993 the government published its White Paper on Science, Engineering and Technology.[18] This placed considerable emphasis on improving the country's economic competitiveness. The ESRC responded by pressing for even closer links with business by using them as referees on research proposals and insisting that researchers consult with users of research at every stage.

This switch in policy was consolidated with the appointment of Dr Bruce Smith as part-time chair of the ESRC. He has a degree in theoretical physics, worked on the Apollo space programme and is both chair of an engineering company and the Smith Institute for Industrial Mathematics and System Engineering which was established to "stimulate innovation in industry and commerce by encouraging greater technology transfer from academia and by enabling post-graduate students to become immersed in a business culture while continuing their degree courses".[19] In taking up his position Dr Smith had accepted a remit from William Waldegrave, then Minister for Science, "in line with the policy of making science and technology more 'useful'". He was particularly concerned with shifting from "a one-dimensional world where intellectual inquiry is the only ambition to a two-dimensional world where the utility of research also counts and see through the management implications of that".[20]

The switch was further consolidated with the development of Research Users Fora. In socio-legal studies the ESRC set up a Research Users Forum in 1994. It was comprised of over 30 members drawn mainly from key institutions of government from bodies representing legal services and from private sector institutions. There were no sociologists and no social policy analysts involved in the forum. Nor were there any representatives from those social groups who have been "disempowered by the law".[21]

As a result of these developments government departments and other key institutions have gained a far greater influence in determining the research agenda within British universities. This is perhaps best illustrated in relation to the ESRC Whitehall initiative entitled *The Changing Nature of Central Government in Britain*. In an annexe to the documentation distributed to academics it was made clear that the Cabinet Office would assist:

> by advising on the feasibility of the research in general, *participating in the selection of research projects* and in the organising management of the programme, facilitating to the best of their ability *legitimate research approaches* to Government Departments. They will take an interest in the relevant outcomes of the research and advise on the best practice for the dissemination of results.[22] (emphasis added)

The other major recent development in the ESRC strategy has been to spell out what it considers to be future research priorities. After 'the largest ever consultation exercise' it arrived at nine broad themes.[23] It is argued that the new themes will ensure that "Council decision-making achieves greater clarity and transparency." It is also argued that the themes will enable "the Council to shape its longer term research agenda and ensure that the research continues to be relevant to the needs of the users." Each theme will have an indicative budget and it is proposed that over two-thirds of the research and training budget will be devoted to the nine themes. One of the nine themes is entitled Governance and Regulation and the purpose of research, much of it covering socio-legal areas, is "To assist in establishing forms of governance and a regulatory framework which adequately balance economic incentives with the protection of the wider public interest".

Government Contracting For Research

Much government research has also become more pro-active and more competitive. Most government departments now draw up a list of research projects which they wish to see conducted during the year and then they invite tenders not only from academics but also from a wide range of other potential applicants including private research organisations and large commercial companies who have moved into research. A blurring of the distinction between consultancy and research has taken place coupled with a downgrading or deskilling of the research role. It is now widely assumed by government departments that anyone can do research and it is no longer necessary to display years of expertise in a particular area. Indeed being an expert may be a distinct disadvantage compared with a proven track record that the work will be completed on time.

The terms and conditions of a government contract are typically very stringent. They require that the contractor treats as confidential all information which may be derived from or obtained in the course of the work. In addition the contractor cannot publish or arrange press releases about the contract or the work without prior permission and all publications arising from the project must be approved. There is an almost universal expectation that the results should point to clear and direct policy implications. As a result most government research is short-term and principally focused on the questions determined by the government and their civil servants. The terms and conditions of the contract will define the objectives and often the methods so closely that there is no opportunity to stray from the predetermined set of goals. In any event, a Research Advisor Group - a body set up to supervise the research - will ensure that the research objectives are being met. There is little or no opportunity to obtain government monies for long term research or for research which raises more speculative and agnostic questions.

Control And Dissemination

The prospects for constructing a critical socio-legal research agenda are being made difficult by the continuing centralisation and management of an increasingly supine mass media which together with the lack of a culture of investigative reporting and the trivialisation of the social world has facilitated the dissemination of official research findings while marginalising research and writing which challenges the prevailing orthodoxy. The rise in the number of public relations and information officers working within the state is a key aspect of this process. These official 'spin doctors' play a central role in mediating between state agencies, the publication of research and public attitudes towards, and consciousness of social problems and policy issues. There has been a significant rise in the number of these individuals employed by the state in the last 15 years. For example the Ministry of Defence employs more information officers than the number of journalists employed by *The Times*, *Independent* and *Today* newspapers. The number of information officers employed by the Scottish Office increased from 25 in 1979 to 41 in 1995.[24] Clearly it is important not to postulate a deterministic position in terms of the relationship between the mass media and popular consciousness but as a range of sociological work has demonstrated that relationship exists and is built on a system of power which has the capability to define in as well as define out what is newsworthy, important and relevant. The influence of the war in Northern Ireland has been particularly important in the institutionalisation of news management.[25]

As the media has become more supine the Conservative government ruthlessly ensured that the control of key institutions in Britain is in safe hands, or held in Mrs Thatcher's famous phrase by 'One of Us' - a phrase, which as Hugo Young has pointed out, she coined long before she became Prime Minister. She applied it to the cadre of "politicians and other advisors on whom she felt she could rely".[26] Since 1979 the strategic and political implications of this phrase have become visible particularly in relation to the quangoisation of our society. At the level of local government there are 3,000 unelected bodies with over 40,000 government or self-appointed members who control over £30 billion of former local government controlled services.[27] Over 70,000 public appointments can now be made at the discretion of government ministers. Many of those appointed have a background in businesses and/or politics. Businessmen and women chair 75 per cent of NHS Trusts.[28] This strategy has become increasingly influential in relation to social and natural science research. It can be seen in the appointment of particular individuals to key positions of power and authority in various research councils.

Being 'one of us' operates at three levels to influence research. First, it can be seen in the kind of social (and natural) science research which the majority of Conservative Home Secretaries have been prepared to consider when they make major policy statements. Second, it also is related to who conducts the research. This has become as important as what the research identifies. In May 1990, the Centre for Policy Studies (CPS) established by Sir Keith Joseph in August 1974 with Margaret Thatcher as president,[29] held a conference on 'crime culture'. Among those in attendance were Kenneth Baker who was soon to become Home Secretary, Lord Thomas, an advisor to Mrs Thatcher, Lord (formerly Sir Keith Joseph) and a Deputy under-secretary from the Home Office who apologised for the non-attendance of David Waddington the then Home Secretary. David Walters, the Director of the Centre, told the audience that British social research was "at worst Marxist, at best state Fabian". He rejected sociological and environmental views on crime and instead pointed to the work of the American geneticist Richard Herrnstein, author of "Crime and Human Nature". Herrnstein told the conference he could

58

not believe that "our ability to anticipate crime from a person's parents early in life or even before their life had begun will be ignored. Somewhere down the road this knowledge ...will be applied". Kenneth Baker, told Charles Murray the populariser of the underclass thesis: "I am just at the moment reading your brilliant latest book with the greatest of interest".[30]

Third, the ideology of 'one of us' has both propelled and legitimated greater ministerial intervention into the research process itself particularly in relation to research which contradicts monetarist policy prescriptions for criminal, civil or family justice. It has to be said that this is not a new phenomenon in the UK, a point which may disappoint those who wish to attribute every authoritarian advance to the devastation generated by Margaret Thatcher's apocalyptic arrival as Prime Minister in May 1979. Twenty years ago Stan Cohen and Laurie Taylor highlighted the various strategies involved in the regulation and control of their research which challenged the policies being developed for long-term prisoners by a coterie of Home Office officials and professionals who had secretly established the notorious Control Units for those labelled difficult or recalcitrant. These strategies included the centralisation of power, the legalisation of secrecy, the standardisation of research, the mystification of the decision-making structure and the appeal to the public interest.[31]

The attempt to suppress research conducted by the Home Office's own research unit in the summer of 1994, the plans to market test the unit's policy research work and the role of ministers in deciding whether the results of projects should be published provide some indication of the intensification in the process of regulation since Cohen and Taylor's time. A further example of this process emerged in March 1995 when it was revealed that Home Office ministers had suppressed a report which contradicted the claim that the introduction of boot camps for young offenders would have a deterrent effect on the crime rate. Ministers took a month to construct a 13 word response to a Parliamentary question about the effectiveness of boot camps in the USA. The report which was not placed in the library of the House of Commons was "deeply sceptical" about the effectiveness of such camps. It revealed that "rates of reoffending were little different from those in prisons and their introduction had more to do with political imperatives than penal ones".[32] In Barbara Hudson's view ignoring and marginalising critical research in this area can be explained in terms of the switch taking place in the criminal justice system in the 1990s:

> The key signs of the shift from legitimation to risk management are the shift in objective from 'justice' to 'safety' and from concern with offenders to concern with victims ... it becomes easy to see why evidence on ... the effectiveness of boot camps is so easily ignored - such evidence is irrelevant if the goal of criminal justice is no longer to bring about change in offenders.[33]

The Impact Of The Changes On Socio-Legal Research

Before examining the possible impact of the some of these changes in the research environment on socio-legal research, a few comments need to be made about the current state of socio-legal scholarship in Britain. The subject was reviewed by the ESRC in 1994 and Hunt has provided an excellent, though pessimistic, commentary on it. What emerged from that review was a discipline which was highly fragmented in focus and apart from a few outposts in the social sciences was mainly located in law departments. Although interesting work was being conducted in various sub-areas, such as criminology, the legal profession, civil and family justice, and mediation, there was little or nothing in common between these different areas. As Hunt has commented: 'the field of socio-legal studies is now constituted by a discrete set of investigations which is determined by their immediate object of inquiry, usually institutional, such as the courts, dispute processes, professionalisation, and so on".[34] He has drawn attention to the 'abiding sense of self-limitation" of socio-legal research commissioned by state agencies and pointed out how it has reinforced pressure towards narrow empiricism.

All the various changes in the research environment have combined to have varying degrees of impact on socio-legal research. But four broad consequences can be identified: the creation of different forms of binary divisions, consolidation of the legal, the politics of pragmatism and the further commodification of research.

Binary Divisions

The Research Assessment Exercises (RAEs) which we discussed above will create new forms of binary divisions within the higher education system. First, as most commentators seem to agree they will produce an institutional separation between research and teaching. Already, however, it is possible to observe the pernicious separation between the two areas within institutions. All universities have taken the RAEs seriously, particularly the 1996 exercise, and have invested, some heavily, in recruiting 'research active' staff. These individuals are seen as scholars who have a good track record in obtaining research monies in contrast to those who have more a balanced teaching and research profile, those who have conducted mostly unfunded or more long term research or those who have rejected outside funding as politically and ethically problematic. One consequence has been the creation of a 'transfer market' in which institutions have been competing with each other to attract staff. Some individuals have benefited considerably by significant increases in their salaries. Others, who have been pursuing a research career on soft money, have been given longer term contracts. A few people have entered the university system not as teachers and researchers but primarily as researchers.

The benefits for individual universities and the university system are much more problematic. We will have to wait and see whether those universities which adopted an aggressive recruiting policy for the 1996 RAE will go down in history as shrewd investors or disastrous gamblers of the nation's higher educational capital. There is a strong view that the amount of monies to be distributed is unlikely to increase significantly and there will probably be only small adjustments to the current distribution.

As a consequence a number of institutions may find themselves in financial difficulties. For the university system as a whole, the exercises have created a number of unforeseen costs. In particular they have forced up salary costs by paying significantly more to a few without any significant expansion in the number of staff. Certainly no extra resources have been made available. To cover the increase in salary costs resources have been switched from teaching.

In any event the outcome of the 1996 RAE is unlikely to alter radically the huge difference in the amount of research monies going to the old and new universities. In 1992 the ratio of total funding council research income to total funding council grant varied greatly across institutions from the LSE at 56 per cent to less than 1 per cent for some of the new universities and colleges. The research income of the best placed of the new higher institutions was only 10 per cent of its overall funding compared with 16 per cent of the worst placed old higher education institution.[35] While the binary divide between the old universities and the new ones has been abolished, a new binary division has been introduced by the RAEs.

The policy has also had a significant impact on morale of staff in individual departments through reinforcing and exacerbating divisions between colleagues. It has led to situations in which 'transferred in' researchers have become 'free floating' with little or no teaching and administration which is then picked up by others in their department. Furthermore, the transfer market reinforces the divisions between established names and those attempting to break into academic life through securing a permanent post. These individuals are likely to remain on short-term contracts as resources are moved towards attractive package deals for those who have been bought and sold on the market.

The strategy of increasing competition for research resources has been wasteful - a fact that has received remarkably little attention. The 1992 RAE exercise is estimated to have cost over £13 million and the 1996 RAE is expected to cost more. At the same time an increasing amount of staff time is being consumed in writing research applications which are then rejected. For example, consider the number of applications to the ESRC in recent years. In 1988/89 there were 601 applications for individual research awards of which 181 were granted awards - a failure rate of 70 per cent. In 1994/95 the number of applications increased to 878. Of these only 178 were granted awards - a failure rate of 80 per cent. If it assumed that it takes at least two weeks to write a proposal, this means that in 1994/95 over 27 years of academic staff time was taken up writing proposals which were rejected. This would amount to an annual cost of around £1 million. This estimate makes no allowance for all the applications submitted for ESRC programmes or bids to the large number of other research funders such as the Nuffield Foundation or government departments.

It is argued, of course, that the competitive research strategy will improve the quality of the research. But this assumes that the assessment process is able to select out not only the quality applications but also the high quality researchers. As the whole process is opaque - ESRC publish no information on how people are selected to comment upon an application or even their names nor how Committees reach decisions on receipt of the comments - it is impossible to conclude that increased competition will improve the quality of research. On the contrary, it may have the opposite effect.

In any event the major result of the strategy to increase competition has been to increase the amount of control over research by forcing more of it through the research grant mould and hence make it subject to intensive vetting. At the same time it has reduced the space for academics to pursue 'unfunded' research and develop their own research agendas free of peer group review until the point of publication. In short, the space for independent and critical scholarship has been colonised by a disciplinary project of classification, categorisation and assessment. For some time the critical academic, like the leper, had a space of exclusion. He or she was left to get on with their work independent of outside interference. Now all is changed. This space has been invaded by the project associated with the plague victim where "meticulous tactical partitioning" takes place and where there are multiple "individual differentiations".[36]

In short, new binary divisions are everywhere: between the research active and the non-research active, between the scholar who attracts research funds and the one who does not, between the international and the national scholar, between the scholar who publishes in the prestigious journal and the one who writes in more popular outlets. But perhaps most importantly, academic freedom has been undermined more by the competitive research strategy than by the change in law under the Education Act 1988 abolishing tenure. This illustrates Foucault's point that "We must construct an analytics of power that no longer takes law as a model and a code".[37]

Consolidating The Legal

At department level the RAE has also led to important changes. In particular, it has encouraged expansion of socio-legal research in law departments. As lawyers are not normally trained in social science research, a number of law departments have adopted the strategy of recruiting social scientists from social policy, sociology, economics and history to work with lawyers to help in the expansion of the socio-legal research profile. This has had two important consequences. First, it has done little to encourage inter-disciplinary research across departments and has further consolidated the autonomous position of law departments within British universities. Second, it has further weakened the already marginalised position of law and socio-legal research in social science departments. This means that instead of the socio-legal research agenda being primarily determined by social scientists it will be increasingly determined by lawyers. Thus the social in socio-legal will be further marginalised as legal forms of thought and problematisation construct the issues to be researched.

This shift will further consolidate what Hunt describes as the 'legalisation of social relations' in modern society - the process whereby an increasing number of activities are analysed within a legal framework and where law, legal institutions, or legal ideology are seen as having a part to play in the solution to an increasing range of problems. This phenomenon owes much to the very rapid expansion in the training of lawyers and their subsequent deployment not only in law but in many other occupations. The RAE has therefore not only consolidated the autonomy of law departments and isolated them even further from inter-disciplinary challenges but it has also given lawyers more control in determining the socio-legal agenda. The ESRC too has played its part by insisting on the relevance of the users of research. As we have seen most of the members of the Socio-Legal Forum are lawyers and hence are unlikely to pose any challenge to the hegemony of legal thought and legal thinking.

The Politics Of Pragmatism

The eclipse of the social and consolidation of the legal is also likely to be helped by the reaffirmation of the politics of pragmatism in the shift towards a more thematic research agenda. Although the thematic approach has the potential of providing an over-arching framework and general organising categories, such as Governance and Regulation, the strong emphasis throughout all the priorities on economic performance and the expectation that the research should help improve the country's economic competitiveness will militate against the development of theoretical paradigms which could pull together the individual and diverse research projects. The Governance and Regulation theme, which cuts across a number of substantive areas and has the potential of bringing together theoretical paradigms from politics, law, economics and sociology, may not do so because of the emphasis on the need for relevant research and partnerships. In the past the emphasis on relevance certainly discouraged the development of theoretical integrative work in favour of empirical study of some discrete aspect of the law or legal institutions and this is likely to be exacerbated with the added criterion of the need for a partnership.

Furthermore the demand for research to be conducted within a pragmatic paradigm has affected research in a range of areas. This demand leaves little room to pursue the idealistic paradigm within which critical theorists are thought to operate by government ministers, state servants and a number of influential academics. Managerial pragmatism has become the mantra of the mid-1990s in the same way that left realism was the academic chant of the 1980s. What unites both discourses is an accommodation with power. This is not the place to develop a full elaboration and critique of their philosophical links. However, as the mantra of pragmatism becomes progressively louder, for example, in the debates around crime and punishment, it is important to acknowledge two points made by Elizabeth Frazer and Nicola Lacey. First, while pragmatism has its roots in American hermeneutics, its contemporary manifestation is built on the "unacceptably reductionist view" that different sociological positions articulated by theorists of whatever political persuasion concerning issues as diverse as slavery, sexual harassment and racism have an equality of moral legitimacy so that "each simply competes for attention in the cacophony of human discourse". Second, they maintain that contemporary pragmatism conflicts with the need to be committed "to exposing, analysing and struggling against the *social reality* of women's oppression and that of other powerless and dominated groups".[38] (emphasis in the original)

Comodifying The Social

The final significant impact of the changing strategies in the management of research has been what Alan Hunt has called "the commodification of research". Hunt maintains that we are witnessing a "shift within academe from 'publication' as the currency unit of value to 'grants'". This is tied in with a wider process involving the "monetarisation of intellectual labour" which is built on:

> the penetration of neo-liberalism into the governance of academe ... it is unambiguously harmful in that it intensifies the comodification of research in the sense that the link between intellectual or social worth and its 'value' becomes increasingly indeterminate ...[it] should be understood as an attempt to govern both the internal relations within

departments and universities and their external relations (assessment, comparability, league tables and so on).[39]

Hunt also notes that there has been a shift in, and a disruption to, the traditional categories of left and right 'which has resulted in the lack of both theoretical and programmatic consensus".[40]

This point is particularly apposite in relation to critical criminology whose fragmentation has been compounded by the disappearance of what Peter Young has called "the utopias in criminological thinking".[41] Richard Ericson and Kevin Carriere have captured the implications of this fragmentation. Criminology, they write:

> has ... expanded enormously in the past decade ... Criminologists help myriad institutions construct suitable enemies, control the irrational by rational means, and apply insurance - formatted technologies. As such criminologists contribute to an increasingly destructured, fragmented and reflexive existence in risk society.[42]

The monetarisation of intellectual labour is affecting a wide range of decisions including the award of PhDs, the assessment of journal articles or comments on research projects. No longer are the ideas themselves being assessed for their own intellectual worth because they carry a new currency.

Researchers on short term contracts have long recognised the realities of the monetarisation of intellectual labour and the need for self-censorship or face unemployment. Making an intervention into the media for these researchers could result in the termination of their contracts and the certainty of becoming a socio-legal untouchable as far as future contracts are concerned. Indeed this process extends to the presentation of conference papers where self-censorship for short-term contract workers (understandably) has become as important as the contents of the paper itself, particularly when those involved in the funding of the research are members of the audience as frequently happens, for example at the British Criminology Conference.

The commodification of research is also affecting where findings are published. Rumours have been circulating since the last RAE that some panels made assessments on the basis of the relative quality of the journal in which a paper was published. As Griffith has pointed out:

> ...the device of reading the titles and reputation of journals instead of the articles themselves is academically and professionally disreputable. It should have received its coup de grace when some panellists suggested that lists should be produced of 'more highly regarded journals'.[43]

It did not and hence articles for civil libertarian journals, activist newsletters and quality newspapers have become secondary to publishing in 'respectable' academic journals. There is clearly merit in writing for academic journals but when this becomes the principal goal on the road to generating funds for university and college departments then by definition interventionist work which is worth much less in monetary terms but often more in political terms becomes secondary. Powerful institutions and individuals have therefore increasingly become protected by the blanket of comodification thrown over them by state bureaucracies in a world where the trade in intellectuals is as subversive to human potential as the operation of the free market in all other spheres of social existence.

What Is To Be Done?

It is often easier in any circumstances to offer critiques of social processes and institutions than to suggest solutions. However, we want to conclude by offering some solutions to the problem of reform and research in the 1990s. These solutions may appear idealistic but as Peter Young[44] has noted in relation to criminology, theorising has been deeply marked by utopian and idealistic thinking and therefore we are not indulging in anything new. Indeed we would say that the glib dismissal of utopian and idealistic arguments in which a range of conservative, liberal and radical scholars engage, as well as state servants, would be easier to take if their research policy solutions and reforms of the criminal, civil and family justice systems appeared to be working. The abject and parlous state of the prison system in the UK and the fact that it may be close to such a serious breakdown in control that individuals are likely to be killed, in our view hardly provides strong evidence to support the position of those who criticise radical scholars for their idealism.

First, we want to come back to Foucault and his argument about the relationship between criticism, reform, thought and social transformation. In 1981 he noted that simply arguing for reform to be carried out was not enough:

> ... *the work of transformation can only be carried out in a free atmosphere, one constantly agitated by a permanent criticism* ... It is a question of making conflicts more visible ... out of these conflicts, these confrontations, a new power relation must emerge, of whose first, temporary expression will be a reform. If at the base there has not been the work of thought upon itself and *if, in fact. modes of thought, that is to say modes of action, have not been altered, whatever the project for reform, we know that it will be swamped, digested by modes of behaviour and institutions that will always be the same.* (emphasis added)

Despite the usual elliptical ambiguity in Foucault's arguments he is getting to a fundamental point namely that real social transformation requires changing the assumptions and unchallenged modes of thought on which practices and policies rest. Penal policy provides a clear example of this argument. The various calls for reforming prisons while important, in our view will always fail, unless the centrality of the prison itself in the everyday thoughts and practices of politicians, policy makers and the wider society is challenged and changed. This means attempting to transform and transgress the current bleak situation in which unthinking reformist politics, policies and research have become part of the problem rather than part of the solution. Pat Carlen put this point well:

My fear is that present trends in the study of women's and men's prisons are getting us further and further away from understanding the power of the prison both to promise and deliver pain as punishment. Unless investigation of that most specific power is put back on the research agenda, studies of both men's and women's prisons will continue to produce either, short-term reformist exposés, or the deconstructionist diversions wherein important questions about the prison's punitive capacity lie are left unasked. The danger then is that unchallenged, triumphant, and transcarceral, the power of The Prison to punish will increase, both in and out of context - indefinitely ....[45]

Second, it should be recognised that scholarly research does not have to be investigated and completed through funding from traditional research bodies. There are numerous examples in socio-legal studies of scholarly research projects which have been as rigorous and as challenging as the many informal projects funded by the state and other official agencies. Moving research away from these agencies involves academics, particularly critical intellectuals, making some difficult choices and taking a small but important step to challenge the processes of governmental control exercised by gatekeeping technicians. It means recognising in the words of C. Wright Mills, that 'by the work they do not do intellectuals uphold the official definitions of reality, and by the work they do, even elaborate it".[46]

This strategy may be problematic in the eyes of some who will argue that it is important to obtain formal funding in order to influence state policy. This may be so but if Hunt is correct in his argument about the comodification of research then it may be time to recognise that formal funding often reinforces the legitimacy of the gatekeepers in the regulation of the research agenda and by extension reinforces official definitions of reality. This point can be put in the form of a question. Would the issues surrounding the impact of the state in Northern Ireland,[47] the question of deaths in custody,[48] the operation of the Prevention of Terrorism Act[49] the standard of prison medical care,[50] the work of the security services,[51] the nature and extent of racist policing,[52] and the destructive power of male violence[53] - to name a few - have been highlighted, discussed and responded to if academics and community groups had gone through the formal process of state funding? Posing this question does not mean dismissing the often excellent work done by critical academics who receive formal funding. However, we would maintain the funded research has been elevated to a position of veneration which often over-estimates its own achievements and influence while underestimating the achievements and influence of those who have rejected the world of formal funding - or who have been rejected by it.

Third, as David Brown has argued, it is important to realise that there is "no 'natural' constituency for 'social justice' or 'progressive law reforms' merely waiting to be realised".[54] Like Foucault, he maintains that reform endeavours should be aimed both at reconstructing popular culture and common-sense ideas about the law as well as securing some particular amendment to formal legal instruments. This in turn can only be done through a "reflexive understanding that knowledge and research are produced through certain institutional and material practices infused with power relations".[55] This position comes close to that articulated by David Garland and Peter Young.[56] In particular, they argue for a social analysis of penality which "would play a pedagogical role" through clarifying and identifying specific areas in which progressive social forces would intervene and struggle around. Such a strategy in their view:

> would be concerned to render visible - and therefore open to challenge - such features as the ideological relations implicit in penal practice (its rampant individualism, the class divisions it both presupposes and reproduces, its racism and sexism, the popular 'opinion' it constructs accordingly), its political forms (of unaccountable 'expertise', hierarchy, exclusion, secrecy) and the legal isolationism imposed by separating the institutions which 'deal with' offenders from those which can intervene to transform the offenders' social conditions. All of these identifications can form the basis for an informed political practice which challenges the unacceptable ideologies, institutions and techniques and which mobilises people around an alternative programme of penal reform.[57]

Finally, Barbara Hudson maintains that introducing reforms and making policy statements will have little impact until contemporary penal practice begins to satisfy standards of social justice and "deliver justice in the sense of justice as fairness and equity". Thus penal discourse:

> if it remains confined within the present parameters it offers little real hope of altering the differential impact of penal policy on rich and poor, black and white, conventional and unconventional. Just as penal policy can only have minimal impact on crime without broader social strategies of crime prevention, so it can have little impact on justice without broader policies to reduce inequalities and social divisions and to increase social provision.[58]

Hudson is pointing to the need for a reorientation of the criminal justice system in the context of a fundamental restructuring of the deeply embedded social divisions which underpin that system. Therefore while it is important to recognise that the rise in the female prison population in England and Wales in 1994 to its highest ever level was in part due to the numbers being incarcerated for non-payment of TV licences,[59] any research and reform in this area can only be seen in the context of the hierarchical ordering of gender in our society and the feminisation of poverty that has intensified in the 1980s and 1990s.

Hudson's remarks are equally relevant to all areas of socio-legal studies. Currently there is a recognition that the whole area of civil justice is under-researched. We know, for example, very little about how the system operates. While there is certainly a considerable potential for research in this area, if current proposals for research continue to be framed within legal and governmental parameters, there will be little understanding of the role of civil justice in maintaining and extending the position of marginalised and dispossessed sections in the population. Issues of civil justice must be theorised and researched within the context of social justice. As with the criminal justice system, there is a need for the reorientation of the system in the context of the deep social divisions and fractures which underpin it. Otherwise law and legal institutions will be continue to be seen as benign rather a central part of the fractured modern social order.

Taking this position does not mean constructing a deterministic argument about human behaviour that denies agency, subjectivity and responsibility. Nor does such a position deny the often appalling crimes committed by the powerful which are clearly not the result of deprivation, desperation and exclusion. However, it does mean recognising that the issue of social justice cannot be separated from the wider divisions which underpin and give meaning to social life and out of which arise key questions of power and powerlessness. This point has not registered with the technical managerialists and pragmatists who are increasingly influential within academic and state circles. Until such a recognition occurs then much of the intellectual work pursued in this country will be dominated not by the quest for social justice but by the competitive rush to devour the crumbs of research dropped by those who sit at the table of power. Perhaps intellectuals should begin to think about overturning the table and give consideration to the moral and political role that social science research can play as an empowering discourse and strategy in a country where brutalising reforms in a range of social institutions have only intensified the social and psychological immiseration of many of its citizens.

Notes

1   For a useful discussion see ESRC, *Review of Socio-Legal Studies* (1994) Chapter 1, and Chapter 1 of this book.
2   S. Hall, *The Hard Road to Renewal* (1982), p. 2.
3   P. Scraton, J. Sim and P. Skidmore, *Prisons under Protest* (1991) , pp. 156-158.
4   See Liberty, *Criminalising Diversity, Criminalising Dissent* (1995).
5   The decision of the High Court on 4th January, 1995 to quash the convictions of Margaret Jones and   Richard Lloyd who were convicted under section 70 after staging a protest at Stonehenge on the grounds that no trespassory assembly could occur on the highway has provided a strong legal challenge to the Act and returns to people some of their rights which were abolished under the CJPO Act. Unfortunately, the High Court was overturned in the Court of Appeal in January 1997.

6   F. Pearce and S. Tombs, 'Hazards, Regulation and Class: Contextualising the Regulation of Corporate Crime', Unpublished Paper (1995).

7   S. Edwards, *Policing 'Domestic' Violence* (1989).

8   E. Curtis, *The Cause of Ireland: From the United Irishmen to Partition* (1994)

9   P. Townsend, 'The need for an International Welfare State' in A. Jenkinson and K. Livingstone, et. al. (eds) *The Future of the Welfare State* (1994)

10 W. Hutton, 'Why they want to put down older generation', *The Guardian*, 6 February, 1995.

11 HMSO, *Higher Education: Meeting the Challenge*, Cm 114 (1987).

12 HMSO, *Higher Education - A New Framework*, Cm 1541 (1991).

13 CVCP *The Growth in Student numbers in British Higher Education*, February (1995).

14 Department of Education, University Statistics (1994).

15 Ibid.

16 J. Griffith, *Research Assessment*, Council for Academic Freedom, Report, No. 4 (1995), p.45.

17 A. Warde 'The Effects of the 1992 Research Assessment Exercise', Network No. 64, January 1996, pp.1-2 See also, R. Brownsword, "Teaching Quality Assessment in Law Schools" 21 (1994) Journal of Law and Society 529.

18 White Paper, *Realising Our Potential: A Strategy for Science, Engineering and Technology* (1993)

19 ESRC, *Social Sciences, News from the ESRC*, Issue 23 March (1994)

20 ESRC, *Social Sciences, News from the ESRC*, Issue 24 June (1994)

21 P. Hillyard, 'Definitions and Directions for Socio-Legal Studies - The Social Dimension,' SLSA Newsletter, 15, Spring (1995) p. 4.

22 ESRC, *The ESRC Whitehall Programme: The changing nature of Central Government in Britain* (1993).

23 ESRC *Thematic Priorities* (1995)

24 *The Guardian*, 19 April (1995).

25 D. Miller, 'The Northern Ireland Information Service and the Media: Aims, Strategy, Tactics in J. Eldridge (ed.) *Getting the Message: News, Truth and Power* (1993),

26 H. Young, *One of Us* (1991), p ix.

27 *The Guardian* 23 September (1995)

28 W. Hutton, *The State We're in* (1995) p. 38-39.

29 D. Kavanagh, *Thatcherism and British Politics* (1987) p. 89.

30 O. James, 'Crime and the American Mind', *The Independent*, 21 May (1990).

31 S. Cohen and L. Taylor, Talking about Prison Blues in C. Bell and H. Newby (eds) *Doing Sociological Research* (1977) pp. 67-86.

32 *The Guardian*, 20 March (1995).

33 B. Hudson, *Penal Policy and Social Justice* (1995), p. 6-11.

34 A. Hunt, 'Governing the Socio-Legal Project: Or What Do Research councils Do?', Journal of Law and Society, 21, (1994), p. 522.

35 C. Craddden, 'The Research "Poverty Trap"', AUT Bulletin, April (1995)

36 M. Foucault, Discipline and Punish (1975), p 198.

37 M. Foucault, *History of Sexuality: Volume 1: An Introduction* (1978)

38 E. Frazer and N. Lacey *The Politics of Community* (1993) p. 184.

39	Hunt (1994) op. cit. p 520-521.
40	Ibid. p. 525.
41	P. Young, 'The Importance of Utopias in Criminological Thinking', British Journal of Criminology, 32, 4 (1992).
42	R. Ericson and K. Carrier, 'The Fragmentation of Criminology' in D. Nelken (ed) *The Future of Criminology* (1994) p.10.
43	Griffith (1994) Op. cit. p. 30-31.
44	Young (1992) Op. cit. p. 436.
45	P. Carlen, 'Why Study Women's Imprisonment? Or Anyone Else's? An Indefinite Article', in R. King and M. Maguire (eds) *Prisons in Context* (1994) p. 138.
46	Cited in I. Horowitz, *Power, Politics and People: The Collected Essays of C. Wright Mills* (1967) p. 612.
47	K. Boyle, T. Hadden, P. Hillyard, *Ten Years on in Northern Ireland* (1980).
48	P. Scraton and K. Chadwick, *In the Arms of the Law* (1987).
49	P. Hillyard, S*uspect community: People's Experience of the Prevention of terrorism Acts* (1993).
50	J. Sim, *Medical Power in Prisons* (1990).
51	P. Gill, *Policing Politics: Security Intelligence and the Liberal Democratic State* (1994).
52	Independent Committee of Inquiry, *Policing in Hackney 1945-1984* (1989).
53	J. Hanmer and M. Maynard (eds) *Women, Violence and Social Control* (1987).
54	D. Brown, 'The Politics of Reform' in G. Zdenkowski, C. Rowlands and M. Richardson (eds) *The Criminal Injustice System* (1998) p. 280.
55	Ibid. p 280-1.
56	D. Garland and P. Young 'Towards a Social Analysis of the Penality' in D. Garland and P. Young (eds) *The Power to Punish* (1983), p. 34.
57	Ibid. p 34.
58	Hudson (1993) p. 179.
59	Home Office Research and Statistics Department, *The Prison Population in 1994* (1994), p.1.

4 Socio-Legal Research - What's The Use?

ROBERT LEE

As Martin Partington documents in his chapter,[1] June 1994 saw the convening of a meeting of potential users of socio-legal research which thereafter established itself as a socio-legal research users forum. The forum sought to represent the views of 'commerce, government and the professions' and this paper will therefore consider both public and private funding of research. As Partington points out the drive towards a more 'market driven' approach to research funding is viewed by many as a sinister development. It is likely, then, that the establishment of such a group will not be universally welcomed whilst 'statements that research funding must give "value for money", or provide work of value to research users are regarded by some as attempts by Government to direct the research agenda, and thus attack academic freedom'.[2] This chapter will attempt to show that in recent history governments have always sought to influence the research agenda, so that what is important about this development is that it opens the debate about the applied nature of much socio-legal research. It suggests that there are some particular and some more general problems of commissioned socio-legal research, and that it is time for these problems to be addressed in the interests of the research community, and even of the users themselves.

Support For Social Science - A History

In Britain, the activity of the Labour administration in the aftermath of the Second World War led to a demand for social research to support and monitor the social legislation introduced. The Clapham Committee[3] was asked to review "whether additional provision was necessary for research into social and economic questions". Reporting in 1946, the Committee suggested that what was needed was expertise in the social sciences within the universities. Bolstering university staffing in these areas would lead to "routine research". The expansion which followed the publication of the Report has been described as "modest".[4] Nonetheless work emerged in the following years, doubtless stimulated by the post-Clapham expansion, of which the best examples may include that of Social Administration, led by Titmuss at the LSE, Industrial Relations at Oxford and Keynesian Economics at Cambridge.

One particular recommendation of Clapham withered under the Conservative Administration of the 1950s: the Standing Interdepartmental Committee on Economic and Social Research. It does not seem to have reported after 1956 or to have met after 1960.[5] It followed that during this time there was no effective survey or co-ordination of social science research. The task of devising a system to "support and co-ordinate" what was described as "social studies" fell to the Heyworth Committee.[6] The recommendations of this Committee should be considered alongside a number of other contemporaneous commissioned reports to fully appreciate its significance. Under the previous Conservative administration an equivalent report on non-military science recommended separating out from Government the control of science funding and the formation of autonomous research councils.[7]

Not surprisingly Heyworth recommended a research council for the social sciences, and the Social Science Research Council (SSRC) was born. The remit of the SSRC as recommended by Heyworth included the requirement to "keep under review the state of research, to advise the Government on the needs of social science research, to keep under review the supply of trained research workers...". In addition the pool of social scientists working within universities, in accordance with Clapham principles, grew rapidly thereafter as a consequence of the Robbins Report[8] and the expansion of social sciences and the university system generally. However the growth of 'teaching numbers' in these areas did not of itself meet the need for trained researchers at a time of increases in public welfare expenditure and growing concerns with the impact and equity of social programmes.

One striking feature of the Heyworth Committee Report was the instrumental view taken of social science and the focus on the use of research in policy making. The Report speaks of the need for social scientists to work alongside administrators in identifying emerging problems and dealing with them. For their part, administrators should look to identify some of the longer term problems and to "penetrate behind the curtain of everyday decisions". To assist this, the Report called for administrators to be familiar with "the scope and value of social sciences". In relation to the administration of central government, this matched the tone of the Fulton Report[9] which called for a more specialist civil service to allow for better informed decision making.

As Thomas has pointed out, in spite of this policy orientation at its inception, " in the Council's early days the desire to be useful was not always translated in a wish to influence policy".[10] However, this was to change and without doubt a turning point was the election of a Conservative Government in 1979. The SSRC faced a series of cuts in expenditure from £25.1M in 1979 to £21.9M by 1982.[11] In addition, in December 1981, Sir Keith Joseph ordered an urgent review of "the scale and nature" of the SSRC's work. The review was conducted by Lord Rothschild, Head of the Government 'Think-Tank' in the Heath Administration. More interestingly in relation to this discussion, Rothschild had introduced the formal procedures for commissioning scientific research[12] and in particular had devised the 'consumer/contractor' principle whereby 'the customer says what he wants; the contractor does it (if he can) and the customer pays'.[13] This principle was widely adopted by government departments[14] and has proved in many ways to be a limiting factor on the social research commissioned which became pragmatic rather than strategic.[15]

The background of the Rothschild Enquiry into the SSRC,[16] is a more significant historical development than the publication of its findings. Two leading social scientists[17] have suggested that the commissioning of the Report was born out of a particular hostility towards social sciences by Keith Joseph rooted not simply in his 'All Souls' snobbery'[18] but rather in the history of 1970s research on 'the cycle of deprivation' which Joseph commissioned while Secretary of State for Education and Science. According to Klein, Joseph sought to locate what he viewed as a cycle of deprivation (from generation to generation) within the families themselves, whereas social scientists conducting the studies treated this concept with scepticism and viewed the problem as relating more strongly to the structure of British society. As Klein points out the deprivation research itself makes "an illuminating study between social scientists and policy makers which...(was) destined to end in a mutual sense of betrayal...".[19] If this analysis is correct in that Joseph thought that "the programmes of research had been subverted, and used by the research community to pursue its own ideological preoccupations",[20] then suppositions that it was the experience of the deprivation study that led to the political campaign against the SSRC may be correct, and indeed may provide the best possible example of the dangers of failing to fully explore the user's expectation.

Nonetheless, when Rothschild reported, it backed the work of the SSRC, unequivocally describing any attempt to wind up the Council as "an act of intellectual vandalism with damaging consequences for the whole country". In spite of this 1982 was to prove a watershed when judged in the light of subsequent changes. The firm recommendation that the budget of the SSRC be maintained was ignored. It was cut further. Its name was changed dropping the word 'science'.[21] Several major research centres lost out. For example the Keynesian Department of Applied Economics at Cambridge had its grant reduced whereas Patrick Minford's Monetarist Department at Liverpool gained increases. Warwick's Industrial Relations' Research Unit was the subject of an examination into allegations of left wing bias which were found, eventually, to be unsubstantiated.[22]

In a much quoted passage of the Rothschild Report, independence from government was asserted as important because of the potentially subversive nature of submitting "policies to empirical trial with the possibility that the judgement may be adverse". These words were warmly welcomed in the research community but they do reflect the disposition of the Report towards applied research. While recommending independence from government the Report maintains a view that research should be directly useful to Government and elsewhere suggests closer links with users such as industry. A revision of the committee structure in the new ESRC certainly seemed designed to produce this relevance and was much more problem-oriented in its approach.

In many ways, although it sought to protect social sciences and saved the Research Council from abolition, following the Report, the Government was no less free to pursue its new orthodoxies and to re-shape the research community to support the effort. After 1982, there was a sharp shift away from a model of research grants to one of research contracts. These are issued in competition, must address a pre-determined theme, and may become the subject of detailed negotiation as to the scope, methods, deadlines and costings of the study. The American writer, Bailey describes this model as 'the strictest form of research funding' in which 'the application of findings is given first priority'.[23]

Ten years after the Rothschild Report came a series of developments which are likely to have profound developments for socio-legal research even though they arise out of the establishment of an Office of Science and Technology. As happened with the Trend Report and the first Rothschild Report it seems likely that social science will be fundamentally affected by policies devised primarily to direct research in the sciences generally. The Office of Science and Technology has given rise to a White Paper on Science and Technology,[24] which places the Research Councils under the direction of a Director-General, and the launch of 'Technology Foresight with its emphasis not only on dialogue between the research community, industrialists and 'users', but also on wealth creation".

The Steering Group of Technology Foresight will determine areas favoured for research and it describes their approach as 'market-driven' (which is in any case apparent from the panels which it has appointed and which reflect industrial sectors rather than academic disciplines). The aim is to incorporate the priorities established by the initiative into the objectives to be pursued by the Research Councils. This move did not meet with opposition from the ESRC whose Chairman described his support for the White Paper as 'fervent'.[25] Since the Office of Science and Technology was transferred to the Department of Trade and Industry in July 1995 hopes of maintaining the governmental independence proposed by Heyworth and supported by Rothschild are fading fast.

This historical analysis demonstrates that from the outset there was an instrumental purpose in supporting the social science community, and that there was an early but growing notion that social research should be capable of application to decisions which face policy makers. This raises the question of whether in more recent times the objection has not so much been to the application of the research to policy objectives but rather to those policy objectives themselves. Certainly it seems to be the case that much wider use seems to be made of social scientific research, and that it has wandered some way from its immediate post war origins of supporting welfare initiatives. However, whatever the ultimate policies pursued, perhaps it was always likely that an academic community would find objectionable forms of funding which tightly shoe-horned funded research into narrowly defined programmes.

From the funder's viewpoint, since the funding is provided by those seeking to illuminate a practice or policy in which they have an interest, this may seem unsurprising and unobjectionable. However the danger is that the expectations of the user are destined to be thwarted either because of the time taken to produce meaningful data can never match the immediacy of the policy imperative,[26] or because in the longer term the trend is "to perpetrate the narrow empiricist mode of research with which administrators are most familiar, and which so limit the potential contribution of the social scientist".[27] This raises the central question of how and why researcher addresses the social research task.

The Purpose Of Social Science Enquiry

Some researchers may perceive their enquiry as simply a search for the truth. May[28] suggests that in this approach: "the discovery and transmission of knowledge ... is the fundamental good of academic life, just as healing is the fundamental good of medicine, and justice is that of the law." He goes on to suggest that those adopting such an approach would feel no obligation to justify their enterprise by reference to its contribution to some other good. It may be that other goods or purposes are realised but "knowledge need not always look beyond itself for its justification".[29] Researchers subscribing to such models are hardly likely to shape their research in order to influence policy, or to express their findings in a manner which advocates particular change, even though the findings might well be employed to advocate or oppose certain positions.

This approach can be characterised in various other ways. It emphasises the 'science' in social science[30] and asserts neutrality as the norm. It favours a separating out of personal values from the professional task of social science and the type of ethical neutrality suggested by Weber.[31] In sociology this approach is typified by Bierstedt: "as a science, sociology is necessarily silent about questions of value; it cannot decide the directions in which society ought to go, and makes no recommendations on matters of social policy".[32] This positivist approach mirrors that of the 'pure' researcher in the physical sciences, but it may be impossible to sustain - just as it is in practical terms in the physical sciences.[33]

Although applied research is often taken as the opposite of this approach, this is more true of the critical school of research. Significantly critical scholars such as Habermas[34] have been influential in trying to expose this pretension to scientific method by highlighting the hidden interests underpinning this 'pure' approach. It is this exposure of a commitment to existing modes of social control inherent in the 'scientific' research which allows the critical scholar to abandon attempts at supposed neutrality. This is replaced not merely by an admission of personal interest or values in the subject researched, but with a declared interest in emancipation and advocacy in the interest of the researched subject. As such it focuses on the disempowered and dispossessed. Critical legal study follows in this tradition, and Alan Hunt, in asking what is critical about critical legal theory quickly points to the distinctive characteristic that "many proponents wish to espouse an explicit political commitment in that their work seeks to contribute towards some political goal. A typical formulation expresses a commitment to overcoming 'domination' and 'hierarchy'. This concern involves a rejection on one hand of the prevalent apolitical stance of much legal scholarship founded on the belief of in the possibility of value neutrality which portrays the lawyer as technical expert. The concern with politics within critical legal studies involves a commitment to some conception of 'praxis', of the interaction of theory and practice".[35]

This critical approach places itself outside the mainstream and separates itself from the establishment (including the academic establishment) which it would seek to change. As such it cannot expect invitations to bring its radical critique to bear on social problems which have found their way to the policy agenda, and nor would it particularly wish to - perhaps preferring to "travel light...(and) avoid acquiring the obligations and inclinations that make large scale funds necessary".[36] If one detects here a note of moral superiority, then it may be a defensive mechanism against those who would denigrate the activity as partisan and promote their own moral superiority in terms of traditional claims of the neutrality and intellectual rigour of scientific method.

There is nothing which is necessarily critical in socio-legal study as many critical legal theorists would readily agree. There is, however, some wish to challenge traditional orthodoxy in approaches to law and legal research and in particular a desire to move away from seemingly meaningless searches for coherence and consistency in law as laid down by the judiciary or the legislature. Indeed it is true to say that there is often a move away from consideration of substantive law in favour of analysis of the processes of law.[37] This is borne out of a long held perception of difference between law as represented in the Law School syllabus and law as it operates in society.

In order to examine the content and workings of law, understandably it was necessary to adopt some mode of analysis other than that rooted in law itself, and it was to the social sciences generally that the socio-legal studies movement turned. From the earliest days this attracted criticism by those who accused socio-legal scholars of eclecticism and almost intellectual burglary.[38] Since that time, criticism of socio-legal enterprise on these grounds has been more muted perhaps because of the power of the work in reshaping accepted doctrinal perspectives on law. But a criticism emerges that the socio-legal approach focuses too sharply upon the instrumental nature of law. Alan Thompson has argued that the identification of reality is in what "a direct empiricism reveals" and that the shift has been one from "the internal concern with coherence, determinacy and non-contradiction in the rules shown by the expository tradition to an external critique of the rules in terms of their practical effects and efficiency in realising policy objectives".[39]

Socio-Legal Study And The Advocacy Tradition

This leaves socio-legal study occupying difficult territory. Critical legal theorists can openly advocate radical change since they make no pretence of value neutrality and explicitly reject notions of objective and interest free research. Indeed post-modernist scholars would reject the very idea of a search for an objective 'truth' arguing that knowledge or insight about truth is itself socially or politically determined. From such a perspective socio-legal research may be seen as serving the needs of policy makers in a highly utilitarian form. It may be that this criticism could be made of much of social scientific research, and disputes about precisely these types of issues have long been conducted in subjects such as sociology. However, there is an added problem when dealing with law, and one which is exacerbated in the present context of limited resources available to fund socio-legal research.

The first training of most socio-legal researchers is in law. As such they form part of a tradition of legal service provision, and much of their training is directed towards the development of aptitudes to inquire into problems, advise on solutions and advocate causes. This advocacy takes a much wider form than representation or even oral presentation of arguments. It encompasses training in the construction and defence of a line of argument, gathering and marshalling evidence to strengthen the case. In the course of modern commercial legal practice such work is undertaken in a variety of contexts, not merely in litigation, but also in commercial negotiation, lobbying, and situations of non-contentious advocacy. Clients increasingly deploy these lawyerly skills in defence of an organisation's position alongside public relations and other media consultants. On the other side of the fence, plaintiff cause lawyers have been long aware of the benefits of using the media to propound their case and to win public support.

Many of the socio-legal community as law teachers are employed to develop skills of constructing argument and collating and presenting supporting material. Equally the competence of students in this area is assessed, and law teachers have traditionally focused on the persuasive power of the argument of the case made, talking openly of students developing the capacity to 'think like a lawyer'. To this traditional pattern has been added in recent years a more overt acceptance of the importance of skills and skills training within the law syllabus. Again much of this skills teaching centres around the notion of a trained advocate.

Commercial and governmental organisations regularly employ the graduates of such programmes. Often they do not employ them directly, but hire them, by the hour or for a fixed fee, from the larger law firms. They form a lawyer client relationship in which a particular view or case should be propounded. The lawyer will not choose the case, and even the line of argument to be pursued may be a matter of client instruction. From the outset the training of those hired, through mooting, debate, and assessments which demand the presentation of a chosen case ('advise X') is to dispassionately advocate the required cause. Institutional rules such as the cab-rank principle make a virtue out of accepting the hire, whatever the task. So when an organisation commissions or sponsors research from within university law schools, and from the very people responsible for the training and development of the professional advocates regularly engaged, why suddenly assume that the organisation is engaging a social scientist rather than yet another paid advocate?

It might be thought that sponsoring organisations would clearly differentiate university based research from professional legal services, but is this really so obvious? Many research tasks are now conducted by management consultants, accountants and even law firms.[40] It may well be that these organisations value the status of the researcher or the institution.[41] It may be that the location of the work adds value or even an apparent neutrality, in that the findings are more readily accepted than if produced by in-house resources, even where the Government department or the company has ample skills to complete the task. However none of this in itself means that the neutral pursuit of the research task and of the presentation of the findings is what the sponsoring body wants or expects. Indeed it is probable that any expenditure will be justifiable only in terms of some instrumental goal of the organisation.

This is doubtless true in a public sector facing increasingly strong budgetary pressure and heightening financial accountability. In the private sector, it is unusual to give money away and much more customary to seek to invest it. Short term shortfalls in profits can be justified to shareholders or partners but only where there is a promise of longer term reward. It seems likely, then, that both private and public sector will be driven by anticipated returns on the money ploughed into research. These may take a number of forms but there are a number of prominent possibilities. The organisation may wish to support a position which it is minded to adopt. The research may assist in laying the ground for a particular policy or in developing a market for a particular product or service. Indeed it might assist such initiatives by filling an information gap, or uncovering new needs or markets. Finally it is likely that the research could prove valuable in the launch of the policy by assisting the argument with legislators or the government machine, and could be of no less value in the commercial sector in approaching a potential client market.

Little of this is surprising and there are countless examples of social scientific and socio-legal research which can and has been used in such ways. The danger is, however, that the expectation of the sponsor is not simply that the research be conducted, but that it does indeed support a policy line and advocates as powerfully as possible a pre-determined interest. Indeed the research may be evaluated by the sponsoring organisation in terms of how effectively this is done. This is the measure, after all, of other professional legal services which the sponsor also purchases. Since the researcher never intended such a purpose, an expectation gap may appear, and may lead inevitably to disappointment on both sides as the researchers dispassionate attempt to summarise research findings is met with a cold response from the funder who sees little return in the research when measured against the instrumental goals which drove the funding forward.[42] What seems to one party to be skilled and painstaking research work is viewed by the other as a wasted investment.

Research Sponsorship And Competing Interests

Beyond these particular concerns of the socio-legal community lie more general worries particularly in relation to commercial funding of research. The researcher may argue that there are other interests to serve beyond that of the commercial sponsor. These are many and varied and include responsibilities towards the employing institution, the community of scholars within the discipline, and potential audiences for the disemmination of research findings. Not surprisingly the researcher may feel conflicts of interest. Yet again, however, there may be particular problems for the socio legal researcher. Those who purchase legal services in other contexts expect and experience full commitment by the lawyer to their cause. Any doubts about representation or conflicts of interest are resolved at the earliest stage, and thereafter the paymaster assumes unconditional support for the position to be advocated. Wider attachments or loyalties on the part of the legal researcher may not be readily understood.

More than this, there are surely dangers arising out of this mis-match of expectations and goals. The response of the sponsor in such

87

circumstances might well be to take greater control of the research agenda as preliminary reports are made or as the methods of the researcher are observed. Ultimately, the sponsor may claim some element of ownership or confidence in the research material, and be able to restrict publication, or otherwise control the dissemination of the results of the research.[43] If the researcher has agreed to allow the sponsor to control the publication of findings, what is the purpose of the research? The researcher is isolated from an audience, will lose critical appraisal of the work, becomes unaccountable (except to the sponsor) in the research undertaken, and may fall victim of the selective publication of the work which may distort the research findings. As Eisenberg points out, traditional notions of academic freedom, which focus upon the employment relations between researcher and university may be ill-suited to protect against this external threat to academic values in the face of the sponsor's interests.[44]

It is also possible that the researcher may be forced to present findings in a particular manner to suit the sponsor. Richard Posner has written that:

> The closer knit the interpretive community ...the simpler the interpretive task. In economic terms one might say that the more homogenous the interpretive community is, the lower are the costs of overcoming the inevitable 'noise' in communication.[45]

This is unquestionably so, and it may follow that the presentation of research findings, however thorough, alters as an aid to interpretation for the sponsoring audience, and becomes subject to distortions as a result. Certainly there are greater dangers of 'noise' when the audience is comprised of a commercial or a policy-making body rather than an audience from within the research community. Indeed there may be dangers of exaggeration in presenting findings or pressure to respond to questions not fully covered in the scope of the research as originally conducted.

Rather oddly given the centrality of research to the work of the academic, there is surprisingly little literature on the potential conflicts which may arise out of funded research. In what is written, most writers focus on issues of publication when addressing concerns of sponsorship. Some of the literature concerns non-disclosure of interests when presenting material for publication. Much of the writing is in the USA where deliberate attempts have been made by commercial organisations to influence anti-trust policy by commissioning articles by paid authors for presentation to law reviews without any disclosure of interest.[46] Writers have advocated that law journals adopt policies of full disclosure of interests at the time of submission.[47] Commentators have dwelt on problems which may arise from sponsors controlling, restricting, or preventing publication.[48] Davis has argued that 'secrecy, however justified outside the university is inconsistent with that commitment to spreading knowledge'.[49] Others would argue that where a sponsor has paid to gain some commercial advantage traditional notions of autonomy may need to be put aside to accommodate the needs of the sponsor.[50] A much cited instance in the literature is the enforced delay in publication to protect commercial secrecy such as a pending patent application or the need to suppress findings on grounds of national security. Even where such instances arise in scientific research, however, some writers would be strongly protective of rights to publish. Rabban for example argues that these are "unrelated to scholarly concerns" and must be seen as compromises justifiable only in order to obtain funding and where such restrictions "do not unduly diminish the value of research upon eventual dissemination to fellow scholars and the general public".[51]

Certain writers have taken particularly strong lines in arguing against the acceptance of contracts which restrict dissemination of results. A Havard Law school member and university Vice President has argued that: "if an institution decides that it is willing to give up its academic freedom to be more directly connected to its sponsors and to serve their purposes, it cannot pretend to be a true university".[52] A similar line is followed in an accompanying paper where the authors argue that "one cannot make the autonomy of professors regarding published research absolute and at the same time guarantee that universities will continue to be primarily committed to the increase of public knowledge".[53] Rather, "if a university is to be an open forum committed to the pursuit of knowledge it cannot allow ...prior restrictions on the normal and necessary discourse among participants in the research process".[54]

All of these comments raise a much wider issue than that of the suppression of research findings. Where sponsored research takes place in a research community such as a university, the community may be altered in a number of ways by that involvement. It is only necessary to look at the number of researchers, even in law schools who exist on 'soft' research funding to realise the pressures to acceptall sources of funding. Over the long term it is necessary to ask whether the university community will be harmed by pursuing projects by reference to commercial necessity rather than intellectual curiousity, by evaluating a scholar's worth by the amount of funding brought in rather than by the quality of the scholarship, by the pressure on young researchers to shape their work along the lines of available funding, and by the possible neglect of other university duties in the face of more profitable activity.[55]

On the other hand it has been argued that the academic community is freer with available funding than if it were not available, and that on the whole research funds have extended academic freedom rather than restricted it.[56] In pursuing this argument, Kidd shares the doubts of Eisenberg as to how free researchers are in practice to engage in research in an unresticted manner. Resource, including time constraints might thwart other research ideas. Researchers may carry allegiances to causes which are impossible to set aside. Views might be compromised in order to make it into print.[57] It may even be that research efforts are constrained by the requirement to please the scholarly community,[58] although as McDowell points out, the audiences for legal scholarship may be diverse - which may itself affect the level of sophistication which one adopts.[59] Rubin argues that legal scholarship is limited by the adoption of a unified discourse with their subject matter. Arguing that legal researchers speak like judges in the course of their work, he would claim that legal scholars lack a distinctive voice or independent research agenda which would constitute a more relevant contribution and speak to a wider audience.[60]

Whether or not Kidd is right to suppose that wider research funding has extended opportunity and freedom to research it is clear that dependency on outside funding from an increasing number and variety of sources is inevitable. In the USA federal funds for university research grew annually by between 12 and 14 per cent during the 1950s and 1960s, but between 1968 and 1974 the funding freeze began what has now become an active search for commercial funding.[61] Such shocks to the system have a lasting impact, and in the UK as well as the USA many see the move to new funding sources as a way to insulate oneself against the vagaries of government funding policies. Even where governmental funds for research are forthcoming, it is clear that little of this money will come without strings, or be available outside initiatives which governments will promote to support ideological or even party political stances.

Robertson writing of more formal protections potentially afforded by freedom of expression under the First Amendment in the USA concludes that:

> If the Government is not directly interfering with the research, it has much leeway to influence or encourage scientists to take the paths that maximise the values it chooses. The constitutional right to research will seldom protect against the power of the purse. That power allows government to choose the science it wishes to sponsor and the knowledge it wishes to produce.[62]

Writing of socio-legal studies, Hunt would point to similar constraints, but goes on to point to a more significant problem.

> There should be no illusions about the tight constraints which surround the researcher working on projects commissioned by state agencies. Irrespective of whether or not the research produces 'useful' results that in any way influence the policy outcomes, the research undertaken bears an abiding sense of self-limitation.[63]

91

Thus for Hunt the problem is not merely the type of projects which are financed, but the inhibiting influences of the funder not only in the prescription of objectives and method, but also upon a researcher who knows the limits of acceptable responses and who thus faces 'enormous realpolitik restraints on the policy options which can be canvassed'.[64] One result of this in Hunt's view is that socio-legal studies contribute little to wider intellectual exchange, being confined in originality and insight from the outset.

Conclusion

It may be clear from the historical analysis at the beginning of this chapter that it is hardly possible to deny Hunt's assertion that there are real and tight constraints upon the socio-legal researcher. However the chapter also argues that socio-legal scholars concerned with exploring the processes of law and the workings of the legal system, usually by empirical analysis, already occupy a difficult territory which is not so free as the space enjoyed by the critical legal scholar. The commitment to this type of work, and to securing the funding to make such research possible, does create a problem for social scientists. A number of significant ethical dilemmas arise in accepting sponsorship whilst protecting wider freedoms and values. For the socio-legal scholar, however, more particular problems arise which relate to the perceived ability of the legal community to advocate causes. This may place significant pressures upon the researcher's control of the project, and at the very least threatens a mismatch in expectation between funder and researcher.

In the early 1960s the University of Reading accepted sponsorship, from the diamond industry for a Chair in the Physical Properties of Materials. The terms of the sponsorship allowed (but did not mandate) the holder to act as a consultant to the sponsor on condition that any patents resulting from the consultancy were to remain the property of the sponsor. These terms 'met with a great volume of protest' and a subsequent motion of condemnation in the Council of the Association of

University Teachers was almost unanimous.[65] We have moved a long way since then. Many would say in the wrong direction. Issues such as the sponsorship of a Chair from the tobacco industry may still cause comment, but in many areas of educational provision we have grown to accept that academic goals may be practicable only with the benefit of some form of sponsorship.[66]

This certainly has become true of the socio-legal community - if only in terms of the pressure for research council support. Hillyard and Sim[67] are right to point out that in this pursuit we endanger the type of work which might make real breakthroughs by challenging assumptions upon which practices and policies rest. But as they point out we know very little, for example, of how the civil justice system operates. There is a need for a process of discovery, and they argue powerfully for one which seeks to examine the position of the marginalised and dispossessed about whom, almost by definition so little is known. Yet coming from an institution with a Unit committed to researching the increasing criminalisation and marginalisation of travellers, it is clear how little can be done without funds and how difficult funding can be to obtain where projects not only do not feature on the policy agenda but challenge the very content of the agenda itself.

So it may be that resources remain vital to certain research undertakings, and that available sources are limited to governmental or commercial sponsors. Unless we are to reject such sources completely, then the socio-legal community must face the inherent difficulties, tensions, conflicts of interests and ethical issues into which we are inevitably drawn. This problem exists over and above that faced by social science generally given the centrality of law, the close alignment of socio-legal research to legislative and regulatory initiatives, and the advocacy tradition within legal education and practice. These problems - which raise uncomfortable issues for funders and researchers alike, and which threaten rather than advance funding - have not been faced but have been swept aside. The time for opening up a dialogue is long overdue. Indeed it should be the responsibility of every researcher at the outset of the research to fully explore the confines and constraints of the sponsorship offered - even if that leads to the withdrawal of the funding. It may be that a users' group could begin the dialogue. What matters is not whether a users' group is convened, but what it talks about.

Notes

1   Partington M, "Socio-Legal Research in Britain: Shaping the Funding Environment" infra p.23.
2   Ibid p.23.
3   Clapham, Report of the Committtee on the Provision for Social and Economic Research Cmd 6868, HMSO, (1946).
4   See Bulmer M, "Governments and Social Science: Patterns of Mutual Influence" in Bulmer M (ed) Social Science Research and Government : Comparative Essays on Britain and the United States Cambridge U P (1987) at p.2. Bulmer, here, is comparing the parallel development in the USA in the post war period.
5   For the background to the work of this Committee, see the Heyworth Committee Report - Heyworth, Report of the Committee on Social Sciences Cmnd 2660, HMSO (1965).
6   Supra.
7   Trend , Committee of Enquiry into the Organisation of Civil Science Cmnd 2171, HMSO (1963). The Report is entirely silent on the support for and funding of social science.
8   Robbins Higher Education : Report of the Committee appointed by the Prime Minister under the Chairmanship of Lord Robbins 1961-1963 Cmnd 4814 HMSO (1963).
9   Fulton, Report on the Committee on the Civil Service : 1966-1968 Cmnd 3638, HMSO (1968).
10   Thomas P, "The Use of Social Research: Myths and Models" in Bulmer (op.cit.) Social Science Research and Government.
11   Figures at constant 1983 levels and taken from Brannen P, "Research and Social Policy: Political, Organisational and Cultural Constraints" in Heller F (ed), The Use and Abuse of Social Science Sage (1986).
12   Rothschild, The Organisation and management of Government R & D Cmnd 4814, HMSO (1971).
13   Ibid para 6.
14   This was never intended, as Rothschild makes clear in his 1982 Report into the SSRC (infra) social sciences were excluded from the 1971 Report. Indeed in the 1982 Report Rothschild draws a distinction between the objective of R & D in the natural sciences (finding out 'whether and if so how something can be done') and social science research, even of an applied nature (providing 'the material upon which it is possible to conduct more informed debate and make better decisions') - at p.11.
15   See Blume S, The Commissioning of Social Research by Central Government SSRC (1982).

16   Rothschild, An Enquiry into the Social Science Research Council Cmnd 8554, HMSO (1982).

17   See Klein R, 'Pinpointing the Poor' Times Literary Supplement 7 December 1982, p.1401, and Cherns A, 'Policy Research under Srutiny' in Heller (ed) op.cit. p.185.

18   For this explanation and a full account of the episode see Flather P, 'Pulling Through - Conspiracies, Counterplots, and How the SSRC Escaped the Axe in 1982' in Bulmer (ed) op.cit. :"Joseph's dislike also seemed to derive from an All Souls' snobbery...which holds as suspect any discipline that does not have its roots in antiquity, such as history or the classics, or is not empirically testable,like the natural sciences".

19   Op.cit.

20   Ibid.

21   Which Cherns (op.cit.) points to as yet more evidence of the deep scars left by the deprivation research findings.

22   Berrill K, Brown E P H, & Williams D G T, Report of an Investigation into Certain Matters arising from the Rothschild Report on the SSRC   SSRC (1983).

23   Bailey K.D., Methods of Social Research Free Press (2nd Ed. - 1982) p.22.

24   Office of Science and Technology, Realising our Potential (Cm 2250) HMSO (1993).

25   See Griffiths J A G, 'Open Letter to the CVCP' 12 January 1996. This section of the paper has derived much assistance from this letter which also considers the equally serious issue of the incorporation of the priorities into University research funding through the research Councils - but such policies lie beyond the ambit of this paper. See also ESRC Annual Report 1993/4 at p 2 where the Chief Executive of the ESRC states that the Council is committed to the goals of the White Paper and that "it is social science ... that studies the process of wealth creation itself".

26   This point is powerfully made by Thomas (op. cit.) pp.52-53. She argues that although social science research can be influential it is rare that this influence is direct, and that too little attention has been paid to the means by which research can influence policy and too much time spent on commisssioning yet more research which appears to fill an immediate policy gap.

27   Walker R, "Perhaps Minister: The Messy World of 'In-House' Research" in Bulmer (ed.) op.cit. p.153.

28   May W F, "Doing Ethics: The Bearing of Ethical Theories on Fieldwork" (1980) 27(3) Social Problems 358.

29   Ibid.

30   Rather in the manner of Durkheim E, Suicide: A Study in Sociology (translation) The Free Press (1951).

31   Weber M, The Methodology of Social Sciences (translation) The Free Press (1949). However, Weber, unlike Durkheim accepts that methods pursued in the natural sciences cannot always be adequate for social research, and can be supplemented by direct understanding (sympathetic empathy) arising out of the experiences of the researcher.

32   Bierstedt R, The Social Order, McGraw-Hill (1957).

95

33   See Kuhn T, The Structure of Scientific Revolutions, University of Chicago
      Press (1962) and the wide body of literature in the sociology of science which
      asserts the value laden nature of the scientific process - for an introduction see
      Whitley R 'The Context of Scientific Investigation' in Knorr K D et al., The
      Social Process of Scientific Investigation Reidel (1980).

34   Habermas J, Knowledge and Human Interest Beacon (1968).

35   Hunt A, "The Critique of Law: What is Critical about Critical Legal Theory?
      in Fitzpatrick P, and Hunt A, Critical Legal Studies Blackwell (1987) p.6.

36   Becker H S, and Horowitz I L, "Radical Politics and Sociological Research:
      Observations on Methodology and Ideology" (1972) 78 American Journal of
      Sociology 48.

37   See "New Trends in Research Interests of SLSAs Growing Membership" 17
      Socio-Legal Newsletter 1 (Autumn 1995) and also Cain M, 'Rich Man's Law
      or Poor Man's Law' 2 Brit J Law and Society 61 (1975)

38   For an early view of some of these issues see the very first issue of what was
      then the British Journal of Law and Society and the opening essays: Willock,
      ID, 'Getting on with Sociologists' and Campbell C, 'Legal Thought and
      Juristic Values' (1974) 1 British Journal of Law and Society 3 and 13.

39   Thompson A, "Critical Legal Education in Britain" in Fitzpatrick and Hunt
      op.cit., p 183 at 186.

40   See Willis CF 'Research at the Law Society' 13 Socio-Legal Newsletter 4
      (August 1994). The author was involved with four funded legal research
      projects whilst Director of Research with a London based Law firm.

41   See Bok D, "Universities: Their Temptations and Tensions" 18 Journal of
      College and University Law 1 at 14: "the mere aura of a well known university
      can have a commercial value." See Willis CF 'Research at the Law Society' 13
      Socio-Legal Newsletter 4 (August 1994).

42   This is a point forcefully made by Michael King on pp 3/4 of his open letter to
      Martin Partington dated 23 November 1994 and attached to 14 Socio-Legal
      Newsletter (Autumn 1994).

43   The author is aware of two instances in which publication of the research
      finding of sponsored research have been supressed by the sponsor.

44   Eisenberg R S "Academic Freedom and Academic Values in Sponsored
      Research" (1988) 66 Tex L Rev 1363. and see the reply by Rabban D "Does
      Academic Freedom Limit Faculty Autonomy" (1988) 66 Tex L Rev 1405.

45   Posner R A, "The Jurisprudence of Skepticism" 86 Michigan L R 827 at 850
      cited in McDowell B, "The Audiences for Legal Scholarship" 40 Journal of
      Legal Education 261 at 262.

46   Douglas W O, "Law Reviews and Full Disclosure" 40 Washington Law
      Review 227 (1965): Newland J. "The Supreme Court and Legal Writing:
      Learned Journals as the Vehicles of an Anti-Trust Lobby" 48 The Georgetown
      Law Journal 105 (1959); and Closen M L, "A Proposed Code of Professional
      Responsibility for Law Reviews 63 Notre Dame Law Review 55 (1988).

47   Douglas (op. cit.) and Closen (op. cit.).

48   Eisenberg R S, "The Scholar as Advocate" 43 Journal of Legal Education 391
      (1993); Davis M, "University Research and the Wages of Commerce" 18
      Journal of College and University Law 29 (1991): and Robison W L, &

Sanders J T, "The Myths of Academia: Open Enquiry and Funded Research" 19 Journal of College and University Law 227 (1992).

49   Davis ibid. at p.38.

50   This is clear from Eisenberg's review of sponsored research (op. cit. Texas Law Review) in which she points to academic institutions in the USA which have adopted policies of allowing increasing degrees of secrecy for sponsors willing to pay more money: cf. Shattuck J, "Secrecy on Campus" 19 Journal of College & University Law 217 (1993) who states that Harvard's policy is to prohibit research done using university facilities or in university time if the findings cannot be openly published.

51   Rabban D, "Does Academic Freedom Limit Faculty Autonomy" 66 Texas Law Review 1405.

52   Shattuck (op.cit.) at 225.

53   Robison and Sandars (op. cit.) at 237.

54   Ibid at 232.

55   These concerns are largely those addressed by The American Association of University Professors, Academic Freedom and Tenure: Corporate Funding of Academic Research (1983) Academe Nov/Dec p 18a.

56   Kidd CV, 'The Implications of Research Funds for Academic Freedom' (1963) 28 Law and Contemporary Problems 613.

57   For a fuller account of these concerns see Eisenberg R, 'Scholars as Advocates' (1993) 43 Journal of Legal Education 391.

58   Getman J, 'The Internal Scholarly Jury' (1989) 39 Journal of Legal Education 337.

59   McDowell 'The Audiences for Legal Scholarship' op.cit.

60   Rubin E L, 'The Practice and Discourse of Legal Scholarship' (1987/8) 86 Michigan Law Review 1835.

61   The American Association of University Professors 'Corporate Funding of Academic Research' op. cit.

62   Robertson J A, 'The Scientist's Right to Research: A Constitutional Analysis' (1978) 51 Southern California Law Review 1203, 1279.

63   Hunt A, 'Governing the Socio-Legal Project: or, What Do Research Councils Do?' (1994) 21 Journal of Law and Society

64   Ibid.

65   For an account of this episode see Lord Chorley, 'Academic Freedom in the U.K.' (1943) 28 Law and Contemporary Problems 647, from where the quotation is taken.

66   On Oxbridge links with Japanese companies see Pitman J, 'Tokyo Blues' Times 22 October 1994 at p27; on creeping commercialisation see Gerard L, 'Why top dons are the business' Independent 2 March 1995; for an interesting perspective on the controversy surrounding Flick's proposed donation to Balliol see Jenkins S, 'Sins of the Founders Revisited' Times 16 March 1996; finally for an argument that honorary degrees are being traded for favours from the rich see Moreton C 'You've got the money, we've got the degrees' Independent on Sunday 26 January 1996 p 5, but cf 'Dons veto business school' Higher 8 November 1996 at p 5.

67   Hillyard P and Sim J, 'The Political Economy of Socio-Legal Research' infra p 45. 983) Academe Nov/Dec p 18a.

5 Sense And Sensibility: Debates And Developments In Socio-Legal Research Methods

ALAN BRADSHAW

Introduction

What distinguishes socio-legal research from traditional legal research? There can be no absolute answers to this question, but there is a single two-part answer that can perhaps best give orientation. Socio-legal research takes legal study outside the legal 'office', with office used broadly in its multiple senses. First, socio-legal research considers the law and the process of law (law-making, legal procedure) beyond legal texts - i.e. the socio-politico-economic considerations that surround and inform the enactment of laws, the operation of procedure, and the results of the passage and enforcement of laws. Second, in studying the context and results of law, socio-legal research moves beyond the academic, the judicial and the legislative office, chamber, library and committee room to gather data wherever appropriate to the problem. In summary, in both topic and locus of study, socio-legal research moves beyond legal text to investigate law-in-society. Consequently, traditional legal reasoning and the focus on codes and cases of law are not the primary concerns of socio-legal study. This vision beyond legal reasoning, codes and cases demands different methods of working from socio-legal researchers.

Some examples illustrate what *are* typical concerns of socio-legal research. In what follows I am using an implicitly broad definition of *socio-legal* to include criminology and the sociology of law. I am not much concerned with boundary disputes which, I know, have informed the structure of research efforts (the separation of *socio-legal* from *criminological* research centres at the University of Oxford being a case in point).[1] Rather quickly boundary disputes become stale.

One landmark socio-legal study in Britain is the prison survival research of Cohen and Taylor. In *Psychological Survival*, Cohen and Taylor study how men survive long-term high-security imprisonment.[2] The research is not of the law per se, but of how a role imposed by the law (that of prisoner) is coped with in different ways by those who occupy that role. The Cohen and Taylor study is interesting not only for its content but for its methods (largely qualitative interviews or conversations, some in groups), for its genesis (out of a prison education project), and for its political history. Clearly, Cohen and Taylor needed various permissions to be able to enter prisons and talk to prisoners. Prisoner communications to outsiders by letter are also censored in Britain. The support of those who rule the prison system - prison governors and the Home Office of central government - was therefore crucial.[3] The research of Cohen and Taylor offended some elements of the prison authorities and the researchers were denied further access to the prisons to complete the project in the way they wanted. At the same time, the British Home Office was also interested in coping tactics and strategies among long-term prisoners, and commissioned another team, of psychologists, to investigate the same subject with more 'conventional' quantitative attitude or opinion scales.[4] There were therefore rival projects on the same theme being pursued at the same time, one being official, the other failing to get full official cooperation. The Cohen and Taylor example illustrates one sort of concern that socio-legal research can have, and one sort of method strategy. It also illustrates how some socio-legal research is 'dangerous' and politically controversial.

A second famously controversial example of socio-legal research is afforded by *Negotiated Justice*, a study of plea bargaining in a British court.[5] The authors, Baldwin and McConville, were concerned with the actual operation of the law in the court arena rather than the letter of the law itself. The research involved questioning those charged with criminal offences, and those charged with defending them - barristers and solicitors. The study focused on a phenomenon that was thought to be rare in Britain - the process of plea bargaining in which a defendant pleads guilty to a charge in the hope of a lower sentence than that likely to be imposed by a (higher) court if the defendant pleads not guilty and insists on a full trial. The study concludes that forms of plea bargaining and of bringing pressure to bear on the defendant are common, that some innocent defendants are brought to plead guilty, and that some guilty defendants are persuaded by their professional advisors to plead guilty even where there is little likelihood of the prosecution mounting a successful case against the defendant. The authors regard much of the 'advice' given to defendants as *undue* pressure.[6] Some parts of the legal establishment were offended by the findings of the research because it seemed critical of legal professionals, who are unused to detailed criticism from outside the establishment. Some rather noisy pressure was brought against the publication of the results of the investigation. The vice-chancellor of the university where the two authors were based decided to submit the manuscript to independent assessors in order to judge the criticisms of lack of respectable scientific method that had been made of the research. The assessors found that the conduct of the research had been within one style of investigation, that it would have been possible to undertake research in a different way, and that - no doubt - it would have been possible to have reached other conclusions. However, the independent assessment concluded that the Baldwin and McConville study had been respectably undertaken, with conventional methods, and had reached honest conclusions in a properly self-critical manner. The vice-chancellor then - and very unusually - had the book published with his introduction which outlined the violent disagreement which had surrounded the study.[7]

A longer summary of the quarrels surrounding the Cohen and Taylor research and the Baldwin and McConville study is given in Jupp.[8] Such research disputes are illuminating because they throw some light on the state of various parts of the legal establishment as well as on the matters directly investigated (prisons, criminal justice procedure). However, it would be wrong to give the impression that noisy

LIVERPOOL JOHN MOORES UNIVERSITY
LEARNING SERVICES

disagreements are common. It is more usual for the legal and administrative establishment to prevent the production of threatening research by denying access to needed interviews, observation or records. To some degree the severity of gatekeeping is a function of individual personalities, and of the perceived status of the intending researchers. I have known legal professionals deny Polytechnic (now 'new university') researchers, whom they had themselves commissioned to do research and who sought appropriate permissions from subjects (clients of a divorce mediation service), while opening up records to an official research group which proposed no such approaches to seek the permission of the agency's clients. Of course, not all research initiatives are prevented, and there has been a healthy tradition of socio-legal research in Britain. Much of this would not have been possible without legal establishment gatekeepers giving researchers access to study sites. There is some evidence that UK police forces have become markedly less secretive over the last 20 years, for instance.

Of course, not all socio-legal research requires access to individuals for interview, postal questionnaire or direct observation. Some socio-legal concerns can be investigated at the aggregate level via the analysis of official statistics. We pass over here any discussion of the problems associated in general or particular with runs of official statistics in order to give this section's final example of the concerns and methods to be found in socio-legal studies. This example moves away from the broad criminological area to the effects of a road safety reform. Again the example is from British experience. Ross et al ask the question whether the introduction of the UK breathalyser legislation reduced road deaths and casualties.[9] UK casualty figures for years before and after the introduction of roadside breathalyser tests are presented by Ross et al (a *time-series* design). However, the intriguing nature of the analysis is that it is quasi-experimental. A quasi-experimental analysis is one in which the experimental technique of fair comparison following some intervention or 'treatment' is attempted even where a fully 'controlled' experimental procedure is not possible, often because the reform or 'treatment' is introduced in a real-life setting, i.e. outside the psychology laboratory. In the Ross et al breathalyser analysis the road casualty and road fatality data are presented, then cunningly disaggregated. If the breathalyser law worked as a deterrent, then we would expect casualties to reduce most during or after peak drinking times. Ross et al divide the data in this way (between peak drinking times, and hours when bars are closed) and reveal that the law *did* seem to make a difference in reducing death and injury, initially at least. Other administrative reforms have come to be routinely analysed quasi-experimentally, including British probation arrangements. Largely in the USA, some quite enormous social reforms have been mounted and analysed experimentally or quasi-experimentally - for example the New Jersey 'negative income tax' reform.[10]

Some Personal Provocation

At this point we move more provocatively into the area of the methods of research in socio-legal study. It is a conceit, but perhaps a fruitfully provocative one, to believe that the research methodologist should be paid something extra, above and beyond normal salary. This bonus would not attach to any pretence to greater technical expertise. It would be, quite simply, danger money.

What dangers are there in social research methods? In certain of the social sciences the research methodologist is frequently in danger of a severe beating, on both the teaching and the research fronts. Any decent social science research methods course - to take the teaching issue first - deserves to tackle overtly technical issues (sampling, experimental design, computer software packages), some of which are quantitatively detailed (descriptive statistics) and/or apparently quantitatively mysterious (notably inferential statistics, i.e. the process of generalizing from sample results to populations via hypothesis testing). These technical issues deserve to be taught so that undergraduates and postgraduate researchers can access technical literature even if they have no intention of themselves employing more structured or quantitative techniques. However, UK educational culture often produces students lacking in mathematical confidence - sometimes lacking simple arithmetical self-confidence - and consequently afraid of and thus hostile to research methods courses. The issue is more acute in some disciplines than others. Psychologists, for example, on average appear more quantitatively fluent than sociologists, political scientists, social workers and students of social/public administration. The danger for research methods specialists is that their courses are more likely to be resented by students and fought over by colleagues than are other core elements of degree schemes.

A second typical danger, in the research act itself, is that - notwithstanding the previous paragraph - many commentators consider themselves to be methodologically qualified when confronting the work of others. The result can be a rather casual indulgence in methodological critique. I have frequently heard the over-ready criticism that 'X's sample seems rather small' without any justification of what would constitute an adequate size of sample within an appropriate design. It is easy to forget that sophisticated sample designs require fewer sample members to reach a required level of precision (likelihood of achieving an accurate population estimate). There is nothing magical about the 'ten percent sample' - in many circumstances it would be plainly silly, as in national opinion polls. Methodological criticisms sometimes appear to be the proxy for substantive criticisms. If you do not like the results, then you can always criticise the method. It is difficult to avoid the conclusion - but equally difficult to demonstrate this claim conclusively - that the barrage of ethical and technical objections to the 'obedience to authority' experiments of Stanley Milgram was, in fact, a response to the unpalatable findings of his experiments.[11] The telling question is whether Milgram, had he found ordinary citizens much less likely than he did to inflict apparent pain in obedience to authority, would have endured so much *methodological* criticism.

A third danger, this time in the research acts of others, is the 'impossible advice syndrome'. The syndrome takes many forms, but what the varieties have in common is that the research methodologist and/or statistician is called in too late for optimum research procedure. Frequently, mid-year, the postgraduate research supervisor sends the postgraduate student to the methodologist 'for a spot of guidance' when what the student really requires is attendance at the introductory methods course which has been running all year, or was run at the ESRC (Economic and Social Research Council) Essex Summerschool last summer vacation. One of the difficulties of truly cross-disciplinary research of the socio-legal type is the need for supervisors to understand the styles and procedures of the other disciplines. For those brought up on classical law library research it is not always easy to get to grips with the different technical, time, ethical and gatekeeping demands of primary empirical field research. Equally, postgraduate and undergraduate dissertation researchers typically underestimate how long such empirical research - frequently of the interview or postal questionnaire sort - takes to accomplish. I normally suggest to students that they about quadruple the time estimates that they typically at first give me for their questionnaire survey. Some of the time management problems stem from the need to get to grips with unfamiliar software packages [for example 'SPSS' (Statistical Package for the Social Sciences)] and the processes that surround them (such as, production of a coding-friendly questionnaire, coding of the data, data-entry into the analysis package, data validation). Some of the time management problems are 'political', residing more at the organisational level. Postgraduate researchers easily underestimate the time needed and the complexity of decision when an organization is approached as the gatekeeper to a research area (for instance, a police force was asked to give permission for approaches to interview individual officers). Similarly, debutante researchers, and some of us older ones, can be naive about how a questionnaire will be received when it arrives in the offices of a bureaucracy - perhaps a large law firm or a local authority. That the knowledge we seek from the survey questions is fragmented, elusive, expensive to manage and record, sensitive in the public relations sense, and slow to be transmitted even within the organisation approached often escapes the postgraduate researching on a first empirical (i.e. non-library) foray and expecting rapid, accurate, straightforward answers. Telling students that they should have started the preparations some months ago, that their surveys are unlikely to be answered, or that their suspect hypothetical questions ('How would your organisation react if a law ABC were to be enacted?') will most probably produce self-serving and suspect answers and puts the methods advisor in danger of being seen to be a negative, carping critic.

A fourth major danger, or rather pair of dangers, lies in the status of socio-legal research methodologists in the production of knowledge. On the one hand, socio-legal research is likely to be seen by the legal establishment as a simple technical instrument at the service of legislation or legal administrative process. This familiar peril is the legal stripping of social research to its technical (usually quantitative or structured research) components - i.e. the socio-legal is removed from its *social* theory (as opposed to purely legal theory) components. In this guise socio-legal research becomes the technical servant of lawyers, whether academic or practitioners. This tendency is not limited to UK socio-legal studies. In a series of *festschrift* interviews Jean Carbonnier, one of the major post-war figures of French sociology of law, views socio-legal research as the helper of the three other parts of the legal project - systematization, interpretation and, most notably, legislation.[12]

The paired danger in the status of the socio-legal research methodologist in the production of knowledge is also an opposing one. The attack here - and it is very often an attack - comes from those with a conventional social science background who prefer that all social research, including socio-legal empirical work, should self-consciously advance social theory. An associated preference of such critics is that empirical research should be self-conscious about its epistemological presumptions. In this tradition of criticism, where theory and epistemological introspection rule, modest policy-generated empirical work as is often found in socio-legal studies (and other social science areas) runs the risk of being cast aside as naive fact-grubbing empiricism.

Current Review

The above section rather mischievously sets out some of the dangers in the professional life of the methodologist within socio-legal studies. Perhaps inevitably, empirical (again, non-library) research methods have an uneasy relation to a field of study - the law - where the classical form of research has been within the archive and where the practitioner professions are high in social status but usually ill-trained in methods of enquiry outside the library. The disciplines which provide the empirical methods, the social sciences, have been lower in status and general political and social influence. Also, most of the major social sciences (notably sociology) are also prone to methodological and theoretical disputes which do little to establish the credibility of empirical methods of investigation.[13]

It is as well to reflect on what legal institutions and legal academe are doing when they allow in the *socio* to create socio-legal enquiry and research. (And in Britain it is hard to resist the perception that the poor relation, social enquiry, is a guest in the grander and more traditional house of the law.) Socio-legal study of course examines the law, its derivation and its operation, in the social context. But we need to move beyond these bland assertions to determine how and why social enquiry engages with the law. Crudely, what do social researchers have that lawyers want? And this identification of two parties - social researchers and lawyers - to the socio-legal project in Britain is self-conscious and deliberate. In part, and in a less dramatic way, the incomplete duality of socio-legal study in the UK is acknowledged in the recent Economic and Social Research Council review of the socio-legal area.[14] This ESRC report is considered at more length below.

Social researchers certainly have some insights and skills that lawyers need, directly or indirectly. Social researchers, particularly sociologists, have some of the technical means for conducting quantified research, notably the sample survey via questionnaire or interview. Psychologists have available highly sophisticated experimental designs, including techniques for dealing with the reactivity of social research (i.e. where the fact and consciousness of the research process change what is

107

being researched). Such experimental designs can be applied to field conditions - for example psychological testing in experimental and 'control' (comparison) prison regimes, or in novel probation programmes. Psychologists tend to be more quantitatively sophisticated than sociologists, employing complex regression and factor analysis statistical tools in the analysis of data.

The apparently 'scientific' tools of the probability sample, the structured questionnaire, and the personality scale seem to appeal to lawyers engaging in or commissioning research. Such tools seem respectable and safe. It is no coincidence that two highly contentious pieces of socio-legal research of the last 25 years were contentious for their *findings*, and yet mostly criticised for the 'looser' more 'qualitative' research *methods* employed. These two pieces of work, given longer treatment above, are *Psychological Survival*, a study of how men survive long-term imprisonment in a high-security environment, and *Negotiated Justice*, a study of plea bargaining in a British court.[15]

In Europe socio-legal study appears in the mid 1990s to have reached a point of self-conscious redefinition in which empirical study and research method are issues to the fore. In the UK the ending of Economic and Social Research Council (ESRC) research centre core funding for the Oxford Centre for Socio-Legal Studies has - not surprisingly - prompted questions of 'where now?'. In continental Europe the International Institute for the Sociology of Law (Oñati, Basque Province, Spain) gathers strength and moves towards complementing its founding impulses with an increasing directly empirical interest.[16]

The UK experience is instructive, not least because UK social enquiry has been very definitely more empirical than the social study traditions of many continental countries - notably France and southern Europe. Despite this, university socio-legal study in the UK has been dominated by law faculties and law lecturers rather than sociologists, economists, psychologists and other social scientists. The position in the USA is perhaps rather more balanced between jurists and other types of social researchers. In the UK the 1994 ESRC review of socio-legal studies drew attention to the major locus of activity in Britain:

socio-legal studies tend to be concentrated in law departments rather than in social science departments. The research community should strive to increase the opportunities for collaborative work between lawyers and social scientists and to develop interdisciplinary research clusters within universities.[17]

The ESRC review of socio-legal studies puts repeated emphasis on the methodological under-preparation of British socio-legal study:

This Review has established that the current output of identifiable trained researchers is inadequate if socio-legal research in the UK is to flourish. Only a fraction of those currently being appointed to academic positions in law will have received any proper socio-legal research training. ... The training of undergraduate lawyers must be firmly grounded in social, economic and political issues. ... A coordinated strategy for training in socio-legal studies is required in order to develop the skills of academics already in post, and to provide a comprehensive network of law and social-science departments competent to provide training in socio-legal studies to the next generation of socio-legal scholars.[18]

The stress of the ESRC is on methods training, but the Council's conclusions make it clear that the training needs pointed to go beyond the purely methodological to integrate with social and economic theory.

There is nothing special about socio-legal research methods, just as socio-legal enquiry is not so self-contained, well-defined or distinctive that it could unambiguously or uncontroversially be defined as a separate 'discipline'. Socio-legal research methods are broadly the general methods of social research, particularly those of sociology, plus the case research techniques of traditional legal research. On another level, however, the situation of research methodology within socio-legal studies is rather special. Research methods training has been a neglected area, a shortcoming amply pointed to by the Economic and Social Research Council's 1994 Review. On a more personal note I have been surprised at

109

the number of Ph.D/M.Phil research students, including those who define themselves as traditional legal scholars, who want to launch into empirical "socio-" research (usually a postal questionnaire) without any survey training and - more worryingly - without informed technical support from the supervisor. Indeed, many supervisors in law schools appear self-consciously defensive about their lack of familiarity with empirical (i.e. non-library) research methods.

The existence of research methods training gaps identified by the ESRC is somewhat surprising given the near 40-year history of the Home Office Research Unit (established 1957) and the tradition of sophisticated, usually quantitative, empirical research established there. In the UK, university socio-legal enquiry has been dominated by academic lawyers located within law schools.[19] This has had the consequence of severely containing the volume of empirical research and of interest in empirical methodological issues. All this is further surprising when it is remembered that many of the most adventurous, controversial, memorable and developmentally significant of all social research studies have been directly or indirectly of interest to the law, particularly to criminology. The crime interests of the US Chicago School produced many participant observation and diary studies, often still cited if not much read.[20] The self-report deviance studies of Hirschi mark a high point of the sophisticated use of simple percentage tables to analyse complex multivariate interactive relationships.[21] Stanley Milgram's ingeniously duplicitous laboratory experiments investigated the limits of obedience to authority in extreme circumstances (a study inspired by the problem of war crimes, and relevant to war crimes prosecutions).[22] Milgram's work threw up huge technical and ethical problems, and the issues of the ethical boundaries of doing, reporting and using research have likewise dominated socio-legal research projects using radically different methods of investigation. Such ethically sensitive and much criticised projects would include Laud Humphreys' investigation of illegal homosexual acts (semi-participant observation, plus interviews) and the Stanford role-playing prison simulation.[23] Curiously, many academic lawyers appear ignorant of these studies.

110

Research methodology has not deserved the relative neglect into which it has fallen. A good knowledge of techniques of research design, implementation and analysis is necessary, and can be acquired quite painlessly. Several of the general social research methods primers appearing for the US undergraduate market in the 1980s and 90s are highly readable and appropriately wide-ranging (i.e. they go well beyond the interview and questionnaire survey).[24] Importantly, these texts are as illustrative and inspirational as they are directive. They give varied examples of research in a way which genuinely conveys the dynamic and excitement of discovery. Although these texts are presumably written for the general sociology degree they take many of their examples from areas explicitly and implicitly relevant to the law. Conversely, the explicitly socio-legal *Research Methods in Criminal Justice* (Fitzgerald & Cox, 1994) is much less entertaining and much more narrowly statistical.[25]

This issue of statistics is perhaps part of the key to the relative UK neglect of socio-legal research methods training and development. British education is notoriously poor at developing in the average citizen confidence, facility and liking for quantification.[26] The 'quantified' parts of research (probability sampling, computer packages and statistical analysis) tend to be treated with a measure of exaggerated respect, fear and loathing. There is no denying that classical inferential statistics (generalizing from sample to population) and multivariate analysis (examining the covariation of more than two variables simultaneously) become technically demanding, but the underlying concepts are straightforward. They are made available through increasingly simple 'cookbook texts' of statistical procedure, and through general educational/inspirational primers on statistics, some of considerable vintage.[27] Ronald Meek's hugely entertaining *Figuring out Society* begins in macabre fashion with public hangman James Berry's use of the regression method to develop the 'humane' drop method of execution.[28] As improbable as it may seem, Meek went on to make the socio-legal use of matrix algebra and markov chains accessible to the lay reader in his reworking of the Mahoney and Blozan data on prison population prediction.[29]

Two Contributions

One of the disappointing features of the use of socio-legal research is the contrast between the level of presentation of evidence and of argument in academic discussion on the one hand and in public debate on the other. The disappointment derives in part from the fact that well-written social and legal analyses, while remaining technically and theoretically sophisticated can remain highly accessible to the intelligent lay reader and serious journalist. Cynics may claim that in the arena of political conflict we must expect the partial presentation and use of evidence. 'It was ever thus' is the claim. Yet it is legitimate to ask, on occasion, who benefits from rather sloppy and insensitive presentations of data.

The case of Sir Paul Condon, Metropolitan Police Commissioner, in the summer of 1995 is a case in point. In August 1995 Sir Paul Condon launched a London police operation to combat street robberies - 'muggings' - in the context of a rising number in London of recorded crimes of this type - from 19,000 in 1993 to 22,000 in 1994, with a rise of 9,000 in the five years up to 1995. He paved the way for this Operation Eagle Eye by writing to black community leaders to invite them to a briefing. The Commissioner's letter points to a reduction in London of recorded crime in general, but goes on to remark that over the two previous years:

> crimes of violence against people showed a marked and unacceptable increase. Most crimes of violence are committed by people who are well known to their victims, but there is a worrying upward trend in the number of street robberies - the kind of offence we generally call "mugging" and which nearly always involves some form of violence. It is a fact that very many of the perpetrators of muggings are very young black people, who have been excluded from school and/or are unemployed. I am sure I do not need to spell out the sensitivity of dealing with this crime problem which is, of course, much more than just a police problem.[30]

112

The letter provoked and outcry in which Sir Paul was variously accused of a racist outburst, of reflecting the racism of his police force, of encouraging or supporting racism in the white population, and of well-meaning but insensitive handling of a difficult issue. It is difficult to tell what Sir Paul Condon hoped to achieve, beyond, perhaps, building bridges internally with police colleagues who already considered him too liberal and sensitive.

The Sir Paul Condon affair can be contrasted with the best of policy-oriented or policy-relevant work to be found in the UK. Clearly, careful explorations of difficult areas are to be found, and are written succinctly and clearly enough, free of unnecessary technical and theoretical ornamentation, to be available to policy makers and intelligent citizens in general. I have chosen as an exemplar of clear and careful work an article by James Nazroo that was published just at the time that the Condon initiative was being debated.[31] Nazroo's article on 'Uncovering Gender Differences in the Use of Marital Violence: the Effect of Methodology' is significant in that it continues the long debate on marital violence that took on particular vigour in the 1970s; it advances the body of evidence within the context of theoretical discussion; it tackles anomalies in present understandings via an analysis of research methods employed; the article reports new research findings; it is self-critical of the boundaries of inference which arise from the limitations of its own sample and method; and the Nazroo article has obvious but unlaboured implications for charging and sentencing policy in the field of domestic violence prosecutions, and for the general legal regulation of marital disputes.

Nazroo reviews the way in which feminist findings of the greater violence done to wives, as opposed to violence done to husbands by wives, have been mainly associated with 'in-depth interviews with relatively small samples of women who were usually selected into the research because of their experience of marital violence'.[32] Conversely, much self-consciously 'gender-neutral' research has highlighted violence against husbands as well as wives. This research has typically relied on surveys of both men and women, using the fixed-format questionnaire, and has often employed the Conflict Tactics Scale (CTS). Users of the CTS scale criticise much feminist research for neglecting the experiences of men, and for investigating violence against women in self-selected or clinical samples which are atypical of marital and cohabiting relationships. Feminist research criticises the CTS research for leaving too much to respondent rating (for example the meaning of 'very often' or of 'beating up' may well vary between respondents in general, and may vary systematically between the genders or other subgroups of the sample). Feminist researchers also point to the lack of contextual understanding of acts of violence in many CTS studies. According to this view CTS studies typically ignore the social and individual differences of interpretation of violent acts, and also neglect the meaning consequences of violence, especially the question of intimidation through fear of recurrence.

Nazroo addresses the contradiction of opposing findings by designing research that takes account of the criticisms levelled by each camp at the other. In essence, Nazroo's survey combines semi-structured open-ended interviewing with systematic and quantitative data gathering. Nazroo comments:

> The advantages of this methodology for the purposes of this research is that it allows three approaches to be used in the measurement of marital violence. First, sufficient information is collected for any incidents of marital violence to be explored in a *qualitative* way. Second, this information is collected in a systematic but detailed enough way for it to *be quantitatively coded in the context specific way ...* . Third, the systematic collection of basic information allows it to be *quantitatively coded in a purely act-based way* similar to that used by the CTS.[33]

The sample used by Nazroo is also sensitively constructed, although not very large. Nazroo questions ninety-six couples originally contacted from GP patient lists for a study of gender differences in stress. The sample therefore gathers *couple* information, not purely unrelated individual data, and is neither self-selected nor 'clinically' selected with reference to prior reports of marital violence. The sample was disproportionately inner-city working class. Because some degree of couple cooperation was needed for the study to be completed, the sample probably underrepresents couples whose relationships were weakest and/or most violent.

On the results gained from this sample Nazroo concludes that:

> These data suggest that purely act-based measures of marital violence, such as the CTS, are highly misleading and that this is a result of their failure to consider the context in which violence is used and the meaning of such violence. ... A more detailed exploration of men and women's accounts emphasises that men's experience of violence in marriage is not as victims, even when they are being hit, while women's experience of violence is almost always as a victim.[34]

Nazroo further suggests that among the women, but not among the men, there is a strong relationship between the experience of violence from husband and anxiety symptoms - i.e. the discovery of an *interactive* association between violence, gender and anxiety. Nazroo concludes by looking back to feminist theories of violence and patriarchy.

There are many interesting features in the Nazroo article, and it may help to draw some of these out here. Theory, finding and methodological consciousness are clearly integrated. More particularly, the starting point of the article is the association between rival theory/finding bundles and the typical research method employed by these competing approaches. The research is designed to cut through these rivalries, with the research method that is chosen by Nazroo explicitly developed to answer the questions posed by each camp - i.e. Nazroo will not accept that there is no solution to the puzzle. More specifically, Nazroo combines different methodological styles within his research (notably the quantitative and the qualitative). Thus he implicitly rejects the notion that different research methods are incompatible because ineradicably value laden and indissolubly wed to rival approaches in social study. The analysis not only combines the qualitative with the quantitative, but within the quantitative register embraces the familiar two-way percentage table (to measure strength of association), the familiar but frequently misunderstood 'p' value of statistical inference (to assess confidence of generalisability from sample to population), and the more complex tabular analysis techniques of 'logistic regression' and 'odds ratios'. And, not least, Nazroo is conscious of the disadvantages as well as the advantages of his sample.

Safe Bets For The Future

Distinctions between the quantitative/qualitative formal/informal styles in social and socio-legal research are both useful and at the same time generally overused and overdrawn. However we shall use the conventional distinction between quantitative and qualitative here in this section in order to point towards interests and skills that the developing socio-legal researcher may well want to pursue (should pursue ?) in the next ten years.

On the quantitative side, statistical computer packages will clearly expand, will become technically more sophisticated, and at the same time will be easier to use. There will be more point-and-click with the mouse, more visual displays, less obvious need to know how to write short programs or 'runs' of command lines to get the statistical software to operate on the cumbersomely structured data. In short, data construction and access within statistical packages are ceasing to be the mysterious and frustrating concerns that they were before the arrival of *Windows*-type operating systems. Such developments are, of course, welcome dangers. They are *welcome* because the simplicity of operation makes for more rapid, happier and less error-prone working. They are *dangers* because it becomes even easier to process large amounts of data inappropriately. If you put the wrong questions (inappropriate statistical procedures) to 'correct' data then you are bound to arrive at wrong answers, however much care has been taken to enter and validate the data into the package. It was always that way - only now more so.

For socio-legal research the one big quantitative advance of the last decade or so has been the development of more sophisticated statistical techniques to deal with simple tabular data. We are most concerned here with data at the 'nominal' level, i.e. where simple categories (male/female, guilty/not guilty) are created and heads counted. The new techniques are 'loglinear' and 'logistic' techniques. Previously, the development and testing of sophisticated models of how the social world is best expressed were largely associated with higher level data at the 'interval' or 'ratio' levels of sophistication (for example psychological test scores, income, years of experience). Higher level data of this sort are often processed using computer algorithms which explore the *structures* present within the data. Popular techniques include *factor analysis* (for example for personality test scores), *path analysis* (for testing causal models) and - perhaps more familiarly for those who completed undergraduate research methods courses, general *multiple regression*. The 'data reduction' ambition in such techniques is to determine which (necessarily simplified) working model of social processes best fits the complexities of large volumes of data. Loglinear and logistic model techniques do a similar job, but for the sort of data which typically appear in 'crosstabulations' (tables like those of the old joke about a population 'broken down by sex and smoking'). In such tables characteristics are typically classified and *counted* rather than *measured*. New statistical techniques have been developed and expressed in software, notably the GLIM package, for the analysis of data at this simple 'nominal' level of sophistication.

Many variables in socio-legal research will be at this nominal level (name-and-count) or at the next higher 'ordinal' level (order-and-count data of the 'high', 'medium', 'low' sort). The general diffusion of loglinear and logistic modelling, plus the software to accomplish this, is therefore likely to aid socio-legal research over the next decade, particularly as these methods spill over from allied areas (notably sociology and institutional evaluation research). The wider adoption of loglinear and logistic modelling must in turn prompt greater understanding in socio-legal studies of inferential statistics - i.e. that general and important question of calculating the security or confidence that we feel in generalizing the result found in a randomly selected sample to the broader population that the sample claims to represent. In the more accessible literature, model building/testing via crosstabulation is explored in general in Ottar Hellevik's *Introduction to Causal Analysis*.[35] More specifically, social research loglinear and logistic modelling techniques are the particular focus of Nigel Gilbert's *Analyzing Tabular Data*.[36] Although the variety of analytical techniques available to the researcher may at first seem bewildering, there are a small number of common themes and there are many linked foundations among them. Logistic regression, for example, is merely one special form of loglinear regression in which the model tested is one in which one of the variables is 'caused' or conditioned by the others in the model.

Our second 'safe bet' that a socio-legal researcher might want to invest in is another computer software package, but this time for the analysis of data derived from the qualitative techniques of observation, diary-keeping and unstructured/less structured interviewing. The next decade will see the routine use of *qualitative data analysis computer packages*, not just for the analysis of empirical field data but for the analysis of formal archival data and informal researchers' library notes in many disciplines. Hence, qualitative analysis packages of the sort described below may be of interest to the traditional legal scholar, as well as to the socio-legal investigator.

Properly speaking, the qualitative data analysis package does not actually *analyse* data in the familiar way of quantitative statistical packages. Rather, the typical qualitative data analysis package answers the storage and cross-referencing problem that has been a simple but profound difficulty of that sort of data which is gathered by the yard of text or reported speech rather than by the summary statistical digit. Now you have all those taped interviews transcribed, how can you make sense of the data, find patterns there? The qualitative data analysis package answers this need.

Typically, the qualitative data analysis package allows the researcher to electronically mark with keywords or titles passages of stored free-format text. Occurrences of the same theme in large volumes of text can later be easily traced via a keyword search. Some programs allow the creation of multiple markers on the same portion of text, and of overlapping or nested thematic sections. The problems of retrieval for comparison of like-themed sections in a large volume of data are therefore reduced. More powerfully, some of these new packages allow cross-referencing, so creating a qualitative analog of the two-way statistical table in quantitative analysis. With some qualitative packages there are facilities for modifying keywords or codes, just as in statistical packages data transformation routines allow for the recoding or computation of variables.

Nigel Fielding (1994) who co-directs CAQDAS (see below) divides the new qualitative data analysis software available into three types - text retrievers, code-and-retrieve packages, and theory-building software.[37] Examples of code-and-retrieve software which characteristically help the researcher to divide text into coded sections are *The Ethnograph*, *Kwalitan*, and *QUALPRO*. Fielding comments that some of the more sophisticated theory-building software (for example NUDIST) also has more powerful code-and-retrieve facilities. The theory-building software is:

software that is primarily concerned with relationships between the categories themselves. ... For example, they might help you to make connections between codes (i.e. categories of information), to develop higher order classifications and categories, to formulate propositions or assertions that imply a conceptual structure which fits the data and/or to test such propositions to see if they apply. These packages are often organised around a system of rules or based on formal logic, offering Boolean searching or hypothesis-testing features. ... some add the ability to code or retrieve data other than text, like picture or video. ... Some enable you to display your code names as nodes in a graphic display (for example a 'tree structure') and to link them to other nodes by specified relationships such as 'belongs to', or 'leads to', 'is a kind of' and so on.[38]

An older but fuller treatment of the possibilities of such qualitative analysis software is given by Fielding & Lee.[39]

The UK Economic and Social Research Council has funded an organ to disseminate understanding of the practical skills required for such computer-aided data analysis. The project is CAQDAS (Computer Assisted Qualitative Data Analysis Software Project), co-directed from University of Surrey and from Royal Holloway, University of London. CAQDAS includes an e-mail discussion group, and has a place in the *ESRC Data Archive Bulletin.* Clearly, a new era has opened up for the qualitative researcher via that arch-tool of the statistician, the computer.

Concluding Note: Some Optimism

The ESRC has taken a lively interest in socio-legal studies over the last few years, and has pushed the issue of research methods training and sophistication to the fore. There is no way of preventing the sometimes rowdy debates of the sort that surrounded the Condon letter, but there is evidence that good empirical work with thoughtful methodological input is present in the UK (the Nazroo article described above). At the same time, the increasing use of computers to facilitate qualitative analysis is likely to bring a mingling of the hitherto numerate-cum-computerate with the formerly qualitative-cum-card file. This in turn may lessen the unhealthy and false virulence of the quantitative-versus-qualitative squabble that became so tiresome within some social science areas. Perhaps we can look forward to a time when the research methodologist no longer deserves that 'danger money', and when socio-legal researchers are a little less isolated from traditional lawyers.

Notes

1   I am grateful to Andrew Ashworth of the School of Law, King's College London, for his comments here.
2   S.Cohen and L.Taylor, *Psychological Survival: the Experience of Long-Term Imprisonment* (1972).
3   id., pp. 35-40.

4   id., pp. 201-207

5   J. Baldwin and M. McConville, *Negotiated Justice: Pressures to Plead Guilty* (1977)

6   id., see, for example, p. 35.

7   id., the dispute is outlined in the Foreword, pp. xv-xvi, and in the authors' own Introductory Note, pp. vii-xii.

8   V. Jupp, *Methods of Criminological Research* (1989). This volume blends methodological reflection with copious, well-chosen examples of research. The series in which it appears is an excellent introduction to the technical, logical and value aspects of empirical research - George Allen & Unwin's *Contemporary Social Research* series, edited by Martin Bulmer.

9   H. Ross et al., 'Determining the social effects of a legal reform' (1977) 13 *American Behavioral Scientist* 493

10   The classic statement of this approach to the analysis of legislation and social reform is D. Campbell, 'Reforms as Experiments' (1969) 24 *American Psychologist* 209.

11   S.Milgram, *Obedience to Authority* (1974). By the time that Milgram published his book, methodological and ethical criticism of the experimental series was already developed thanks to article publication. In his book Milgram conducts a lively counter-attack against the critics. In the experiments Milgram had ordered US citizens, volunteering supposedly for an experiment into the effects of punishment on learning, to give ever stronger electric shocks to another volunteer, the 'learner'. The 'learner' was, in fact, an actor and confederate of Milgram, and received no electric shocks. The real purpose of the experiment was to determine how far, and in what conditions, citizens would administer apparently harmful shocks under mild pressure from a voice of 'authority'.

12   S. Andrini and A-J. Arnaud, *Jean Carbonnier, Renato Treves et la sociologie du droit* (1995). The volume considers both Carbonnier and Treves as founders of the sociology of law in France and Italy respectively. It is, in itself, an example of the qualitative interview method.

13   See, for example, A. Dawe, 'The Two Sociologies' (1970) 21 *British Journal of Sociology* 207, reproduced in *Sociological Perspectives*, eds. K. Thompson and Jeremy Tunstall (1971) 542. The basic epistemological and methodological positions are set out, usually in an over simple and antagonistic way in myriad sociological primers, for example M. Haralambos, *Sociology: Themes and Perspectives* (1980), especially ch. 12.

14   Economic and Social Research Council, *Review of Socio-legal Studies* (1994).

15   Cohen and Taylor, op. cit., n. 2; and Baldwin and McConville, op.cit., n. 5.

16   Within Spain itself (the Oñati centre is international in character, although its Spanish home gives Hispanic socio-legal studies much influence there) Pompeu Casanovas in Barcelona, and Manuel Calvo García in Zaragoza are particularly active. See, for example, M. Calvo García, *Los Fundamentos del Método Jurídico: una Revisión Crítica* (1994).

17   Op cit., n.14, p. 46

18   id., p.45

19   I am not at all convinced that the arrival of non-lawyer criminologists in UK law schools since the mid-1980s has been of sufficient volume to change the fundamental research and teaching orientations of law schools.

20   An outline of the Chicago School is given in K. Plummer, *Documents of Life* (1983) ch. 3.

21   T. Hirschi, *Causes of Delinquency* (1969).

22   Op. cit., n. 11.

23   See L. Humphreys, *Tearoom Trade* (1975). For the Stanford prison simulation see C. Haney et al., 'Interpersonal Dynamics in a Simulated Prison', (1973) 1(2) *International Journal of Criminology and Penology* 69.

24   See, for example, T. Baker, *Doing Social Research)* (1988, 1994); L. H. Kidder and C. Judd, *Research Methods in Social Relations* (1986).

25   J. D. Fitzgerald and S. M. Cox, *Research Methods in Criminal Justice* (1994).

26   Evidence of weak average British educational standards in mathematics has been available for some while. Much of the recent evidence comes from Professor Sig Prais of the National Institute for Economic and Social Research. See, for example, 'British children trailing in maths', *The Times*, 19 January 1996.

27   An understandable and non-intimidating 'cookbook' introduction to statistics is given by F. Caswell, *Success in Statistics* (1982). For a general education statistical primer (an intelligent lay person's guide) see, for example, W. J. Reichmann, *Use and Abuse of Statistics* (1961, 1964).

28   R Meek, *Figuring Out Society* (1972).

29   See the posthumous R. Meek, *Matrices and Society* (1986).

30   Sir Paul Condon, letter from the Metropolitan Police Commissioner to black community leaders, reproduced in the *Guardian* 7 July 1995.

31   Nazroo, 'Uncovering Gender Differences in the Use of Marital Violence: The Effect of Methodology', (1995) 29(3) *Sociology* 475.

32   id., p. 476.

33   id., p. 480, emphasis in the original.

34   id., p. 490.

35   Hellevik, *Introduction to Causal Analysis* (1984). Crosstabulations (two-way tables, and more complex tables) are common in survey research. The use of data to properly explore theory is less practised. For a sophisticated example see Nazroo, op cit., n. 31.

36   Gilbert, *Analyzing Tabular Data*, (1993).

37   N.G. Fielding, 'News from the CAQDAS Networking Project', (1994) September *ESRC Data Archive Bulletin* 5.

38   id., p. 7.

39   N.M. Fielding and R. M. Lee (eds.), *Using Computers in Qualitative Research* (1991).

6 Fem-Legal And Socio-Legal: An Incompatible Relationship?

KATHERINE O'DONOVAN

Depicting the relationship between feminist legal theory and socio-legal studies creates not just one moment of interrogation for the writer, but such a series of moments that interrogation almost becomes all. For not only is feminist theory currently characterised by pluralism and diversity, but British socio-legal studies appears to suffer from a continuing identity crisis. That the previous statement is an expression of opinion is evident, although there is a measure of agreement amongst feminists about the first assertion. The point is that a commissioned essay such as this inevitably requires that the writer has a theoretical position, implicit though it may be. In writing this essay my perception of the relationship under discussion is analogous to that between painting and photography. Feminists acknowledge that their depictions of law are painted from their perspectives, based on experiences, connections, empathy, and sometimes anger.[1] Ethnographic methods, which create an understanding of law in everyday life provide much of the material on which feminist legal theory draws. Painting is also about imagination; feminist theory often imagines how things might be in a new world. And, in addition to utopianism, painting offers the space for self-criticism and new paintings. On comparison, socio-legal studies has, I suggest, an uneasy relationship with the past positivism of social sciences, the Olympian views of lawyers, and current epistemological doubts. According to Roger Cotterrell, "[i]ts concern has been to supplement lawyers' interpretations of the world in ways that could be considered useful by legal professionsal, legislators and law enforcers".[2] The hope of providing a series of photographs of law and society still snaps or flickers. This is not a critical tradition, although there are signs of change.[3]

This essay confines itself largely to the developing conversation in British feminist legal theory and to the longer established British socio-legal studies movement. It is worth noting that the former does not have an association nor even an annual conference. For these reasons, and because I see the conversation as characterised by fluidity, I have not used the word 'movement'. The geographic confinement is for reasons of brevity. Influences from Europe, from North America, and from Australasia, can be read in feminist writings in the British Isles today. However, it is arguable that a tradition is developing, as evidenced by an increasing number of published papers and books.[4] Feminist 'streams' at conferences, such as that of the Socio-Legal Studies Association or the Critical Legal Conference are further evidence of the growth of feminist work.

In the course of its pictorial art feminist legal theory challenges many accepted conventions of legal scholarship. This happens at a number of levels, and can be summed up by using the concept of 'disorder'.[5] The creation of order is a necessary goal of any legal system. As explained by Peter Fitzpatrick law's role is to make society possible.[6] Ordering is a major part of that. Ordering in terms of creating hierarchies, excluding disavowed qualities, effecting closure of what can be known and said, dictating re-presentation, is disordered by feminist theory.[7] That the breaking of silence by women, that their insistence on recognition and hearing, has disordered the order of men is well established.[8] Disordering of legal scholarship occurs through the introduction of new categories to stratification theory; through challenges to claims of neutrality and justice; through the introduction of subjectivity by 'ecriture feminine'; through questioning of established methodologies of research.[9] Disordering is accompanied by destabilizing.[10] Not only does feminist legal theory insist that past scholarship is flawed in its claim to truth by its dismissal or ignorance of a social category, but this insistance has led to questioning of the tools of law and of social science. Concepts, categories, methods, of the recent past, are indicted as flawed. Sceptics might argue that this attack on past scholarship and on its methods leads to doubts about feminist scholarship; for might it not also be a blinkered creation of its times? It is likely that those working on feminist legal theory will answer 'yes' to that question. This does not undermine a methodology that insists on continuous questioning of itself and its achievements. For in its current form feminist work takes place as a conversation amongst scholars. Disordering of the accepted order points up the contingency and mutability of laws, legal and social arrangements and practices. I think we are prepared to assert that our ideas are in flux. Just as a painter may paint a subject again and again, so too may a theorist continue to see different aspects of what she presents and her representation, and in different ways, and from other angles. In the present essay, the very juxtaposition of two purportedly different legal 'approaches' or 'fields' permits the expression new textures, perspectives, plural and varying illuminations. "[M]eaning is constructed within language, through a process of differentiation. Meaning is not absolute or fixed in relation to a referent, but is arbitrary in that respect. Meaning is constructed through the counterposition of differing elements, whose definition lies precisely in their difference from each other".[11] But the painting of an outline, or even a picture, as a set task cannot be evaded. The painting is not finished and is not intended to be so. Paradoxically, part of my task is to paint the connections and intersections between two 'fields'. Having described socio-legal studies as presenting photography as its modus operandi, I am already caught in a contradiction. Furthermore, even an impressionistic painting gives some form of definition; but a definitive approach is precisely what I propose to put in question. We need to ask a series of questions: a definition for which purposes? whose definition? who or what is excluded by the definition?

In painting my picture I must first draw an outline. My objective is to see what feminist legal theory and socio-legal studies have in common, how they differ, and what they can learn from one another. In so doing I shall present a sketch of both areas from my perspective, despite my reservations about definitions. My work should not be regarded as hard-edged or outlined in black, but as fluid and impressionistic. Because

I believe that critique leads to engagement and understanding my views are critical. Yet there are commonalities, particularly of method, in the two 'fields', and I shall argue that a representative perspective must draw on both commonalities and differences.

The Continuing Identity Crisis Of Socio-Legal Studies: A Critique

A return to the 'foundational' writings of the British law and society movement of the 1960s and 70s reveals an absence of and silence about women.[12] Despite a large academic investment in stratification theory, this theory was seen in horizontal terms.[13] The idea that stratification might also be vertical took time to arrive. With hindsight it is easy to condemn this. Yet it is not so long since legal scholars interested in introducing information about social conditions and the impact of law into legal studies were regarded as suspect.[14] One way of coping with that suspicion is to make positive claims about empiricism and objectivity; mirroring claims made by 'real' lawyers about law. Arguments about socio-legal research have been largely conducted around issues of model building, methodology, cause and effect Policy setting and implementation could thus remain within the control of lawyers. To some extent the legal academy and policy-makers looked to socio-legal studies to find out 'how law works', the impact and consequences of legislation, the social effects of particular laws. So, although the multidisciplinary agenda of the socio-legal studies movement was a reaction against blinkered legal orthodoxies, its role was to be supplementary, to provide information. Critique was not a goal. The subjects of law and society research are people where they touch on law, but there is an assumption of stasis about such subjects.[15] This assumption about the 'fixedness' of legal subjects may be conditioned by empirical research. Reflection on this, in the presentation of findings, could challenge the frequent criticism of socio-legal studies as failing to be informed by social theory.[16]

The common criticism of the socio-legal studies movement advanced by unsympathetic members of the academy in the past concerned its hybrid nature, the critic's definition of 'law', or some other agenda from the British academic legal tradition.[17] It is only very recently that socio-legal studies has, in its own eyes, attained acceptance in the eyes of the legal and academic establishment.[18] My reflections concerning the initial resistance of the movement to feminist analysis must be placed in the context of tentative analysis in the early years of the movement in Britain, and in the context of stratification being seen in terms of class. Because the feminism of the seventies was primarily a political movement, the development of theory followed somewhat belatedly.[19] Furthermore the ethnographic method drawn upon by feminism has not been seen in law and society studies until recently. There have been other consequences of positivism in the work of socio-legal researchers, for example, the much-debated question whether empirical findings were 'value free'.

Emphasis on group and individual cultural identities, gender, race, ethnicity, in the eighties, and the birth of subjectivities, has created further problems for socio-legal studies. For with this birth, the identity crisis deepens. Not only has the positivist ground been evacuated, not only has the 'value free ' paradigm been acknowledged as false, but claims to universality are under pressure. Yet the empirical mission to find out, for example, how people are using a particular piece of law, or how regulatory legislation affects conduct, or the impact on peoples' lives of legislative change, depends on being able to generalise about the findings. It is not only socio-legal work that is faced with this problem of generalization. The critique mounted by post-structualist thinkers such as Derrida and Foucault of the main assumptions on which much social scientific research was based has laid a minefield for claims to knowledge, certainty, and generality.[20] Concepts such as 'society', 'community', 'social structure', labour market', 'role', are shown to contain assumptions about persons and their relationships, about a social totality, about the existence even of 'community'.[21] However distorted the ideas of these theorists have been by their popularization, a return to innocent use of abstract concepts is unlikely: the questions 'whose society?', 'whose community?', 'whose definition?' will not go away. An understanding of

127

the power of naming and of language has been pioneered and developed by feminist theory.[22] Acknowledgement by researchers of the past invisibility of women, their construction in reports and empirical studies as male appendages, contributes to the destabilization of the old certainties of research. If the erstwhile solid idea of 'social structure' is built on shifting sands what else may collapse? Who is silent who may yet speak? With doubts and contentions entering in at a variety of levels, sociology is under pressure. Its mission to explain is beset by internal and external disarray. Sociology's authority has been based on its claim to generality , if not universality, in its findings and theories. Law and society research is affected by this crisis, as it draws extensively on sociology as part of multidisciplinary work.

Post-structuralist arguments have influenced the development of 'post-modernism'. This term reflects certain commonalities in movements in cultural studies, aesthetics, philosophy, the arts and humanities, but with plural resonances. For our purposes, its significance seems to be a rejection of the grand projects, the *'grand recit'*, of rationalist Enlightenment. Michele Barrett says of sociology, "since most sociology owes much to rationalism, sociologists must choose between a sociology of post-modernity and a post-modern sociology".[23] The choice is presented as between studying post-industrial society in the context of the micro-electronic revolution and the globalization of communication and information systems, and developing a sociology with new methodologies which acknowledge the end of grand narrative. Either path puts general claims into question. Furthermore the democratization of information that has followed from the micro-electronic revolution has reduced the monopoly of scholars on information and explanation. Their findings can be contested by those with counter experiences. Again, the birth of subjectivities creates spaces for such challenges to authority.

Both socio-legal studies and feminist theory are affected by these changes. My argument is, however, that the latter, because of its emphasis on contingency and flux, and because of a practice of self-criticism, is better placed to react. The consequences for the former of contentiousness over concepts and methodology and suspicions about universalist claims are unclear. Having already suggested a socio-legal identity crisis, and having expressed suspicion about claims to authority, it is difficult for the writer to claim to be able to present a picture. My personal view of socio-legal studies is that it is interested in the intersection between law and the lives and experiences of subjects. The reasons may be instrumental, in the provision of information to policy-makers; more recently, other projects have been undertaken; for example, the demystification of law and its return from the monopoly of professionals to the places where ordinary people encounter it in everyday life. The law and society movement has a mission to generate understanding and explanation. Consequences of law making, how a particular piece of legislation works, how decision makers set about interpreting and applying legislation, the impact of this on lives, the relationship between social and legal practices, provide particular foci, alongside more general questions of law and society. It may be that the age of unreflexively theorised empiricism is over, but there is an important contribution that law and society research can make to debates about the nature of law, about the diversity of experiences of forms of regulation, including informal mechanisms. This can be done by treating law as a field of social experience, seen from the perspectives of communities, groups and individuals.[24]

The instrumentalist aspect of socio-legal studies, and its emphasis on detailed empirical studies has long been criticised by researchers in the sociology of law and in social theory. There are a number of reasons why these criticisms are made. The role of the grants awarding systems and the funding of empirical research by government and policy-oriented foundations is one. The failure to problematise categories, structures and concepts, referred to earlier, is another. The lack of reflection on the researcher's perspective on the social world "as no more 'true' or 'false' than is the colour of the landscape seen from a certain vantage point and at a certain time of day", is a third.[25] Nevertheless, socio-legal studies has its own values.[26] Some studies take humanist photographs of a compassionate kind, through which perspectives can be compared and contrasted, and find their acceptances.

There is an intersection between the humanism of socio-legal studies and feminism. Empirical studies informed much of early feminist legal studies. Although it is often said that liberalism gave birth to feminism, socio-legal studies can also make a claim to parentage. Initially the feminist case concerning inequalities drew on empirical evidence, in order to ask that liberalism live up to its promises of equality under law.[27] As a form of 'immanent critique' feminism challenges contradictions within law and legal practices. This not only draws on statistics and specific studies, but is a drawing on socio-legal methodology also. Engagement with governmental, legal, and social practices, was relatively straightforward in the early days; but it had a radicalising effect. For it became evident that beneath issues of treatment lay a complexity of issues of concepts, language, and presentation. In short, feminists developed an epistemological critique, but retained an articulate major premise of equality as a major social value. It is worth repeating that this is a value that law purports to instantiate, and that specific political discourses and practices draw on some concept of equality as inspiration and justification, and for their own legitimacy. Notwithstanding a gradual deconstruction of concepts and structures, feminist theory has been able to avoid loss of identity. This is because a moral commitment to equality, however criticised as a concept, has been retained. Confronting legal discourse with its own rhetoric, with its self-justification in terms of 'equality under law', with its claims to legitimacy on grounds of generality, has been a powerful tool. The accusation of failure to live up to its own standards places legal administration in some difficulties. In exposing the evident contradictions , certain gains have been made.[28]

Feminist Legal Studies: Fluidity, Mutability And Contingency

If socio-legal studies has been marked by a continuing identity crisis, feminist legal theory has been marked by its awareness of contingency and flux. In that sense it is difficult to capture in a painting. Empiricism informed early work on feminist theory as it had done earlier for socio-legal work.[29] But whereas socio-legal studies sets out to answer defined questions, feminist legal theory uses empirical evidence to prove a case. In this sense it can not claim ever to have been 'value free'. The findings of social scientists grounded much early argument about inequalities and were used effectively. There is a continued awareness that things can change. Indeed, change is the practical and political commitment of feminism.

Initially feminist argument started from a premise about equality, drawing on liberal and Marxian philosophies. The starting point was explicitly value based. There was no difficulty in finding evidence with which to challenge what Albie Sachs called 'the myth of judicial neutrality' in the legal denial in the courts of the status of 'persons' to women.[30] There was thus an early awareness that judicial power must be demystified. The institutional arrangements of the welfare state, such as the treatment of women not as equal under the law, but as dependents of men were easily exposed. Legal history, legislation, case law, have been implicated by scholars in a denial to women of full legal subjecthood, and as not living up to law's self-description as neutral and objective.[31] Legal doctrine, legal reasoning, legal method, and legal education are under indictment.[32] Family law offers examples gendered law affecting women, men, lesbians, gays, transsexuals; and unequal treatment such as abuse, marital rape, the feminisation of poverty, particularly after divorce.[33] Analysis of labour law reveals that the worker written into statute is gendered.[34] Criminal law displays its assumptions about provocation and reasonableness as based on patterns culturally associated with masculinity.[35] Legal regulation of sexuality is analysed as constructing the male subject and excluding the woman as Other.[36] Even a seemingly neutral area, such as property has been shown to operate on gendered assumptions.[37] The list goes on. It covers international law,[38] human rights discourse,[39] public law,[40] legal method and language,[41] the conventional curriculum and assumptions of legal education.[42] The picture is painted in the depressing colours of inequality. Yet it is illuminated by hope: the hope of change, underpinned by a belief in the values of equality.

At one time, in an attempt to emulate the expository tradition of other branches of sociology or law, feminist writing delighted in establishing typologies. An initially favoured taxonomy went from liberal (assimilation to the male model),[43] to Marxist (examination of the material base),[44] to radical (the problem is patriarchy).[45] Other taxonomies contrast equality feminism (procedural or substantive?),[46] with difference feminism (taking account of sex and gender).[47] Cultural feminism has been identified as a claim for a women's culture, with its own language and values, morally superior because it was characterised by an ethic of care.[48] Later taxonomies see theory as having developed through three positions:'law is sexist'; 'law is male'; 'law is gendered'.[49] I have deliberately summarised these positions in one phrase, because what emerges from attempts at definition and delineation has a fairly short life. The creation of these positions, the ordering by an immediate history, the establishment of a taxonomy, is a sign of academic respectability and arrival. To communicate what feminist legal theory is about it is necessary to have such classifications. But they miss contingencies, mutabilities and subjectivities. No sooner published and taught for a short period such categories became obsolete, for the conversation moves on . Taxonomies are open to disagreement and criticism. As more and more women find their subjecitivities local doubts intensify. Conventional academia is dismayed by such lack of theoretical unity and purity, but within feminsm it is a source of strength. For it counters exclusion, it allows for diversity and plurality.[50]

A counter-argument to flux and contingency is that academics do need to paint a finished picture, even if the next painting goes over it.. In other words, it is only by hanging the painting, by having the expression that we can move on. The debate on meanings of sex-gender provides an illustration of both the counter-argument and my argument, in that, the painting and re-painting of this issue, its presentation and representation, has increased understanding, even though there is no definitive version.

Contemporary Western feminism has been affected by theories drawing on deconstruction and post-modernism. Categories of analysis such as 'patriarchy', 'mysogyny', 'sex/gender', have been put in question.

Discourse theory challenges the primacy of materialism. Understanding that positivistic searches for the origins of 'women's oppression' are a futile attempt to resurrect grand narrative makes spaces for other concerns. Self-criticism facilitates movement and change. A corresponding interest in language and texts as creating and constructing meaning leads to increased focus on difference where definition lies precisely in the delineation of elements different from each other. But the expression of differences and consequent definitions are unresolved.

Into the disagreements about definitions of sex/gender, and significant theories which inform these, enters the realisation, as expressed by Nicola Lacey, "that there is, by definition, no language unmarked by gender configurations of power".[51] Language remains a particular problem. As stated earlier, feminist legal theory speaks in moral voices, drawing on the concept of 'equality'. Feminist writings document disillusionment with the use of this concept and with the concept of 'rights'.[52] The questions asked earlier, 'whose community?', 'whose justice?' about the deployment of social scientific concepts, have been also asked about feminist drawings on concepts such as equality.

Disagreement amongs feminist and post-structuralist writers about the meaning of gender dominates much of the theoretical literature of those for whom *'difference'* is pivotal to their theoretical frameworks. The definition of gender is derived from theory, and therefore lack of agreement is hardly surprising. This disagreement can be documented from the writings of de Beauvoir, Irigaray, Foucault, and Wittig. For de Beauvoir man is subject, woman is other.[53] For Wittig, man is universal, woman is sex; only men are 'persons', and there is no gender but the feminine.[54] To Irigaray, woman is the sex which is not one.[55] These phrase-summary, crude one-liners though they be, reveal disagreement. With Judith Butler's shift to a new framework, that of 'performance', the issue of *the definition* , or *the meaning* of gender is not resolved, but is moved on.56 Thus the painting continues.

The debate about the meaning of gender also touches on debates about the subject and about identity. One of the achievements of feminist legal theory has been an analysis of law's subject. Drawing on theories of

Irigaray and Cixous, amongst others, theorists argue that the legal subject is male. Luce Irigaray states:

> even when aspiring to a universal, neutral state, this subject has always written in the masculine form, as man... It is man who has been the subject of discourse whether in the field of theory, morality or politics.[57]

Deconstruction of law's subject in a variety of legal discourses has revealed that the dominant subject is male, and that the female subject is a projection of male imaginings. Evidently there is a possibility of other imaginings. The trouble is that the language of gender is not vacated.

The argument goes like this: the neutral figure, upheld as a projection of all legal subjects, and therefore as universal is a particular kind of person with a set of characteristics associated with masculinity. But as noted by Simone de Beauvoir, he depends on woman as 'other';[58] to be his mirror. As Ngaire Naffine says:

> on the one hand our man of law is assumed to be a freestanding, autonomous creature, rationally self-interested and hard-headed; on the other hand he is a being who is assumed both to have and to need access to the values of Gemeinschaft, the family values, ... Women's domestic labours sustain the paradox of the man of law.[59]

Nicola Lacey[60] identifies difficulties in this type of analysis which she views as depending on an assumption of a binary system marked by gender. In this system masculinity is associated with reason, self, mind, public; femininity is associated with emotion, other, body, private. It is true that feminist analysis has drawn on the Derridean notion of *differance,* containing the idea not only of binary oppositions but also of deference,[61] superiority and inferiority. However there is an historical basis in legal materials for the application of such analysis to law. Empirical evidence can be found to support the theory.[62] It is true that there is a danger of reifying gender differences, and of appearing to accept them as an essential aspect of subjects, but readings of the work on law's

134

subjects and interpretations may differ. But the significance of gender in the constitution of social relations, and in the subordination of women is central to feminist analysis. It is important therefore to separate a method of analysis, based on historical and empirical evidence, from a substantive position of stating that this is how thing *are in essence*. A utopian position of imagining how things might be must be further differentiated.

If we apply Judith Butler's notion of gender as performance to the debate on law's subject, it may be possible to heed the warning about essentialism given by Lacey. To a certain extent the idea of performance calls on earlier work on the 'presentation of self in everyday life' by ethnomethodologists. Gender role prescriptions are avoided, as are issues of definitions, in a fluid, anti-essentialist approach. It is unlikely however that issues of power will so easily be dissolved. This is the lesson of history, and the work on law's subject brings this home to us.

Issues of power return us to critiques of law's siren call for feminism. Carol Smart argues that law has delivered little to feminists, that its power should be resisted, and that legal reformist strategies create conditions which might be used against women's interests.[63] It is self-evident that this argument depends on particular definitions of law, although Smart gives detailed empirical evidence in support. Action depends on the theory informing it and on foreseeable consequences. Nicola Lacey is less pessimistic in seeing a place for reformism and for utopian imaginings, despite an awareness of the interrelationship of the legal with economic, social and political relations. Smart's rejection of law and her view of its over-inflated view of itself leads her to argue for a de-centreing of law. This is based on her belief that law's power closes; and her view of its high status in the establishment of knowledge and truth. But if law is so powerful and controlling, this argument might support the work which challenges this power and status, particularly critique and deconstruction. Lacey's disagreement with Carol Smart is not just about definitions of law, but over Smart's closure of possibilities. As Lacey says, we "cannot yet imagine what law would look like in a genuinely equal world peopled by relational subjects connected to each other by mutual respect for each others' irreducible difference".[64] This is a debate about law's connections with other social sciences, its power, methods and closures. It suggests that the specific work of deconstruction of particular doctrines, rules, and areas of law in feminist theory may be drawing to an end, and that more general jurisprudential questions may be developing. As generations of younger scholars enter the conversation, new debates are conceived, and hidden aspects of present concerns are revealed.[65]

Concluding Question: An Incompatible Relationship?

In making the contrast between painting and photography I have been drawn into issues of difference, but I have also drawn out relationships. Counterposing socio-legal studies and feminist legal theory with a view to drawing meaning out of their relationship leads me to my contrast of stasis and flux. The similes of photography and painting and the differences between them are intended to catch the idea of snapshot as opposed to art. Closer scrutiny shows flaws. Some subjects can be photographed as constantly changing in a series of stills. Some paintings try to emulate photographs. Yet we understand the similes. One catches the idea of stasis, of reality; the other the idea of interpretation, of change of what might become. This relates to a general critique of socio-legal studies as instrumental and policy oriented. Whilst the critique, in its generality, underestimates the influences on the law and society movement of feminist legal theory, critical legal studies, sociology of law, and social theory, nevertheless there remain difficulties. These can be best expressed through analogies with photography: perspective, medium and snapshot.

One lesson of feminist work is that there is no theoretical perspective from which social research can be mounted. Even specific empirical studies confined to narrow technical issues contain views and values, and should be enlarged by reflection on their implicit theories. Such enlargement leads to connections with social theory and the sociology of law. Where the research agenda addresses issues of legal impact, law's instrumental role in change, questions soon arise which go to social theory. Even the conceptualization of the research cannot take

136

place without reference to social theory, however disguised. The medium of research is similarly problematic. Choosing and designing methodological forms, deciding on the subject to be interviewed , or to act as reporters, leads to theory. Will the perceptions of officials and administrators of the 'problem' of violence towards women be compared to those of the abused? Does the project conceive of law as a 'top-down' affair, a protection? Or does it rely on a methodology such as diaries and reports of those who seek help? Behind these questions lie broad issues of citizenship, representation and democracy.[66]

What empirical studies have offered to feminism is data from research on which arguments about values such as equality can draw. It would be wrong therefore to imply, or for the reader to infer, that there are no commonalities between the two fields. Fruitful and mutually beneficial relationships are in existence. For reasons of continency and flux, and my resistence to contributing to the early obsolescence of typologies, further specification is unnecessary. However, that feminist legal theory has brought new questions, self-criticism, new methods and a salutary corrective to the law and society movement is evident, despite fluidity and shifts in perspectives.[67]

Feminist paintings of new visions range from the utopian to strategic policy proposals. The latter proposals may often be supported and advanced by socio-legal work. Whereas that may be sufficient for socio-legal scholars, feminists may regard such reforms as necessary but insufficient. Thus the utopian moment after deconstruction, so important to feminist visions, has not yet figured , and may never do so in socio-legal work. A series of questions pervade feminist utopianism, in which issues of representation in both the presentational and democratic sense are pressing. Because of the necessity to provide information to policy-makers, precisely in order to document the impact of legal change and law's role as an instrument of change, socio-legal studies' snapshot model dominates unless tempered by reflexive theory. There is a practical task to perform. Yet the snapshot may be out of date by the time it is developed; or at least by the time the legislative outcome is printed on the Parliamentary order paper. Whereas feminist theory can allow for changing subjects, for new conceptions of selves, this has not yet been built into the socio-legal camera. Perhaps because feminism has generated and lived with a major social revolution, it has a heightened awareness of the mutability of subjects and selves. The challenge to socio-legal studies is to re-think its conceptions of selves,[68] to open up the pluralism of experiences of modes of regulation, to set its own priorities free from agenda set by law/government, and to reconsider the participation of citizens in the legal process.[69]

Changes in conceptions of selves are possible, as the recent histories of many women, and of women as a category, testify. Before this can happen ontological ideas of possibilities, of other selves, of becoming, must develop. The general flourishing of subjectivities has increased the spaces, opened up by feminism. Thus feminist theory itself is open to challenge as exclusive, non-representative, unable to represent plural subjectivities. Feminist scholars have attempted to meet this challenge in reflective and self-critical writing, by acknowledgement, by modification, and by admission that isues of universality and generality are problematic. However, insofar as critique of exclusion, hope for equality (however reconstructed as a concept), unites both theorists and their feminist critics, common ground is shared. In other words, there is a shared hope and a common concern about exclusion. Underpinning this is a shared ethics; an explicitly agreed starting point of the values of understanding, mutual respect, and empathy. Continuing to argue among ourselves, and with others who share these values, concerns and hopes, may yet create greater appreciation of the contribution of feminist legal theory to the law and society movement.

Notes

1   Feminist theory takes a similar view to critical legal theory, that the Olympian vantage point does not and cannot exist, although some seem to forget this when it comes to their own writing. Debates have taken place about viewpoints and perspectives and the distinctions between the two. The suggestion has been made that the perspective of the oppressed is preferable to that of the oppressor, as the former has to understand the latter in order to survive, but also retains her own subjectivity. See A. Jaggar, Feminism and Human Nature (1983). Anger has been a driving force of feminism, and has

given energy to critique and argument. See R. West, "The Difference in Women's Hedonic Lives: A Phenomenonological Critique of Feminist Legal Theory" (1987) 3 *Wisconsin Women's Law Journal* 81. For an important argument that feminist writers should resist the lure of the dominant academic discourse with its insistence on authority, and embrace particularity, fluidity, and diversity, see, E. Jackson, "Contradictions and Coherence in Feminist Responses to Law" (1992) 20 *Journal of Law and Society* 398.

2   R. Cotterrell, "Introduction: The Law and Society Tradition" in R. Cotterrell (ed.) *Law and Society* (1994), xiii. Cotterrell sees the American law and society movement and the British socio-legal movement as almost exactly equivalent. Because I agree, and for stylistic reasons, I shall use the terms interchangeably.

3   S.S. Sibley and A. Sarat, "Critical Traditions in Law and Society Research" (1987) 21 *Law and Society Review* 165. For an assertion of the value of a self-critical, reflexive sociological perspective on law which recognises the limited nature of the legal perspective see R. Cotterrell, "Sociological Perspectives on Legal Closure", in A Norrie (ed.) *Closure or Critique: New Directions in Legal Theory* (1993).

4   A brief review of the numbers articles containing references to feminist theories or writings published in seven general British legal periodicals, published in 1994, reveals as follows: *Cambridge Law Journal* 0/22; *Journal of Law and Society* 2/28; *Law Quarterly Review* 1/17; *Legal Studies* 1/21; *Modern Law Review* 2/23; *Oxford Journal of Legal Studies* 2/31; *Social and Legal Studies* 3/22. This is evidence of work at United Kindom universities, and of interest on the part of readers and editors.

5   In the phallocentric order women are a source of disorder because they disrupt. See C. Pateman, *The Disorder of Women: Democracy, Feminism and Political Theory* (1989).

6   P. Fitzpatrick, "Being Social in Socio-Legal Studies", (1995) 22 *Journal of Law and Society* 105. Fitzpatrick's argument is that law enter in to make society possible. Its generalities are intended to overcome the social problem of exclusion. But law's methods of categorization and classification mean that law excludes (and arguably cannot do otherwise, as expressed in the maxim of statutory construction expressio unius ext exclusio alterius). For these reasons both law *and* society are impossible.

7   Feminist theory in its initial second wave argued for the extension of rights possessed by men to women. It was gradually realised that such a process of assimilation was impossible for those embodied and situated differentially. At that point feminist theory had to challenge the existing order. It became disruptive. See Pateman op. cit., n.5, and C. Pateman and E. Gross (eds.) *Feminist Challenges: Social and Political Theory* (1986).

8   L. Finley, "Breaking Women's Silence in Law: the Dilemma of the Gendered Nature of Legal Reasoning" (1989) 64 *Notre Dame Law Review* 886.

9   On the critique of law as not living up to its promise of neutrality and objectivity see K. O'Donovan, "Engendering Justice; Women's Perspectives and the Rule of Law" (1989) *University of Toronto Law Review* 127; on subjectivity and 'ecriture feminine' see L. Irigaray, Speculum of the Other Woman (1985) ; on feminist epistemology see C. MacKinnon, Feminism

Unmodified: Discourses on Life and the Law (1987); Williams, "Feminist Legal Epistemology" (1993) 8 *Berkeley Women's Law Journal* 63; for challenges to law's methods and closures see M. J. Mossman, "Feminism and Legal Method: the Difference it Makes" (1986) 3 *Australian Journal of Law and Society* 30.

10   N. Naffine, *Law and the Sexes: Explorations in Feminist Jurisprudence* (1990); C. Smart, *Feminism and the Power of Law* (1989). A. Young, *Femininity in Dissent* (1990). Carol Smart is critical of the project of 'feminist jurisprudence' and (by implication) of feminist legal theory. I use the term in a broad sense to include the various strands of feminist work that makes a pattern; whether of 'trashing', of critique, of reformist proposals, of utopian visions. To me theory is not confined to abstraction, but is present in concrete work, even if the author thereof does not recognise it.

11   M. Barrett, "Words and Things: Materialism and Method in Contemporary Feminist Analysis" in M. Barrett and A. Phillips (eds) *Destabilising Theory* (1992) 203, referring to the work of Roland Barthes. See also G. C. Spivak, "Displacement and the Discourse of Woman" in Easthorpe and McGowan (eds) *A Critical and Cultural Theory Reader* (1992).

12   Examination of the first ten volumes of the *British Journal of Law and Society*, now the *Journal of Law and Society* (1973-1983), reveals that articles on feminism, or with women as subjects, appeared as follows: vol.1, 0/21; vol.2, 2/19; vol. 3, 1 /18; vol.4, 0/19; vol.5, 3/18; vol.6, 0/15; vol.7, 1/15; vol.8, 0/14; vol.9, 1/15; vol.10, 1/15.

13   Thus standard academic texts on the family automatically assumed that the wife was a shadow of her husband and shared his social class position. See for example, M. Young and P. Wilmott, *Family and Kinship in East London* (1957). Later work has questioned this assumption, some studies showing that it is possible for women and children to be poor despite sharing a home with a man classified as 'middle class'. See J. Pahl, *Money and Marriage* (1989).

14   See the (1973) 1 *Journal of Law and Society*, where the editor Philip Thomas explains the existence of the new journal.

15   For example, the reform of the law of divorce in England and Wales is currently going through the following stages; first, research was conducted in the early to mid-eighties and published by G. Davis and M. Murch, *Grounds For Divorce* (1988); a consultation paper by the Law Commission followed: *Facing the Future, a Discussion Paper on the ground for Divorce*, No. 170 (1988) ; a Law Commission report was next: the *Ground for Divorce*, no 192 (1990); a green paper from the Lord Chancellor's Department followed, Looking to the Future: Mediation and the Ground for Divorce (1993) Cm 2424.

16   For this criticism see, for example, N. Lacey, "Normative Reconstruction in Socio-Legal Theory", address to the Socio-Legal Studies Association Conference, Leeds, 1995; R. Cotterell, op. cit., n. 2, xviii.

17   Resistance to the entry of socio-legal studies into legal education can be deduced from the 'manifestos' published by the new law schools of the 1960's. See (1967) IX *Journal of the Society of Public Teachers of Law*, pp.344-359. See also W.L. Twining, *Blackstone' Tower* (1995).

18	A. Hunt, "Governing the Socio-Legal Project: or What Do Research Councils Do?" (1994) 21 *Journal of Law and Society* 520.
19	The story has yet to be told of the hostility faced in the seventies by legal academics who undertook feminist analysis. Because many of these scholars are now successful in terms of the conventions of academic life, it appears that feminist work was a 'career move'. At the time, however, the rejection slips told another story.
20	M. Foucault, *The Archaeology of Knowledge* (1989); M. Barrett, *The Politics of Truth: From Marx to Foucault* (1991);
21	M. Barrett, op. cit., n.11.
22	On the power of naming see A. Rich, *On Lies , Secrets and Silence* (1980).
23	M. Barrett, op. cit., n.11, p. 206.
24	I see the move away from 'grand recit' not as a rejection of theory, but as an espousal of theories. Simon Jolly in this volume argues that the age of empiricism in family law is over. Although studies have been carefully theorised, I agree with Simon Jolly's analysis because such work has not been reflexive or self-critical. For the agenda which socio-legal studies, including those on family law , might espouse see R. Cotterell, *Law's Community: Legal Theory in Sociological Perspective* (1995) Ch. 14. the final sentences of this paragraph have drawn on this work.
25	R. Cotterell, op. cit., n. 2, xv.
26	N. Lacey, op. cit., n. 16.
27	K. O'Donovan, op. cit., n. 9.
28	This is a matter of debate amongst feminists. Some, for example Carol Smart, take the view that law offers 'a siren call' for feminists. Others, such as Nicola Lacey suggest that reform can be part of a feminist strategy of change. This will be discussed later in this essay. For an excellant analysis which sees a place for law reform, see R. Sandland, " Between "Truth" and "Difference": Poststructuralism, Law and the Power of Feminism" (1995) 3 *Feminist Legal Studies* 3. See further E. Jackson, op. cit., n.1. My own work has pointed out the gaps between , and contradictions in law's own declared values such as equality under law, and the actual performance of legal institutions.
29	Feminists give a broad interpretation to empiricism, relying on specific studies, government and official research, such as Social Trends, participant accounts. It has been possible to use empirical studies not written in sympathy with women, or which did not 'see' women, for such accounts spoke for themselves, although not necessarily as their authors intended. See for example Ngaire Naffine's deconstruction of Professor Glanville Williams's treatment of rape in his Textbook on Criminal Law; N. Naffine, "Windows on the Legal Mind; The Evocation of Rape in Legal Writings (1992) 18 *University of Melbourne Law Review* 741; N. Naffine, "Possession: Erotic Love in the Law of Rape", (1994) 57 *Modern Law Review* 10.
30	A. Sachs and J. Hoff Wilson, *Sexism and the Law: A Study of Male Beliefs and Judicial Bias* (1978).
31	S. Sheldon, "Who Is the Mother to Make the Judgment? the Constructions of Woman in English Abortion Law" (1993) 1 *Feminist Legal Studies* 3.

32	M. J. Mossman op. cit.,n.9; P. Goodrich, "Twining's Tower: Metaphors of Distance and Histories of the English Law School" (1995).

32   M. J. Mossman op. cit.,n.9;   P. Goodrich, "Twining's Tower: Metaphors of Distance and Histories of the English Law School" (1995).

33   K. O'Donovan, *Family Law Matters* (1990).

34   N. Lacey, "Legislation against Sex Discrimination: Questions from a Feminist Perspective" (1987) 14 *Journal of Law and Society* 411; K. O'Donovan "Labour Law's Subject: A Hidden Agender? in Y Kravaritou (ed) *Le Sexe du Droit du Travail en Europe* (1996).

35   D. Nicholson, " Telling Tales: Gender Discrimination, Gender Construction and Battered Women Who Kill" (1995) 3 *Feminist Legal Studies* 185; K.O'Donovan, "Defences for Battered Women who Kill" (1991) 18 *Journal of Law and Society* 219; K.O'Donovan "Law's Knowledge: The Judge, The Expert, The Battered Woman and Her Syndrome" (1993) 20 *Journal of Law and Society* 24; C. Wells, "Battered Woman Syndrome and Defences to Homicide: Where Now?" (1994) 14 *Legal Studies* 266; A Young, "Conjugal Homicide and Legal Violence: A Comparative Analysis" (1991) 31 Osgoode Hall Law Journal 761.

36   S. Duncan, "Law's Sexual Discipline: Visibility, Violence, and Consent" (1995) 22 *Journal of Law and Society* 326; S. Duncan, "'Disrupting the Surface of Order and Innocence': Towards a Theory of Sexuality and the Law" (1994) 2 *Feminist Legal Studies 3*.

37   A. Bottomley, "Self and Subjectivities: Languages of Claim in Property Law (1993) 20 *Journal of Law and Society* 56; A. Bottomley, "Women, Family and Property" in M. Maclean and J. Kurczewski (eds.) *Families, Politics and the Law* (1994); K. Green, "Thinking Land Law Differently: Section 70 (1) (g) And The Giving of Meanings" (1995) 3 *Feminist Legal Studies* 131. L. Flynn and A. Lawson, "Gender, Sexuality and the Doctrine of Detrimental Reliance" (1995) 3 *Feminist Legal Studies* 105.

38   H. Charlesworth, C. Chinkin and S. Wright, "Feminist Approaches to International Law (1991) 85 *American Journal of International Law* 613. C. Chinkin, "Women's Rights as Human Rights under International Law", paper given at the W.G. Hart Legal Workshop 1994.

39   S. Wright, "Human Rights and Women's Rights" in K.E. Mahoney and P. Mahoney (eds.) *Human Rights in the Twenty-first Century* (1993).

40   K. O'Donovan, "Gender Blindness or Justice Engendered?" in R. Blackburn (ed.) *Rights of Citizenship* (1993); K. O'Donovan, "A New Settlement Between The Sexes?" in A. Bottomley (ed.) *Law's Subjects and The Core* (1996).

41   J. Wallbank, "Returning the Subject to the Subject of Women's Poverty: An Essay on the Importance of Subjectivity for the Feminist Research Project" (1995) 3 *Feminist Legal Studies* 207. R. Martin, "A Feminist View of the Reasonable Man (1994) 23 Anglo-American Law Review 334*.

42   P. Goodrich, op. cit., n. 32.

43   B. Hoggett and S. Atkins, *Women and the Law* (1984).

44   C. Smart and B. Smart, *Women, Sexuality and Social Control* (1978); M. Barrett, *Women's Oppression Today (1980)*.

45   S. Wright, "Patriarchal Feminism and the Law of the Father" (1993) 1 *Feminist Legal Studies* 115.

46   J. A. Sohrab, "Avoiding the 'Exquisite Trap': A Critical Look at the Equal Treatment/Special Treatment Debate in Law" (1993) 1 *Feminist Legal Studies* 141.

47   For example Nicola Lacey, "Feminist Legal Theory; beyond Neutrality" Current Legal Problems (1995) marks out 'difference' feminism as problematic, and attributes this position to Naffine, op. cit. n.10, and (to some extent) to Luce Irigaray, discussed below notes 53 and 55.

48   C. Gilligan, *In a Different Voice* (1982). M. J. Larrabee (ed.) *An Ethic of Care* (1992). For a critical account, which sees Gilligan's position as 'essentialist', see M.J. Frug, *Postmodern Legal Feminism* (1992).

49   C. Smart, "The Woman of Legal Discourse" (1992) 1 *Social and Legal Studies* 29.

50   M. J. Frug, op. cit., n.48, advises "a decentred, polymorphous, understanding of the subject", at p.126. However, there is room for doubt about the achievability of such for those trained in the methods of the Enlightenment. See K. O'Donovan, (1995) 3 *Feminist Legal Studies* 249.

51   N. Lacey, op. cit., n. 16, p.12.

52   E. Kingdom, *What's Wrong With Rights? Problems for a Feminist Politics of Law* (1991). D. Herman, *Rights of Passage: Struggles for Lesbian and Gay Equality* (1994) Ch. 4. D. Herman, "Beyond the Rights Debate" (1993) *Social and Legal Studies* 25. A. Diduck, "Legislating Ideologies of Motherhood" (1993) 2 *Social and Legal Studies 461.*

53   S. de Beauvoir, *The Second Sex* (1960).

54   M. Wittig, "The Point of View: Universal or Particular?" (1983) *Feminist Issues* p.64: "Gender is the linguistic index of the political opposition between the sexes. Gender is used here in the singular because indeed there are not two genders. There is only one: the feminine, the 'masculine' not being a gender. For the masculine is not the masculine, but the general".

55   L. Irigaray, *Ce sexe qui n'en est pas un* (1977). See M. Whitford (ed) *the Irigaray Reader* (1991); M. Whitford, *Luce Irigaray: Philosophy in the Feminine* (1991).

56   J. Butler, *Gender Trouble: Feminism and the Subversion of Identity* (1990).

57   L. Irigaray, "Sexual Difference" in T. Moi, *French Feminist Thought* (1987) 119.

58   S. de Beauvoir, op. cit., n.53.

59   N. Naffine, op. cit., n.10. p.148.

60   N. Lacey, "Feminist Legal Theory: Beyond Neutrality" *Current Legal Problems* (1995).

61   J. Derrida, "Force of Law: the 'Mystical Foundations of Authority'", n D. Cornell, M. Rosenfeld and D.G. Carlson (eds.) *Deconstruction and the Possibility of Justice* (1992). See also, M. Davies, *Asking The Law Question* (1994), Ch.8.

62   K. O'Donovan, *Sexual Divisions in Law* (1985) Ch. 2.

63   C. Smart, *Feminism and the Power of Law* (1989).

64   N. Lacey, op. cit., n.16, p.18. For Lacey's critique of Smart's pessimism, see "Closure and Critique in Feminist Jurisprudence" in A. Norrie (ed.) *Closure or Critique?* (1993), and op. cit., n.60.

65   R. Sandland, op. cit., n.28.

66   M. Mahoney, "Legal images of Battered Women: Redefining the Issue of Separation" (1991) 90 *Michigan Law Review* 1; M. Thornton, "Embodying the Citizen", in M. Thornton (ed.) *Private and Public; Feminist Legal Debates* (1995) 198.

67   Many legal scholars, including readers of the Journal of Law and Society, do not read the feminist literature. This is because of perceptions that it is 'narrow' or 'sectarian', or that it is not for them. This is a pity for a number of reasons, of which I shall mention two: first, if my thesis in this paper is correct, feminist theory and method does offer a way out of certain theoretical *impasses* experienced by, for example, socio-legal research; second, ignoring feminist work continues the assumption that the male or conventional point of view is universal.

68   Cotterell, supra n.24.

69   R. Collier, *Masculinity, Law and the Family* (1995) applies a socio-legal analysis to gender in the constitution of relations in the family, and to forms of regulation, legal and informal.

7 Distant Relations: The New Constructionism In Critical And Socio-Legal Studies

PETER FITZPATRICK[1]

'... the already established, already stifling reign of society.'[2]

Introducing Ambivalence

My generous brief encompasses 'issues of the role of theory in socio legal research'. As the reach of theory is always incomplete, so my criticism of others for limits in their theories should not detract from my obvious regard for their work. Conciliation at the outset seems advisable since my sub-brief could be seen as provoking conflict, covering as it does two somewhat opposed fields, critical legal studies (CLS) and socio- legal studies (SLS). My concern, however, will be more with a similarity - between these fields - with their common resort to a 'new' social constructionism as a, if not the, basis for their further advance. Yet the need for conciliation remains because social constructionist claims will be extensively criticised here. The criticism is not aimed ultimately at the rejection of such claims but, rather, at their possible refinement. The general argument is that social constructionism is incapable of sustaining any theoretical stand that does not divide against itself and, in so doing, indicate its incompleteness and its dependence on another position. Might it not, then, be more revealing to explore terms of these divisions rather than constantly to insist on a monadic unity 'in theory'?

Such is the conclusion but first a few things must first be covered. Social constructionism, as we will see, is voracious in its claims both to antecedents and to achievements. It incorporates so much of classic social science that venerable theoretical issues will have to be considered. Although this may lead to a questioning of social constructionism's claims to being 'new' there remains something of novelty in its joining together issues about law's relation to the social with questions of agency and structure, of resistance and power. So, social constructionism carries with it not just a particular theoretical development but also a wider range of persistent issues in SLS and CLS.

Critical Legal Studies

The story of CLS has been told well and often. This account will simply set the scene, orienting CLS towards SLS and towards questions of constructionism. CLS is an intellectual and political movement originating in resistances to the orthodox study of law in doctrinal terms. Consistent with its roots in the radical political culture of the 1960s, CLS has sought to effect libertarian reforms in legal education, but its success with this has been less conspicuous than the large impact it has had on legal theory.

CLS has thrived on opposition. Rarely can an intellectual endeavour so diverse and eclectic have caused such hostility within an academic orthodoxy. CLS has been a persistent provocation to mainstream legal scholarship from its earliest guise as variants of phenomenology and critical social theory to its later inclusions of postmodernism, feminism and anti-racism. This conflict is in one way unsurprising. What has united the several strands of CLS has been a radical interrogation of the academic adequacy and the operative autonomy of doctrinal approaches to law. In another way the opposition to CLS does seem surprising because there are social perspectives on law, such as those provided by the sociology of law, which have long questioned the self-sufficiency of the legal domain. This questioning has, however, largely taken the integrity of law as given and then related law to various social influences or determinations. The dangerous dimension of CLS has consisted in its 'applied theory'[3] - in its scrutiny of law from within, a scrutiny that has revealed basic division and contradiction within law itself, not just as an academic field but as the very rule of law held necessary for the viability of liberal society. In particular, by looking closely at legal doctrine in operation, CLS has shaken law's claims to consistency, certainty and predictability.

The cunning of law, however, knows no bounds. The disorientation of law effected by CLS does raise the issue of why such a precarious entity as law endures. CLS has in ways added to law's mystery, and even its potency, by showing, at least obliquely, that law survives in the face of its own incoherence. Perhaps this is why postmodernism has begun to prosper within CLS and why CLS has come to explore the arcanum of law's distinct 'force' and its (paternal) authority by resort to deconstruction and psychoanalysis. Another influential response in CLS to law's radical uncertainty has been the discovery that there is an ineluctable place within law for ethics and justice - elements which were supposedly excluded in doctrinal claims to completeness. But, in all, origins prevail and the old enemy of doctrine persists; and CLS continues to provide expansive protocols of combat which themselves would find coexistence impossible without this common adversary.[4]

The divide between postmodernism and earlier 'critical' versions of CLS remains chasmic and constructionism has been advanced to overcome it, or at least to provide common ground. Constructionist claims in CLS are usually of a kind that law constructs some social form or division - gender and property, for instance. This elevation of law seems, at least implicitly, to derive from the assimilation of two dimensions of constructionism. First, CLS would here accord with the classic claim of constructionism - for some its prime claim[5] - that seemingly natural things like gender and property are socially constructed. Most brands of constructionism would add a refinement in which the social is not allowed existence apart from its being apprehended in a specific discourse or language or cultural interpretation. If we were to add 'legal' to these things, then legal discourse and such could be said to construct gender, property and so on.[6] There is, in all, something of a shift from the bad old realist days when law was determined by everything else to the new interpretative dawn when everything else is determined by law.[7] The postmodern tinge given to CLS by interpretation is considerably heightened by another variety of constructionism. It usually goes under the names of constitutive or relational theory and would see law not only constituting but

147

being constituted by that to which it relates.[8] This plurality yet reciprocity of relation entails, so it is claimed, 'a postmodernist stance'.[9] I will be querying the adequacy of these various positions but first SLS must be introduced to the argument.

Socio Legal Studies

A brief that covers theoretical aspects of SLS would, for some, smack of the oxymoron. As an applied field, one in which an inviolate law is related to its social context, SLS is often seen as needing neither explication nor justification in theory. Yet SLS has also been haunted by apprehension about its intellectual coherence. Recent attempts to demarcate the field confess to failure.[10] Resolution, at first sight, is hardly helped with the expansion of 'socio-legal studies' as it takes on something akin to its broad North American meaning, a meaning which accommodates the diversity of work on 'law and society' and the sociology of law. Yet two constructionist, or proto-constructionist, lines of resolution have emerged from this extension and the outcome seems similar to the type of constructionism inhabiting CLS.

The emphasis in SLS on how law is socially constructed - an emphasis that resonates with the debunking of legal positivism within CLS - has been creatively combined with an 'interpretative turn' so as to focus on how law is socially interpreted or culturally produced.[11] This focus tends to be set against official, positivistic renditions of law. Yet perspectives within SLS which would see law as socially constructed, manifestly potent as they have been, have never succeeded even in their widest ambit in eliminating a distinctiveness, even autonomy, of law in its relation to society. There are, I have argued, good historical and theoretical reasons for this since society depends every bit as much on law for its identity as law depends on society.[12] Oblique support for this could be found in the claim now so often made in SLS that law constructs or constitutes or, more weakly, shapes various social entities - gendered or sexual identity, consciousness, community, a putative custom, and so on - or that law 'construct[s] social and cultural life' in general.[13]   Almost inexorably, and much as with CLS, there has been a combining of these two dimensions - the social creating law and law creating the social - in a relational or constitutive theory of mutual determination.[14]   In all, the 'constructed' similarity between SLS and CLS is a strong one.

Lineaments Of Social Constructionism

Part of the problem in talking about social constructionism is that, although its antecedents can be venerable, it has only recently been configured into something of a new approach. It can indeed be difficult to discern. Take its claim that entities and relations usually conceived as natural can be shown to be socially constructed. For some that would be the whole wisdom of social constructionism.[15]   But, manifestly, such a claim is neither unique nor oven-fresh. Another approach is to list the numerous possible attributes of social constructionism and to say that it corresponds to any of them.[16]   Sorting this out is not helped by the promiscuity of sources claimed for social constructionism - classic sociological, phenomenological, poststructural, postmodern and more.[17]

Yet something must be resolved if we are to talk of the creature. And talk of it, it seems, we must. James Davidson would discern constructionism's 'comprehensive takeover of the academy' from 'the eighties' onwards.[18]   Velody is a little more restrained in describing the 'ever-growing spread of the theme of social construction'.[19]   If only to ease alarm at having been taken over or spread to surreptitiously, it should immediately be stressed that constructionism is more evident in some areas than others. It has been particularly prominent in studies of identity - gender, racial and self-identity - and in the sociology of scientific thought. However, its presence in legal studies has not been inconspicuous. Lacey has referred to 'the constructionism to which most legal theory is now committed'.[20]   This commitment must have been somewhat *sotto voce*. Strong as it may be operatively, explicit commitment to constructionism has been even more rare and more recent in legal studies than in the academy at large.

This still leaves the problem of resolution and although my criticism of social constructionism will say more fully what it may be, it has to have some initial palpable presence. This, I now suggest, can be endowed in two ways. One is to say, that out of the multitude of origins and attributes of social constructionism, there seem to be a couple that are central and definitive. The other is to engage with a recent, perhaps unique, elaboration of constructionism in legal studies and that engagement will occupy much of the remainder of this chapter.[21]

As for definitive attributes, social constructionism would fuse social determination with 'the interpretative turn' or 'the linguistic turn' in a way that would secure the inviolability of the social. The ancestral claims which constructionism makes to social determination would, at first, seem to be challenged by such 'turns'. After all, the primal perception that we construct putatively natural states - sexuality, science, intelligence, the body, madness, childhood, and so on - and that we do this interpretatively would seem to extend as readily to 'social' facts or identities, even to the idea of the social or society itself. Put another way, one would have thought that social determination would have been undermined in the vaunted claims that constructionism is anti-essentialist and anti-realist, that constructionism accommodates agency and contingency, and that it elevates language and the performative force of language, even language 'as a pre-condition for thought'.[22] If for example, we followed Foucault in this - and he is high in the hagiography of constructionism - then an 'object', social or otherwise, would 'emerge only in discourse'.[23] This outcome, is, however, not to be countenanced. The social silently outflanks the interpretative and the most common conduit for this is the invocation of Berger and Luckman's *The Social Construction of Reality*.[24] As that famed title indicates, society endures adjectivally and a more substantive clash between it and interpretation is, in a way, avoided. Thus, to take a recent paean to constructionism, 'the social practices engaged in by people' are 'the proper focus of our enquiry', or the focus is 'the dynamics of social interaction', or it is social 'processes'; and society remains all-encompassing in the dubbing of the very constructionist endeavour as a form of 'social enquiry' - and it is, after all, 'social' constructionism.[25]

This outline of social constructionism is coming close to a more purposive criticism of it, but before presenting that criticism some further focus must be provided to accommodate law. The most explicit and most extensive accommodation is Elizabeth Mertz's offering of 'a new social constructionism for socio-legal studies'.[26] Whilst doing no more with social constructionism than incorporating its omnium gatherum of sources and claims, Mertz adroitly orients these towards prominent concerns in the social study of law. So, whilst placing emphasis on the salience of 'interpretive social-scientific perspectives' and on 'skeptism regarding the fixed or natural character of categories' such as 'customary law' and 'rationality', Mertz also places particular emphasis on how constructionism can overcome 'dichotomous, either/or thinking about law, society, and epistemology'.[27] Such dichotomies would include those between 'people's perceptions' and the 'constraints of the social structures surrounding them', or those between 'idea and action, meaning and material life, constraint and creativity, power and resistance, stasis and change'.[28] This vaulting ambition may be qualified in that social constructionism is most extolled when it adopts perspectives that are 'moderate', or 'pragmatic', or 'empirically grounded', or where it provides 'a reasoned middle road between the Scylla and Charybdis of choices ... between hegemony and resistance, between purely theoretical accounts and data-driven research reports'.[29] All of which could stand as a qualification of the criticism which I now present if the claims Mertz is making for social constructionism as theory are not meant to sustain the rigours of coherence and comprehension usually associated with theoretical explanation. In defence of my critical criteria, it would seem to be inconsistent to set one's concern purely in theory-laden terms and then to suggest that something inexplicitly less than theory is what it is all really about.

Constructing The Social

Fanciful as it may seem, the initial argument here is that the diverse and extensive claims of constructionism can only be made because, to borrow Latour's title, 'we have never been modern'.[30] The moderns arrogate a uniform reality which supposedly has no need of a transcendent reference to give it meaning. 'Society' and the 'social' become that transcendent reference or they provide an operative compensation for absence. The resolution of impossible opposition or 'dichotomies' is made possible in a blithe and perpetual reference to the social. As we have already seen, social realist assertion about what is constructed enables us to take what Mertz calls 'strong positions about the relative soundness of different constructions of social reality' and enables us to judge what 'is not well grounded'.[31] And we can do this whilst affirming that constructionism exists in the realm of people's interpretations of the social because the social, as we saw, folds the interpretative into itself. That is, the social constructs the very modes and abilities of interpretation. With the resulting construct being social, as opposed to being a natural or essential ascription, the self- generating circuits of social constructionism are complete.

This is but an application of Lefort's more general point that there is 'an illusion that lies at the heart of modern society: namely, that...the social can account for itself', that it is 'transparent to itself' or 'intelligible in itself'.[32] The pervasion of the social excludes or expels consideration of the construction of 'society' or 'social' itself. Inquiry is blocked into the construction of the 'autonomously''social in its historically specific, and presumably contingent, modern form. The contingency of the social has nonetheless been established from within, as it were, by showing that the social itself exists in people's interpretations of it and in their acting in accord with those interpretations.[33] Yet it has also been cogently shown that such interpretation and such acting on it themselves depend upon an element of the social that subsists beyond them.[34]

A similar impasse seems to be reached if we consider not just the failure to 'construct' the social but also the failure to 'construct' the process of construction itself. In its usual mode, social constructionism instantly eschews theoretical comprehensiveness by calling for some primal constructor outside of itself. This agent is sometimes seen as an all-powerful actor constructing a distinct and passive other - masculine force creating female entities, the Occident creating the Orient, and so on. Or it is a matter of 'us' constructing our own social reality or our own interpretation of it. Here also there is a distinction between constructor and constructed: the interpreter is 'somehow estranged' from what is being interpreted.[35] The argument could also be put somewhat in reverse. If construction were complete and, it would follow, we were constructed within it, then there would be no position from which we could know of the construction or see and interpret it as a construction. Social scientists could hardly deny themselves this capacity.

If, alternatively, we locate our theoretical force in the constructing position apart - by, for example, following that 'interpretative turn' so often said to impel social constructionism - then we cannot have a constant construction. We would rather, and in Goodman's terms, be 'confined to ways of describing whatever is described. Our universe, so to speak, consists of these ways rather than of a world or worlds'.[36] Indeed, such an outcome, such an irresolution, is exalted by constructionism in its moments of 'anti-essentialism' and 'radical relativism'.[37] Goodman ruins such a happy espousal by adding that, since these are only versions of a world, we 'cannot test a version by comparing it with a world undescribed, undepicted, unperceived'.[38] But this is exactly what social constructionism has to do. As Mertz puts it, 'analysing events as cultural constructions requires that we imagine the possibility of stepping outside of particular constructions of the world, asking what the assumptions and entailments of those constructions look like'.[39] Constructionism confirms the contingent, even precarious, even ungrounded nature of that which is constructed - constructed as hegemonically solid and normal. It imports another realm, the possibility of a position besides itself, from which the construction cannot just be known and effected but tested and evaluated for its adequacy. Furthermore, without this reality beyond there could be no construct as such because, in Goodman's terms, there would simply be competing versions. Any one of these could be interpreted in farther version and so on into an infinite regress.

153

Another variation on the position apart would be the frequent claim that social constructionism involves an element of 'reflexive awareness'.[40] More extensively, 'social constructionism itself is not exempt from the critical stance it brings to bear on other theories', and it 'therefore must recognise itself as just as much a social construction as are other ways of accounting'.[41] This seemingly courageous, not to say reckless, stand is nothing of the sort. It none-too-covertly accords social constructionism the capacity of ultimate self-constitution. Or, at least, social construction can only be made to appear in terms of social construction. We thus arrive at a point of self-generating and unassailable origin, at another god-substitute, similar to the self-presentation of the social.

Distance And Relation

In short, with social construction, whether we consider the elements of the social or of construction, we seem to arrive at the same kind of outcome. The constructed and the constructor evoke even provoke each other. They orient themselves towards and depend on each other. This analysis can be seen as supporting or complementing Mertz's account, particularly her large concern with 'dichotomies'. The divide between the constructed and constructor is reflected in the dichotomies between structure and agency, power and resistance, the material and interpretation, and perhaps others. However, in my argument it is not initially a matter of 'overcoming stale opposition in a single bound', or of 'overcoming analytic dichotomies' or of 'provid[ing] a reasoned middle road'.[42] True, we have seen that constructionism does occupy something of a space-between two sides of an opposition, but it neither overcomes the opposition nor provides a resolving *via media*. For a start, the opposition on closer observation proved less than completely dichotomous. Each side of the opposition seemed to open to and involve the other. But they did so whilst retaining a distinctiveness from each other. This, in turn, was not just a matter of their being distant from each other and thence having to be related or mediated. It was also a matter of the distance or distinctness being sustained in the relation.

This little economy of distance and relation will now be placed in two settings which Mertz particularly emphasises. As my analysis of constructionism would lead us to expect, of all her dichotomies Mertz puts considerable emphasis on that between structure and agency, along with the opposition between imposed power and resistance which is treated as a variant. That will be the first setting. The second setting which Mertz particularly emphasises is that branch of social constructionism called relational or constitutive theory. Its attractions will be evident in the light of my analysis since it seems to enable a promiscuity of relation which transcends the niggling division asserted in the analysis. The division between structure and agency replicates and reinforces constructionism's resident opposition between interpretation and the social. It also affirms the implicit resolution in favour of the social. Mertz may well be minded to find a middle way overcoming the 'impasse' produced by such 'dichotomies' but her formulations do favour the structural and the social. We are told that 'people's perceptions are important' and 'so are the at times iron constraints of the social structures'.[43] Even if a precarious parity survives this ferric quality of structure, it then evaporates when we are told that people's very perceptions are 'surrounded' by these 'social structures' - an outcome similar to that usually reached in social constructionism, as we have seen.[44] When structural elements are accessible to the agent, this is only as an optional extra attached to their perduring structural character. So, whilst 'law plays a constitutive role in the world of the everyday, ... it is *also* available as a tool to people as they seek to maintain or alter their daily lives'.[45] Then there is a compounded assurance of structural domination when 'social actors ... refract and reshape' legal 'frameworks' and do this 'in structured ways'.[46] The importance of agency even its 'reshaping' capacities, is always set about with structure.

The subduing of agency and interpretation is predicated also in the treatment of resistance. Mertz opens and closes her accounts with an intense focus on resistance.[47] It is also significant in that an 'approach' based in structure and agency 'of necessity combines analysis of ... imposed power and active resistance' among other 'dichotomies'.[48] Further than this Mertz does not go in explicitly linking sets of dichotomies to each other but she floats them contiguously in a way that connects them up consistently enough. In the result, resistance sits on the agency side of the divide and power on the structural. This is somewhat countered by a type of social constructionist claim that academics as well as 'local people can see beyond the structuring framework.'[49] As always, ambivalence then re-enters when people's very perceptions are 'surrounded' by 'social structures', when 'struggles' are waged only 'within the framework set by law'.[50] Further, the local is constituted within 'legal discourse' and 'local resistance needs to be understood within the broader context of wide-scale social changes and structures'.[51]

Much of the *de facto*, and it is very much *de facto*, resolution of the 'dichotomy' between power and resistance comes from the dimensions accorded resistance. It is, for a start, etymologically compliant: resist being *re-*, back and *sistere*, to stand - hence *resistere*, stand back, withstand.[52] 'Resistance' serves to elevate that which is, in relation to itself, resisted and it imports a place where one stands in order to resist. Mertz and others who join her in 'celebrating resistance uses' always place or situate resistance - it is something done by 'agents' and 'people': it is 'local' and 'everyday'; or it is situated in 'practice'.[53] These constraining dimensions are set in Mertz's extolling empirical research as the way to study resistance, and this in castigation of more self-indulgent 'critical' forms of enquiry.[54] As particular and evanescent, as always parasitic on that which is resisted, resistance by itself comes from and goes nowhere. It is allowed neither enduring structure nor effective history. So, whilst studies of resistance tell us how it 'shapes' law as power or structure, it is only able to do this within the constraints of the local or the everyday. Such studies also reveal much about law influencing or shaping or constituting the local and the quotidian. In the result, the dimension of power or structure remains virtually aloof and inviolate in its own terms. Its mysterious force is obliquely confirmed. My analysis would offer a position from which power could be opened to resistance, structure to agency. This does not entail overcoming dichotomy or impasse, either in Mertz's indefinite terms or in terms of the higher banality of 'structuration'. [55] The academic maintenance of a distinct structure and a distinct agency can be seen, in Adorno's terms, as 'correct insofar as it registers more intransigently the split that has actually taken place in reality than does the premature unification at the level of theory'.[56] We saw, nonetheless, that social constructionism revolved around aporias in which interpretation and the social and, we can now add, structure and agency or power and resistance could be opened and shown to be responsive to each other.

Relational or constitutive theory would claim to accommodate some such responsiveness. Mertz inveighs against 'the inadequacy of a model that posits a simple one-way causal link between law's intended effect and social change'; and she advances 'a relational approach' to accommodate 'the role of law and the construction of social identity', a taking 'account of the complexities of the interrelationship between law and social change', of 'the complex, mutually constitutive relationships that form between legal processes and social identities'.[57] Whilst not wishing in the least to dissent from this relational approach, it does encounter problems as a variety of constructionism - problems that were rehearsed earlier. If construction is to be 'taken seriously ' as an explanatory principle, then we seem to be plunged into circularity and a certain inconsequence if we purport to explain something as constructed and say it is constructing of that which has constructed it. To take a conspicuous example, for Said the identity called the Occident constructs the Orient but the Occident takes its identity from its oppositional construction in relation to the Orient.[58] To counter a simple circularity or an infinite regress, we would have - in the aporetic terms of constructionism - either to adduce adequately conjoining *social* relations between the constructing and being constructed or advance some *interpretative* perspective integrating them. Either resolution would face a considerable challenge as we have seen. Further, to constitute each other, law and society or other paired objects could not relate simply as a matter of marginal or vague influence. If this is all they did, then the distinct integrity of the objects would be simply affirmed and they would not be constituted relationally. The objects must, then, be related in a necessary way to the effect that one would be 'constitutively' different or non-existent without its relation to the other. But if objects are produced in 'their' relation what is there to keep them distinct and, as it were, objectified? Why should they not simply submerge in the relational soup? The object seems always to have resisted or persisted beyond even the most resolute efforts to account for it in constructionist terms.[59]

Conclusion

As abrupt and unresolved as that may appear to leave the argument, it is an apt if open point at which to conclude. A parallel could be drawn with the earlier account of CLS where law was found to persist despite the most supposedly resolute efforts to render it indeterminate or deconstructed. Such efforts have provided a facile justification for the charge of nihilism often levelled at CLS. Within SLS as well, Mertz for one is concerned to 'make a case for a moderate social constructionist approach as a solution to ... the potentially nihilist consequences of deconstructionist approaches'.[60] My engagement with social constructionism in SLS and CLS has tried to reverse this orientation. Rather than rescuing deconstruction, social constructionism could be seen as rescued by it. This may be deconstruction of a certain dispensation but it is, I suggest, a deconstruction that accords with Derrida's work - his 'Force of Law' providing perhaps the most strongly delineated example.[61]

This is a deconstruction which makes two 'constructive' contributions that would, counter the attribution of nihilism. These things I take to be related or even the same. For Derrida, it is true, any asserted construction can always be deconstructed to reveal its incompleteness, the trace of another possibility, or its dependence on a supplement excluded in its making. But this does not produce a simple dissolution, a nihilistic nemesis. As Derrida more than once proclaims, presence does persist and deconstruction depends on this persistence.[62] Put another way, we could readily reverse focus and see any deconstruction as an explication of the particular construction, as a revelation of the process creating and stored in the construction. Deconstruction and construction are coeval. This is the first constructive contribution which deconstruction offers beyond the charge of nihilism. The second would bring the construction into a relation with other constructions. That which is excluded or rendered supplemental in the making of a construction does not dissipate into an ominous void from which it can return and reduce the construct to incoherence or nothingness. The excluded or the supplemental attach, as it were, to other constructs. The construct is thence 'set in relation' to these other constructs.[63]   So, whilst my essay could be roundly read as fomenting division and disintegration within social constructionism, a gentler reading would find a constructive linking of its otherwise estranged elements of interpretation and the social, agency and structure, and so on.

Notes

1   Colin Perrin thoughtfully helped me to see much of the 'new' social constructionism as orthodoxy. Some of the themes in this essay are developed differently in his 'Approaching Anxiety'.

2   J.-L. Nancy, The Inoperative Community (1991).

3   C. Perrin, 'Approaching Anxiety: The Insistence of the Postcolonial in the Declaration on the Rights of Indigenous Peoples' (1995) VI Law and Critique 55.

4   Contrary claims to completeness are made, however. In a recent survey of CLS Boyle has described the field, without irony or the hint of paradox, as 'a fragmented and heterodox whole': id., p.xxix. His account can only begin to assume coherence because of a series of drastic, usually implicit, exclusions, not least being the mute limitation of reviewable work to that produced in the United States. The outcome nonetheless, and miraculously, lives up to the demand he makes of good theory - that it exhibit a 'prejudice against parochialism': id.

5   See T. Sarbin and J. Kitsuse, 'Prologue to Constructing the Social' in Constructing the Social, eds. T. Sarbin and J. Kitsuse (1994).

6   See the examples provided by Boyle op. cit., n.3, pp.xxii-xxxvi.

7   The reference here is not to legal realism even if one variant could fit the point. There may appear to be a bridge across this divide in CLS via the claim that critique in CLS is 'deconstruction', presumably because of its making legal artefacts indeterminate. If the argument in the last section of this present essay is accepted, however, this is not deconstruction since deconstruction is as much about rendering determinate as it is about making indeterminate.

8   See e.g. A. Hunt, Explorations in Law and Society: Towards a Constitutive Theory of Law (1993), pp.174-5, 224-6.

9   S Henry and B. Milovanovic, 'The Constitution of a Constitutive Criminology: A Postmodern Approach to Criminological Theory' in The Futures of Criminology, ed. D. Nelken (1994) 117.

10   See P. Thomas, 'Socio-Legal Studies in the United Kingdom' in Precaire Waarden, ed. F. Bruisma (1994) 229.

11   See e.g. C. Harrington and B. Yngvesson, 'Interpretive Sociolegal Research' (1990) 15 Law and Social Inquiry 135; S. Merry, Getting Justice and Getting Even: Legal Consciousness among Working-Class Americans (1990); A. Sarat '"... The Law Is All Over": Power, Resistance and the Legal Consciousness of the Welfare Poor' 2 Yale Journal of Law and the Humanities 343; B. Yngvesson, Virtuous Citizens, Disruptive Subjects: Order and Complaint in a New England Court (1993).

12   P. Fitzpatrick, 'Being Social in Socio-Legal Studies' (1995) 22 Journal of Law and Society 105.

13   S. Merry 'Resistance and the Cultural Power of Law' (1995) 29 Law & Society Review 11, at p.14.

14   These various positions will be considered shortly.

15   E.g. Sarbin and Kitsuse, op. cit., n.5, chapter 1.

16   E.g. V. Burr, An Introduction to Social Constructionism (1995) pp.2-9.

17   E.g. id., pp.8-10, 12-14; Sarbin and Kitsuse, op. cit., n.5, pp.2-6.

18   J. Davidson, 'It's Only Fashion' (1994) 24 November London Review of Books 12, at p.12.

19   I. Velody, 'Unnatural Acts - Or nature expelled from her garden: how constructionism came to pass' (1994)

20   N. Lacey, 'Normative Reconstruction in Socio-Legal Theory' (1996) 5 Social and Legal Studies 131, at p.151.

21   That elaboration is provided by E. Metz, 'Legal Loci and Places in the Heart: Community and Identity in Sociolegal Studies' and 'A New Social Constructionism for Sociolegal Studies' (1994) 28 Law & Society Review 971 and 1243. These will be cross-referenced as one work. This and the other sources already referred to on social constructionism (or constructivism as it is sometimes called) explore it as something almost exclusively Anglo-American. For another perspective see V. Villa, 'La Science Juridique entre Descriptivisme et Constructivisme' in Théorie du Droit et Science, ed. P. Amselek (1994) 281. It is also treated as a matter of the social sciences, including social psychology, but it does exist elsewhere such as in the 'new historicism': see J. Copjec, 'Introduction' in Supposing the Subject, ed. J. Copjec (1994). For a different use in the arts see S. Bann ed., The Tradition of Constructivism (1974).

22   See Burr, op. cit., n.16, pp.1-16 and Sarbin and Kitsuse, op. cit., n.5 for accounts of social constructionism along these lines. The specific quotation about language is from the former at p.6.

23   M. Foucault, The Archaeology of Knowledge (1972) 47.

24   P. Berger and T. Luckman, The Social Construction of Reality: a Treatise in the Sociology of Knowledge (1971).

25 Burr, op. cit., n.16 pp.4-9. There is also resort to 'cultural', 'historical' and the 'everyday' as society-substitutes: id..

26 Mertz, op. cit., n.21.

27 id., pp.1243-4, 1258.

28 id., pp.975, 1244.

29 id., pp.934, 1258-9.

30 B. Latour, We Have Never Been Modern (Trans. C. Porter) (1993).

31 Mertz, op. cit., n.21, p.1258.

32 C. Lefort, The Political Forms of Modern Society: Bureaucracy, Democracy, Totalitarianism (1986) 184, 201, 207. Since society is an 'empty place' (to borrow Lafourt's phrase) devoid of transcendent reference, it invites repletion in other terms - in scientific or natural terms such as those provided by evolutionary development or by economy. So, social constructionism, although set against natural ascription and essentialism, would seem to import such things in its being social: cf. J. Dollimore, Sexual Dissidence: Augustine to Wilde, Freud to Foucault (1991) 227. The social itself is also essentialized, as the text now goes on to indicate.

33 P. Winch, The Idea of a Social Science and its Relation to Philosophy (1958 -1st edn).

34 S. Lukes, 'Methodological Individualism Reconsidered' in Sociological Theory and Philosophical Analysis, eds. D. Emmet and A. MacIntyre (1970).

35 S. Fuller, 'The Reflexive Politics of Constructivism' (1994) 7 History of the Human Sciences 87, at 89.

36 N. Goodman, Ways of Worldmaking (1978) 3.

37 See e.g. Burr, op. cit., n.16, p.5 and Sarbin and Kitsuse, op. cit., n.5, p.10.

38 Goodman, op. cit., n.36, p.3.

39 Mertz, op. cit., n.21, p.1249.

40 id., p.1261.

41 Burr, op. cit., n.16, p.41.

42 Mertz, op. cit., n.21, pp.974, 1244, 1259.

43 id., p.975.

44 id.

45 id., p.1260 (emphasis added) adopting A. Sarat and T. Kearns 'Beyond the Great Divide: Forms of Scholarship and Everyday Life' in Law in Everyday Life, eds. A. Sarat and T. Kearns (1993) 61.

46 Mertz op. cit., n.21, pp.1246-7.

47 id., pp. 972, 1261.

48 id., p975.

49 id., pp.1251, 1256.

50 id., pp.975, 1246-7.

51 id., pp.1245, 1260.

52 W. Skeat, A Concise Etymological Dictionary of the English Language (1962)444. Thanks to Hans Mohr for endowing me with a copy.

53 Mertz, op.cit., n.21, p.1261.

54 id., pp.973-5, 1261.

55 A. Giddens, A Contemporary Critique of Historical Materialism: vol 1: Power, Property and the State (1981) 26-9 for a summary version.

56 T. Adorno, 'Sociology and Psychology' (1967/8) 46/7 New Left Review 67 and 79 at p.78.

57 Mertz, op. cit., n.21, pp.972, 978, 1048. Whilst having to accommodate the social construction of law, this approach has tended to see itself more as a corrective emphasis on law's constructing or shaping the social, as to which see R. Cotterrell, Law's Community: Legal Theory in Sociological Perspectives (1995) 7-14.

58 E. Said, Orientalism (1985) - cf. Perrin, op. cit., n.2. There are venerable difficulties here. How can we say 1 constructs 2 when 2 is an undelimited part of 1? It is not clear with these claims what the causal universe may be. If it is more extensive than 1 and 2, how do we know that a relation between 1 and 2 is not influenced of perhaps determined by the relation of either or both to 3, 4, 5 or 47: see e.g. H.B. Acton, The Illusion of the Epoch: Marxism-Leninism as a Philosophical Creed (1955) 160-6.

59 Cf. Foucault's failed attempt to delimit the object's construction in discourse, 'to substitute for the enigmatic treasure of "things" anterior to discourse, the regular formation of objects that emerge only in discourse': op. cit., n.23, p.47 - see E. Laclau and C. Mouffe, Hegemony and Socialist Strategy: Towards a Radical Democratic Politics (1985) 111-12.

60 Mertz op.cit., n.21, p.1245.

61 J. Derrida, 'Force of Law: "The Mystical Foundation of Authority"' in Deconstruction and the Possibility of Justice, eds D. Cornell et al. (1992).

62 The phrase, aptly, is adapted from Nancy op. cit., n.2, p.4. It may be more difficult to derive this second constructive contribution from Derrida but he seems in 'Force of Law' to present it as a general dynamic of deconstruction - op. cit., n.61, Part 1, especially at p.28. For a development of the argument see my 'Governmentality and the Force of Law' (in press) Teoria Sociologica.

63 id., Part 1 and J. Derrida, 'Limited Inc abc' (1977) 2 Glyph 162, at p.248.

8 Lessons From The Classroom: Some Aspects Of The "Socio" In "Legal" Education

ANNE BOTTOMLEY

I am aware of a weight of history and a sense of foreboding. What can I possibly say about legal education which has not been said? Even as I pose this question, I realize that, mixed with my fear of simply being entrapped in yet another critique of the twin demons of the expository tradition and vocationalism; I am not sure of the thing called legal education and the assumptions we make of it. It is as if we have continued to thrive on a reductionalist model, continued to feed from a fear of being caught within it, and continued to spin fantasies of escape into a terrain of authenticity. Authentic to what? I suspect that, for most of us, this is answered by recognising a kind of craving; a craving to be truly academic. To find a place in the academy in which we seek a respect for our identity; or rather seek an identity.

In one sense circumstance, a contingent factor brought to bear on our history, has helped. Along with the rest of the academy we are now subjected to research reviews. Our research profile begins to look much more like that of our colleagues; research degrees become the norm for faculty and our students have a greater sense of their teachers having a life outside the classroom.[1]

But at the same time, other contingencies are brought to bear. As funding of institutions becomes more problematic, growing numbers of students become a priority and, as we know, law can still recruit students.

The law school has become central to the economy of the academy. The impact in terms of teaching loads, size of classes and simple need for "through-put", has left many law schools reeling. Whilst we respond to the innovation of having our research profile taken seriously (at least by us), we also feel the impact of the institution requiring of us a capacity to take on more students. Initiatives to find new recruitment patterns are welcome; direct entry candidates came from feeder programmes or as graduates from other disciplines taking exemption degrees on fast track programmes. Access courses mobilize mature entrants. Still more sources of student supply are found and tapped. The institutions managers are happy; deals are struck with the deans of law schools to make them happy; a degree of control over some of the resources coming in, recruitment of more teachers (albeit often on short term contracts) and limited protection for research space (albeit often for the established or senior members of staff). An obvious possibility emerges; legal education becomes a major source of funding for the institution, the law school works with this and establishes a trade off; the protection of research.[2] Delivering a research profile as well as student out-put provides us with a security that many other faculty members envy. But, and it is a very big but, there is a cost. It reinforces the idea that lawyers gain entry to the academy as simply that...as lawyers, or rather as the producers of lawyers. The underlying rationale and presumption is that we are able to recruit students because, and only because, legal education is a route to the legal profession. And increasingly we are recruiting people who do reinforce this profile; the two year degree student concerned only with the professional exemptions. The temptation is to collude; why bother with innovations in legal education when the academy, the student body and the imperative to research make it simpler to adopt a minimalist approach to teaching?

Vacating, as far as possible, the undergraduate curriculum, especially that which we used to know fondly as "the core", has a respectable tradition. Establishing margins away from the terrors of students expectant of orthodoxy, comfortable only with certainty and closure and focused on a dream of being a lawyer (here to undergo the

164

pain to allow for the deferred pleasure of the real world and the pot of gold) was a strategy for trying to find space (and a few "real" students) to be an academic.[3]

And now we can feed our fears with another compelling story; the present is becoming so much worse. Students are increasingly demanding; of grades, of solutions, of accessible material, of proof (or at least promise) of relevancy and of anything which will make them more marketable. For they are very scared. Burdened by debt or family obligations, they know that there is not enough room in the legal profession for all of them.[4] They want to make it but are fearful that they will not. We, knowingly, take many who will not, their profile too obviously against them. Increased student recruitment has diluted quality; but it has also brought in able candidates who in periods of growth would have had a chance but in a period of contraction will not - most notably mature students. Out of ease, out of feeding their desires, out of, sometimes, simple fear of student pressure, we teach them as if they are to become lawyers. It is a simple currency; an easy exchange. It is fundamentally dishonest.

It is a gloomy picture. It reflects contingencies which are beyond our control and therefore, we could argue, we are simply engaged in a series of survival strategies. But we are failing to take responsibility for our own role in this scenario if we do not now begin to re-engage with the issue of legal education. And, it is my contention, if we do not struggle with that engagement we will leave a crucial weakness in our attempt to be part of the academy as academics, rather than simply purveyors of legal education who buy space and toleration because of our economic strength. A weakness which comes from not only how we are viewed but how we view ourselves.

We cannot escape law. We do not need to. What we do need to escape, or rather turn and face, are the myths and demons of our own making. Three particular demon myths should be confronted (or are they hydra-heads of the same fantasy?).

Hydra One: Black Letter

The first is the fear of Black Letter; seduction back into the comfort and pleasures of rule and doctrine, of closure and completeness or at least the promise of imminence, of the presence of law about to be revealed. We have spent so much energy distancing ourselves, protecting ourselves through critique and expose, that we have continued to need and feed Black Letter. Without the bogy of Black Letter, we are lost in trying to reveal to our students our own identity, our own promise of imminence. The easiest form of critique was revelation:

> ...to identify the reality beneath the law...would become the basis of a critique of law..[5]

And, of course, and correctly, the expository style of teaching law, of presenting/constructing law within this image, was a primary object of critique. But it became predicated on needing the continuation of this style of teaching as the presumed dominant form; the orthodoxy to be revealed as false consciousness, the purveyor of the orthodoxy to be revealed as the purveyor of false consciousness. Black Letter....what we have escaped but that which still holds sway. The thing to reveal and the thing to fear. The seduction to be resisted.

Seductive because we secretly knew of its pleasures. Seductive because it had been a currency of identity for us as academic lawyers. Seductive because we were not sure what would (could) take its place; in the very act of negation we required its presence. Meanwhile, a familiar pattern emerged, we projected our desire/fear onto another and into another place. Black Letter became the site of all that was worst; the fearful warning.

The oppositional history was necessary; a break with an orthodoxy which had become stagnant and had not responded to developments in either the broader academy or the discursive practices associated with "law". Weakness in its origin were exacerbated by time:

> Because nothing but assertion supported the law-as-science ideal, it soon took on the trappings of revealed truth.. The belief that law existed beyond the reported cases, awaiting some legal explorer, helped sew a confusion among those who sought a scientific basis to law.[6]

A confusion which forced an increasingly assertive style to the project which, partly because of the reception of the expository style into law schools formed originally around professional courses and only latterly turned to degree work, added the extra assertion that this was a suitable training for lawyers.[7] The confusion within the academic project became, weirdly, displaced into a trajectory which suggested that if the revelation of law was not to be found in the academy it would be found in the practice of law. Displacement and deferral; another place for imminence and promise. (Of course, many of those who we now hold responsible for this inheritance may have been seeking survival strategies in circumstances similar to our own.)

To create distance, to find space away from the dead hand of history, to be able to participate in trends within the academy (and to be able to explore law untrammelled by legal education), these things seemed possible and necessary in the period of expansion of the then new universities in the late 1960s.

I was an undergraduate student in the early 1970s attending one of the "new" campus universities, I was (naive as I was) surprised and confused to find that the presence of law teaching was considered contentious by many of the academics, especially those in the social science faculty. Law was dismissed as having no academic credence; it had no discipline base, it could only exist for vocationalist reasons. Lawyers, on the whole, remained strangely silent when faced with this challenge (often trying to convey, in my experience, a smug superiority rather than trying to explain or defend).

167

What did I experience as a "legal education"? Other than the freedom of total choice in courses taken and a wide range of subjects studied alongside my major, the actual law courses followed the expository tradition. Indeed there seemed a strange disjuncture between our lives as law students and our lives as students enrolled on other courses; the ideas, debates and academic developments resounding through other disciplines simply did not touch our legal studies. So powerful was this division that many of us who wanted to go on and ask questions of what law-out-there was really like, or to pose ethical and policy questions outside of jurisprudence courses (and indeed there were even those of us who felt that those courses did not really allow key issues to be discussed.

That potential space was found in the expanding social sciences, was made even more attractive to lawyers who hankered after proper respect in the academy as here was a "discipline", a methodology, a way of testing ideas and posing possibilities about a social structure with real social consequences. So in the 1960/1970s many "lawyers" simply left, resurrected themselves as criminologists or "socio-legal" scholars and met sociologists who, looking for new terrain to explore, had found the study of legal institutions and processes a virtually open field.

The message seemed simple...stay in law departments and stay a lawyer, doctrinal work and the potential of the route to the profession kept open; or go elsewhere and study "law" in its full, complex social glory and the potential of the route to the wider academy opened.

This involved a double move. Firstly a vacation of law departments, a distancing from legal education, and secondly an implicit denial that the study of "law" (rather than simply legal education) was possible within "law".

But the period of vacation was not long. Even in a period of expansion, there were insufficient jobs in criminology and sociology of law; the recruitment areas were primarily in law departments structured around legal education. I wonder, also, how secure many of the ex-patriate lawyers actually felt when they presented themselves as resurrected academics. What did they have to offer? Whereas, on their return to law departments, their currency was sure. Here they could present themselves as importers of academic knowledge, offering a future, a new vision for law within the academy, for, indeed, legal education or rather an education through (and out the other side of) law. But I run ahead of myself...I need to freeze the frame of this period of externality.

In some ways, I am constructing a historical fiction. Out of a tangled pattern, I try to draw one thread of narrative. I want to locate a moment which seems to have passed so quickly, but has left such a strong legacy, that the pattern is difficult to discern. It was an encounter with the social sciences, and in my narrative most specifically with sociology. It was a small space in which people talked of the sociology of law; in which the talk was presumed to be either a kind of dialogue or a kind of kindly education. We were either to become conversant with the methodologies of social science or to indeed become social scientists ourselves. Locating this moment might take into account 1965, with the establishment of the then Social Science Research Council and the decision to allow funding through this body for work on law. The funding body for the humanities (The British Academy) would continue to fund law research as it fitted into a humanities brief and the SSRC would take funding for research into law as it fitted into a social science brief. "Two bites at the cherry" for lawyers, but also a division of law into two, seemingly distinctive, patterns of scholarship.

Sumner, writing in 1973, puts forward the case for a partnership between sociology and law:

> Law must be integrated with sociology in teaching and research.... The barriers to this project are not insurmountable and can be cleared with will and self-consciousness. The vocational, practical teaching ideology of the lawyer and the more, abstract, educational teaching ideology of the sociologist do not raise impossible barriers....Eventually we must aim for the drastic revision of most law courses in this country and the inclusion of the work of sociologists of law in most general sociology courses. The complete revision of most law courses in this

country is long overdue; as has been the examination of the attitudes, beliefs and purposes of most law teachers which this revision entails. We must act now: there can be no compromise.[8]

But it was not a real partnership. The task for sociologists was to offer courses on sociology of law; for lawyers it was to completely rethink their courses. Partnership in research was more easily accomplished; the establishment of the Oxford Centre for Socio-Legal Studies in 1972 marking a beginning.[9] But even here a slippage is indicated; was socio-legal simply deemed to be a more graceful rendering of sociology of law? If so, in what sense, more graceful? It was, of course, the beginning of one identity crisis: what did socio-legal mean, or rather, what did we want it to mean? In Sumner's article "socio-legal" is used as a short hand, indicated in his first footnote.[10] But the tone of his paper, his audience indicated by its place of publication, clearly mark that the "legal" is to be read through "socio"; it is a move more important to lawyers than sociologists. What this opened up was a territory which could be negotiated; however clear Sumner was about the "socio" representing sociology he (or others committed to a possible partnership) could not over-determine, or limit, the many ways of reading a meaning, or identity, into "socio-legal".

I have a sense that the slippage from sociology of law to socio-legal was significant; it allowed much greater scope of play for lawyers, a reference to difference from their past but not a commitment to a shared future with sociologists. Did it simply come to represent the regrouping of the ex-patriate lawyers? It signalled, perhaps, a rite of passage. An escape from law, an engagement with social sciences and a return to law protected by the shield of "socio". (The engagement with social sciences did not become a marriage because it would have required either a partner of equal status, a contract of exchange, or lawyers subsuming their identity into sociologists, coveture. Some did; they became the sociologists of law. Most didn't; they returned to the their family of origin). Could the shield be a sword?

I am struck looking back on such papers as Sumners' with the prescriptive tone so often adopted; the certainty of the project and the good it will bring. What actually transpired seems a poor shadow of the possibilities; a series of moves to accommodate the "socio" to the "legal". Our knowledge is limited, we do not have a clear account of the attempts made in legal education to achieve a socio-legal project for undergraduates; all we can do is record the more visible trends and patterns.

Further, many of those records are now written by people often wanting to achieve distance from the socio-legal to acclaim another project, critical legal education.[11] Narratives often become confused as they move from a future to a past without any real moment of present. However themes do emerge and are readily visible; it may be that we should learn that to over-characterise is dangerous as both an account of actual practices and as rendering possible futures.

The opening up of a terrain named as socio-legal allowed access to questions, issues and materials which had not been part of the established curriculum...an emphasis on process, policy and possibilities (of which law was only one option) breathed life into the subject area. It critically challenged and in many ways undermined key tenets in the way in which law was thought and taught to undergraduates; the separation of substantive law from procedure, a focus on the contingent rather than simply a presentation of the coherence of legal argument, on dispute resolution rather than simply litigation, of the realities of life in the lower courts (or indeed in the corridors of the higher courts) rather than simply the outcome of cases taken on appeal. All this was essential as part of our learning process as we attempted to come to grips with this strange baggage called "law". But there was also a more negative aspect to this fresh wind. First of all it blew either in directions away from the core curriculum, or in as far as it did blow in that direction many were not really sure how to deal with this new found knowledge. Again, a compromise emerged; the teaching of doctrine could be accommodated along with aspects of the "reality" of law in (or as) process. The "in context" approach. This took as given the need for (or at least the necessary continuation) of doctrinal work but presented it wrapped with a packaging of "reality".

This approach thrived at undergraduate level and was reflected in undergraduate text-books and associated series. The approach was and is not without its problems. How far should one go in displacing the study of torts by a discussion about compensation alternatives, or contracts by arbitration, or land title by registration, or offenses tried in the higher courts by regulatory offenses etc. How far should one be teaching "law out there", the law of the profession and the market and the state, rather than the basic models of legal relations, rights and responsibilities?

I am afraid, despite innovative ideas and programmes, that legal education is currently in a mess. We have in practice too often produced a kind of "add on" approach to our subjects. Keeping the methods and material which have been deployed for years and adding to that a "context" of policy, procedure or possibilities which become a sugar coating on an otherwise familiar pill. Students aren't fooled; especially when many course innovations are not reflected in examination papers which return to the safety of the tried and tested.

There remains an uneven approach to different areas of core teaching; an inheritance of presumptions that some aspects of the curriculum are "freer" than others. Common law (especially torts), criminal law and administrative law are the heady subjects which excite the inheritors of the 1970s project. I still meet colleagues who presume that land and trusts are both too doctrinally bound and too vocationalist in orientation, to be truly interesting. The consequences of these attitudes is reflected in many law schools which produce some innovative courses but abandon other courses to the full rigours of the traditionalists. An uneven programme at its best, at its worst it fails to produce a coherent account of academic work to the student body:

A preliminary evaluation of contextualism recognises its significance as challenging the expository tradition in its own arena of substantive law. It is this feature which attests to its real but generally unspoken critique of orthodox legal education. Its lack of apparent attention to its own methodology has resulted in its impact being very uneven..[12]

I agree with Farmer that much of the work characterised as "law in context" continues to produce:

the divide between law and context (which) is unhelpful and artificial, and perpetuates the margin of context....we should abandon certain of our attempts to teach law in context.[13]

Farmer's argument parallels my own in a concern that too often such work is not sufficiently theorised:

theoretical neglect of their subject tells us more about their own anxieties and insecurities than it does about law...(they have)..neither confidence in the path being followed nor wholehearted enthusiasm for interdisciplinary study..[14]

Which results in an academic confusion. Farmer concludes:

The law must be understood and presented as a series of shifting rationalities which demands that we as teachers abandon and challenge, however temporarily, our own received understanding of the law. How after, after all, can we go beyond existing theory if we do not understand it properly?[15]

This means taking responsibility for the academic project. It calls for, and makes possible, an engagement with legal discourse. Losing the fear of doctrine. Not being seduced by doctrine; but taking doctrine seriously. Ways of giving meaning; ways of talking law; ways of talking ideas.

It is, in one sense, simply taking ourselves seriously. We have accumulated enough evidence to know that no closure is complete; that the repressed returns; that the excluded is only a projection of exclusion; that the more assertive the project of an identity the more likely that this assertion hides a fundamental fragility.

A need to distance ourselves from truth-claims, from a positivism which no longer holds, is one thing. To continue to demand of legal discourse that it, or rather we, conform to this model, is another expectation.. We no longer need to present a picture of:

> .. break(ing) the legal mould which is essentially jurisdictional, institutionally linked to the law and its personnel. Doctrinal lawyers operate through closure and exclusion... [16]

...except as a representation of history and a cautionary tale. We certainly can no longer trade on revelation of doctrine as false consciousness ("to identify the reality beneath the law"[17]), if that counters legal positivism with a positivist account of "reality", a simple dialectic of truth claims.

If "law" no longer holds a stable identity for critique, except as a fiction of our own making, a continual reworking of our heritage; neither does the "socio" offer a stable site to launch that critique.[18] Not merely has distance been created from the social sciences as methodology; the very concept of society becomes problematic as a working concept, and along with it the ease of reference to "reality" as somehow the "law" as it is, rather than the "law" as constructed for study.

Current debates about the identity of socio-legal studies generally focus on theoretical questions, and rightly so. But there are clues as to some of the factors which constitute the conditions for that debate. They are found by looking at the heritage of socio-legal studies within the practices of law schools. Funded research projects have tended to focus on the impact of law in practice and the possibilities of law reform; the scale and methodologies of such projects often require close co-operation between lawyers and social scientists. On the other hand, legal education has remained the province of lawyers; albeit lawyers influenced in numerous ways by the "socio". However not only has the "socio" tended to continue to reproduce the "legal" as the core to be studied and/or critiqued; it has also provided credibility to one mode of critique as "law in practice" as opposed to "law in books". Reading through material produced in different law faculties suggests that many have opted to present a "skills" programme as their most innovative contribution to legal education in recent years. This is where we come full circle. Ironically this is often presented as a new realism brought about by a meeting of socio-legal work with a new vocationalist perspective. Education, reduced to training as a technician, has been reproduced through a different alliance but sharing a similar heritage with that which at one time many of us tried to escape. (I sometimes wonder whether at some later date, we shall look back on "skills programmes" as quaintly ridiculous in their pretensions to realism and preparation for life, as we now view the once innovative training of "problem solving").

What has to struggle for an identity, a place, between these two poles is still the idea of the lawyer as academic; of scholarship in law. As Scott concludes:

> ..much contemporary legal research is social-scientific rather than scholarly in its ethos, because it is increasingly dependent on external grants and consequently undertaken by a self-sufficient cadre of fullish-time researchers. This trend..is likely to create a greater gap between legal research and professional practice. In these circumstances legal education, because of the vocationalist fix of most law students, is almost bound to identify with the latter, consigning legal research to a semi-detached and quasi-oppositional role.[19]

Hydra Two: Law Student

"The vocationalist fix" of the law student is the second great myth but as with all myths it holds a truth. As education becomes, for the student, a more costly enterprise, the choice of undergraduate study becomes more vocationally orientated. A job is the goal; humanist aspirations for education are replaced by an orientation towards skills for the market place. For those who choose law, the vocationalism seems focused; the ironic twist being simply the paucity of jobs available in the profession. We face students who are increasingly fearful of fulfilling their desires. They experience more pressure and consequently exert more pressure. In many faculties the commendable concern to encourage student feed-back as part of the monitoring of teaching standards, becomes another aspect of a consumerist ethos in which student demands reflect, and continue to reproduce, a reductionist account of what an education in law might be about. Results and relevancy, an assurance that what is being taught will enhance their prospects of a career in law, becomes a currency of exchange within the law school.

As in the language of the documents coming from the professional bodies and the Lord Chancellor's Committee on Legal Education and Conduct, this is "the initial stage", the first step on a road which focuses beyond the undergraduate degree, beyond the academy.[20]   Twining characterises this approach as a "primary school for the profession";[21] for Douzinas *et al* it is:

> ..literally, a finishing school; one that finally stops the
> possibilities of a textual exploration that could bring text
> towards ways of reading other than those imposed by the
> discipline of legal and educational institutions.[22]

In institutions where the "Law School" has developed as the site of lawyers within the academy, students and faculty spending the majority of their time separated from other groupings; the character of a specific (vocationalist) orientation is likely to be exacerbated. It becomes much easier to develop a Law School culture. Some law departments struggled out of a servicing relationship with other departments. Now many Law Schools are encouraged into a servicing relationship with professional bodies, offering not merely professional training courses but short courses for the professionals themselves. For undergraduates this means more contact with "lawyering" rather than other undergraduate studies. Further, more degrees are becoming tailored to meet not only the undergraduate profile but also the graduate profile; fast track exemption routes for those who already have degrees and seek only professional qualifications.

All of this suits the academy; more students mean more money. The fact that it might dilute the academic enterprise can be ignored provided the faculty presents a research profile. But for those teaching increasing numbers of students, morale has hit a new low. One hears anecdotal evidence of the "vocationalist fix" taking a stronger hold. Today students select electives on far more conventional lines than a decade ago; resisting courses overtly concerned with theory or critique; willing only to engage with "relevant" courses and material. There is a new realism afoot which dismisses and displaces the academic enterprise.

This can easily become an excuse for retrenchment; give them what they want and find what space we can, for what we want to do, elsewhere.

There are many arguments for resisting this position. Firstly, I think that it would reinforce a view of us in the academy that we are, for all our attempts to be "researchers", not really "scholars". A claim for the lawyer as academic must include, crucially, the presentation of our subject to our students; amongst whom will be found the next generation of academics. It is a reworking of the challenge to a lack of discipline base in the 1970/1980s, but now it is not focused through a frame of discipline base because, simply, the academic world has moved on from being quite so certain about the very notion of clearly defined and separate disciplines based on distinctive methodologies. It is more amorphous; a claim to being part of an academic project which produces scholarship of value to the academic world. But as with funded research projects, as Scott pointed out, if that scholarship is not reproduced at undergraduate level, it cuts itself loose, not because, as Scott argues, it moves away from professional practice, but because it has no firm institutional base. It fails to confirm an academic identity for ourselves, for our students, for the rest of the academy.

Secondly, by vacating legal education to vocationalism we fail the student body. On simple statistics, the majority of undergraduate law students will not become lawyers. Yet we continue to teach them as if that is the focus of our mutual endeavour.

In my experience the strongest, most often used and most powerfully emotive word used by students when questioning a course is "relevant". Is this "relevant"? By implication this suggests a measurement and an immediacy which can be tested. It can be experienced as a challenge or as an opportunity, to justify what is being taught. How that challenge is met, an answer framed and justified, is crucial in our attempts to negotiate and influence the student conception of what a degree in law is, or can be, about. Two major justifications of "relevance" in substantive law are proferred; this may be boring and hard but the professional bodies insist that we teach it and, this is not in the text books and is therefore difficult to follow but it is at "the cutting edge" of what is going on in practice and isn't that exciting. Recourse to these two explanations re-enforces not only the centrality of "relevance" as the touch-stone for our enterprise but also reproduces the key operational image/fantasy of undergraduate work; that our text comes from another place and that the justification for our enterprise is found elsewhere. This modus vivendi, the duality of displacement and deferment, is a crucial clue which leads us straight to questions not of our students but of ourselves.

I suggest that one of the reasons why so many law students still aspire to becoming lawyers is because of the messages we give our undergraduates in the process of our teaching and the presentation of our subject to them. We are still, essentially, uncomfortable with "law" as the focus of our own identity as academics. Farmer's reference to "our insecurities and anxieties" is all too apposite. What our students pick up is our own defensiveness; we find it easier to collude with them in being lawyers than to try and "bring them over" to an academic project; because we are not sure of that academic project. When we are faced with a student body demanding relevance, we counter by displacing our responsibility onto others (is this a key legal skill?). We have constantly failed to take responsibility for setting an academic agenda. Now we fail to identify our projections on to them and, so easy an inversion, begin to blame them for our condition.

What do students want? We make so many presumptions of them....but have we enquired? We presume of them a "vocationalist fix" and then presume that this is a demand for a menu of black letter main course and plenty of skills on the side. If this is so where does this culture, this heritage, come from? This conflation of old-style "real law" with new style "real law"? It can only be from us; we may like to think that some strong student tradition carries this forward but my suspicion is that it receives daily confirmation in the class-room. We presume rather than enquire, we project on to them our heritage and our insecurities. Their inheritance is tragic; closure for a promise many will not benefit from and those who do succeed...how will they look back on their legal education?

Hydra Three: The Profession

There is one basic fact seldom expressed to our students. It is that we have been unable to persuade the legal profession that a law degree should be the only route into the practice of law. Whatever good arguments we present, however much we try to adjust courses to new versions of a vocationalist ethos; it remains the case that our colleagues in practice are unconvinced. A recent remark from a member of the Law Society involved with education, suggested that currently about one third of training contracts go to non-law graduates. This is despite the large numbers of unemployed law graduates. It is not a question of supply. It is a question of judgment of quality which reinforces a judgment that a law degree is not a necessary part of legal education. There are many lawyers, and senior judges, who hold degrees in other academic disciplines and believe in a broad academic education. They have the evidence of their own careers to prove that committing ones undergraduate studies to law is unnecessary.

However, to keep what hold we have, we necessarily allow the professional bodies to continue to determine the content, the process of examination and to some extent the style of our undergraduate degrees in order to achieve exemption status. Our presentation of this scenario is still often one in which we cast ourselves as passive victims. As Moffat points out:

> The increased freedom in structuring courses recently permitted by the profession.... carries with it burdens of responsibility and insecurity: the overly prescriptive syllabus is no more..[23]

Further the successful challenge to the proposed disappearance of equity and trusts as a separate foundation subject, proved that when academics make a stand and construct an argument the professional bodies may well respond.[24]

I believe, I can put it in no higher account, that to be taken seriously by the profession we need to present ourselves as academics. Not as pale imitations of the real thing: the lawyer in practice, but as having an identity in our own right. I believe that a starting point in this is to bring scholarship into legal education; not to allow them to become two different enterprises in the law school. Despite the many pressures on us within the academy; we have to create the space to think about what we want to do with our "burden of responsibility and insecurity". To again try and think about new patterns for legal education; because we have been given the space to do so by the profession. We must take that space and make our own agendas; to be able to return and renegotiate in strength from a sense of our own priorities. We can no longer protect ourselves with the story of the "prescriptive syllabus"; and if we do not respond now the final shred of clothing torn from us, will reveal our nakedness.

Turning Back...Facing A Future

I have landed in the trap I sought to avoid. Not only have I focused on the twin orthodoxies; I have also adopted a hectoring and prescriptive tone. I wanted rather to be exploratory; to talk of the moments of opening, of engagement and of possibilities. Why does "legal education" seem so over-determined to the point where one is always brought back to repeat the same patterns?

Paradoxically, I am far more optimistic than my paper might suggest; I have overdrawn for the sake of argument the "present conditions" of legal education. I have constructed cautionary narratives rather than attempted a full history. It would be easy for me to construct the final step in this narrative; the future of critical legal education as opposed to the limitations of the socio-legal project. Given that my own sympathies lie in the direction of the humanities; it is very tempting to argue that critical legal education recovers a project for the academic study of law which allows access to all the thriving areas of the academy and, in particular, the resurgence of a focus on systems of meaning and access to ethical questions. It is also tempting to point out that in the recovery of text and the focus on intertextual play, critical legal education allows for, indeed demands, a struggle with doctrine, the production of doctrine, and the place of discourse as one aspect of discursive practices. It takes law seriously; as practice, as text. Such an approach might be a bridge between scholarship and teaching, as is any scholarship which takes text seriously. It might also be a bridge between those interested in the text of law and those interested in the practice of law; because it isn't predicated on the need to deny either. It is certainly a bridge towards the rest of the academy.

However I do not believe in absolutism. It is clear to me that marking a territory called "socio-legal" not only made a great deal of sense in its origins but also allowed for considerable growth in work around law. I do not believe that this territory needs to be, or indeed should be, constructed or defended against the traditions of academic law, as exemplified in legal education. Neither do I believe that this territory need take on the role of object of critique. Rather we should be reaccessing the academic values of those traditions as revealed through both the study of them as well as the practice. Examining the philosophical ideas behind the core conceptual tools of law, examining the different processes of argumentation and reasoning, including the academic search for doctrinal clarity; these are part of a study of the discourse of law. Socio-legal work has, to date, tended to focus on the discursive practices rather than the discourse itself. There is no reason why it should not turn to discourse itself. The discomfort of focusing on the discourse is that it means focusing on ourselves as academics; as those who have in part constructed, and in greater part, reproduced this heritage. If the rubric "socio-legal" is to remain a signal for careful, concise, clear thinking about law in all its manifestations then this must be part of the terrain. In which case it will mean a collection of people working on different aspects of law who are interested in each others work and do not feel limited by out-moded histories. A starting point for access to this is found in the classroom; in confronting our role there as researchers as well as teachers. In studying us and what we do, and taking responsibility for how we present what we do to the next generation. In one sense, to be more conscious about the conflicts we operate within and to use them more productively. To be more transparent. To face and place our fears and to understand what it means to search for an identity. [*With many thanks to Nick Jackson and Chris Stanley.*]

Notes

1   Of course "(an)other life" claim was often found in holding the professional qualifications; a source of authority and mystique (otherwise known as

"reality") for the student body. How far will a research/publication profile begin to pose an alternative to this? Many young academics still come with Bar examinations behind them; was this keeping their career options open, or did/do they see it as part of an academic profile?

2   Successful bargaining is seen by the lawyers as simply the rightful outcome of their contribution towards the financial health of the academy, but it leaves tensions. A retreat into Law Schools may help an external profile and internal bargaining position, but it also often marks a move away from other academics, and limits initiatives based in inter-disciplinary work.

3   W.T. Murphy, "Reference Without Reality; A Comment on a Commentary on Codifications in Practice" (1990) 1 *Law and Critique* 61; Christopher Stanley, "Killing Them Softly With My Words?" (1990) 1 *Law and Critique* 39.

4   Philip Thomas, "The Poverty of Students" (1993) 27 *The Law Teacher* 152

5   Alan Thompson, "Critical Legal Education in Britain" (1987) Vol. 14 *Journal of Law and Society* 183, at p.186.

6   Richard Cosgrove, *Our Lady The Common Law: An Anglo-American Legal Community 1870-1930* (1987) pp.31-32, quoted in W. Murphy 'The Oldest Social Science? The Epistemic Properties of the Common Law Tradition' (1991) 54 *Modern Law Review* 182, at n.4

7   For a history of legal education in this country see William Twining, *Blackstone's Tower: The English Law School* (1994).

8   Colin Sumner, "Law and Sociology - The case for Partnership" (1973) *The Law Teacher* 7, at p.19

9   See Special Issue on the Oxford Centre (1995) 25 *Journal of Law and Society*. On questions of funding socio-legal research see Alan Hunt, "Governing the Socio-Legal Project: Or What Do Research Councils Do?" (1994) 21 *Journal of Law and Society* 520

10   Sumner, *op.cit.* n.8, p.7

11   See, eg Alan Hunt, "The Case for Critical Legal Education" (1986) 20 *The Law Teacher* 10; Alan Thomson, "Critical Legal Education in Britain" (1987) 14 *Journal of Law and Society* 183

12   Hunt, *op.cit.*, at p. 15. For an example of transparency in thinking through the problem in relation to trusts (to counter the prejudices of some of my colleagues) see Graham Moffat, "Trusts Law: A Song Without End?" 55 *Modern Law Review* 123.

13   Lindsay Farmer "Bringing Cinderella to the Ball: Teaching Criminal law in Context" (1995) Vol. 58, *Modern Law Review* 756, at p. 756

14   *op.cit.*, at p. 757.

15   *op.cit.*, at p.756.

16   Philip Thomas, "Speaking Truth to Power" (1995) 15 *Socio-Legal Newsletter* 3, at p.4.

17   Thomson, op.cit., n. 5.

18   See David Nelken, "Beyond the Study of Law and Society?" (1986) 2 *American Bar Foundation Research Journal* 323; Peter Fitzpatrick "Being Social in Socio-Legal Studies" (1995) 22 *Journal of Law and Society* 105

19   Peter Scott, review of William Twining "Blackstone's Tower: The English Law School" (1995) 22 *Journal of Law and Society* 429 at p. 431

20   See Lord Chancellor's Advisory Committee on Legal Education and Conduct, *Consultation Paper on the Initial Stage* (June. 1994)

21   William Twining, "Remembering 1972: The Oxford Centre in the Context of Developments in Higher Education and the Discipline of Law" (1995) 22 *Journal of Law and Society* 35, at p.44

22   Costas Douzinas, Shaun McVeigh and Ronnie Warrington, "Postlegality: After Education in the Law" (1990) 1 *Law and Critique* 81, at p.91

23   Moffat, *op.cit*, n.12, at p.123

24   See Peter Birks, "Villany with a Smiling Cheek (1995) 10 *S.P.T.L. Reporter* 16

9 Criminal Justice: The Development Of Criminal Justice Research In Britain

ANDREW SANDERS

Socio-legal studies in 1960s and 1970s Britain began, in part, as a reaction against the legal formalism of traditional legal scholarship. Traditional legal scholars were, and still are, almost wholly interested in the content of legal rules and principles. Socio-legalists were interested in the origins and effects of laws, the interests they serve and the way they actually work. As part of the eschewing of 'law' per se the rules were generally treated as unproblematic. This was as true of most early criminal justice work as it was of other socio-legal work.[1] But there were several streams of research in the 1960s and 1970s.

First there was what one might call 'administrative criminology'. This type of research aims to improve the running of the criminal justice system and includes work on, for instance, prediction scores, and sentencing disparity.[2] Second, there was civil liberties-inspired research. This aimed to expose how the system worked in inegalitarian or non-libertarian ways with a view to legal reform. Examples include work on access to solicitors for suspects in police stations, and on unrepresented defendants. Third, there was socio-legal 'gap' research which sought to identify gaps between the legal rules and the reality the rules purported to portray. This was also often of an 'expose' kind, and often overlapped with the civil-liberties oriented work, and included work on plea bargaining and police rule breaking. Finally, there was sociological research on, for instance, the role of the police and legal profession, and on court processes as status degradation.[3]

The first three of those streams of research shared an inadequate conception of law: administrative criminology did not address it: the civil liberty stream assumed that the rules in question were deficient and should be improved, taking it for granted that this would alter reality;[4] and 'gap' research assumed that there was nothing wrong with the law, the blame for 'gaps' being laid at the door of the officials who were supposed to operate the law. Only the sociological stream had the potential to go further, although it usually did not do so even in the best work. The earliest major example of sociological work actually treating legal rules as an object of inquiry and relating their structure and content to the totality of criminal justice is Doreen McBarnet's *Conviction*, which did not appear until 1981. McBarnet showed that what is often assumed to be a gap between rules and reality in police behaviour is sometimes a gap between rhetoric and reality.

In recent years there has been an explosion of criminal justice research. This has encouraged the growth of criminal justice courses and, belatedly, teaching materials, including several new socio-legal texts in 1994 and 1995.[5] But the pattern remains the same. 'Administrative criminology' - criminal justice management, crime prevention, police performance measures, evaluation of new inter-agency networks, bail schemes, evaluation of new policing routines - has expanded fastest. Not all this research is necessarily mundane and anti-intellectual: crime prevention and inter-agency work, for instance, raises major theoretical, sociological and political questions. And so I shall argue later that to be 'policy-related' is not in itself a problem, but that the category should be divided into two: policy-led research (which is problematic) and intellectually-led policy-relevant research (which is not).

This is not to say that path-breaking work has been entirely squeezed out in the later 1980s and 1990s. Some of the work on policing, 'regulation', 'white collar' crime, diversion as corporatism or part of the 'surveillance society', the delivery of legal services and on those at the receiving end of criminal justice has been stimulating and resourceful.[6] But this is not the centre of gravity of the discipline, of criminal justice courses, or of practitioners' concerns. Thus, as Jefferson and Shapland point out, *Policing the Crisis* - clearly sociological in its multi layer analysis of 'mugging', social reaction, state and media - appeared at the time of publication (1978) to be a seminal work.[7] Yet very little research has been inspired by it, and overall there has been a narrowing of focus despite increased empirical research activity. Without feminist-inspired work and, to a lesser extent, work on racism and criminal justice, the field would have almost completely divided into two grossly unequal parts: empirical work characterised by the first three streams (in particular of the 'administrative' variety), and largely theoretical sociological work.

I would crudely sum up the shortcomings of British criminal justice research as follows. First, topics of short-term significance to administrators are given priority over matters of more fundamental significance. Second, and more important, the *approaches* adopted are those which are geared to the short-term interests of administrators. Research is, in 90s jargon, consumer-led. The 'consumer' is usually defined as the administrator. But even when it is the victim or suspect, as in 'expose' research, the problem - failure to stand outside categories defined *for* the intellectual rather than *by* the intellectual - is fundamentally the same. Finally, there is a widespread failure to subject the law to scrutiny: to see the law as both part of the phenomenon requiring explanation and as part of the explanation for the problem under examination.

Take, for example, guilty pleas. These raise questions which go to the heart of the adversary system and, indeed, of the Rule of Law itself. The broad topic is capable of leading to policy-relevant fundamental research as well as superficial policy-led research. Most attention is given to 'cracked' trials, ie late plea changes. The aim of such work is to identify ways of securing guilty pleas at an earlier stage and avoiding cracked trials. This of course raises simpler theoretical questions (and safer political questions) than asking why and how people come to plead guilty in the first place. One of the most famous pieces of British research on plea bargaining, *Negotiated Justice*, precisely concerned 'cracked trials' and was an unsophisticated example of the fourth stream of research. Like *Policing the Crisis*, though, its classic status did not inspire a stream of research to follow up its insights. Only recently has plea bargaining been subjected to detailed scrutiny - now that the *cost* of cracked trials is seen as a significant problem. The fate of the defendants, which concerned Baldwin and McConville, is usually ignored.[8] This exemplifies what is wrong with the preponderance of current research. Of the two groups of actors in the system - those working *in* it, and those being worked on *by* it, it is the former which is being assisted by research, arguably at the expense of the latter.

The Weaknesses Of British Criminal Justice Research

In order to illustrate these points concretely I subject a number of pieces of research to closer scrutiny. I concentrate on five, even though this risks being unfair to the authors. In the interests of even-handedness I include two of my own pieces of research. They are my early research on prosecutions[9] and my research with Lee Bridges on legal advice to suspects in police stations.[10] The other studies are: Baldwin and Hill on 'Green Form' legal advice,[11] Moston and Stephenson on informal interrogation,[12] and Brown et al on the revised PACE Code of Practice.[13] There are certain faults shared by these studies, which are common to criminal justice research in general:

Assuming Social Constructions To Be Fixed Entities

My early prosecution research was consumer-led. The professionals' problem was the prosecution of weak cases. My task was to find them, discover the reasons for their prosecution, and recommend the reforms which could eliminate them. Since I discovered that the reason was often that of police policy, the obvious solution was to remove prosecution decisions from the police and give them to an independent prosecution service. Only later did I realise, by standing outside the policy question and the police frame of reference, that 'weakness' and 'strength' are constructions and that only institutions with the power to construct their own cases could be truly independent of the police.[14]

Similarly, the research on access to legal advice saw the decisions of suspects, lawyers and police officers as largely discrete. Making the police - or, better still, another agency - inform suspects more clearly of their rights was the obvious policy implication. Only later did I (with Richard Young) realise, first, that these decisions are hugely dependent on structural circumstances, particularly the fact of coercive custodial detention. What matters is not so much who offers advice to the suspect, as the conditions under which the suspect has to wait and receive the advice. Advice is not intrinsically valued or not, and nor is it encouraged or discouraged in a vacuum. Its value, and the level of encouragement, is in part a product of the immediate environment in which suspects find themselves, and that environment is controlled by the police. Second, these same conditions structure the nature of the advice and assistance provided by lawyers to clients. Under these conditions legal advice to suspects could as often be functional for the police as for the suspect.[15]

Similar analyses could be made of Brown et al and of Moston and Stephenson. Both studies attempted to discover the extent of interrogation outside the police station, something which would rarely be lawful under PACE Code of Practice 'C'.[16] The method sought to explore this was to ask the police officers who, not surprisingly, often described their exchanges as 'information seeking' (which is lawful). Remarkably, the propensity of police officers to construct unlawful encounters as lawful in other contexts (such as 'gilding the lily')[17] was not seen as an instructive parallel by these authors.

It is often thought that data collection and analysis must involve counting whatever it is that is being studied. This, however, begs the question of what it is that one is really studying. All five pieces of research considered here tried to quantify some data but drew conclusions about something different. Thus I used my own counting of 'weak' cases (in my prosecution research) and police 'ploys' to discourage requests for advice (in the research with Lee Bridges on legal advice for suspects in police stations) to draw conclusions about how often the police 'abused' their position. This, of course, was naive. Counting these breaches of the rules simply counted how often the police abused their position by breaking certain rules. The police had, and still have, many perfectly legitimate ways of achieving the same objectives. This illustrates the importance of the point in the chapter's opening section about both understanding the law and treating it as problematic: lawyers generally understand what the law says rather better than do social scientists, but tend to be more easily misled into believing that what is lawful is not problematic.

Both issues - use and abuse of position, and rule breaking - are interesting, but they should not be confused. The latter, whilst usually easier to quantify than the former (hence sometimes, mistakenly, used as a surrogate for the former), is not easy to count (as illustrated below in the context of the other studies). Is it necessary to quantify rule-breaking in order to demonstrate its importance? Critics of *Case for the Prosecution* feel that it is.[18] But again it depends what it is one is trying to study. In this research we were trying to show that when the police needed to break the rules to pursue their working rules they could do so. Even one proven case of rule breaking would 'prove' a limited version of this hypothesis, although not, of course, a more powerful hypothesis that the police always - or even often - do so in such circumstances. The only quantification that would make sense would be to isolate those situations where rule breaking is required for the achievement of police objectives, and see if that is what they do. But this would be extremely difficult to carry out. More limited exercises may obscure the issue. Thus Roger Evans, in his Royal Commission study, suggests that we exaggerated police case construction through interrogation because 77 per cent of interrogated juveniles confessed at the start of their interviews before the police even needed to raise their voices.[19] All this proves, though, is that most of the time the police do not *need* to construct cases in this way, and leaves unilluminated the more interesting question of how the police react when things do not go their way. As it happens, Evans notes that some of these interviews begin so bizarrely that they almost had to have been preceded by informal interviews - where, of course, all sorts of case construction techniques may have been brought to bear.

In essence what is being quantified can be so partial that quantification can be more misleading than enlightening. This was so in the other three studies under consideration here. Brown et al, Moston and Stephenson, and Baldwin and Hill; all asked the subjects being studied how often they broke various kinds of rule. It is true that this can produce an estimate of minimum rule-breaking, but it is all too easy for this to be elided into a simple estimate of rule breaking. These studies also illustrate the further problem of surrogacy: low estimates of rule breaking are taken as low estimates of abuse of position in each case. One result was that the Royal Commission on Criminal Justice, which relied heavily on the research of Brown and of Moston and Stephenson, confused the two: "...the effect of PACE and of Code C has been beneficial. Research shows general compliance with Code C...".[20] Neither the Commission nor most of its research investigated the effect of the legislation and Codes, and the conclusion was reached on the basis of this research's conclusions about rule-adherence. Finally, by asking the subjects about their own rule-breaking these researchers did not actually quantify the amount of rule-breaking occurring, but how often these subjects *admitted* it.

Not all research requires that more than one perspective is examined as long as it is clear to researcher and reader that the conclusions to be drawn relate only to one perspective. Obvious though this may sound, it is remarkable how often broader conclusions are drawn. Thus the methodology of both Brown et al and Moston and Stephenson did not, as we saw above, allow them to discover how often the police actually carried out informal interrogations (although this did not stop Brown et al describing as 'findings' in their conclusion what they correctly describe as 'claims' earlier in the study). Similarly, Baldwin and Hill asked solicitors what was wrong with the Green Form Scheme: 'rates of pay', most solicitors replied. It is true that Baldwin and Hill also asked clients what they thought of the services which had been provided, but it is still only a perspective. The essence of a successful 'sting', as Paul Newman and Robert Redford demonstrated in the film of that name, is not to let the stung victims know when they have been had. Many clients think they are getting a good service, but triangulation - with reality, and not just with those providing the service - should still be sought. Thus in our legal advice research we found many cases where suspects were satisfied with a very poor service because they did not have any yardstick or experience by which to expect better.[21] Comparing what solicitors did with what they *said* they did produce a dramatic contrast.

Wherever people are asked about their own performance, in particular, there are vested interests. It is so obvious that such matters should be approached with caution that it should not have to be spelt out, but the same mistakes are still being made.[22] This is not to suggest that triangulation will always work positivistically to enable 'the truth' to be revealed. Different communities have different truths. However when one community - usually the professions and other elites - represent orthodoxy, gathering other perspectives can at least challenge those orthododoxies.

I have argued that much research falls into the classic 'gap' category, often with a crusading 'expose' zeal to show that police and other state agencies break their own rules. My counting of weak cases and the use of 'ploys' fell into this tradition. The tempting, though not inevitable, next step is then to blame this rule breaking either on the organisation in question or on individuals within it (the 'rotten apple' theory). The former is now usually preferred over the latter, as in most of the studies under scrutiny here, because of the recognition that individual behaviour is generally shaped by organisational goals. However, if individual behaviour is shaped by its environment (specifically, organisational goals), is it not probable that organisational behaviour and goals will, in turn, be shaped by the environment in which the organisation operates? Thus in *Case for the Prosecution* we argue that police working rules are derived from a crime control ideology intended to keep the lid on a society structured on race, class, power and privilege. Researchers with different theoretical perspectives might identify different origins for these working rules,[23] but it is naive to assume, as so much criminal justice research does, that there are no origins beyond the organisation.

The explanation for rule infraction is crucial to the recommended cure. If the organisation or its personnel is to blame, the prescribed cure might be a new organisation (in my own flawed works, the CPS to replace the police prosecution function; someone other than the police to tell suspects their rights). Sometimes the cure prescribed - even by sophisticated researchers such as David Dixon and his colleagues[24] - is the promulgation of 'best practice' guidelines, the development of better training, and so forth. Witness the growth in 'ethical interviewing' by the police.

But how much difference have such reforms made? Dixon argues, in a critique of *Case for the Prosecution* that training and work patterns could affect the way custody officers do that aspect of their job that impacts upon the rights of suspects.[25] Our argument is that the working rules operated by custody officers which often deny suspects their rights derive from basic police functions which largely over-ride any effect which training and work patterns might have. This argument has received empirical support from Brown et al, who found that on this point it made no difference what the custody officer arrangements were. But it was just good fortune that Brown et al happened to examine this issue. Where there is no empirical research we must extrapolate from what we know of criminal justice and the way we understand it. That can only be done by research which incorporates at least an element of the fourth strand of research outlined in the first part of this chapter.

Failure To Investigate The Experiences Of The Subjects Of Criminal Justice

We observed that research concentrates on those working *in* criminal justice at the expense of research on those worked on *by* it. Although this appears not to be true of three of our five chosen studies, these appearances are deceptive. In these studies suspects were interviewed, but not in an attempt to understand how it felt to be a suspect, or what it was like to be subjected to police power. Suspects were generally asked to confirm or deny what the police/solicitors said or to evaluate rule adherence. And in the fourth study (Baldwin and Hill), where clients were interviewed, again no attempt was made to understand their experience. Instead they were, in effect, asked to evaluate the performance of solicitors. Thus even when the powerless are given a voice, as in four of the five chosen studies, it is generally only to shed light on the powerful. As an exercise in triangulation this is acceptable, but that is not the only point of discovering the voice of those 'below'. As long ago as 1977 Baldwin and McConville showed that the subjective experience of pressure - in this case to plead guilty - was as important as objective factors.[26] But few studies have followed in its wake, one notable exception being Paddy Hillyard's *Suspect Community.*[27]

It is significant that some of the most important findings of the five chosen studies emerge from suspect interviews which related to their experience rather than to evaluation of official agencies. One such finding is that detention in the cells is subjectively experienced by suspects as far worse than anyone imagined, hence affecting their decision making in important ways; another, linked, finding is that half the suspects who refuse legal advice would not do so if it were readily available.[28] Studies which made such experiences the centre of attention could advance our understanding immeasurably, but only if the questions such research seeks to answer are appropriate. *Suspect Community*, for instance, did not make the mistake made by Baldwin and Hill of asking for an evaluation of the actions of officials.

Future Directions For Criminal Justice Research

Now let me turn around the criticisms made in "The Weaknesses of British Criminal Justice Research" to present in summary form some suggestions for strengthening future research on the lines identified as the fourth stream of research in the first section of this chapter. First, there is a need for research which can investigate the power and interests of criminal justice agencies. The goals of these agencies need to be discovered by research, and not merely accepted on the basis of a mission statement or set of official guidelines. When rules are broken, or individuals are left ignorant, perhaps making apparently foolish choices, the broadest environment within which this happens should be examined. The power of the law in structuring the environment, in for instance, facilitating the abuse of position, has to be investigated and not simply accepted as a back-drop for the 'real' factors.[29]

There are social-structural issues such as class, race, and gender to be considered. One way of understanding the significance of these issues is to research the perspectives of victims, suspects and defendants. Arguments which put class and race, for instance, at the forefront which are currently somewhat speculative could be thereby strengthened (or indeed undermined).[30] Another way of doing this is to mount multi-level and inter-disciplinary research on the lines of *Policing the Crisis*.[31]

Can policy-oriented research ever fulfil the ambitions set out here? I think so. Much Home Office research, for instance, has moved on from the early days of purely descriptive or statistical administrative criminology to more sensitive work. A study of public order policing, for instance, recognised and used some of the insights and advances outlined here: McBarnet is cited on the permissiveness of the criminal law, and arrest is seen as a resource for enforcing order and authority.[32] Although little is made of these insights, here or elsewhere in Home Office work, there is sometimes enough for a secondary analyst to use.

There is a problem, though, with researchers collecting empirical data a-theoretically, and other academics using that data in different theoretical ways. Take my prosecution research which positivistically attempted to identify weak and strong cases. One of my objectives was to see why domestic and non-domestic violence cases which were similarly weak or strong were treated differently. Identifying the crucial factors requires that those factors be thought to be worth investigating in the first place, and without a theory to guide one's search the process is almost arbitrary. My conclusion - that it is order and authority, not the domestic nature of an incident that counts - is therefore suggestive only, because no data was systematically sought along that dimension.[33] Ultimately though, if cases are constructed to be strong or weak, it makes no sense to see why strong and weak cases are treated differently without seeing why cases are weak or strong in the first place. My initial positivistic approach could reveal no more than some insights into this process.[34] Its systematic pursuit required a different project.[35]

Making a different point, Jefferson and Shapland observe that survey research tends to draw conclusions from averages and minorities.[36] This is acceptable for certain purposes. But if the aim of the research is, for instance, to ascertain points of conflict or to relate the opinions of minorities to their experience of policing, this is not merely useless but actually misleading. If the survey is done first, and then these issues are raised, it might be found that insufficient demographic data were discovered to delineate differences between majorities and minorities. So appropriate questions need to be generated in order to shape one's research, and it is an important role of theory to prompt researchable questions even if the data these questions seek are not quantifiable.

It is not just theorists and 'new left pessimists' (in Dixon's phrase) making these points. Pawson and Tilling have called for theoretically driven evaluation research ("the dourest, most matter-of-fact corner of the literature") where theory and empirical work would be developed together.[37] Similarly, Crawford argues for a 'corporatist' analysis of multi-agency initiatives which would be neither managerialist nor conspiratorial.[38] It is not that criminal justice research has to be 'new left pessimist' to be any good, but simply that it needs to make its theory explicit. What we cannot do is to simply 'let the facts speak for themselves'.

Some Concrete Proposals

What does all this mean in concrete terms? I shall briefly outline two research ideas which take the critique presented here as their starting point, and which are situated in the fourth stream of research identified in the first part of this chapter.

Withdrawals Of Complaints By Victims Of Domestic Violence

Most research on this topic is policy-led. One line of work, from the perspective of criminal justice agencies, seeks to identify such cases early in order not to 'waste the time' of agencies in cases that are 'going no-where'. Another approach is that of critics of the apparently poor response of the criminal justice system, who either characterise withdrawal as a myth or who argue that the police and CPS persuade victims to withdraw and/or create the conditions which encourage it. To a greater or lesser extent all the faults discussed in 'The Weaknesses of British Criminal Justice Research" can be observed here: withdrawal is largely seen as a fixed entity, debate centres on 'how often', individuals or groups (rather than laws and socio-economic conditions) are blamed, and the perspective of the subject - in this case the victim - is not taken seriously.

There are two pieces of research which help us to turn these problems around and develop a new research project. First, recent D. Phil research by Carolyn Hoyle suggests that many women who call the police to domestic disputes withdraw their complaints because they do not want their partners to be arrested and/or prosecuted, and would not want this even if (or especially if) there were tougher penalties.[39] Second, David Ford presents an argument as to why this may be so: he argues that women sometimes use the threat of prosecution as a power-resource to persuade their partners to desist from violence. For these women, police intervention without prosecution may not represent case-failure, but case-success.[40]

To investigate this Carolyn Hoyle and I propose to examine this from the viewpoint of the victims. Rather than asking them to evaluate the actions of the police and courts, with the pitfalls identified in 'The Weaknesses of British Criminal Justice Research", we propose to ask directly about reasons for withdrawal (or not), what victims wanted from the police and courts, and how far those agencies were able to provide what they want. By taking police areas with different arrest and prosecution policies we will be able to see how far policies which serve different *agency* interests also serve the interests of the victims. Although not policy-led, this research would be highly policy-relevant, because it would help to evaluate near-mandatory arrest schemes. Insofar as victims do use the threat of prosecution as a resource, maintaining this situation requires that choice be left with victims. It would therefore reduce the power of victims in relation to their violent partners to introduce near-mandatory arrest schemes such as now exist in some areas of the USA.

Over the last 15 years or so there have been sporadic outbursts of rioting in a large number of inner-city areas throughout Britain. For example in December 1995, Brixton flared up again. Much of this anger and disorder is directed at the police, and often appears to be 'triggered' by a particularly insensitive act of policing. Theoretical questions to which these events give new urgency include: how far people obey the law (and its most visible representatives, the police) only when they view it as legitimate; the extent to which people accord legitimacy to the police and criminal justice system in general; by 'legitimacy' do we mean fair results or fair process; whether we can talk about 'people' in general in this context or whether class, gender and ethnic distinctions are important.

Tom Tyler's work suggests that legitimacy is a vital element in adherence to law, and that legitimacy is accorded to the system only when the process is perceived to be fair.[41] Carolyn Hoyle and I propose to see how far this thesis is true of Britain using different methods to those used by Tyler. Whereas he employed questionnaires, we propose to interview suspects. Again, this would be 'bottom up' research, rather than 'top down', but would not aim primarily to evaluate what the police do. In fact we hope to interview the officers, not so much to see how far different accounts match, but to explore the different perceptions of police-suspect encounters held by the two groups. Further, as noted in 'Future Directions for Criminal Justice Research', different communities have different experiences. Thus, rather than seeing suspects as one homogeneous group, we would look at suspects from very different communities and try to map not only their different types of encounter with the police, but also how far the gaps between their perceptions and those of the police differ across different communities.

Like the domestic violence project, the fact that this research would not be policy-led does not mean that it is not policy-relevant. If the police are serious about community policing, and if one aim of that is to reduce the tensions which contribute to riots, then the police need to understand how the community - or communities - see the police and their encounters with the police. And if Tyler is right about the importance which people ascribe to fair process, perhaps we will be able to re-cast the old debate about 'crime control v due process': it may be that greater police adherence to due process would, rather than get in the way of policing, enhance it. But it *would* get in the way of confrontational styles of policing. It may be, of course, that the State would not be willing to enhance community policing at the expense of confrontational policing, but that would be a matter for another research project. At present this is all speculative because astonishingly little research has actually been carried out which takes seriously the perspective of the suspect.[42]

Future Prospects

I have emphasised the distinction between policy-*related* research and policy-*led* research. Many of the weaknesses identified in this chapter, which are true also of socio-legal studies in general, are a product of research being policy-led rather than being theoretically-led. We need, for instance, to continue with a staple of socio-legal studies: the analysis of legislative change and its effects. But it is equally important to study the effects on *suspects and defendants* as on criminal justice *agencies*; to study *why* change occurs as well as *what* has occurred; to study controls *over* the system as well as controls *within* the system.[43]

Why, then, does socio-legal research display so many limitations? The ESRC Socio-Legal Review blames isolation and the inadequate training of researchers with legal backgrounds. However, the shortcomings of criminal justice research cannot be blamed on lawyers, for social scientists predominate in this sub-field (casting doubt on this explanation for the weakness of socio-legal studies in general). The only lawyer involved in any of the five studies scrutinised in "The Weaknesses of British Criminal Justice Research" was myself, and none of the researchers were isolated from other social scientists. Nor is there a resource problem, for the Home Office, whose research has been especially criticised, has tremendous resources.

Chapter 7 of the ESRC Review hints at another reason: performance is judged in large part by grants, and it is difficult to secure grants for theoretical work.[44] In many institutions there is now an academic Catch-22 for lecturing staff: if you don't get grants your time for solid intellectual work is eaten away by teaching and administration; and if you do, your time is eaten away by organising and carrying out the kind of work for which grants are available. For contract research staff the situation is worse. While carrying out one project a typical researcher will be trying to write articles or a book out of the previous project and be preparing the grant application for the next. Small wonder that so much socio-legal research fails to situate itself in its intellectual context. However, just in case this purist argument fails to cut ice, frenetic grant-getters should beware Jefferson and Shapland's warning: "The message of the decade has ... been that activity does not necessarily equate with influence".[45] Those who seek influence are - I would like to believe - as likely to wield it through the quality of their work as their readiness to dance to the tune of the piper.

And so we can urge researchers to be theoretically driven and not policy-driven, and urge ESRC to encourage and fund such research. But if a key argument of this chapter is that criminal justice individuals and organisations under-perform (or fail to perform according to their mission statements) because of structural pressures and the real objectives of those organisations we should also consider the application of this argument to the academic world. The weaknesses we have identified should be attributed to the powers and interests of four groups: policy-makers, agencies with the power to 'gatekeep' access, funders (these three often being the same bodies), and the research community itself. Just as education and training for police officers has little of the intended effect, the same will be true of the education and training of researchers. The 'consumers' of socio-legal studies are those who control the market for this work: not the neglected suspects, defendants and victims, but criminal justice agencies. Now that the Socio-Legal Studies Association is recognised by government agencies, ESRC, the universities, and other relevant bodies, it has an interest in legitimising itself and the work of its core members. That means doing precisely the policy-led type of work which has been criticised here. Alan Hunt observes that the key elements of Chapter 7 of the Review - criticisms of the theoretical shortcomings of SLS and its excessive subservience to policy concerns - were dropped from the Review's Conclusion.[46] Was it naive to expect anything else? And will ESRC grasp the nettle and pick up its intellectual mission? We will not see criminal justice research develop intellectual depth until this depth is sought by institutions with the power and money to exert the necessary market influence.

Notes

1   eg M. Banton, *The Policeman in the Community* (1964) Tavistock Publishers and M. Zander, *Legal Advice and Criminal Appeals: A Survey of Prisoners, Prisons and Lawyers.* (1972) Crim LR 132. For an instructive general review see M. Cain, *Trends in the Sociology of Police Work* (1979) IJ Soc Law 7:143. Many shortcomings observed by Cain remain true of the wider field of criminal justice research, showing just how far this field has not come.

2   The criminal justice research to be discussed in this paper will not hereafter include penal research. This is partly a matter of convenience and lack of expertise. It is also because most penal system work is not so much socio-legal as criminological ie. with the former, law is (or should be regarded) as part of the phenomena to be investigated, while with the latter law is largely the backdrop against which the study is carried out as with any other criminological research (eg the study of armed robbery or car theft).

3   Some historical work emerged a little later. See especially D. Hay et al, *Albion's Fatal Tree: Crime and Society in Eighteenth-century England* (1975) Allen Lane; E.P. Thompson, *Whigs and Hunters: the Origin of the Black Act* (1975) Penguin.

4   This is the 'legal reform' model which is criticised by M.McConville et al, *Case for the Prosecution*, (1991) Routlege, Ch 10

5   The main texts are: A. Ashworth, *The Criminal Process*, (1994) OUP, A. Sanders and R. Young, *Criminal Justice* (1994) Butterworths, S. Uglow, *Criminal Justice*, 1995, Sweet and Maxwell; N. Padfield, *Criminal Justice - Text and Materials*, 1995, Butterworths.

6   I will not attempt the impossible task of picking the 'best' works. Jefferson and
        Shapland ('Criminal Justice and the Production of Order and Control', *BJ Crim*
        1994, 34:265) have already made their attempt, with which I broadly agree.
7   S. Hall, C. Critcher, T. Jefferson, J. Clarke, and B. Roberts, *Policing the
        Crisis: Mugging, the State, and Law and Order* (1978) Macmillan.
8   J. Baldwin and M. McConville, *Negotiated Justice*, (1997) Martin Robertson.
        For a critique of the Royal Commission on Criminal Justice's treatment of this
        issue, see M. McConville and C. Mirsky: 'Redefining and Structuring Guilt in
        Systemic Terms' in M. McConville and L. Bridges, ed *Criminal justice in
        Crisis*, (1994) Edward Elgar.
9   The earliest write up of this was 'Prosecution Decisions and the Attorney-
        General's Guidelines' (1985) Crim LR.
10   A. Sanders and L. Bridges: 'Access to Legal Advice and Police Malpractice'
        (1990) Crim LR 494.
11   J. Baldwin and S. Hill, *The Operation of the Green Form Scheme in England
        and Wales* (1988) Lord Chancellor's Department.
12   S. Moston and G.M. Stephenson, *The Questioning and Interviewing of
        Suspects outside the Police Station* (1993) Royal Commission on Criminal
        Justice, Research Study 22. HMSO.
13   D. Brown, T. Ellis and Larcombe, K. *Changing the Code: Police Detention
        under the Revised PACE Codes of Practice* (1992) Home Office Research
        Study No 129, HMSO.
14   A. Sanders, *Constructing the Case for the Prosecution* (1987) 14 Journal of
        Law and Society 229.
15   A. Sanders and R. Young, 'The Rule of Law, Due Process and Pre-Trial
        Criminal Justice' *Current Legal Problems* (1994) Vol 47. For a fuller
        discussion see A. Sanders, 'Access to Justice in the Police Station: An Elusive
        Dream?' in R. Young and D. Wall, ed, *Access to Criminal Justice*, 1996,
        Blackstone.
16   This Code of Practice, for the Detention and Treatment of Persons in Police
        Custody, was revised in 1991 and again in 1995.
17   For one of many examples see M. Young, *An Inside Job*, 1991, OUP. This,
        anthropological study, incidentally, is a fine example of research of the fourth
        kind described earlier.
18   M.McConville, A. Sanders, R. Leng, et al. See the critiques by Dixon, Reiner
        and Morgan, and the replies by Leng and by McConville and Sanders
        reproduced from the 'authors meet critics' session of the 1993 Cardiff British
        Society of Criminology Conference. The papers are collected in L. Noaks, M.
        Levi, and M. Maguire, ed, *Contemporary Issues in Criminology*, U of Wales
        Press, 1995.
19   R. Evans, *The Conduct of Police Interviews with Juveniles*, HMSO, 1993.
20   Royal Commission on Criminal Justice, *Report*, Cm 2263, HMSO, 1993, p.25.
21   A. Sanders et al, *Advice and assistance in police stations and the 24 hour duty
        solicitor scheme* (1989, LCD). For a more recent study showing that poor

services are still the norm see M.McConville et al, *Standing Accused*, 1994 OUP.

22   A. Rutherford, *Criminal Justice and the Pursuit of Decency* (1993) Oxford University Press, is the latest offender. See my review of it in *MLR* (1994) 57:675.

23   See eg the anthropological approach of Malcolm Young, op cit, and Max Travers' critique of *Case for the Prosecution* and *Standing Accused*: "Improving Criminal Justice Research" (paper given at the SLSA Conference at Leeds, 1995).

24   D. Dixon, A. Bottomley, C. Coleman, M, Gill and D. Wall *Reality and Rules in the Construction and Regulation of Police Suspicion* (1989) *International Journal of the Sociology of Law*, 17:185.

25   D. Dixon, "Legal Regulation and Policing Practice" *Social and Legal Studies* (1992) 1:515

26   *Negotiated Justice* op cit.

27   To which this part of the paper is indebted.

28   A. Sanders et al, op cit. D. Brown et al, op cit. See A. Sanders and R. Young, 'The Rule of Law...', op cit, for a discussion of the theoretical significance of these findings. A parallel find in *Suspect Community* is that examinations under the PTA lasting even less than one hour are often experienced as highly intrusive. This would not be obvious without doing the research, yet officially such intrusions do not even exist for examinations need be recorded only if they last over one hour.

29   Something we try to do in A. Sanders and R. Young, 'Rule of Law...' op cit.

30   See M.McConville and L.Bridges, *Criminal Justice in Crisis* (eg chapters by Singh and by Sanders).

31   op cit

32   D. Brown and T. Ellis, *Policing Low-Level Disorder* (HORS 135, 1994). For other examples of sophisticated or sensitive Home Office work see C. Willis, *The use, effectiveness, and impact of police stop and search powers*, Home Office RPU Paper 15 (Home Office, 1983); L. Smith, *Domestic violence: an overview of the literature* (1989) Home Office Research and Planning Unit. HMSO; and B. Bowling, 'Racial harassment and the process of victimisation' *BJ Crim*, 1993, 33:231

33   A. Sanders, 'Personal Violence and Public Order' *IJ Soc Law* (1988) 16:359

34   Discussed in A. Sanders, 'Constructing the Case for the Prosecution', op cit.

35   Which was carried out in the work which led to *Case for the Prosecution*, op cit.

36   op cit

37   R. Pawson and N. Tilley, "What works in evaluation research?" *BJ Crim* (1994), 34:291

38   A. Crawford, "The partnership approach to community crime prevention: corporatism at the local level?" *Social and Legal Studies* (1994) 4:497

39   C. Hoyle, "Charge and prosecution decisions in incidents of domestic violence" (SLSA Conference, Southampton University, 1996). This is based on *Responding to domestic violence: the role of the police and the criminal justice system* (D.Phil Thesis, University of Oxford Centre for Criminological Research, 1996). The two research projects outlined in this section have both been developed with Carolyn Hoyle and, at the time of writing, we have applied for funding for both projects.

40   D. Ford, 'Prosecution as a victim power resource' *Law and Society Review* (1991) 25:313-334

41   T. Tyler, *Why People Obey the Law* (1990) Yale UP

42   P. Hillyard, *Suspect Community*, op cit, is, of course, a notable exception here. This work, along with that of Tyler, was the main inspiration behind this research proposal.

43   See eg M.McConville and L.Bridges (ed), op cit; S.Field and P. Thomas (ed), *Justice and Efficiency? The Royal Commission on Criminal Justice*, Blackwell 1994; R. Young and A. Sanders, *The Royal Commission on Criminal Justice. A Confidence Trick* (1994) Ox J Legal Studies.

44   See Hillyard in this collection. And A. Hunt, "Governing the Socio-Legal project" *JLS*, 1994, 21:520 at 524.

45   op cit, p.284

46   A. Hunt, op. cit.

10 Public Law

DENIS GALLIGAN

Introduction

If we are to judge the contribution socio-legal research has made or might
make to public law, it is necessary to begin with a sketch of the scope of public
law. Twenty years ago it might have been taken to mean constitutional and
administrative law in the sense that those subjects form part of the core of a
law degree.   In that sense, public law meant the general doctrines and
conventions of the Constitution for the one part, and the doctrines of judicial
review of administrative action for the other part. Now, in the light of two
important changes, the subject should be construed much more broadly. The
growing awareness that there is more to administrative law than the doctrines
of judicial review signals one line of change. Judicial review retains a position
of great prominence in the students' reading lists but at least some attention is
now paid to other institutions, doctrines, and procedures, including such
matters as the ombudsman, appeal tribunals, complaints procedures, public
inquiries, rule-making, and policy-formation. Just what is included and the
degree of coverage of any subject will vary, but   such matters are now
regarded as properly within the subject of administrative law.

The second shift in the broader construction of public law is marked
by an expanding interest in specific areas of administrative law and
government, such as urban planning, social security, immigration, and mental
health. It is coming to be recognised that, in addition to such discrete areas of
administrative law, there are many spheres of public activity which raise
interesting issues of public law; the criminal justice system, for instance,
although traditionally left to criminologists, can also be seen as a set of public
institutions conducting activities within a framework of public law. Similarly,
the exercise of discretion by the prosecutor is as interesting to the public
lawyer as it is to the student of criminal justice. The expanding scope of

public law is added to by the widespread practice of the privatization of public functions by transferring them to the private sector, but then constructing a special regulatory regime in order to protect the public interest in the conduct of those activities are conducted. Another sphere of expansion can be seen in the area of self-regulation where certain activities, such as the conduct of professions or policing of the financial world, have a public element and yet are left to be controlled by the practitioners in that area themselves. In short, these various factors and movements give some idea of the great and broadening scope of public activities and the corresponding need for them to be conducted within a framework of public law.

The result is that public law must now be regarded as a large subject which ranges across all spheres of activity of institutions, authorities and officials of a public or a semi-public kind exercising a public or semi-public function. Debates might rage about a more precise definition of public law, but for our present purposes I shall take the widest view to be the most useful. With that wide view in mind, I shall now consider the state of progress of socio-legal research and then offer some suggestions as to its future direction. The analysis will be divided into the following two issues: (i) the areas of research covered; (ii) the approaches to research. In discussing these two issues, I shall indicate some of the lines that future research might take.

Areas Of Research

Amongst the many issues which might be raised concerning the exercise of state authority through administrative institutions, four stand out as especially important and interesting. The first concerns the nature and composition of the authorities and institutions which comprise administrative government. A second focuses on the way those authorities and institutions exercise their powers. This in turn can be divided into two different sets of questions. One concerns the standard-setting role of the authorities; the other relates to the making of decisions or the taking of action in individual cases. However, public law does not stop with the exercise of powers, but tries to ensure that authorities and institutions are accountable for their actions. Accountability takes many forms, from methods of supervision such as that exercised by the Audit Commission through complaints procedures and related forms of recourse triggered by individual grievances, to the heavy artillery of judicial review. The fourth issue then for research centres on the forms and methods of accountability and recourse.

Nature Of Administrative Government

The first of these areas leads to an analysis of the nature, structure, and composition of administrative government. It raises many issues: the kinds of bodies comprising administrative government; their internal structure and composition; their relationship with other authorities such as Parliament, the executive and ministers. It also extends to the ideas and ideologies which inform and influence administrative government. To raise these issues is, of course, to ask about the nature of British government and administration, a subject which has been much written about by political scientists and students of public administration. But while socio-legal researchers can learn much from that literature, the socio-legal perspective itself adds to our understanding of administrative government by paying attention to the legal framework within which it operates, by identifying and analysing the doctrines and conventions which underlie that framework, and by showing the relationship between doctrine and convention on the one hand and the practical workings of the institutions and authorities on the other hand. Moreover, while there is an extensive literature on the nature of British government and institutions, two recent developments show the need for old issues to be revisited with a fresh eye.

One is the increasingly intricate and complex relationship between British government and institutions on the one hand, and the institutions and ideas of international organizations and systems, especially the European Union, on the other hand. The result is that British administrative government is no longer in complete control of its own activities, but it is greatly influenced by the demands of the laws and institutions of the European Union and to a lesser, but nevertheless serious degree, by the decisions of the European Commission and European Court of Human Rights. Since lawyers are well aware of the inter-relationship, the standards of discussion and analysis at the doctrinal level is already high; the same cannot be said of socio-legal analysis where awareness of this dimension is barely aroused and the issues for research are hardly formulated. The inter-relationship between national laws and institutions and those deriving from extra-national sources raises many important issues and should become an area of absorbing research.

The second matter which opens up many new lines of research is the changing face of administrative government is the United Kingdom. The idea that ministers and their advisers develop policies, that those policies wind their way through the legislative process to emerge as statutes, and that the statutes then go back to ministers and their departments for implementation, for which the minister is then answerable to Parliament, is often taken as expressing the heart of British government and administration. The reality is that British government has fluctuated between the high centralization inherent in this image and the severe fragmentation of authority to special boards, agencies and other institutions. A centralized departmental system with ministerial accountability to Parliament, supported by a staff of well-educated, professional civil servants, may have emerged in the early part of the twentieth century as the near perfect system of government and administration, but as the end of the century approaches a number of major shifts and changes are under way. These are broadly threefold: the fragmentation of central government, contraction of the administration, and the infusion of private sector notions into the public sector.[1]

The fragmentation of central government consists in breaking up departments into special agencies to carry out administrative tasks previously performed within the departments. Each of these Next Step Agencies has a framework document which defines its objectives, its relations with the department, the minister and Parliament, and a range of other matters relating to finance, personnel, and performance.[2] The basic idea is that each agency has well-defined aims that should be confined to implementing policy not making it; policy matters are for ministers, putting them into operation for the agencies. The ethos for the agency is good management and efficiency and effectiveness in realising its aims.[3] The idea is that central government should be broken down into agencies and at present more than one hundred have been created.

The second change noted, the contraction of the public sector and the consequential reduction of administrative government, has several parts: the privatization of public industries, the conversion of public agencies into private bodies, and the transfer of public services to the private sector. Privatization of public industries consists of converting the old public service corporations relating to such matters as power, communications, and transport into private corporations and then creating a regulatory agency to oversee aspects of the industry's activities. The second form of privatization process consists in an administrative body, whether department, local authority, or other agency, entering into a contract with a private firm or company under which the latter will perform a certain service. While contracting out certain aspects of public service is not new, the determination to extend the contracting out to a range of matters traditionally regarded as properly performed by public bodies is novel. Examples are the running of prisons, aspects of police work, various services performed by local authorities, and parts of the civil court system.

The third part of this shift is the introduction into the public sector of private sector ideas. [4] This contracting-in process consists in introducing contractual relations between different parts of an administrative authority for the delivery of a public service. The Next Steps Agencies are good examples where the chief executive of each enters into a contractual arrangement with the minister under which the duties of the agency are set out. Perhaps the most notable example is the National Health Service within which different parts of the service enter into contracts with each other for the provision of health care. Some parts, such as hospitals, provide health care, while other parts, such as district health authorities or general practitioners, buy health care. Contracting-in is, of course, very different from contracting-out, but the underlying idea common to both is to entrust the provision of a public service to a distinct body, whether public or private, where the terms and conditions, the levels of performance, and the criteria of success, are spelt out in a contract-like document.

The second area of research in public law is the making of administrative rules and policies. While the policy-making process at the highest levels of government and the legislative functions of Parliament are both well studied, the same cannot be said of policy-making at the lower levels of administration. Policy-making at these levels, which is sometimes authorized formally by the parent statute but at other times simply implicit in the exercise of discretion, offers ample opportunities for socio-legal research. Some important and interesting studies have been conducted. On policy-making on specific issues, R. Baldwin's study of the Civil Aviation Authority is a notable example,[5] while G. Richardson[6] and K. Hawkins[7] have uncovered many of the features of administrative policy-making in the environmental sphere. Much can also be learnt about administrative policy-making from case studies of the Health and Safety Executive, the Office of Fair Trading, the Monopolies and Mergers Commission, and the Commission for Racial Equality - case studies of each of which are contained in R. Baldwin and C. McCrudden (ed), *Regulation and Public Law.*[8] These studies show how policy is shaped, sometimes in advance, but often in the course of deciding a specific issue. Policy may also be made in order to formulate general standards, principles, rules, etc. to be applied in specific cases. This rule-making process raises distinctive issues which have long been a subject of socio-legal research. Much has now been written about the different kinds of administrative rules that may be created[9] and case studies are beginning to emerge of rule-making in particular contexts, an important study being J. Black's analysis of agencies in the financial services industry.[10]

Although there is now a steady flow of studies of policy formation and rule-making by administrative bodies, one is left with the feeling that the areas are still not attracting from socio-legal research the attention they deserve. One reason for this may be that, in the United Kingdom at least, much administrative policy making, whether on a specific issue or in creating rules, is informal and largely unregulated by law. There is no general procedural code and in many areas the process takes place without guidance from the parent statute. Administrative policy-making is poised at the crossroads of political science, economic analysis and administrative theory, and, if there is no law, it may be argued, there is nothing specifically for socio-legal research to do. While there is some force in this point, it would be a pity if socio-legal researchers were to abandon the field. For one reason, other jurisdictions, including Australia and the United States, are developing refined procedural frameworks within which administrative policy-making takes place and it must only be a matter of time before this influence is felt in the United Kingdom. A second reason is that, while policy-making may be sparsely regulated by formal procedures, it nevertheless proceeds according to patterns of informal rules and standards. The study of those patterns and the identification of different procedural models is a suitable matter for socio-legal research, not only because the principles are important, but also because a greater awareness of what happens in practice may stimulate a more systematic approach at the policy level.

Another major theme in the policy-making process is the activities of interest groups and their relationship with the policy-making authorities. The study of interest groups by political scientists is well advanced, but little has so far been done to consider their activities in relation to administrative procedures.[11] Socio-legal research, could play a major part in understanding the role of interest groups in different contexts of administrative policy-making, and in relating that role to the emerging political and legal principles concerning participation, consultation, openness and transparency, access to information and the rational basis for action. This could be complemented by research directed towards attaining a better understanding generally of the policy making process, of the factors which influence it, and the social constraints upon it.

Individualized Decisions And Processes

The one area of public law in which socio-legal research has outstanding credentials is in understanding the decision processes within administrative agencies. This is particularly so where the decision processes relate to individualized decision-making. Hence, there is a long tradition of deep empirical research which began twenty or so years ago with studies of environmental law [12] and culminated most recently in penetrating accounts of decision-making in social security, [13] mental hospitals, [14] and housing homeless persons. [15] These studies and others have been of great importance in showing how administrative agencies apply legal rules and standards, and what factors influence their actions. The concept of discretion has been prominent in several of these studies; it has proved to be a useful way of focusing on the way officials approach their tasks and how they translate an external legal environment into patterns of practical decision-making. Indeed, the literature on discretion, both theoretical and empirical, is extensive. [16]

The study of administrative decision-making is also notable for the way in which the disciplines of social science, especially sociology, administrative and organisational theory, and psychology, have been put to good use. [17] Each discipline, with its own theoretical framework and accumulated experience, helps in displaying aspects of decision processes and the variables at work within them which might otherwise be missed. The result of these techniques is an understanding of administrative decision-making which is many-layered and deeply contextual. Outstanding examples of how the wider perspective enhances and enriches our understanding of decision processes are Baldwin, Wikeley and Young's study of social security, Peay's research into Mental Health Review Tribunals, and Loveland's work on decision-making in the housing context.

In view of the high achievement socio-legal research has already made in the study of administrative decision-making, the main object for the future ought to be to continue to explore, through deep empirical research and by drawing on the disciplinary insights and traditions of the social sciences, the complex social world of administrative institutions and officials. Considering the huge array of administrative bodies and processes, this may seem an endless task. The object, however, should not be just to assemble more and more case studies on unrelated topics; it should be rather to use case studies of specific areas and issues to accumulate knowledge and understanding of administrative processes generally. [18] A case study of decision-making in social security is at one level concerned with the variables specific and local to that context; at another level, however, knowledge and understanding gained there can be generalized to be equally applicable to other areas. The process of generalization is the beginning of theory so that eventually local knowledge becomes the basis for theoretical speculation. I shall return to this point in the final section.

Within this general objective, however, one or two other points of added focus ought to be identified for the purpose of future research. The first is the need to articulate and understand more about the different forms which administrative processes may take. Much of the empirical work so far is concerned with the application of legal standards and the discretionary variations around those standards. A natural extension of this work would be to pay attention to different kinds of standards, particularly those of a professional or specialist kind.[19] Similarly, the elements of investigation, consultation, and informal negotiation, which are often very central to administrative processes, await fuller study than they have so far received.[20] A second point of focus for further research in this area is the quality of primary decisions. The chance for a party to appeal from a decision or to seek some other form of recourse is an important part of administrative processes, but it is clear that, no matter how extensive those possibilities may be they will always be of limited effectiveness in correcting poor decisions.[21] A major concern for policy makers, legislators and administrators, therefore, ought to be to improve the quality of decisions and actions in the first instance. The attainment of that objective would be helped by empirical study of the variables which shape particular administrative contexts. Some of these variables, such as the standard of training and the level of resources, may point to the need for drastic structural adjustment and, therefore, are beyond the reach of socio-legal activities; within those constraints, however, the close study of different contexts will help to reveal the influence of other variables on the quality of decisions and guidance may be given as to how quality can be improved. Examples can be given to illustrate this approach. One is the study of closed institutions which has proved invaluable in remodelling decision processes in such contexts as the police station whilst another is the improved understanding we have of the variables within low level, front line, social welfare decision-making which also points to the ways in which quality control can be introduced at those levels. In general, the concern for quality at the most rudimentary levels of administration should stimulate and give direction to extensive and penetrating empirical work.

Two concepts at the heart of administrative law are accountability and recourse. Accountability suggests that one body explains and justifies its actions to another on the basis of certain standards which the former is expected to apply. Recourse refers to the means available to a party to take action against a primary decision or action. The two concepts are related and overlap, since forms of recourse may also be ways of bringing the authority to account. Accountability, however, is a broader concept than recourse, embracing a variety of processes which do not depend on a party bringing an action or complaint. Although accountability is a fundamental concept in the understanding and workings of administrative government, it is surprising how little research exists both into the concept itself and into the way that different systems of accountability work in practice. A programme of socio-legal research into accountability is timely. The main task would be to analyse the different forms of accountability occurring in different contexts. The fragmentation of central government and the attempt to introduce ideas based on the market into areas of administration, such as the National Health, undermine some of the traditional ideas of accountability; they pose interesting questions as to exactly what forms of accountability prevail in these new contexts and how adequate they are.

Socio-legal research has tended to concentrate on forms of recourse rather than more general issues of accountability. Indeed, we live in an age in which substantial resources are devoted to providing ways by which an aggrieved citizen may appeal against or complain about the actions of public or semi-public bodies. The heavy artillery of judicial review has always been prominent in administrative law text books, but in practice it plays a small role in the total arsenal of recourse. Since the Franks Committee Report in 1948, special tribunals have been created to hear appeals from a great range of administrative decisions. Twenty years later, the idea of the ombudsman took root and has since flourished with various special and general ombudsman responsible for a range of matters, including the operations of central government, the conduct of the prisons, the running of the national health service, and the performance of the police. Most recently, a renewed interest has been taken in creating more informal and internal systems of complaints, partly as a result of the Citizens' Charter introduced in 1991[22] and partly the result of a more general sense that those subject to the actions of a public or often semi-public body ought to be able to express their dissatisfaction easily and informally. The result of these various movements and innovations is a complex and extensive system of appeals, complaints and reviews.

One form of recourse which is becoming more widespread is internal complaints procedures. They have received, however, little attention,[23] although a recent study in the area of social security has shown how interesting and fruitful the study of internal procedures can be.[24] This can be linked to a parallel line of research into the psychology of complaining within the national health system which has wider implications for our understanding of why parties seek recourse and how their claims can best be dealt with.[25] Since the burgeoning of the tribunal system, following the Franks Report, a good range of research has been devoted to understanding the workings of appeal tribunals.[26] Although the variety of tribunals is enormous, a steady flow of research in areas such as social security, immigration, industrial relations and mental health, has revealed many of their strengths and weaknesses. We know that a tiny fraction of parties who are subject to administrative action lodge appeals; that legal representation and advice makes a great difference both to bringing an appeal and the outcome;[27] that various factors enter into and constrain the actions of tribunals;[28] and that there is often a severe tension between inquisitorial and adversarial approaches within tribunals.[29]

While research into the workings of tribunals is well-developed, the same cannot be said of ombudsmen, for although the first ombudsmen have now been in place in the United Kingdom for nearly 30 years, little empirical work has been done. Much has been written about what the role of ombudsmen should be,[30] but few attempts have been made to study what they actually do.[31] Amongst the basic issues to be considered is how the investigation is conducted, what obstacles are encountered, the attitude of the officials, and how bargaining and negotiation enter into relations between the investigators and the officials in resolving an issue. Another matter concerns the impact and influence that investigations by ombudsmen have on the authority being investigated, while the attitudes of parties themselves and their perceptions and expectations in relation to ombudsmen open up another major area for enquiry.

Similar remarks may be made about judicial review of administrative action. On the one hand, judges are proclaiming judicial review to be one of the great success stories of the age in protecting citizens against the state, while on the other hand there is little serious research to show just what its real impact and significance is.[32] The first attempt to fill the gap is a study by Sunkin, Bridges, and Mazeros into the use and effectiveness of judicial review.[33] This is an important study for its findings and for the effect it is likely to have in stimulating further socio-legal research in this area.

It can be seen from this brief survey that the general issues common to the various forms of recourse are to what extent are the different mechanisms used, how do they work in practice, what are the expectations of those involved in them, and what effect do they have on the primary administrative bodies whose decisions and actions are under scrutiny. Socio-legal research has been undertaken in each of these areas, but in most of them, with the possible exception of tribunals, research is still in its early stages. Internal complaints procedures, ombudsmen of various kinds, and judicial review all raise questions of great importance, from the standpoint of general public interest and also from the point of view of citizens affected by them.

Approaches To Research

Socio-legal research is first and foremost directed at ascertaining the facts about the workings of law and legal institutions. At their simplest, empirical studies provide information about the legal world which may be rather different from the assumptions we readily make and which may reveal that world to be more complex than we expect it. That a tiny percentage of first level administrative decisions is subject to any form of review or appeal; that compliance with standards controlling pollution is achieved less by the threat of prosecution than by bargaining and negotiation between inspectors and polluters; and that judicial review provides only very limited protection against executive and administrative action, are all interesting and important in increasing our knowledge of how law works in practice. Socio-legal research in public law has been very much along these lines: studies have been directed at gathering basic facts about administrative officials and institutions, and about the legal framework within which they work. Such studies are local and particular, but may be the basis for formulating generalizations about administrative processes. Knowledge is of interest from two points of view: it is important simply to know what happens, but it is also on the basis of such local and particularized knowledge that conclusions can be drawn which have general application in other areas.

Now while such first order empirical studies are the foundations of socio-legal research, there are two points to be made which call for reflection by socio-legal researchers in general and especially in public law. On the one hand most socio-legal research is done by lawyers, while on the other hand in order to delve beneath the surface of the social world, socio-legal research needs the contribution of the social sciences. The disciplines of social science, whether sociology, political science, psychology, or economics provide the means for penetrating and comprehending the social world at levels and in ways which are beyond simple common sense and curiosity. To take some examples: by concentrating on motives and intention, psychologists are able to reveal much about the roles and expectations of the actors in legal processes; by understanding the political environment and the forces at work within it, political scientists can show the interconnectedness of institutions and practices; while sociologists help us to identify and understand a whole range of social constraints and influences on administrative acts and decisions. Social science is simply indispensable, not just in helping to reveal factors which would otherwise be unnoticed, but also in providing a set of disciplinary frameworks within which the significance of those factors can be understood. One major challenge, then, is to broaden the net of socio-legal research by encouraging more social scientists to become involved.

The second point to be made concerns the process of generalization, by which I mean the process of moving beyond local facts about this or that area of law to a more general understanding of legal phenomena. Generalization can of course be conducted at different levels of complexity.

Let us take an example: a study of people appealing to tribunals has shown that they have a better chance of winning their appeals if legally represented than if not. On the grounds that the reasons for this hold not just for the few tribunals studied but for tribunals generally, the hypothesis may be advanced that legal advice and representation before any tribunal is likely to improve the appellant's chances of success. In other areas, generalization may be more complex, but the reasoning process remains the same. The general point to be made here is that socio-legal research in public law ought to engage more in this process of generalization. For to generalize is to theorize, since theorizing consists in being able to move from the facts particular to our situation to the claim that those facts will hold true in other situations. An intensive study of judicial review might enable us to theorize about the conditions under which it will be seen by aggrieved parties as a desirable and viable remedy. A different kind of study might provide the basis for theorizing about the impact of judicial review on administrative bodies. The short point is that the gathering and interpreting of information is necessarily the basis for generalizing and theorizing. My suggestion is that research in the public law context ought to pay more attention to developing middle order theories about law and administration.

The last point to be made about the approach taken by researchers in public law is perhaps a little less obvious and more arguable. The point may be stated briefly research in public law in the Anglo-American tradition rarely reaches beyond middle order generalizations to make contact with the more abstract and speculative theoretical traditions of social theory. This is both a puzzle and a loss. Why is it that the rich and varied traditions of theoretical speculation, which are to be found in the most basic text books on the sociology of law, appear to play almost no part in the conceptual apparatus of socio-legal researchers, especially in public law? Whether it be the traditions of American realism, the sociological jurisprudence of Ehrlich and Malinowski, the socio-historical theories of Marx and Weber, or the post-modern formulations of Habermas and Luhmann, it is only rarely that one finds any reference made to them let alone inspiration being derived from them. The lack of regard for more speculative theory is a loss; it is a loss, first, because the more speculative theoretical traditions can illuminate and inspire and, secondly, because it separates socio-legal research from any other area of social science, where the theoretical traditions of the discipline constitute the frames of reference within which research is conducted. This is a bigger issue than can be done justice in a few remarks, but I wish to conclude by suggesting that socio-legal research in public law would be greatly deepened and enriched if it displayed a better awareness of its own theoretical bearings and drew on the rich traditions of speculative theory.

Notes

1   A fuller analysis of these changes is contained in the Introduction in D.J. Galligan (ed), *A Reader on Administrative Law* (Clarendon, Oxford, 1996).

2   Further discussion of Next Steps Agencies can be seen in the following: N. Lewis, "Change in Government: new public management and Next Steps" (1994) *Public Law* 105; P. Greer, "The Next Steps Initiative: an examination of the Agency framework document" (1990) *Public Administration* 89; P. Kemp, *Beyond Next Steps* (1993).

3   See further Dr. S. Zifcak, *The New Managerialism* (Open University Press, 1994).

4   An analysis of several forms of contracting-in is contained in I. Harden, *The Contracting State* (Open University Press, 1992).

5   See R. Baldwin, *Regulating the Airlines* (Socio-Legal Studies, Oxford, 1978).

6   G. Richardson et al, *Policing Pollution* (Socio-Legal Studies, Oxford, 1984).

7   K. Hawkins, *Environment and Enforcement* (Socio-Legal Studies, Oxford, 1984).

8   Weidenfeld and Nicholson, London, 1987.

9   See R. Baldwin, *Rules and Government* (Socio-Legal Studies, Oxford, 1995) and G. Ganz, *Quasi Legislation* (Sweet and Maxwell, London, 1986).

10   J. Black, *Regulators as Rule Makers* (Socio-Legal Studies, Oxford, forthcoming) and "Which Arrow?: Rule Type and Regulatory Policy" (1995) *Public Law* 94-118.

11   Amongst the literature on interest groups, the following are of particular importance: W. Grant, *Pressure Groups, Politics and Democracy* (1989); J. J. Richardson and G. Jordan, *Governing Under Pressure* (1979).

12   See G. Richardson and Others, "Policing Pollution" (Socio-Legal Studies, Oxford, 1984) and K. Hawkins, *Environment and Enforcement* (Socio-Legal Studies, Oxford, 1984).

13   Baldwin, Wikeley, and Young, *Judging Social Security.* (Clarendon, Oxford, 1993)

14   J. Peay, *Tribunals on Trial* (Clarendon, Oxford, 1990).

15   I. Loveland, *Housing Homeless Persons* (Socio-Legal Studies,Oxford, 1995).

16   See further on discretion, D.J. Galligan, *Discretionary Powers* (Clarendon, Oxford, 1986) and K. Hawkins (ed), *The Uses of Discretion* (Socio-legal Studies, Oxford, 1994). Both books contain extensive bibliographies.

17   For an example of this contribution, see D.J. Hickson and others, "Decisions and organisations - processes of strategic decision-making and their explanations"

(1989) 67 *Public Administration 373;* several essays from social science perspectives can be seen in Hawkins, *The Uses of Discretion.*

18   On the relationship between specific studies and generalisation, see further R. Kagan, "What socio-legal scholars should do when there is too much law to study" in D.J. Galligan (ed), *Socio-Legal Studies in Context: the Oxford Centre Past and Future* (Blackwell, Oxford, 1995) and D. J. Galligan, Introduction to *A Reader on Administrative Law.*

19   J. Peay, *Tribunals on Trial* marks an important start in this direction.

20   For an introduction to different forms of decision-making and the variables within them, see D. J. Galligan, *Due Process and Fair Procedures* (Clarendon, Oxford, 1996) chapter 8.

21   For further discussion of the issues here, see D.J. Galligan, Introduction to *A Reader on Administrative Law.*

22   Citizens' Charter (HMSO, 1991).

23   See the review of research by R. Rawlings, *The Complaints Industry: a Review of Socio-Legal Research on Aspects of Administrative Justice* (E.S.R.C., 1986).

24   Baldwin, Wikeley, and Young, *Judging Social Security,* see also R. Sainsbury, "Internal Reviews and the weakening of Social Security claimants' rights of appeal", in G. Richardson and H. Genn (eds), *Administrative Law and Government,* (Clarendon, Oxford, 1994).

25   S. Lloyd-Bostock and L. Mulcahy "The Social Psychology of responding to Hospital Complaints: An Account Model of Complaints Procedures" (1994) 16 *Law and Policy* 123.

26   For further references see R. Rawlings, *The Complaints Industry* and also J. Peay, *Tribunals on Trial.*

27   H. Genn and Y. Genn, *The Effectiveness of Representation before Tribunals* (Lord Chancellor's Department, London 1989).

28   J. Peay, *Tribunals On Trial.*

29   Baldwin, Wikeley and Young, *Judging Social Security.*

30   For example, M. Senevaratane, Ombudsmen in the Public Sector (Open University Press, 1994). P.Brown, "The Ombudsman: Remedies for this information", in Richardson and Gomm, *Administrative Law and Government Action.*

31   One notable exception is the study by N. Lewis, M. Senevaratane, and S. Cracknell, *Complaints Procedures in Local Government* (Centre for Socio-Legal Studies, Sheffield, 1990).

32   An interesting, early study is T. Prossor "Politics and Judicial Review: The Atkinson Case and its Aftermath", 1993 *Public Law* 59.

33   M. Sunken, L. Bridges and G. Mazeros *Judicial Review in Perspective* (Public Law Project, London, 1993).

11 Tort And Socio-Legal Studies.
The Road To Damascus: Paved With Good Intentions But Few Epiphanies

WADE MANSELL

... there are examples of research which though not leading to immediate policy initiative have the effect of changing the nature of the debate so that ideas and opinions begin slowly to change. The work of the Oxford Centre for Socio-Legal Studies into accidents is an example (Harris et al 1984). This did not lead to the rapid adoption of no fault compensation schemes, but has informed the, admittedly slow, development of thinking on the appropriateness of the tort system in the compensation of accident victims.[1]

In this review I focus primarily but not exclusively upon tort and negligence. There are two reasons for this decision. Firstly, the overwhelming majority of research work described as sociological and concerned with torts is directed towards negligence, and, secondly, negligence law dominates the law of tort in terms both of numbers of actions and financial implications. Most of this research and writing has been concerned, to a greater or lesser extent, with the fault principle as a basis for tortious liability, and if its defenders have eschewed socio-legal research, the inability of those who have conducted such research to convince and persuade policy makers of the implications of their research requires consideration. The irony begging explanation is that with unrefuted evidence of the inefficiency, the arbitrariness (or even capriciousness) and indeed the injustices of the fault principle, nevertheless that principle has not, for many years, been in better heart.

When the Butterworths' prize-winning text book on tort, published in 1995[2] feels able to assert not only that there is little prospect of significant change in negligence principles but that even if there were, "it is no longer clear that such reform could count uncontroversially as enlightened",[3] then major questions need to be asked. The Howarth defence of the fault principle simply does not engage with the evidence provided by critics. Only three brief references are made to such critics. The first,[4] to Atiyah's *Accidents Compensation and the Law*[5] simply says of the critique offered "The fault principle was *allegedly*[6] expensive to operate, produced unpredictable results, and did not manage to compensate many people". The second, to a French text,[7] which says that the principle was also "*allegedly* based on a fiction that in, for example, road accidents or medical injuries there had been anything other than momentary inattention whose consequences had been magnified out of all proportion by modern technology".[8] The third reference,[9] in concluding a report of the criticisms, alludes to the claim that instead of the law responding to the moral intuitions of victims, they are often initially surprised by the law's choice of defendant and shift the blame to that defendant in their own mind at the law's suggestion.

While the criticisms are reported briefly, selectively and without engagement, the defences of the fault principle are reported without examination almost as irrefutable truth. Thus the defence refers to the need for incentives for both victims and accident causers, the opportunity to consider the effects of new sorts of behaviour and "the sheer cost of no-fault, social security based schemes".[10] Tunc is dismissed by the statement "the allegation that fault is fictitious confuses a civil law notion of fault, unreasonable behaviour judged objectively, with a criminal law notion of the guilty mind",[11] and Lloyd-Bostock with "the fact that victims response to the law's attribution of blame shows rather that the law is more reasonable and well considered than many believed".[12]

It is not really within the scope of this chapter (nor probably worthwhile) to engage with that author on that level (though it might suggest that a vote for the Liberal Democrats, of which the author is a prominent member, would not be a vote for tort reform!). What is important is that in spite of a considerable and impressive body of evidence provided by socio-legal research it is still possible to ignore the necessary implications of the findings, and to proceed as though they did not exist. Howarth is not alone. He is correct in his assessment of the acceptance of the fault principle by policy makers and, as Jane Stapleton observes of the critiques: "These structural challenges to the respectability of tort still exist but excite less interest nowadays, no doubt partly due to the recessionary times which force expensive reform programmes of comprehensive compensation for, say, personal injuries a long way down the political agenda".[13] This pertinent statement draws attention to what many consider the rather depressing gap between reasoned research and experience, and the policies of the policy-makers which are able to ignore both if they are not emotionally or politically appealing. The ESRC Report[14] is surely correct in observing that "whatever the quality of academic policy - relevant research, the extent to which the recommendations of scholars are likely to be directly implemented depends on political considerations and the decisions of other persons. Researchers are not (and never can be) policy makers". But if this is true it is a depressing conclusion that research which is thorough and persuasive is ignored.

Thus what I want to explore in this chapter is what the reaction to (or apathy towards) a well researched and crucial socio-legal topic in tort tells us about the state of socio-legal studies within Tort.

Since 1970 with the seminal event of the publication of Atiyah's *Accidents Compensation and the Law* socio-legal studies in tort in the UK have never been the same. If the New Zealand *Woodhouse Report*[15] was its harbinger this did not detract from its originality, thoroughness and quality. Although William Twining, the editor of the series in which it appeared, has suggested his acquiescence in the view expressed in the preface that the book was conceived of mainly as a contribution to legal education and legal scholarship, and only incidentally to reform,[16] I think this disingenuous. Twining recognises the book shows the tort system did not fulfil its objectives, and that where the tort system was looked at in the context of the total compensation picture in England and Wales, and compared and contrasted with other compensation systems, the effect was devastating. Indeed he observes that the fact that the book was then in its fourth edition (now fifth) while representing a publishing success, was also an indication of its lack of political success. Whatever the author or his editor may say, most of us who read the book did not see it as concerned only incidentally with reform. The contribution to legal education and legal scholarship was the suggestion that the tort subject, when directed to accidents and compensation, was fundamentally flawed and intellectually incoherent. Surely the necessary inference to be drawn, even if only from the factual material provided, was that justice, however defined, required change. Implicit too in the book was the view that some changes seemed preferable to others. This was not merely a critique, not merely an excellent piece of socio-legal work, it was also a work in which the elicited facts themselves, almost without regard to ideology, seemed to indicate the reform path.

How was such an apparently convincing argument in both weight and coherence refuted? The short answer is that it was not, and never has been refuted, notwithstanding the "Howarthian" perspective. Rather it was almost as though the message the book contained was too complicated and demanding in the solutions it suggested to be taken seriously in a reform debate. While popular, the book, as an educational tool, is generally used, if at all, as supplementary reading rather than as the central text in a torts course. While it has become popular for "black letter" legal academics to proclaim that they have never met a "black letter" legal academic, nor do they believe they ever existed, the propensity of tort academics to use such texts as Winfield and Jolowicz,[17] Street,[18] and Salmond[19] has not greatly diminished.

Of course some claimed to be of the view that the Atiyah perspective had been put to the test in the Pearson Report[20] arising from the Royal Commission on Civil Liability and Compensation for Personal Injury created in 1972 and been found wanting.[21] Not only was this not true but the Royal Commission in its pathetic interpretation of its terms of reference had decided it could not even consider the Atiyah perspectives in their entirety since the Commission was precluded from considering the general question of whether the tort action should be abolished in cases of personal injury and replaced with a universal accident compensation scheme such as New Zealand had adopted in 1972.[22] Atiyah himself challenged this narrow view of the terms of reference but the damage was done.

Almost the only merit of the Pearson report was that it did provide a significant amount of socio-legal research and consequent data. A large household survey teased out a nationally representative sample of injured people who had received medical treatment and whose injury had resulted in at least four days incapacity for work or other normal activities. The result of the survey was to confirm the comparative unimportance (statistically but not in terms of compensation received) of damages as a remedy. Overall only 6.5 per cent of such victims recovered any damages. These consisted of 25 per cent of those injured in motor vehicle accidents, 10.5 per cent of those injured at work and only 1.5 per cent of those injured otherwise.

Given such figures and the many others provided for the Pearson Commission how were they able to report, after six years work, findings which have been almost comprehensively ignored by the legislature? Perhaps the central reason lies in the lack of a coherent and cogent underpinning for their recommendations which seemed piecemeal at best, and scarcely consistent at worst. The almost ad hoc approach they favoured with a new no fault scheme for injuries caused by road accidents; with a special benefit for severely handicapped children; and with a statutory basis for criminal injuries recommended, did not seem to reflect any clear philosophy. While affirming the desirability of a shift from tort towards social security there was no overall coherent structure proposed and no willingness to fundamentally appraise civil liability and compensation for personal injury.

The one positive effect of that Commission however was to stimulate to further socio-legal work which, even if only in retrospect, shed some light on why the problems posed for Pearson could have seemed insuperable. The progress in the debate since the Pearson report has made it clear that, even had the original terms of reference been more sensibly interpreted, not all problems would, or could have been resolved.

What has come to be perceived as a basic flaw in critiques of the tort fault principle, is not simply that personal accidents should be compensated with regard to need rather than fault, but rather that the justification for privileging personal injury or disability resulting from accident itself has to be understood and rationalised. Thus the logical development from a conclusion that personal injury should be compensated on the basis of need rather than fault, immediately begged the question as to why disability occurring without accident, given the new emphasis on need, should not be compensated. Those who argued the legislation through in New Zealand providing for no fault compensation for accidents were not unaware of this dilemma but there it was resolved in a typically pragmatic manner - namely, accident compensation without fault was politically saleable and popular; compensation for all disability at the same level, significantly less so. Thus the view was that accident compensation could be made more rational, and that every improvement ought in due course to be educative of the possibilities of equal compensation for equal disability. Unfortunately, for a variety of reasons discussed by Palmer[23] attempts to broaden compensation provisions foundered politically.

Within the United Kingdom this pragmatic approach was never emulated even though it might well have been politically possible. Certainly by 1984 with the publication of the work of the Centre for Socio-Legal Studies *Compensation and Support for Illness and Injury*[24] there was recognition that compensation for disability was a much more sensible category than compensation for accidents. That work not only provided an impressively devastating array of evidence attesting to the shortcomings of the tort system of compensation for injury, but comprehensively surveyed and considered evidence of compensation and support for illness. The recognition that if cause was to be replaced by need as a criterion, then it made no sense to distinguish injury and illness. But while intellectually irresistible the political difficulties encountered in New Zealand were not ignored. What the researchers concluded in that study was that revolutionary legislation of the sort which would be required to implement their coherent proposals was unlikely but that piecemeal

227

reform directed towards a more acceptable and coherent compensation and support goal was possible with political will.

It is clear however that the gains in coherence were, to some extent at least, at the expense of political realism. How is this to be explained? Before considering this, it is important to record a further improvement in coherence, and deterioration in political practicability. Quoting Beveridge,[25] Stapleton in her book *Disease and the Comparative Debate*[26] observes: "acceptance of (the needs) argument... would avoid the anomaly of treating equal needs differently" and that "a complete solution is to be found only in a completely unified scheme for disability without demarcation by the cause of disability". This of course is fully consistent with Harris et al[27] but both the penultimate and ultimate sentence of Stapleton's book[28] threatened such consensus as did exist among would-be tort reformers.

> Until there is a re-evaluation of such fundamental issues as why, if at all, the disabled should be treated preferentially over victims of other misfortunes, there will not be much gained from formulating detailed designs for schemes of benefits. The daunting lesson to be learned from a disease focus is that the "compensation" debate is fundamentally and disturbingly more complex than we have generally assumed.

In other words the suggestion was that the socio-legal debate required a further broadening. Reason had to be sought not only for prioritising accident victims over other victims of disability but now also for prioritising victims of disability over other victims of the vicissitudes of life. This had already been argued in the USA when Liebman stated:

> Our society may revere medicine and sympathise with the sick, but it holds no views that could explain distinctions between persons totally unable to work according to whether their condition results from an illness or, on the other hand, from limited natural abilities, decades of racism or sexism, homosexuality, family burdens, technological change, a broken home or national fiscal policy.[29]

Thus fundamental questions which at their narrowest had proved too broad for the Pearson Commission are now at large. They are however at large in a world which is preoccupied with limiting government spending, and reducing, at least direct, taxation. If the terms of debate are now clarified, the clarification does not make the path of reform which the socio-legal debate had advocated, any more obvious. It is important to understand why this is so and this requires an explanation of why accident victims, at least those tortiously injured, should be privileged over others similarly disabled, and also why both categories should take priority over the "Liebman disadvantaged". That the answers are more emotive than rational is of fundamental importance for an understanding of the contributions, but also the inherent limitations of purely socio-legal research on the topic.

There are many explanations for the seeming acceptance of the privileging of the victim disabled by a tortious act over those otherwise disabled. The first is purely historical and relates to the tradition of tort damages being the means by which the victim is returned to the state she would have enjoyed but for the tort, and at the expense of the tortfeasor. There is no similar tradition with regard to illness. Also in tort a single tortfeasor is called upon to make good the damage, and clearly the losses of those disabled otherwise are not similarly individually attributable. Thus we have grown accustomed to the idea of full compensation to victims injured through tort and may be offended when victims of similar accidents or mishaps and without a tortfeasor, receive so much less compensation. Thus it may be that we have internalized the idea of full compensation as the obvious response to accidental harm.

Conversely there is no long historical tradition of such compensation for those who have become ill. Before the creation of the welfare state losses and harm caused by illness and congenital disability fell upon the unfortunate victim and family without substantial relief. Thus the receipt of social security in whatever form and under whatever guise was undoubtedly some amelioration of the hardship which had previously ensued. That it was at a

229

level which ensured some sort of independent survival, but little more, did not alter this fact.

Thus we have two very different traditions and the fact that so few accident victims received anything approaching full compensation did not affect the myth which is regularly sustained by the publicity attaching to very substantial awards of damages.

A second reason for different attitudes to differently caused disabilities was highlighted by Calabresi a quarter of a century ago.[30] It was his suggestion that a reason for the distinction in levels of compensation is that it seems possible to reduce the number and severity of accidents, and full compensation ought to affect the accident rate. Thus potential tortfeasors should be deterred from careless activity by the knowledge of the consequences. Again the fact that research has discovered little evidence which supports this thesis is not in itself as significant as the fact that accidents are seen as being caused by people, and illness by fate. To observe this is of course to return to the focus upon cause when the reformers have argued its irrelevance. That view however, is important because it too is *perceived* as indicating different compensation requirements.

There may be other reasons for the different perceptions. Accidents are often public events - unlike illness, with both direct and indirect witnesses. Television shows much more of overturned buses, crushed football crowds and motorway `pile ups' than it does of congenitally disabled children, cancer wards or hospices. Similarly the suddenness of an accident is often contrasted with the onset of illness.

Finally, according to many writers, there is a different emotional response to accidents when caused by another, to other accidents and disabilities. Ideas of blame and separation continue to permeate the popular psyche no matter how extraneous such notions may seem to researchers.

The only other substantial justification for the privileging of accidents with or without fault was that used by Woodhouse J. in his famous report[31] - namely, pragmatism. It was accidents about which, rightly or wrongly, most concern was voiced; and it was a reasonably distinct category; and it represented an opportunity to begin the reform of welfare for the disabled.

Paradoxically, defensible though that argument appeared to be, it carried within it, its own seeds of limitation if not destruction. By bringing to all accidents remedies approaching in value that previously restricted to tortious accidents, any subsequent scheme was likely to prove financially, and perhaps even politically, expensive. Instead of attempting to assess a global figure which could be afforded for accident compensation, and then calculating what that meant in terms of compensation for individual injuries and disabilities, the New Zealand accident compensation scheme sought to raise whatever figure was required to fulfil the expenditure needed to compensate as had been decided. The result in New Zealand has been resistance to the funding of the scheme, and the consequent significant reduction in levels of compensation deemed payable.

Thus to suggest that all accident victims be compensated in ways similar to tortious remedies at once made it unlikely that other victims could be brought within such a scheme. As Stapleton observes.[32]

> The fact of limited resources does not explain why the preferred first and perhaps only step of reform is to provide generous benefits to a class of disabled selected on the basis of cause of disability. Arguably it might make better sense to start with low uniform benefits for all disabled increasing them across the board if and when resources allow.

While that makes sense it does not acknowledge that the political priority of the disabled has never been high and indeed has seldom been lower. It is unrealistic to think that if tort accident victims were treated as all other victims that the result would be a net increase in benefits received by the disabled. And it is true also that advances for accident victims have been made most frequently in response to particular accidental tragedies such as that of thalidomide leading to the Congenital Disabilities (Civil Liability) Act 1976 allowing a right to sue in tort for damage inflicted *in utero*; and that of children damaged by whooping cough vaccine, pertussis, with the Vaccine Damage Payments Act 1979. Thus we arrive at the peculiar position of discovering that while almost all reformers agree that need should oust cause as the criterion for compensation for disability, to achieve this would seem to be contrary to common sense perception and the political reality of the problem. Were common sense to coincide with reformers' reason, the probable result would be an almost certain levelling down of compensation towards benefit rather than vice versa.

But if it is at least possible to have a sensible debate about which kinds of physical disability merit which kinds and levels of compensation, Liebman's disadvantaged seem to dwell well beyond the pale. Those who "merely" suffer from limited or unwanted (in the sense of being superfluous to economic needs) natural abilities, those who suffer from a heritage of racism and sexism, or those, who for whatever non-physical-disability reason, are unable to compete on the labour market, seem to be accepted as the natural losers in the world of the market economy. It could not operate without them. If the concept of alterity has come to excite the post-modern world in its discussions of "foreigners" and "outsiders", it has its use too within the nation state to describe those whose very failures make success possible. The altar of the market economy requires the sacrifice of the "alter". When it comes to compensation, while opinion may be divided over equating all physical disability, it is depressingly uniform in accepting as inevitable what Galbraith describes as an underclass, fundamentally, and for reasons for which it is not responsible, unable to compete successfully in the competition culture.[33]

We have arrived at what might seem to be depressing conclusions about the state of socio-legal research and tort, certainly in its relevance to reform. Before discussing this conclusion and its implications for both socio-legal theory and research it might be pertinent to consider briefly the most recent piece of substantial research into personal injury - the report of the Law Commission entitled "Personal Injury Compensation: How much is Enough?"[34] This is a substantial study of the compensation experience of victims of personal injury. The report is written by Professor Hazel Genn, an authority on empirical studies of injuries and their legal aftermath. Obviously the first point of comment is that the report is restricted to victims of personal injury who received damages - ie. the tort category of disability victims. In itself, in its acceptance of this category, this will clearly lead to findings which reinforce the category as discrete and sensible. The agonizing of earlier studies of "cause versus need" is not a part of this study which comes within a wider review of damages being undertaken by the Law Commission.

The object of the research however was not insignificant. It provided clear evidence that even those within the category of comparatively "fortunate" injury victims (ie those obtaining a tortious remedy) were not necessarily returned to the state they had enjoyed before the injury. In one sense this is inevitable since pain and suffering, and injury, may only be ameliorated and almost never alleviated by money. In another sense, however, it once more was made clear by the study, that the level and often the fact of compensation by damages, remains a lottery. This is partly inherent in the nature of the beast which necessitates the striking of a bargain between lawyers as to the level of compensation after negotiations which resemble nothing so much as (in a greatly prolonged form) the haggling required before purchase in an Oriental market. The price settled upon in each case often has less to do with the quality of the claim (or the carpet!) than with the quality of the bargaining skills of the buyer and seller.

Most disturbingly, with the passage of time between settlement of claim and the time of interview with the survey, between three fifths and three quarters of all those who had received damages expressed themselves as dissatisfied with the level of damages received. This was explained in terms of the money representing inadequate compensation for the impact of the injuries on the victims' way of life and a strongly held view that the damages did not make up the loss of earnings suffered. Additionally the survey accepted the evidence that notwithstanding the principle of full compensation most victims required significant unpaid care by parents, spouses, friends and neighbours. It also found an unmet need for counselling and psychological support for accident victims, and retraining schemes to enable such people to re-enter the labour market. Support in adjusting to new post-injury circumstances was notably lacking.

Thus the findings of this study are important but limited. It accepts earlier findings as to the significance and scope of personal injury compensation but within that category it evidences the short comings of the system in terms of the delay in settlement, the level of settlement, the effect on employment, and indeed in the use of the damages received. The irresistible inference to be drawn however, is that if this dissatisfaction is to be overcome then the cost will be significantly greater, with yet further privileging of one category of accident victims. While the non-financial problems of such victims are acutely observed, I am sure that the author of the report will accept that these conclusions are even more appropiate for those not receiving tort damages.

What have socio-legal studies contributed to an understanding of tort as evidenced by negligence and personal injury? More controversially what have they contributed to reform? The controversy arises from new doubts regularly expressed about the value and purposes of socio-legal study as traditionally conceived. The self-confidence of those who sought to identify the social facts which resulted from legal regulation with a view to righting wrongs and providing justice for the disadvantaged, has withered into an agony of epistemological doubt. Where socio-legal studies once gained their attraction from the practical nature of what they were able to describe and prescribe, more recently they have reverted to a realisation that notions of justice require justification. A central theme of much writing on the sociology of law centres on the question expressed by one writer in the following terms[35]

> ... can socio-legal research say anything about justice? Can it engage directly and effectively with contemporary legal debates, in the sense of debates about what legal doctrine and practice *should be* rather than what legal agencies in fact do?

As will be apparent this worry which is seen by the author as "an especially pressing underlying question",[36] is not one with which I unreservedly identify. Had the Good Samaritan been a modern (or postmodern!) socio-legal theorist the victim of the robbery might well have passed on (to use an inappropriate euphemism) while the Samaritan pondered the meaning of justice. This is not entirely facetious.[37] Socio-legal theory seems to have arrived clearly at a position where the facts as revealed are no longer able to speak for themselves.

Put this way the position is manifestly unsatisfactory but it is important to understand why it has developed as it has and what insights it provides. Seventeen years of Conservative government in the UK, together with the apparent collapse of international alternatives to liberal capitalism, and the ever increasing power of international capital and transnational corporations and institutions, encouraged a reaction of powerlessness. While "empowerment" has become a popular concept, much "disempowerment" has resulted from the internalisation of helplessness aggravated by the emphasis upon individualism. Institutions such as the World Trade Organisation, the International Monetary Fund and indeed the European Community feed this sensation of what used to be called "anomie" or "alienation". Problems which require legislative reform seem too formidable for this to be feasible.

Simultaneously however, there has been a sensible scepticism directed towards sweeping solutions to problems with many nuances. "Big answers" to "big questions"[38] are no longer fashionable for the very good reason that many of the central concepts which informed both such questions and answers have been called into question. "Progress" is now perceived as nothing more than a value judgement from a particular perspective, while "development" has persuaded eminent authors to write entire books exposing the false premisses upon which it is based.[39]

I maintain, that pertinent though these insights are, they nevertheless should not lead to an inability to press for change. The need for change is amply demonstrated in studies which show not only that those compensated by damages have unmet expectations and needs, but also that those uncompensated are often forced into economic penury and degradation. Needless to say the inferences to be drawn from socio-legal research will depend upon the ideology of the inferer but I have yet to meet a law student who thought that the disparity in financial treatment accorded to "Baby A" who suffers blindness through an improperly placed catheter and "Baby B" who is born with congenital blindness anything other than an absurdity. To those who like David Howarth[40] reply that expense alone rules out the equalising of the cases, Jane Stapleton's answer is clear: if there is a limited amount of money available for the compensation of the "disabled" it seems more equitable that it be distributed, such as it is, in accordance with need, even though neither child might receive "full" compensation.

Finally, the fact that misfortune and disability are so complex, in itself does not dictate inactivity. When the political climate changes, as it surely must, the time may come when substantive, rather than formal, equality once more appears as a serious item upon the political agenda. Until then however, a pragmatic, if emotive, approach may still have a logic of its own. Even within the existing political climate a necessary move away from fault, at least in accidents, seems to be the conclusion reached in every serious socio-legal study. In a recent Law Commission Report restricted, as I have stated, to compensated personal injury victims, the author feels bound to remark on the anomaly when, in repeating that the majority of accident victims receive no compensation in tort, she wrote of those victims:

> Although their injuries will have the same impact on their ability to work, the same impact on their ability to function independently, and the same impact on their family and social life as the injuries of compensated accidents, 'uncompensated' accident victims and their families must simply depend on their own savings and social security benefits to cover the losses and extra expenses resulting from their injuries. In focusing on the experiences and perceptions of compensated accident victims, it is important not to lose sight of the wider issues.[41]

The ambivalent conclusion of this brief review of socio-legal studies and tort is that while the academic arguments provided by research have been impressive and show how the position might be at least ameliorated,[42] they have nevertheless been politically resistible at best and unsaleable at worst. It is depressing, but probably true, that one emotive television documentary on the hardship of one appealing case of uncompensated misfortune will have more effect - at least in changing the climate of opinion - than much detailed socio-legal research. But the place of this research is to sustain such a climate and to validate the appeal for change.   Current philosophy which might persuade us that the darkest hour is just before another even darker hour, must be eschewed!

Notes

1   Economic & Social Research Council, *Review of Socio-Legal Studies* (1994) 17. The reference within the quotation is to Harris et al. *Compensation and Support for Illness and Injury* (1984).

2   D. Howarth *Textbook on Tort* (1995).

3   id., p.33.

4   id., p.32.

5   (First ed. 1970).

6   my italics.

7   A. Tunc *Responsibilite Civile* (2nd ed. 1989).

9   op. cit. p.32.

9   to S. Lloyd-Bostock "Common sense morality and accident compensation" [1980] Ins LJ 331.

10   op. cit. p.33.

11   id.

12   id.

13   J. Stapleton "In Restraint of Tort", in P. Birks (ed) *The Frontiers of Liability.* Vol 2 (1994) 83.

14   op. cit., n.1 p.17.

15   Report *of the Royal Commission of Inquiry on Compensation for Personal Injuries in New Zealand* (1967).

16   W. Twining "Reflections on Law in Context" in *Essays for Patrick Atiyah* eds Cane and Stapleton (1991) 1 at p.28.

17   W. Rogers *Winfield and Jolowicz on Tort* (13th ed. 1991).

18   M. Brazier *The Law of Torts* (1988).

19   R. Heuston and R. Buckley, *Salmond and Heuston on the Law of Torts* (19th ed 1991).

20   *The Report of the Royal Commission on Civil Liability and Compensation for Personal Injury* (1978).

21   T. Weir, *A Casebook on Tort* (4th ed. 1979) 3 "The Law of tort has thus been subjected to a critical examination and has passed it".

22   See further J. Conaghan and W. Mansell, *The Wrongs of Tort* (1993) 86-101.

23   G. Palmer "New Zealand's accident compensation scheme: twenty years on" (1994) 44 U. of Toronto L.J. 223.

24   op. cit. n.1.

25   *Social Insurance and Allied Services* (1942) para 80.

26   (1986).

27   op. cit.

29	p.183.
29	L. Liebman "The Definition of Disability in Social Security and Supplemental Security Income: Drawing the Bounds of Social Welfare Estates" (1976) 89 Harv. L.R. 833, 864. Quoted M.J. Stapleton op. cit. 181.
30	G. Calabresi *The Cost of Accidents* (1970).
31	op. cit. n.15.
32	op. cit. p.147.
33	J.K. Galbraith *The Culture of Contentment* (1992).
34	(1994).
35	R.Cotterrell *Law Power and Community* (1995) 297.
36	id.
37	But it may seem gratuitously unkind and, worse still, self-righteous. It is not meant to be. As the Bible makes clear, Samaritans are found in the most unexpected places.
39	See W.Mansell et al., *A Critical Introduction to Law* (1995) 145-164.
39	See e.g. W. Sachs, *The Development Dictionary* (1992).
40	op. cit.
41	op. cit. p.262.
42	But probably no more than that. I have deliberately not entered into a wider discussion of the problems of individual monetary compensation in a world of individualism.

12 Socio-Legal Analysis Of Contract

DAVID CAMPBELL

Introduction

Clear evidence that the socio-legal analysis of contract in the UK is currently in a healthy condition is provided by the recent publication of the second edition of Collins' *Law of Contract*[1] and of Wheeler and Shaw's *Contract Law*.[2] Collins' is the first full length textbook[3] informed by a thoroughgoing commitment to the socio-legal approach and Wheeler and Shaw the first casebook displaying such a commitment. Together with Adams and Brownsword's, Tillotson's and Wightman's introductions to the subject,[4] Adams and Brownsword's commentary on key issues[5] and Beale *et al's* cases and materials[6] of a somewhat different complexion to Wheeler and Shaw, these books mean that those teaching contract have the opportunity properly to base an undergraduate course on the socio-legal analysis of the subject. In this chapter, I will argue that this opportunity has arisen because of the emergence of a solid body of writing which constitutes a watershed in the history of the socio-legal analysis of contract in Britain. After first sketching a brief history of that analysis, I will then present an outline of its main themes in which I hope to show that it has now so established its position that its overall stance need no longer be, as it were, oppositional. The criticisms socio-legal analysis has made of the classical law of contract are widely accepted in high level scholarship at least, and socio-legal contract is now, in its positive statement of the theory of relational or co-operative contract, to the fore of putting forward what the present state of the law of contract desperately needs, a rival to the classical law.

Early Socio-Legal Analyses Of Contract

Mention of Collins' *Law of Contract* allows us to trace a direct line[7] between the present state of the socio-legal analysis of contract and the first sustained such analysis in the UK of which I am aware, that of Wolfgang Friedmann. Though this theme is in fact relatively subdued in the second edition, in which the concept of market failure is central,[8] the first edition of Collins' book turned on a play between the formerly individualistic character of contract law and its present commitment to the "communitarian values...which gave birth to the Welfare State,"[9] "the substantive values of fairness, trust and co-operation".[10] I hope to concede to no-one in the degree of my admiration for Collins' book but, for the purposes of an history of socio-legal contract, it must be recognised that it did in central ways revive an argument which Friedmann first put forward in 1951 in *Law and Social Change in Contemporary Britain*[11] and very considerably revised and expanded eight years later in *Law in a Changing Society*.[12]

Friedmann argued that contract has four social functions: securing freedom of movement, providing insurance against calculated economic risks, securing freedom of will and securing equality between the parties. These functions, Friedmann seems to allow, could once have been performed by adherence to freedom of contract: "The classical theory of contract...was that two or more individual persons freely bargained with each other [so] control over the terms of contract was limited to a few categories of illegality".[13] However, the disappearance of *laissez faire* over the course of capitalist development removed the plausibility of freedom of contract:

> formal equality, to vote, to make contracts, to migrate, to marry, was regarded by early utilitarianism and democratic theory as automatically conducive to social liberty and equality. The increasing gap between this theory and the reality of developing capitalist society...had its particular effect on the law of contract, the legal symbol *par excellence* of this society.[14]

The concentration of business leading to the prevalence of contracts of adhesion, the substitution of collective for individual bargaining, the expansion of welfare provision and an enlarged range of excuses for non-performance to deal with "the spread of such political, economic and social upheavals as war, revolution, or inflation"[15] had given contract a far more collective rather than individualist character:

> it is clear that contract is becoming an increasingly institutionalised. From being the instrument by which millions of individual parties bargain with each other, it has to a large extent become the way by which social and economic policies are expressed in legal form.[16]

Of course, doctrinal legal scholarship had not caught up with the significance of these changes in the way the functions of contract are performed, and so:

> The difficulty of bridging the gap between the formal and substantive aspects of both freedom and equality is evident in the pathetic contrast between the law of contract as it is taught in most textbooks, and modern contract as it functions in society.[17]

Law in a Changing Society was a very considerable success, receiving the strongest market endorsement when Penguin brought out an abridged version in 1964 and (with Stevens and Sons) a second edition in 1972, the year of Friedmann's tragic death. The 1972 account of contract shows no marked change from the 1959 account, just a pleasing accumulation of confirmatory evidence.[18] But, despite the endorsement of Lord Denning in the preface to *Law and Social Change in Contemporary Britain*,[19] this success did not have any significant impact on research in or the teaching of the law of contract, but would appear to have been confined to work on the "sociology of law." Leaving aside Atiyah for the moment, I am unaware of any socio-legal writing on contract after the

241

publication of Friedmann's account in 1959 which pointed either to the divergence of the formal law of contract from business practice or to the way the law was coming to express the values of the welfare rather than the liberal state[20] until the publication of Beale and Dugdale's empirical work,[21] which reached conclusions "broadly similar" to those of Macaulay's 1963 study and so brought the concept of "non-use" into wide British usage. With the partial exception of some related discussions of dispute resolution procedures,[22] work on the sociology of commercial law[23] during this period largely was conducted at levels of abstraction which meant it had little interest for those concerned with the actual law of contract.[24] This to some extent followed from the different cognitive interest of the "sociologist" as opposed to the "lawyer"[25] but also - and perhaps not very differently in truth - was not very unusually an instance of the disregard for its empirical subject matter[26] that has reduced much sociological theorising to its present moribund state.[27]

This lack of work on the law of contract informed by awareness of social context was, of course, to some extent in contrast to the situation in the USA, for the way in which the British reception of legal realism confined it to the ghetto of "jurisprudence" has meant that some of the most compelling, socially conscious criticisms of classical contract ever made went (and continue to be, so we have on occasion to reinvent the wheel)[28] largely unappreciated in contract scholarship.[29] Against the background of highly influential realist treatments of contract leading to the production of the Uniform Commercial Code, what we can now see as the first widely successful campaigns against classical law were beginning to be waged in the USA in this period, with the doctrinal consequences of Macaulay's (and his colleagues at Wisconsins') contribution being pursued to their negative conclusion particularly by Gilmore[30] and to their positive ones in terms of formulating a new theory of contract particularly by Goetz and Scott,[31] Goldberg[32] and, most interestingly, by Macneil.[33] Of course, one should not underestimate the relative marginality, in comparison to the vast industry that was and is the teaching of classical contract in USA law schools, of alternative contract theories even there, but it is clear that it was in the USA that the foundations of the present significance of the socio-legal analysis of contract were being laid.

However, there was one, as it were, applied area in which this picture of British socio-legal accounts of contract as almost non-existent is inaccurate, and that is labour law. Following from the "peculiar" qualities of labour-power as a commodity, the social dimensions of labour law are relatively manifest by comparison to other types of contract and the flat failures of trying to resolve labour issues by classical contractual reasoning are equally so.[34] Under these circumstances, in which welfarist intervention (was, but even now) is the most obvious feature of labour law, the need for a broadly socio-legal approach relatively urgently impresses itself, and English labour law has been fortunate in having a line of very distinguished academic analysts with sufficient breadth of scholarship to deal with the legal issues in a way which is informed by an integral understanding of the social context of those issues.[35] From this line it is invidious to single out even so eminent a person as Sir Otto Kahn-Freund, but that Kahn-Freund was the author of seminal articles work on the detail of English labour law and also saw fit (and was able) to introduce Renner's *The Institutions of Private Law and their Social Functions* to British readership exemplifies the quality I am trying to describe.[36] It has not been until relatively recently that socio-legal analysis has begun to be applied to the basic principles of contract even remotely as widely as it is in labour law and this is because it has taken an event within traditional contract scholarship to allow this to happen.

From the time of the Factory Acts, there has been no hegemony of, as it were, a classical law of employment, for the political dimension of "judicial non-intervention" in labour disputes is clear.[37] Leaving aside any differences between the qualities of the works of Friedmann and Collins, the earlier Collins (and other contributors to the "welfarist critique" of classical contract,) sparked off a major debate in contract scholarship in a way that Friedmann did not, as it were, for an external reason. It has taken the recognition of the degeneration of the classical law of contract to make clear the plausibility of alternative approaches to contract, including the socio-legal, and if the "death of contract" was first recognised in the

USA, it is now also recognised in the UK, largely as a result of the work of P.S. Atiyah.

P.S. Atiyah

It was with a very considerable degree of unfairness that in the list of works I gave at the beginning of this chapter I omitted to mention that 1995 saw the publication of the fifth edition of Atiyah's *Introduction to the Law of Contract*, for, without doubt, Atiyah has been the English scholar most responsible for winning the acceptance of the socio-legal approach to contract. This is so, however, only in an indirect way, and I trust that the reasons for this omission will emerge.

In books and papers which he has published since 1954, Atiyah has made the unproblematic maintenance of the classical law of contract impossible for anyone who wishes to engage at the highest level of English contract scholarship. In essays on the central doctrines of classical law of contract, the principal ones of which are collected in *Essays on Contract*,[38] Atiyah has exposed the internal incoherence of those doctrines and shown how the most important cases simply cannot be reconciled with them. I have discussed Atiyah's criticisms of those doctrines, particularly that of consideration, elsewhere in a way which I trust illustrates their power,[39] and will here say only that they were the major force in creating the possibility, by making clear the necessity, of the radical critique of classical contract in England and Wales.[40]

Atiyah attempted to give a statement of the law of contract in the light of these criticisms in what, at its first publication in 1961, was a 266 page introduction to the subject but which has now grown into a fair sized textbook,[41] and this was, until the relatively recent appearance of the already mentioned works by Adams and Brownsword,[42] Collins, Tillotson and Wightman, the only real breath of fresh air amongst the textbooks on the subject.[43] In particular, in the first two editions of his textbook Atiyah included a chapter on 'The Future of the Law of Contract' which brought an argument comparable to Friedmann's in *Law in a Changing Society* into the heart of contract scholarship.[44] However, this part of the achievement of this textbook has been eclipsed by that of what undoubtedly is the most important work of modern British contract scholarship, *The Rise and Fall of Freedom of Contract*,[45] in which Atiyah complemented his doctrinal studies with a magisterial history of the law of contract between 1770 to 1970, the thrust of which is sufficiently captured in the title of the book. *The Rise and Fall* ends with an explicit statement of 'The Need for a New Theory' in the light of the fall,[46] and all subsequent productive contract scholarship in this country has been an attempt to speak to that need.

Atiyah has not, in my opinion, properly satisfied this need himself. The promised second part of the study of contract of which *The Rise and Fall* was the preliminary first part[47] has not appeared, and between the appearance of the third and fourth editions of his book on contract,[48] he seems to have swallowed a rather large chunk of Posnerite law and economics which sadly seems to have exaggerated what were relatively minor shortcomings in his work and now make his theoretical account of the subject go backwards. I have argued this at length elsewhere,[49] and wish to make only one point here.

Any account of the socio-legal study of contract in England and Wales would happily embrace Atiyah but could hardly, as it were, claim him outright. Atiyah's overwhelming strength is in the analysis of doctrine, handling common law and statutory materials in a way which invites fair comparison with the greatest figures of the history of the common law, and he has not (until recently, in the unfortunate way I have mentioned) developed a background to his views which draws on social scientific materials in any profound way.[50] In *The Rise and Fall*, he argues that the classical law turning on the freedom of contract was once an accurate legal representation of the capitalist economy, and that the breakdown of that law was the product of increasing state interference in that economy. The motive for this interference was that in the 1870s democratic aspiration was consolidated within the British state, and democracy is inconsistent with the socially divisive outcomes of the uncontrolled market.[51] Leaving aside the excellence of the legal scholarship, Atiyah's account of the obsolescence of the classical law is informed by a conventional history of gradual social improvement charted through changing intellectual, political and legal attitudes which measured the classical law according to criteria external to that law and, finding it wanting, changed it from the outside. The general social and economic structure which contract expresses actually plays little part in these changes[52] but changes in response to outside pressures which are, basically, intellectual currents. There is little comparison between this sort of idealist historiography and the thrust of empirical social science. After broadly accepting Atiyah's account, one should go on to ask why the democratic aspiration which led to the development of the welfare state appeared so compellingly at the time it did, and any social scientifically serious attempt to do so has not resided at the level of intellectual expressions but has followed those expressions to the social structure of bourgeois society, to its groups and interests, its characteristic polity and to the nature of the capitalist economy legally expressed in contract. As Atiyah appears to know of this literature only through Marx's thought, and indeed through an insensitive view of that,[53] the resources of social science are not exploited in his work and the structural questions about the place of contract in the capitalist economy which inform socio-legal analysis of contract are not pursued.[54]

The Position Since 1979

Nevertheless, leaving aside those who have just gone ahead in the old way in disregard of the progressive developments in the subject,[55] Atiyah's call for a new theory has been a very effective focus for discontent with the classical law and as such has met with a number of responses. The first of these has been attempts to revamp the classical law of contract, and whilst the main works are American,[56] substantial contributions are being made in the UK, exemplified to undergraduates by the revisions which Professor Furmston is making to Cheshire and Fifoot.[57] A second is, in effect, to give up hope of reviving the corpse of the classical law and give a whole

246

new doctrinal basis to obligations, and this is the thrust of attempts to identify a common law of obligations and of attempts to identify that law not by bringing together the extant law of contract and tort[58] but by giving obligations a novel statement in terms of restitution.[59] These initiatives have, of course, their own novelty and abiding interest, but, although novel in their substance, of which they are often embarrassingly self-consciousness, they remain very conservative in their method, for these are purely doctrinal works and it is the claim of those most critical of the classical law that the fundamental problem of the classical understanding is that it completely fails to grasp the empirical significance of the rules.[60]

The third response is the growth of the critical[61] socio-legal analysis of contract, to the point where now, I think, it occupies a position of indisputable importance within contract scholarship as a whole. That "socio-legal" is a collective noun, embracing contributions from the range of social sciences,[62] is in itself no way a bad thing, but it has led to a difficulty with which I must now deal.

The most significant social scientific intervention in contract has undoubtedly been from within economics, and equally undoubtedly the most influential such intervention has been that of the "law and economics" movement based on work of academics at the University of Chicago.[63] Posner's *Economics of Law*, first published in 1972 and now in its fourth edition,[64] has been the focus of what must be the most powerful theoretical intervention in the common law since realism. However, in Posner's hands, law and economics has become a most remarkably apologetic rationalisation of the common law generally[65] and of specific aspects of the classical law of contract,[66] and in this it is at profound variance with the broad thrust of the socio-legal analysis of contract, which is centrally raising the most profound questions of the adequacy of that law.

Having noted this problem, however, and whilst I can hardly take the issue much further here, two things must be pointed out. First, even broadly Chicagoan law and economics has produced theoretical[67] and empirical[68] work on contract of the greatest interest, and this work demands a productive response even if one disagrees with it. Second,

Chicagoan law and economics is not law and economics *per se*. Not only the older[69] but even strong variants of the new institutional economics[70] are producing some of the most productive research programmes in social science which simply cannot be damned because of the ideological overtones of the likes of Posner, and a strong rejection of these overtones is to the forefront of a sizeable minority of law and economics scholarship in the USA.[71] Posner has, indeed, recently had to suffer the explicit rejection of his interpretations of Coase by Coase himself, and this no doubt was a sobering experience, for I have encountered no writer in all of social science more capable of a tellingly witty attack than Coase.[72] It is my own profound belief that a genuinely productive dialogue which improves both "law and economics" and "socio-legal analysis" of contract may be developed,[73] but in saying this I am conscious that mine is a minority position[74] which would not only be disputed by law and economics scholars but also by many socio-legal scholars.[75]

Though an antipathy between the Chicagoan law and economics of contract and the socio-legal analysis of contract undoubtedly exists, there can be no doubt that in one way the ideological dominance of right wing economic policy has been of assistance to the latter. For a clear, if no doubt unintended, consequence of the reign of Mrs Thatcher has been to promote the British socio-legal analysis of contract because the version of monetarism which she so successfully promoted in the UK has had a central role for "contract" Concentration on the "free market" tends to promote the study of contract amongst all but the most mathematical economists and those who find it comforting to live in their dreamworld, but, on the other hand, contextual awareness of the social conditions for the operation of markets contradicts belief in the, as it were, "pure market" of neo-liberalism,[76] so it very largely has been those who are prepared to view the market in this "pure" way that have benefited from the state's efforts to promote the market since 1979.[77]

But if socio-legal analysis was more or less completely marginal to the expansion of the realm of contract under Thatcherism, socio-legal analysis of the "contract" regimes that have been established have been very significant. The privatisation of formerly state owned corporations[78] and the empirical operation of contracted out former state services[79] have been subject to searching socio-legal analysis. The new forms of public sector contract simply cannot be fitted into the classical contract paradigm,[80] and the need to expand that paradigm to accommodate[81] these new forms[82] has made the value of socio-legal analysis readily apparent. Again leaving aside the, as it were, insider accounts of dealing with these systems which provide interesting data,[83] the volume and interest of the theoretically informed empirical work undertaken on public sector contracting already exceeds that undertaken on private contract, and the ESRC is strongly supporting this work.[84] The socio-legal analysis of public contracting also is being developed in ways which promise important theoretical developments in order to analyse the new public/private "hybrid" governance structures,[85] and in particular there appears to be developing a potentially very productive convergence between contract and public law.[86]

If the need to come to terms with changes in the nature of government has had its main effect in stimulating work on public sector contracting, it is nevertheless the case that the socio-legal study of the private law of contract undoubtedly also has benefited from the simply higher profile which contract has been accorded in public and academic debate since 1979. "Contract" is, in fact, a convergence point for work in those disciplines - principally accountancy,[87] economics of all shades,[88] and management theory[89] as well as law - which are trying, *in a concrete way*, to come to terms with the fundamental problems of organisational governance which the collapse of Keyenesian-socialist policies in the west and state communist policies in the east, together with the continuing manifest unsatisfactoriness of capitalist markets, now poses. In the possible interdisciplinary work which this convergence now makes possible, it should be the case that, by enriching other disciplines' work on contract by deepening their appreciation of the law, the socio-legal analysis of contract can repay the considerable debt which it has incurred by its own borrowings from those disciplines.[90]

The 1995 directory of members of the Socio-Legal Studies Association now shows 21 persons listing contract or a closely related subject[91] as a research interest, and a further 17 persons (in addition to overlapping membership) listing these subjects as a teaching interest.[92] This information is not complete - in what I hope is an unintentional omission it does not include me - and amongst those actively participating in or contributing to a stream of papers on "The Socio-Legal Analysis of Contract" given at the 1994 Annual Conference of the Socio-Legal Studies Association - the first such a gathering in the UK of which I am aware[93] - there were at least 5 other academics who had published in this field.[94] Members of this small but often quite senior group of British academic lawyers are producing socio-legal work on contract which is amongst the leading contract scholarship and is receiving considerable attention within that field.

By no means all of this attention is favourable. The first edition of Collins' textbook received some outright wrecking reviews[95] and Wheeler and Shaw have come in for their share of such treatment.[96] But when Weir saw fit to spend 6 pages of the *Cambridge Law Review* in a diatribe against Collins, one can see that the lack of faith in the power of disdain that led to the expenditure of this amount of effort was the product of a fear that things are not going the way one would like, and two relatively recent events exemplify, I think, the current position.

In 1993 the pending imposition of the EEC Directive on Unfair Terms in Consumer Contracts stimulated a colloquium held at Merton College Oxford, amongst the participants at which were a number of those, from both sides of the Atlantic, who have done most to keep life (and sometimes genuine interest) in the classical law of contract over the last thirty years. The basic tone is that of the conservative attempt to keep squeezing the new wine into old bottles that exemplifies this scholarship, but it is not merely new events but new doctrine that informs the book, and this is a major change. Not only did the editors of the resulting collection on *Good Faith and Fault in Contract Law* feel obliged to introduce the work with essay entitled 'From "Classical" to Modern Contract Law',[97] but the book contained a section on 'Relational and Long-term Contracts'! It is not that these new doctrines are overall enthusiastically embraced in the UK contribution. In one of the essays on 'Relational and Long-term

Contracts', the eminent USA scholar Melvin Eisenberg passes the judgement that:

> The literature on relational contracts has brought home a fundamental weakness of classical contract law, that is, the flawed nature of its implicit empirical premise that most contracts are discrete. The literature has also been illuminating in its economics and its sociology. Legally, it has excelled in the treatment of specific types of contracts, like franchise agreements; specific types of express or implied terms, like best-efforts provisions; and specific types of relationships, like those in which one party must make a transaction- or relation-specific investment.[98]

This contrasts very starkly with the view of the other - British - writer on 'Relational and Long-term Contracting', Ewan McKendrick, that Melvin Eisenberg does more for the understanding of relational contract by sticking to "everyday sense" in this one 13 page essay than Macneil, Goetz and Scott and Harris (and I) have done in their lifetimes of scholarship.[99] But the point is that new perspectives are allowed to be legitimate subjects for discussion.

Even more strikingly, in the House of Lords, Lord Mustill[100] turned to an article written by Harris, Ogus and Phillips[101] to resolve what has been thought to be a vexing problem in damages. This article drew on some interesting microeconomics to set out a concept of "consumer surplus" as a way of identifying some abiding problems in damages, and Lord Mustill adopted it as the basis of resolving a dispute that had caused the Court of Appeal (itself divided) to reverse a first instance decision only then to itself be reversed in the House of Lords. I am bound to say that I cannot regard this as a novel departure in the law as I have been teaching - with success I think - the position now reached by the House of Lords to undergraduates for 10 years,[102] but it is a very welcome recognition that the classical law has become enmeshed in conundra which, though they no doubt can be hedged about and fiddled with by doctrinal word spinning, can be simply resolved only by turning to socio-legal scholarship.

Contemplating the rather dizzying prospect this turn in legal reasoning opens up, I think one can, in sum, say that the increase in the amount of socio-legal analysis of contract being done, and more particularly the wider recognition it is being accorded, is substantial compared with the position even of a decade and certainly of two decades ago. As, as I have mentioned, amongst the group of socio-legal contract scholars there now are a number of senior academics, and of its nature this should mean that the currency of socio-legal analysis will grow. As I will say at more length later, though the research agenda remains dominated by USA scholarship, some emergent themes in the British socio-legal work seem to me to be novel and highly significant contributions.

Themes Of Socio-Legal Analysis

The socio-legal contribution to contract scholarship can be said to have three related features. These are a stress on the empirical reality of business relationships as the fundamental subject of contract; a stress on the problematic relationship of the classical law of contract expressed in legal texts to those business relationships, and a consequent stress on the shortcomings of the law of contract expressed in legal texts coupled with a wish to eradicate those shortcomings by a new statement of the law. Let us take these in turn.

Almost all accounts of the socio-legal analysis of contract in the common law world begin with Macaulay's 1963 article on 'Non-contractual Relations in Business: A Preliminary Study'.[103] The essential import of this article is that the actual conduct of business, and particularly the resolution of disputes, does not rely on formal legal provisions so much as informal, non-legal understandings. This theme of the "non-use" of contract has been explored in a now large empirical USA literature,[104] in comparison to which the volume of the British empirical literature is small. Leaving aside such literature as, say, the "insider accounts" of the conduct of arbitrations or the modification of construction contracts which necessarily testify to, but do not theoretically comprehend, the non-use of formal contract,[105] there have been, to my knowledge, only 5[106] British empirical studies which have produced comparable findings of "non-use". These are the work of Beale and Dugdale already mentioned,[107] the work of Beale, Harris and Sharpe on the franchised distribution of cars,[108] the work of Daintith on iron ore contracts,[109] the work of Lewis on pre-contractual negotiations[110] and the work of Wheeler on *Romalpa* clauses.[111] These studies have all been of pronounced interest in themselves and have led to important reviews of the actual application of the doctrines of contract and the actual working of the commercial legal system in England,[112] to unique suggestions for reform,[113] and have, as I will discuss, been the foundation of significant new lines of contract theory. Under its 'Contracts and Competition' initiative, the ESRC has since 1992 funded 13 major projects all of which should be nearing completion at the time of writing, but of these only - to the mind of an unsuccessful applicant a very disappointing - two look as if they will contribute to this empirical literature on private contracting.[114] Nevertheless, this small corpus of empirical work has been of greater importance within British contract scholarship than its small size would lead one to think, largely, no doubt, because there is no comparable empirical work conducted within the bounds of more traditional scholarship.[115] The significance of this point of difference between socio-legal and traditional scholarship might well be productively discussed by means of a specific example.[116]

One of the conundra used to perplex me as an undergraduate, and still used to torment undergraduates if the contents of textbooks are anything to go by,[117] is the "personality mistake", the doctrine developed at common law to deal with the situation in which a fraudster obtains goods by obtaining credit or purporting to make payment by virtue of adopting a false identity. In *Lewis* v. *Avery*[118] the fraudster purported to be a well known actor and so persuaded the seller of a car to take a cheque which was dishonoured. Between the seller and the fraudster the legal position is clear, though of course the fraudster is hard to find. The position is *not* clear as between the seller and a third party to whom the fraudster may sell the goods, for, in effect, given that the fraudster typically is not available for potential legal proceedings, the common law of contract is faced with the dilemma of leaving the loss with the seller in good faith or the buyer in good faith. If the first sale is enforceable, title will pass to the ultimate buyer who will retain position but if that sale is void (or voidable and avoided in time), as *nemo dat non quod habet*, the original seller will be able to recover possession. The fact of non-payment does not avoid a contract but operative mistake typically does, and so an argument was mounted that the original sale was entered into by mistake as to the personality of the fraudster.[119]

It would be hard to exaggerate the degree of doctrinal confusion to which attempts to resolve this flat dilemma gave rise in classical accounts of personality mistake and I will return to this. Let us concentrate on the real problem. As it arose in connection with the very expensive chattel of the car, fraudulent purchase and resale obviously led to cases of severe hardship. In *Ingram* v. *Little*,[120] the facts of which arose in 1957, the original sale price was £717, a figure which would be at least 10 times higher in 1995 values.[121] The problem must have been viewed as severe indeed, for the Law Reform Committee was stirred to action and it reported in 1966.[122] With the degree of acumen one expects, the doctrinal possibilities were explored but if, as one almost equally expects, the report has not led to action, this cannot be seriously regretted for, with respect, the Committee did not know what it was talking about. If the problem is, say, the wrongful disposition of cars, one does not get to know *anything* about that by considering whether the personality of a buyer was or was not material to the contractual intention a seller, and one can reach *either* conclusion about this second question without getting one whit closer to an informed opinion about the first. What is needed, surely manifestly to anyone other than those who have a training in the classical law of contract but even, with effort, appreciable even by those, is some empirical knowledge of the nature and extent of the problem of wrongful disposition. Atiyah pointed this out in 1966,[123] and subsequent editions of his book on sale of goods have hammered home the point that:

Generally, the Report was a disappointing document largely because of its complete failure to search for any empirical evidence as to the way in which the law operated. The continuing lack of this evidence makes it very difficult to justify positive proposals for change of a fundamental character.[124]

That commercial problems are addressed in the classical law of contract[125] in an abstract fashion divorced from the gathering of empirical evidence about the nature of those problems[126] is a major criticism of the classical law of contract mounted by socio-legal scholarship.

A second theme of the socio-legal analysis of contract is a criticism of the method of the classical law which can allow one to proceed in this way. Again foreshadowed by Atiyah,[127] socio-legal scholars have mounted very persuasive criticisms of the perversion of the common law method that is part and parcel of the perpetuation of the classical law of contract in the face of the overwhelming evidence of its falsification.[128] The central doctrines of classical contract have had to be so twisted in order to retain the appearance of having continuing relevance that they have taken the enormously valuable quality of flexibility in the common law and brought it into disrepute. That those doctrines now provide very limited answers to the basic questions about the nature and extent of contractual liability which they are meant to answer[129] is, an ineluctably established - but hardly dominant - position in the advanced scholarship. It is a position which even informs relatively recent statutory measures and appeal decisions which provide tolerably clear solutions to conundra which go back over a hundred years of the classical law contract by breaking with that law, such as the Unfair Contract Terms Act's effective recognition that offer and acceptance can easily be nothing but a sham in consumer contracts and *Williams* v. *Roffey Bros and Nicholls (Contractors) Ltd's* similar verdict on the existing obligations rule in consideration. To be frank, it is hard to see what socio-legal studies can add to Atiyah (or those who nearly emulate him)[130] he, for this effort is one of doctrinal criticism, but a number of the socio-legal writers discussed here have made important contributions to this effort.[131] Let me try to illustrate this by continuing with my example of personality mistake.

It should just be said that the problem is not one of "personality"; this is a mere accidental feature unrelated to the basic issue of fraud.[132] It is hardly to be expected that the common law would immediately produce the correct solution to, or the correct analytical framework for, the analysis of complex problems such as mistake. But it is a most serious shortcoming to be so wedded to conceptual ratiocination as to procrasinate when questions affecting people's livelihoods are at stake. The bankruptcy of it all surely was confirmed when, in 1991, Waller J. began his judgement in *Citibank NA* v. *Brown Shipley and Co Ltd*[133] by recognising that "there is in issue which of the innocent parties should bear the loss from a fraud", for all he was the saying was that, such has been the achievement of the law of contract over the 113 years between *Cundy* v. *Lindsay*[134] and *Citibank NA*, that it now offered him the possibility of doing the wrong thing knowing what he was doing whereas previously he could have fooled himself into thinking he was doing the right thing. Let us be clear; the problem of the allocation of loss in cases of personality mistake *cannot* be resolved but the loss merely allocated to one or other party,[135] or apportioned between both,[136] or shifted to some background insurance scheme.[137] But cutting through the ratiocination leaves the problem clear of the quite capricious distinctions which have been drawn, with their nevertheless real, and indefensible, consequences, and allows us to address practical measures which might deal with this problem.[138]

Perhaps the most irritating aspect is that it is clear warrant for the maintenance of the rigid distinction between law in theory and in practice that legitimates scholarship which is abstract in the bad sense and practice which is senseless. How can one distinguish *Ingram* v. *Little* from *Lewis* v. *Avery*? As one *cannot* do it on rational grounds, one is thrown back on such conjecture as that the court held the opinion that in the former case the sellers were two retired gentlewomen and in the latter a manifest idiot,[139] and I have had the benefit of having had this analysis conveyed to me many times by practising lawyers who go on to tell me that, in effect, there's more to law than one can find in books.[140] This criticism is hard to ignore because it is true, and will remain true so long as what is in the books is, to speak politely, at variance with reality, or, more accurately in cases like personality mistake, is utter rubbish.

When applied to what passes for the teaching of contract, socio-legal criticisms of the methodology of the classical law have led to exposures of the absurdities of the traditional contract syllabus[141] and of the distorted use of the textbook[142] that have led us to the position where, as I began this chapter by saying, there are excellent "alternative" textbooks now available which make the development of alternatives to that syllabus more easily possible.[143] I cannot improve on the statement of what is at issue here which has been given with sufficient force by Collins in the preface to the second edition of his book:

> Perhaps no other subject in the standard canon of legal education can claim such an august tradition, such rigour of analysis, and such sublime irrelevance, as the law of contract. The multitude of textbooks typically repeat an interpretation of the subject which has remained unaltered for a century or more in its categorisation and organisation of the legal materials. The latent values which inform these works include a priority attached to personal liberty, minimal regulation of market transactions, and a profound divide between private economic transactions and public control over the public order. This fidelity to nineteenth century *laissez faire* ideals, which is unmatched in other fields of legal studies, often remains concealed behind a presentation of the law which emphasises the formal, technical and ahistorical qualities of legal reasoning. The result of this fidelity to tradition is that students learn in their early years a misleading and almost entirely irrelevant set of rules. It is doubly misleading, for the values which support the law have altered, and the emphasis upon the formal qualities of legal reasoning tends to exclude any appreciation of how the law rests upon policy choices at all. The attempt to repeat the past guarantees the irrelevance of the subject, since it can have only rare practical

applications, because most contractual relations will be governed by different rules from those stated in the books.[144]

A response to Collins has been to say that the those who remain committed to the classical law are aware of its deficiencies and of the necessity of dealing with them. This no doubt is true of many, and one is at great pains to recognise the learning and subtlety of even, say, a Treitel. But the point is whether it is better to just go on patching up the classical law, to the point where the patches more than cover the entire original fabric, or to develop, in the interests of coherence and explanatory economy, the new theory for which Atiyah has called. I think it permissible to accept that enough evidence has been accumulated to force the discussion of this issue. But, adapting certain positions in the modern philosophy of science, I have earlier argued that, despite its manifest weaknesses, the classical law of contract will not be displaced until a compelling rival account of contract is developed.[145] In what constitutes its third distinctive feature, socio-legal scholarship is putting forward two such rival theories which have provoked sustained discussion.[146]

The first is the "welfarist critique" of classical law.[147] The argument is largely that of Friedmann and Atiyah, though developed at greater depth than in Friedmann and at a somewhat social theoretically more profound level than in Atiyah. It is in essence that the development of the welfare state imposes a collective character on contract that it did not possess in the liberal form which was the corollary of *laissez faire*. I have certain reservations but what might be said without passing a contentious judgement on the welfarist critique is that, in a sense, it does not get to the heart of the crucial issue in critique of classical contract. What is it about welfarism that makes it so difficult to contain within the framework of the classical law? If the broad answer is collective values, then the crucial question becomes one of showing why collective values are difficult to contain within that framework and what a law of contract able to adequately express those values would look like.

It is in the depth of attention that is being given to the development of the alternative law of contract that is required by the successful critique of the individualistic assumptions of classical contract, the legal corollary of the assumptions necessary for neo-classical economics, that British socio-legal analysis of contract is developing a fundamentally innovative position. This critique of individualistic assumptions has been broadened out into what Adams and Brownsword have called "the embryonic modern co-operative theory of contract".[148] and this co-operative theory promises, in my opinion, to be the successful rival to the classical law of contract. (Though I myself would persist in calling it a relational theory.) This theory is being developed in a number of ways, and many of the British socio-legal writers discussed in this chapter are making contributions. Its doctrinal relationship to classical contract,[149] its relationship to institutional[150] and game theoretic economics,[151] and its philosophical[152] underpinnings are presently being explored in (if I can be excused praise that refers to works of my own as well as others) highly stimulating papers. Instead of repeated piecemeal attempts to accommodate new evidence within what is becoming the predominantly *ad hoc* body of theory that is classical contract in the hands of its sophisticated practitioners, socio-legal contract is showing how a far more coherent and explanatorily economical rival theory to the classical law may be developed. Which of these rival theories should be adopted is entirely legitimately open to debate.[153] The point is that it *is* now open to debate: a novel position in the English law of contract.

Though I have not dwelt on the point in my attempt to confine this chapter to work done in the UK, it will have been manifest to the informed reader at many points in what has so far been said that the basic drive of the British socio-legal analysis of contract has lain in the development of positions originally developed in the USA. Even the theories discussed above display this characteristic, but not, I think, nearly to the same extent as the basic borrowing of the concept of non-use. The "welfarist critique" of the classical law has clear American precedents,[154] and the co-operative or relational theory itself is highly indebted to Ian Macneil's relational work - his first (1968!) casebook was called *Contracts: Instruments for Social Co-operation*.[155] However, the latter theory in particular is being developed in the UK in novel ways which are paralleled by, but not led by, contemporary American developments.[156] And it is at this point, where socio-legal analysis has won its independence from the classical law and is displaying at least quasi-sovereignty in relationship to America, that I believe that the British socio-legal analysis of contract can now properly be said to be making its own contribution.

Conclusion

Any evaluation of the, as it were, institutional position of the socio-legal analysis of contract must begin with a recognition of its continuing relative weakness. Of the British writers discussed in this chapter, almost all are personally known to me, many of them well, and whilst this may speak of a becoming gregariousness on my part, it also speaks of the rather limited number of those actively publishing work on the socio-legal analysis of contract. Nevertheless, I believe it indisputable that the volume of work is growing (albeit from a very small base), that the quality of that work is manifest, and that the work is reaching a wide audience. In sum, whilst I hope I am not deceiving myself, for I am not uninterested in the truthfulness of this belief, I believe that the position of socio-legal analysis within British and common law contract scholarship is rather healthy.

However, I conclude by returning to the beginning; if true this belief leads one to say that the major task of socio-legal analysis of contract is to expand and refashion the undergraduate teaching of contract, which remains, in my experience, often just a disgrace. Moving from credibility and perhaps even in limited areas dominance in the leading scholarship to obtaining a wide audience in undergraduate teaching is a leap. It has by no means been accomplished in the USA.[157] Leaving aside the highly creditable elements of the more sophisticated teaching of the broadly classical law, the flat recitation of silly rules does seem to have some sort of comforting effect on the mind of many law undergraduates which education in Britain now processes, and so appears, for indisputably important if not to my mind ultimately compelling reasons, an easier option when faced with the teaching of larger and poorer classes in shorter terms with fewer books and journals. It may be that the wider reception of the socio-legal analysis of contract is inhibited by the present social conditions of university teaching. If an appreciation of social context allows one to appreciate this, it is nonetheless a reflection which gives little comfort.*

* I should like to thank Hugh Beale, Roger Brownsword, Simon Deakin, Donald Harris, Andrew Harries, Richard Lewis, Willie Seal and Peter Vincent-Jones for their comments on this paper, many of which I have not taken on board as they, entirely legitimately, require substantial changes to my argument

Notes

1 H. Collins, *Law of Contract*, 2nd edn, London, Butterworths, 1994.

2 S. Wheeler and J. Shaw, *Contract Law*, Oxford, Oxford University Press, 1994.

3 The 1st edn (London, Weidenfeld and Nicolson, 1986) was much shorter at 209 pages and really was more of a monograph than a textbook. D. Campbell, 'Review Article on H. Collins, *The Law of Contract*' (1987) 21 *The Law Teacher* 212, 219. This quibble about length allows me to say that the 2nd edn of Collins was the first socio-legal *textbook* on contract and not to grant this honour to the excellent J. Tillotson, *Contract Law in Perspective*, 3rd edn, London, Cavendish Publishing, 1996 (1st edn 1981) which is of 272 pages in total and deals with many issues very briefly. This predeliction over length may well reflect that I have not thought sufficiently about what is needed in a good textbook.

4 J.N. Adams and R. Brownsword, *Understanding Contract Law*, 2nd edn, London, Fontana, 1994; Tillotson, *Contract Law in Perspective* and J. Wightman, *Contract: A Critical Commentary*, London, Pluto Press, 1996. I initially did not include Tillotson in this short list for the 3rd edn is tremendously disappointing and makes no effort to keep up with the scholarship.

5 J.N. Adams and R. Brownsword, *Key Issues in Contract*, London, Butterworths, 1995.

6 H. Beale *et al*, *Contract: Cases and Materials*, 3rd edn, London, Butterworths, 1995. I am grateful to Hugh Beale for letting me see the 3rd edn in proof.

7 I. Macneil, 'Review of H. Collins, *Law of Contract*'. (1987) 14 *Journal of Law and Society* 373.

8   D. Campbell, 'The Relational Constitution of the Discrete Contract,' in D. Campbell and P. Vincent-Jones, eds, *Contract and Economic Organisation: Socio-legal Initiatives*, Aldershot, Dartmouth, 1996, n 17.

9   Collins, *Law of Contract*, 1st edn, p 1.

10   *Ibid*, p. 203.

11   W. Friedman, *Law and Social Change in Contemporary Britain*, London, Stevens, 1951, ch 4.

12   W. Friedmann, *Law in a Changing Society*, London, Stevens, 1959, ch 4.

13   *Ibid*, pp. 93-4.

14   *Ibid*, pp. 94-5.

15   *Ibid*, p. 102.

16   *Ibid*, p. 124.

17   *Ibid*, p. 90.

18   W. Friedmann, *Law in Changing Society*, 2nd edn, Harmondsworth, Penguin, 1972, ch 4.

19   A.T. Denning, 'Preface,' in Friedmann, *Law and Social Change in Contemporary Britain*, pp. ix-x.

20   Of course, a limited number of socio-legal analyses of aspects of contract other than the basic nature of "modern" as opposed to "classical" law appeared during this time, eg the superb analysis of early mercantile law given in R.B. Ferguson, 'Legal Ideology and Commercial Interests: The Social Origins of the Commercial Law Codes' (1977) 4 *British Journal of Law and Society* 18 (and further pursued in R.B. Ferguson, 'Commercial Expectations and the Guarantee of the Law: Sales Transactions in Mid-nineteenth Century England,' in G.R Rubin and D. Sugarman, eds, *Law, Economy and Society 1750-1915: Essays in the History of the English Law*, Abingdon, 1984, pp. 192-208).

21   H. Beale and T. Dugdale, 'Contracts Between Businessmen: Planning and the Use of Contractual Remedies' (1975) 2 *British Journal of Law and Society* 45. I am aware from personal discussions that Hugh Beale is concerned that the extent and nature of "non-use" described in this paper has been overestimated by myself and others.

22   Eg R. Cranston, *Regulating Business: Law and Consumer Agencies*, London, Macmillan, 1979 and R.B. Ferguson, 'The Adjudication of Commercial Disputes and the Legal System in Modern England' (1980) 7 *British Journal of Law and Society* 141.

23   By contrast, this period was one of remarkable productivity in criminology and the extension of criminological work into the detail of the common criminal law and its operation, exemplified by the, to my mind, methodologically pathbreaking D.J. McBarnet, *Conviction: Law, the State and the Construction of Justice*, rev edn, London, Macmillan, 1983 and P. Carlen, *Magistrates' Justice*, Oxford, Martin Robertson, 1976.

24   A very marked exception to this is A.L. Stinchcombe, 'Contracts as Hierarchies,' in A.L. Stinchcombe and C.A. Heimer, *Organisation Theory and*

Project Management: Administering Uncertainty in Noweigan Offshore Oil, Oslo (Norway), Norweigan University Press, 1985, ch. 2.

25   The actual rules as opposed to what is taken to be their implementation and effect do not figure as such even in as fine a book as A. Podgorecki, *Law and Society*, London, Routledge, 1974. Podgorecki does devote chapter 9 of his discussion of the methodology of the sociology of law to the "Analysis of Legal Materials," but by this he means case files which can be used in the statistical analysis of dispute resolution procedures. Cases and statutes themselves do not figure. The authoritative survey by R. Tomasic, *The Sociology of Law*, London, Sage, 1985 concluded with an early and highly welcome insistence that "greater attention needs to be given to the form and content of legal rules as such" (*ibid*, p. 127). Roman Tomasic, however, has a first degree in law (as well as higher degrees in sociology) and indeed now is the author of leading Australian textbooks on company law.

26   Eg though Balibar must be credited with actually mentioning the employment contract in his discussion of wage-labour, he does so only to dismiss it as of no real importance: "Marx shows how the mechanism of capitalist production...produces the labourer's existence as an appendage of capital and makes the capitalist...capital's functionary. There is nothing individual about this connection [and] it is in consequence not a contract but "invisible threads" which bind the worker to the capitalist class". E. Balibar, 'On the Basic Concepts of Historical Materialism,' in L. Althusser and E. Balibar, *Reading 'Capital,'* London, New Left Books, 1970, p. 233. I myself am convinced that wage-labour is a system of exploitation but it is exploitation through a purportedly individual agreement and must be explained as such, and moving from a concrete contract to "invisible threads" (a typically Althusserian abuse of a quotation from Marx) is to move in the wrong direction, to absurdity and irrelevance.

27   It is much to be welcomed, then, that a survey of the now over 500 members of the Socio-Legal Studies Association shows that 30 per cent of the members of that Association are researching in "core areas" (as opposed to the 13 per cent shown in a comparable survey in 1974). Anon, 'New Trends in Research Interests of SLSA's Growing Membership' (Autumn 1995) 17 *Socio-Legal Newsletter* 1.

28   Eg K. Llewellyn, 'The Rule of Law in Our Case Law of Contract' (1938) 47 *Yale Law Journal* 1243: "it is not safe to reason about business cases from cases in which an uncle became interested in having his nephew see Europe, go to Yale, abstain from nicotine, or christen an infant heir 'Alvardus Torrington III'. And it may even be urged that safe conclusions as to business cases of the more ordinary variety cannot be derived from what courts or scholars rule about the idiosyncratic desires of one A to see one B climb a fifty foot greased flagpole or push a peanut across the Brooklyn Bridge".

29   A more understandable but no less regrettable failure to appreciate the significance for contract of institutional economics also denied British scholarship use of what, in my opinion, is a tremendous resource.

30   G. Gilmore, *The Death of Contract*, Columbus (USA), Ohio State University Press, 1974, p. 1. Gilmore's recognition of the strength of the non-use point is coupled with a frank declaration that socio-legal scholarship is completely uninteresting to him, so he will go on using the same old methods of legal scholarship. This academic arrogance is, in fact, rather touching, but that Gilmore's consequent account is rather nihilistic is hardly surprising as he has in this way ruled himself off from contributing in the terms of the scholarship that he himself starts by saying is most compelling.

31   C.J. Goetz and R.E. Scott, 'Principles of Relational Contracts' (1981) 67 *Virginia Law Review* 589.

32   V.P. Goldberg, 'The Law and Economics of Vertical Restrictions: A Relational Perspective' (1979) 58 *Texas Law Review* 91.

33   I.R. Macneil, 'The Many Futures of Contract' (1974) 47 *Southern California Law Review* 627. I have reviewed Macneil's work as a whole in D. Campbell, 'The Social Theory of Relational Contract: Macneil as the Modern Proudhon' (1990) 18 *International Journal of the Sociology of Law* 75. It is my opinion that it is urgent that a readily accessible compilation of Macneil's papers be brought out and it is hoped to do so early in 1997.

34   The titles of A. Fox, *Beyond Contract: Work, Power and Trust Relations*, London, Faber and Faber, 1974 or D.M. Beatty, 'Labour is not a Commodity,' in B.J. Reiter and J. Swan, *Studies in Contract Law*, Toronto (Canada), Butterworths, 1980, study 9 convey the message clearly.

35   Hugh Collins and Simon Deakin are amongst the latest representatives of this line.

36   O. Kahn-Freund, 'Introduction,' in K Renner, *The Institutions of Private Law and their Social Functions*, London, Routledge and Kegan Paul, 1949, pp. 1-43.

37   J.A.G. Griffith, *The Politics of the Judiciary*, 3rd edn, London, Fontana, 1985, ch. 3.

38   P.S. Atiyah, *Essays on Contract*, rev edn, Oxford, Clarendon Press, 1990.

39   D. Campbell, 'The Undeath of Contract: A Study in the Degeneration of a Research Programme' (1992) 22 *Hong Kong Law Journal* 28-41.

40   As I shall go on to say, Atiyah made his criticisms as early as 1961 in the first edition of his textbook, and so was writing at a time in which he actually contributed to the attack on the classical law in the US as well as Britain. Gilmore acknowledged the influence of the 2nd edn of Atiyah's textbook in *The Death of Contract*, p. 7 n. 7.

41   P.S. Atiyah, *An Introduction to the Law of Contract*, 5th edn, Oxford, Clarendon Press, 1995.

42   The 1st edn of *Understanding Contract Law* was published in 1987.

43   I am leaving aside the very fine and innovative attempt to integrate contract into a textbook statement of a general law of obligations made in P.J. Cooke and D.W. Oughton, *The Common Law of Obligations*, 2nd edn, London, Butterworths, 1993. I have noted the substantial influence of Atiyah on this

book in 'Review Article on P.J. Cooke and D.W. Oughton, *The Common Law of Obligations*' (1989) 23 *The Law Teacher* 334.

44   P.S. Atiyah, *An Introduction to the Law of Contract*, 5th edn, Oxford, Clarendon Press, 1961, ch. 25 and 2nd edn, 1971, ch. 25. Atiyah did not include this chapter in the 3rd edn (1981, pref) rather, I suspect, because he thought the welfarist argument was won and so the specific chapter arguing it was superfluous. In the 4th (1989) and 5th edns Atiyah has rather changed his mind about all this, in a way I will briefly discuss.

45   P.S. Atiyah, *The Rise and Fall of Freedom of Contract*, Oxford, Clarendon Press, 1979.

46   *Ibid*, pp. 778-80.

47   *Ibid*, vii. *The Rise and Fall* is prefaced with Keynes' aphorism from 'The End of *Laissez-faire*' that: "A study of the history of opinion is a necessary preliminary to the emancipation of the mind".

48   P.S. Atiyah, 'Freedom of Contract and the New Right,' in *idem*, *Essays on Contract*, ch. 12.

49   Campbell, 'The Undeath of Contract: A Study in the Degeneration of a Research Programme', 41-7. This trend continues to be described by his most recent work. Atiyah, *Introduction to the Law of Contract*, pp. 27-34.

50   The rest of this paragraph is based on Campbell, 'Review Article on H Collins, *The Law of Contract*' 215.

51   Atiyah, *The Rise and Fall of Freedom of Contract*, pp. 581-92.

52   *Ibid*, pp. 24, 572, 592.

53   P.S. Atiyah, *Law and Modern Society*, Oxford, Oxford University Press, pp. 74-7. Prior to his engagement with neo-classical economics, Atiyah's most sustained excursion into theory was into the philosophy of promising. *Idem*, *Promises, Morals and the Law*, Oxford, 1981.

54   An intellectually impressive but really quite extraordinary recent example of the type of historiography displayed in *The Rise and Fall* is J. Gordley, *the Philosophical Origins of Modern Contract Doctrine*, Oxford, Clarendon Press, 1991, in which great learning about legal history and extraordinary implausibility about the historical causality claimed are mixed in a most striking way.

55   J.C. Smith continues to be the exemplar. I have attempted to show this in 'The Undeath of Contract: A Study in the Degeneration of a Research Programme', 24-8 and the appearance of J.C. Smith, *The Law of Contract*, 2nd edn, London, Sweet and Maxwell, 1993 subsequent to my writing this paper this has given me no reason to change my opinion. Indeed, Smith's recent article on mistake, in which he is now going so far, though using circumlocutions that betray his amazement at his own daring, as to hazard that *Bell* v. *Lever Bros Ltd.* is a bad case, is just breathtaking in its wilful disregard of everything that is interesting in the present scholarship. J.C. Smith, 'Contracts - Mistake, Frustration and Implied Terms' (1994) 110 *Law Quarterly Review* 400. This piece is one of the relatively few new articles Treitel has thought fit to include

in the latest edition of his textbook. G.H. Treitel, *Law of Contract*, 9th edn, London, Sweet and Maxwell, 1995, p. 262 n. 1.

56   The most flexible tack taken is to add so many novel elements that one is left wondering just wherein lies the residual classical element of the classical law. Eg M.A. Eisenberg 'The Bargain Principle and Its Limits,' (1982) 95 *Harvard Law Review* 741 and M.J. Trebilcock, *The Limits of Freedom of Contract*, Cambridge (USA), Harvard University Press, 1993. A more principled, but very apparently less persuasive, line is the defence of the classical law pretty much as is. Eg R.E. Barnett, 'A Consent Theory of Contract' (1986) 86 *Columbia Law Review* 269 and C. Fried, *Contract as Promise: A Theory of Contractual Obligation*, Cambridge (USA), Harvard University Press, 1981.

57   G.C. Cheshire *et al*, *Law of Contract*, 12th edn, London, Butterworths, 1991.

58   Cooke and Oughton, *The Common Law of Obligations* and A.M. Tettenborn, *An Introduction to the Law of Obligations*, London, Butterworths, 1984.

59   P. Birks, *An Introduction to the Law of Restitution*, rev edn, Oxford, Clarendon Press, 1989; AS Burrows, *The Law of Restitution*, London, Butterworths, 1993 and A.M. Tettenborn, *Law of Restitution*, London, Cavendish Publishing, 1993. As I write, I learn that the forthcoming 1996 Annual Conference of the SPTL will contain a Specialist Subject Section on the 'Failure of Contracts' which, it would appear, will turn on the offering of a restitution-based alternative.

60   Professor Burrows is, for example, seeking to come to terms with the present confusions of exemplary damages during his current term as a Law Commissioner. His mind is commendably open on the line he should take and he has invited opinion in the normal fashion of the Law Commission and a discussion of his options took place under the auspices of the SPTL in July 1995. A. Burrows, 'Reforming Exemplary Damages: Expansion or Abolition?', paper given to an SPTL Seminar on 'Exceptional Measures of Damages'. All Souls College Oxford, July 1995. Very many erudite and interesting discussions of the possible restitutionary bases for an award of exemplary damages were given, but it would appear that no empirical inquiry into whether commercial parties wanted any such cause of action has been or will be undertaken.

61   I draw no distinction between "critical" and "socio-legal" studies other than that implied in the next footnote.

62   I am ignoring those writers who analyse contractual doctrine after the method broadly known in post-modern cultural theory as textual deconstruction. The postal rule seems to excite a peculiar fascination for these writers. C. Douzinas and R. Warrington, 'Posting the Law: Social Contracts and the Postal Rule's Grammatology' (1991) 4/11 *International Journal of Semiotics and Law* 115; S Gardner, 'Trashing with Trollope: A Deconstruction of the Postal Rule' (1992) 12 *Oxford Journal of Legal Studies* 178-93 and P. Goodrich, *Languages of the Law: From Logics of Memory to Nomadic Masks*, London, Weidenfeld and Nicolson, 1990, pp. 149-74. I am in no way wishing to open up a pointless demarcation dispute when I say that the interpretative

methods used in these and similar writings seem to owe much more to canons of literary criticism than to social science, and so I exclude them from this review of socio-legal analysis. This in itself is not meant to in any way disparage these often interesting contributions (eg C. Dalton, 'An Essay in the Deconstruction of Contract Doctrine' (1985) 94 *Yale Law Journal* 997,) though I perhaps should, in addition, make it clear that I myself find the characteristic methodological statements of post-modern literary criticism irrational and indeed ludicrous, not only in style but in content, and in complete contradiction of the, as I say, often highly interesting results.

63 Recently authoritatively reviewed in N. Duxbury, *Law, Economics and the Legacy of Chicago*, Hull, Hull University Law School, 1994.

64 R.A. Posner, *Economic Analysis of Law*, 4th edn, Boston (USA), Little, Brown and Co. 1992.

65 I have criticised what certainly used to be (it may still be, but it's hard to tell) Posner's main idea here, that the common law was "wealth maximising," in D. Campbell, 'Ayres versus Coase: An Attempt to Recover the Issue of Equality in Law and Economics' (1994) 21 *Journal of Law and Society* 445-9.

66 With Donald Harris, I have attempted to point up the differences by discussion of the specific issue of commercial impracticability in D. Campbell and D.R. Harris, 'Flexibility in Long-term Contractual Relationships: The Role of Co-operation' (1993) 20 *Journal of Law and Society* 171-2.

67 Eg, J.H. Barton, 'The Economic Basis of Damages for Breach of Contract' (1972) 1 *Journal of Legal Studies* 277 and A.M. Polinsky, 'Risk Sharing Through Breach of Contract Remedies' (1983) 12 *Journal of Legal Studies* 427.

68 Eg P.L. Joskow, 'Contract Duration and Relationship Specific Investments: Empirical Evidence from Coal Markets' (1987) 77 *American Economic Review* 168 and P.L. Joskow, 'The Performance of Long-term Contracts: Further Evidence from Coal Markets' (1990) 21 *Rand Journal of Economics* 251.

69 Eg J.R. Commons, *Institutional Economics*, New Brunswick (USA), Transaction Publishers, 1990.

70 Eg O.E. Williamson, *The Economic Institutions of Capitalism: Firms, Markets, Relational Contracting*, New York (USA), Free Press, 1985.

71 'Symposium on Post-Chicago Law and Economics' (1989) 65 *Chicago-Kent Law Review* 1 and 'Non-Posnerian Law and Economics Symposium' (1989) 12 *Hofstra Law Review* 193.

72 R.H. Coase, 'Coase on Posner on Coase' (1993) 149 *Journal of Institutional and Theoretical Economics* 96-8. I leave the reader to enjoy the prose of this article, but, as part of my attempt to proselytise, let me just quote one of Coase's other jokes. Having just exposed to his own satisfaction the utter impracticability of a tax regime designed to reduce pollution, whilst allowing its mathematical coherence given certain ridiculous assumptions, he concludes: "In my youth it was said that what was too silly to be said may be sung. In modern economics it may be put into mathematics". R.H. Coase,

'Notes on the Problem of Social Cost," in R.H. Coase, *The Firm, the Market and the Law*, Chicago (USA), University of Chicago Press, 1988, p. 185. Coase also knows a good joke when he sees one. R.H. Coase, 'The Lighthouse in Economics,' in R.H. Coase, *The Firm, the Market and the Law*, p. 213.

73   Campbell, 'Ayres versus Coase: An Attempt to Recover the Issue of Equality in Law and Economics.'

74   I am gratified that it is explicitly shared by S. Deakin *et al*, '"Trust" or Law? Towards an Integrated Theory of Contractual Relations Between Firms' (1994) 21 *Journal of Law and Society* 330. Something like the position informs the selection of material in Beale *et al*, *Contracts Cases and Materials*.

75   Eg R. Cranston, 'Creeping Economism: Some Thoughts on Law and Economics' (1977) 4 *British Journal of Law and Society* 103. The problem is, in fact, more acute in other areas than in respect of the common law of contract, for when Posner sees fit crassly to pronounce on more directly ethically sensitive issues such as adoption, it is hard not to be disgusted and enraged.

76   P. Gabel and J.M. Feinman, 'Contract Law as Ideology,' in D. Kairys, ed, *The Politics of Law: A Progressive Critique*, New York (USA), Pantheon Books, 1982, ch. 8.

77   Eg G Mather, *Government by Contract*, London, Institute for Economic Affairs, 1991. The British career of Cento Veljanovski is instructive in this respect. Between 1979 and 1989 and Veljanovski produced, under the auspices of the Centre for Socio-Legal Studies at the University of Oxford, very interesting works indeed, in contract and other areas, which promised to explore the possibilities of a productive engagement between socio-legal studies and new institutional economics, though the latter was always most preponderant. In 1989 Veljanovski left the Centre almost immediately to take up work as a consultant on deregulation to the telecommunications industry, and now produces work from which all trace of any such engagement has been expunged.

78   Eg C. Graham and T. Prosser, 'Privatising Nationalised Industries: Constitutional Issues and New Legal Techniques' (1987) 50 *Modern Law Review* 16 and C. Graham and T. Prosser, *Privatising Public Enterprises*, Oxford, Oxford University Press, 1991.

79   Eg P. Vincent-Jones and A. Harries, 'Limits of Contract in Internal CCT Transactions: A Comparative Study of Buildings Cleaning and Refuse collection in "Northern Metropolitan,"' in Campbell and Vincent Jones, eds, *Contract and Economic Organisation: Socio-legal Initiatives*, ch. 10.

80   D. Hughes, 'The Reorganisation of the NHS: The Rhetoric and the Reality of the Market' (1991) 54 *Modern Law Review* 88; D Hughes and R. Dingwall, 'Sir Henry Maine, Joseph Stalin and the Reorganisation of the National Health Service' (1990) 5 *Journal of Social Welfare Law* 296 and J. Michie, 'Institutional Aspects of Regulating the Private Sector,' in J. Groenewegen *et*

al, eds, *On Economic Institutions: Theory and Applications*, Aldershot, Edward Elgar, 1995, ch. 7.

81   Not thereby to approve, for the predominant view taken in the socio-legal scholarship clearly seems to be that the more "contractual" of these forms have led to a deterioration in the quality of transacting in the affected services. P. Vincent-Jones, 'The Limits of Near-contractual Governance: Local Authority Internal Trading Under CCT' (1994) 21 *Journal of Law and Society* 214; 'P. Vincent-Jones, 'The Limits of Contractual Order in Public Sector Transacting' (1994) 14 *Legal Studies* 364 and K. Walsh *et al*, 'Contracts for Public Services: A Comparative Perspective,' in Campbell and Vincent Jones, eds, *Contract and Economic Organisation: Socio-legal Initiatives*, ch. 11. On the other hand see P Fenn *et al*, 'Long-term Contracts in the Market for Health Care,' in Campbell and Vincent Jones, eds, *Contract and Economic Organisation: Socio-legal Initiatives*, ch. 8.

82   D. Hughes *et al*, 'Contracts in the NHS: Searching for a Model?' in Campbell and Vincent Jones, eds, *Contract and Economic Organisation: Socio-legal Initiatives*, ch 9.

83   Which is reaching vast proportions. The bibliography on contracting out/competititve tendering maintained by The Chartered Institute of Public Finance and Accountacy, for example, now runs to hundreds of items.

84   The ESRC Research Programme on Contracts and Competiton has funded research by K. Barker, M. Chalkley, J. Malcolmson and J. Montgomery of the University of Southampton on 'Contracting in the NHS;' by W. Bartlett, L. Harrison, C. Propper and D. Wilson of the University of Bristol on 'Providers, Purchasers and Contracts: The Economic Effects of Institutional Reform in the NHS;' by J. Broadbent and R. Laughlin of the University of Exeter and D. Shearn and H. Willig-Atherton of the University of Sheffield on 'Managing Financial Contracts in the Public Sector: A Comparative Analysis;' by N. Deaking and P. Spurgeon (originally with the late K. Walsh) of the University of Birmingham on 'Contracts and Competition in the Management of the Public Service Sector: A Comparative Study;' by R. Flynn, S. Pickard and G. Williams of the University of Salford on 'Contract Specification and Implementation in Community Health Services;' and by D. Hughes of the University of Swansea and J. McHale of the University of Manchester on 'Contracts in the NHS: The Regulation of an "Imposed" Market.' (Two other empirical projects seem to be of a merely applied nature.) A. Harries, W. Seal, P. Vincent-Jones and I have recently received an ESRC Research Grant for a project on 'Conflict and Co-operation in Contracting for Professional Services: A Comparative Study.'

85   This sense of "hybridity" is not the same as (though it overlaps) the most current use of that term, which is to capture a quality organisation, the structure of which provisionally must be described as somewhere between market and hierarchy. I am grateful to Peter Vincent-Jones for this observation, on which he is expanding in P. Vincent-Jones and A. Harries, 'Conflict and Co-operation in Local Authority Quasi-markets: The Hybrid Organisation of Internal Contracting Under CCT,' *Local Government Studies*,

forthcoming 1996. See n. 145 below for works on the more current sense of hybridity.

86   I. Culpitt, *Welfare and Citizenship: Beyond the Crisis of the Welfare State*, London, Sage, 1992; I. Harden, *The Contracting State*, Buckingham, Open University Press, 1992 and N. Lewis, *Choice and the Public Order: A Jurisprudence for Contemporary Politics*, London, Butterworths, forthcoming 1996.

87   Eg W.B. Seal, *Accounting,Management Control and Business Organisation*, Aldershot, Avebury Press, 1993 and W.B. Seal, 'Security Design, Incomplete Contracts and Relational Contracting: Implications for Accounting and Auditing,' *British Accounting Review*, forthcoming 1996.

88   S.N.S. Cheung, 'The Contractual Nature of the Firm' (1983) 26 *Journal of Law and Economics* 1; O. Hart and B. Hölmstrom, 'The Theory of Contracts,' in T. Bewley, ed, *Advances in Economic Theory*, Cambridge, Cambridge University Press, 1987, ch. 3 and J. Kornai, *The Socialist System: The Political Economy of Communism*, Oxford, Clarendon Press, 1992, ch. 21.

89   Eg M. Aoki, *The Co-operative Game Theory of the Firm*, Oxford, Clarendon Press, 1984; P. Armstrong, 'Contradiction and Social Dynamics in the Capitalist Agency Relationship' (1990) 15 *Accounting, Organisations and Society* 415 and Williamson, *The Economic Institutions of Capitalism: Firms, Markets, Relational Contracting*, ch. 12.

90   Guenther Teubner's work on contract (and company law) (eg G. Teubner, 'Piercing the Contractual Veil: Social Responsibility of Contractual Networks' in .T Wilhemsson, ed, *Perspectives of Critical Contract Law*, Aldershot, Dartmouth Publishing, 1993, pp. 211-38) would appear to be the leading example of such a development, for I am given to understand that this is a major contribution to systems theory. I am afraid that I cannot really pass judgment on this as, whilst I am able to grasp the thrust of Teubner's use of "autopoiesis" (G. Teubner, *Law as as Autopoietic System*, Oxford, Basil Blackwell, 1993) as a modern treatment of reflexivity after Beck (G. Teubner, 'Substantive and Reflexive Elements in Modern Law' (1983) 17 *Law and Society Review* 239), I am so utterly out of sympathy with what I am able to make of his views on systems (M. Hutter and G. Teubner, 'The Parasitic Role of Hybrids,' in Campbell and Vincent Jones, eds, *Contract and Economic Organisation: Socio-Legal Initiatives*, ch. 6) that I fear I am missing the point. Indeed, I am bound to confess to ennui when reading the later Habermas and the later Luhmann in general. For further references on the concept of hybridity on which Teubner is working see n. 145 below.

91   Civil obligations/remedies, commercial law and common law. With all respect to Mr Murray, the compiler of the directory, it would, in my opinion, be better to collect this data using a set list of subjects after the fashion of the Law and Society Association rather than by allowing members to identify their own research interests.

92   Socio-Legal Studies Association, *Directory of Members 1995*, London, Butterworths, 1995 (available only by private circulation).

93   Though one should be aware of the meeting of European critical contract scholars in 1992, the results of which were published in Wilhelmsson, ed, *Perspectives of Critical Contract Law.*

94   The papers are published in Campbell and Vincent-Jones, eds, *Contract and Economic Organisation: Socio-legal Initiatives.*

95   T. Weir, 'Review of H Collins, *Law of Contract*' (1986) 45 *Cambridge Law Journal* 503.

96   A.M. Tettenborn, 'Review of S. Wheeler and J. Shaw, *Contract Law*' (1995) 54 *Cambridge Law Journal* 212. In all fairness it must be said that Tettenborn's criticisms are directed at the approach to the subject and not at the author as was Weir's comments on Collins.

97   J. Beatson and D. Friedmann, 'From "Classical" to Modern Contract Law', in J. Beatson and D. Friedmann, eds, *Good Faith and Fault in Contract Law*, Oxford, Clarendon Press, 1995, ch. 1.

98   M.A. Eisenberg, 'Relational Contracts,' in Beatson and Friedmann, eds, *Good Faith and Fault in Contract Law*, p. 303.

99   E. McKendrick, 'The Regulation of Long-term Contracts in English Law,' in Beatson and Friedmann, eds, *Good Faith and Fault in Contract Law*, p. 308 n. 10.

100   *Ruxley Electronics and Constructions Ltd* v. *Fortsyth* [1995] 3 WLR 118 at 127 per Lord Mustill. Lord Mustill was given a push in this direction by the somewhat exasperated comment on the Court of Appeal decision in H Beale, 'Damages for Rebuilding' (1995) 111 *Law Quarterly Review* 54.

101   D. Harris *et al*, 'Contract Remedies and the Consumer Surplus' (1979) 95 *Law Quarterly Review* 581.

102   One hesitates to think of the costs occasioned by the adjudication of this matter - concerning £2500! - and wonders what price we pay for the slowness of the common law to change in this country.

103   S. Macaulay, 'Non-contractual Relations in Business: A Preliminary Study' (1963) 28 *American Sociological Review* 55. Strangely, Macaulay's other 1963 article to similar effect, 'The Use and Non-use of Contracts in the Manufacturing Industry' (1963) 9 *Practical Lawyer* 13 is widely neglected.

104   The major project now underway is the Wisconsin Business Disputes Group Project. M. Galanter *et al*, *The Transformation of American Business Disputing: A Sketch of the Wisconsin Project*, Dispute Processing Research Programme Working Paper DPRP 10-6, Madison (USA), Institute for Legal Studies, University of Wisconsin, 1991.

105   John Adams has recently indicated how his own earlier work on franchise contracts, guided by extensive practical experience of them, might be expanded into a socio-legal research programme in J. Adams, 'Franchising: The Draftsman's Contract,' in Campbell and Vincent Jones, eds, *Contract and Economic Organisation: Socio-legal Initiatives*, ch 1.

106   D. Yates, *Exclusion Clauses in Contracts*, 2nd edn London, Sweet and Maxwell, 1982, pp. 16-33 and D. Livermore, 'Exemption Clauses in Inter-business Contracts' [1986] *Journal of Business Law* 90, though conducted

with reference to Macaulay and Beale and Dugdale, are, as it were, applied analyses aimed at guiding business and governmental policies towards exclusion clauses. Yates has used his research to produce essentially a practitioner's handbook on exclusion clauses. D. Yates and A.J. Hawkins, *Standard Business Contracts: Exclusions and Related Devices*, London, Sweet and Maxwell, 1986. Livermore's work was conducted under the auspices of the Law Reform Commission for Tasmania, and led to a report which was presented to the Tasmanian parliament in 1983. J Livermore, *Exemption Clauses and Implied Obligations in Contracts*, Sydney (Australia), Law Book Company, 1986. N. Palmer, 'Great Art Living Dangerously: Legal and Empirical Issues in the Lending of Works of Art,' in R. Halson, ed, *Exploring the Boundaries of Contract*, Aldershot, Dartmouth, forthcoming 1996, ch. 6 has a similarly "applied" character. (I am grateful to Roger Halson for letting me see this work in proof.) This is not in any way to disparage these last three excellent empirical studies of which, as I will argue below, there should be many more conducted in relation to law reform.

107   Beale and Dugdale, 'Contracts Between Businessmen: Planning and the Use of Contractual Remedies.'

108   H. Beale *et al*, 'The Distribution of Cars: A Complex Contractual Technique' in D.R. Harris and D Tallon, eds, *Contract Law Today: Anglo-French Comparisons*, Oxford, Clarendon Press, 1989, pp. 301-34

109   T. Daintith, 'The Design and Performance of Long-term Contracts', in T. Daintith and G. Teubner, eds, *Contract and Organisation: Legal Analysis in the Light of Social and Economic Theory*, Berlin, De Gruyter, 1986, pp. 164-89. This paper was a, as it were, theoretical adjunct to work on primary commodities trading of a more applied nature which was variously published elsewhere. Daintith's later work on beer and petrol distribution was based on empirical material taken from official reports. T. Daintith, 'Vital Fluids: Beer and Petrol Distribution in English Law,' in C. Joerges, ed, *Franchising and the Law: Theoretical and Comparative Approaches in Europe and the United States*, Baden Baden (Germany), Nomos Verlagsgesellschaft, 1991, pp. 143-78.

110   R. Lewis, 'Contracts Between Businessmen: Reform of the Law of Firm Offers and an Empirical Study of the Tendering Practices in the Building Industry' (1982) 9 *Journal of Law and Society* 153. R. Lewis, 'Insurers' Agreements Not to Enforce Strict Legal Rights: Bargaining with Government and in the Shadow of the Law' (1985) 48 *Modern Law Review* 275 exposes the unacceptability of an unusual case of non-use but does not bring in any new empirical material.

111   S. Wheeler, *Reservation of Title Clauses* Oxford, Clarendon Press, 1991.

112   Adams and Brownsword, *Understanding Contract Law*, H. Beale, *Remedies for Breach of Contract*, London, Sweet and Maxwell, 1980, nb chs. 1, 10; D.R. Harris, *Remedies in Contract and Tort*, London, Weidenfeld and Nicolson, 1988, nb ch. 2 and Tillotson, *Contract Law in Perspective*, nb ch. 2.

113 D.R. Harris and CJ Veljanovski, 'Remedies Under Contract Law: Designing Rules to Facilitate Out-of-Court Settlements' (1983) 5 *Law and Policy Quarterly* 97.

114 These are the projects of B. Lyons, J. Mehta, C. Starmer and G. Thomas of the University of East Anglia on 'Testing Contract Theory' and S. Deakin, B. Evans, A. Hughes, C. Lane and F. Williamson of the University of Cambridge on 'Vertical Contracts, Incentives and Competition.' A collection of papers produced under the initiative, together with some works of other contributors working in the area whose work was not funded under the initiative, is to be published as S. Deakin and J. Michie, eds, *Contracts, Cooperation and Competitiveness*, forthcoming. Though I must stress again that it is a disappointed applicant who writes, from papers produced under the initiative which have led to draft chapters of this book it seems that though the work of Deakin and his colleagues seems of the highest interst, the work of Lyons and Mehta seems to add nothing but illustrative material,.

115 At the time of the writing of the 4th edn of Benjamin, A.G. Guest was made aware of Wheeler's work on *Romalpa* clauses, which showed that only 15% of *Romalpa* claims were partially, and only 5% wholly, successful. His response, in an otherwise wholly orthodox account emphasising the possibility of recovery, was to include token reference to "considerable difficulties...in attempting to enforce the [*Romalpa*] provision" which may arise "in practice". D. Campbell, 'Review of S. Wheeler, *Reservation of Title Clauses*' (1992) 19 *Journal of Law and Society* 492 n. 27.

116 Still the most compelling unpacking of the philosophical implications of this, as it were, realist criticism of contract doctrine, showing why the law in books just is not enough and the law in practice matters more, is that of Llewellyn. A short statement of the necessity for a "sociology of doctrine" insufficiently widely known to be worth mentioning here is to be found in KN Llewellyn, *The Common Law System in America*, Chicago, University of Chicago Press, 1989, sec 63. One does wonder how far many of the defenders of the *purely* doctrinal method realise that they are committed to the consequences of "validity" taken to their extreme by Kelsen? (whose "pure theory" Llewellyn thought "utterly sterile". K.N. Llewellyn, *Jurisprudence: Realism in Theory and Practice*, Chicago (USA), University of Chicago Press, 1962, p. 356.) In my opinion, Llewellyn's view of legal reasoning - in which the notion of situation-sense plays a key, if difficult, role - remains also the best indication of the jurisprudence that would follow from acceptance of the socio-legal critique of the classical law K.N. Llewellyn, *The Common Law Tradition - Deciding Appeals*, Boston (USA), Little, Brown and Co, 1960, pp. 121-57. For a recent attempt to use situation sense to elucidate default rules in contract see T.D. Rakoff, in Beatson and Friedmann, eds, *Good Faith and Fault in Contract Law*, 1995, ch. 9.

117 The law of personality mistake is given in a distilled form which concentrates its atmosphere of absurdity to a point where one is forced to realise that it

should be appreciated more as an artistic effect rather than a theoretical doctrine in Smith, *The Law of Contract*, ch. 6.

118 [1972] 1 QB 198.

119 *Cundy* v. *Lindsay* (1878) 3 App Cas 459.

120 [1961] 1 QB 31.

121 I am grateful to Kevin Dowd for this information.

122 Law Reform Committee, *Transfer of Title to Chattels*, 12th Report, Cmnd 2958 (1966).

123 P.S. Atiyah, 'Law Reform Committee: Twelfth Report' (1966) 29 *Modern Law Review* 541.

124 *Idem, Sale of Goods*, 9th edn, London, Pitman Publishing, 1995, p. 364.

125 Of course, the same can be said of other areas and the, I think the right word is scandal, is even more naked in tort. D. Harris *et al*, *Compensation and Support for Illness and Injury*, Oxford, Clarendon Press, 1984. Atiyah himself has, of course, done a great deal to make the position clear in tort as well as contract. P.S. Atiyah, *Accidents, Compensation and the Law*, 5th edn, London, Butterworths, 1993.

126 The source of empirical evidence guiding English contract adjudication is the past experience of the better, indeed not unusually excellent, judges of the commercial court, but that this is itself an adequate source of such evidence could not, I think, dare be maintained in public debate, though it undoubtedly is this belief, which is hugely influential within the business and legal establishment, on which the whole system of contract adjudication presently rests.

127 P.S. Atiyah, *From Principle to Pragmatism: Changes in the Function of the Judicial Process and the Law*, Oxford, Clarendon Press, 1978; P.S. Atiyah and R.S. Summers, *Form and Substance in Anglo-American Law: A Comparative Study of Legal Reasoning, Legal Theory and Legal Institutions*, Oxford, Clarendon Press, 1987 and P.S. Atiyah, *Pragmatism and Theory in English Law*, London, Stevens, 1987.

128 Campbell, 'The Undeath of Contract: A Study in the Degeneration of a Research Programme', 24-41.

129 T. Wilhemsson, 'Questions for a Critical Contract Law - and a Contradictory Answer: Contract as Social Co-operation', in Wilhelmsson, ed, *Perspectives of Critical Contract Law*, p. 9.

130 Eg on the case which so confirmed Atiyah's (then) 20 years of argument, R. Halson, 'Sailors, sub-contractors and Consideration' (1990) 106 *Law Quarterly Review* 183; R. Halson, 'The Modification of Contractual Obligations' (1991) 44 *Current Legal Problems* 111 and R Halson, 'Opportunism, Economic Duress and Contractual Modification' (1991) 107 *Law Quarterly Review* 649.

131 The work of Roger Brownsword (often with John Adams) is exemplary in this respect. Merely on consideration, one can point to J.N. Adams and R. Brownsword, 'Contract, Consideration and the Critical Path' (1990) 53

Modern Law Review 536 and R. Brownsword, 'Static and Dynamic Market Individualism', in Halson, ed, *Exploring the Boundaries of Contract*, ch 3.

132   Campbell, 'The Relational Constitution of the Discrete Contract,' pp. 47-8.

133   [1991] 2 All ER 690.

134   (1878) 3 App Cas 459. *Cundy* v. *Lindsay* remained the most influential authority cited in *Citibank NA*.

135   Law Reform Committee, *Transfer of Title to Chattels*, para 15.

136   *Ingram* v. *Little* at 73-4 per Devlin LJ.

137   G. Battersby, 'The Sale of Stolen Goods: A Dilemma for the Law' (1991) 54 *Modern Law Review* 752.

138   I Davies, 'Wrongful Disposition of Motor Vehicles in England: A US Certificate of Title Solution?' (1994) 23 *Anglo-American Law Review* 460.

139   B. Jackson, *Law, Fact and Narrative Coherence*, Liverpool, Deborah Charles, 1988, pp. 105-6.

140   I must convey my particular thanks to Mark Conway in this respect, who at least has the good grace typically to "water" down his advice.

141   R. Lewis, 'Criticisms of the Traditional Contract Course' ((1982) 16 *The Law Teacher* 111.

142   Adams and Brownsword, *Understanding Contract Law*.

143   An early but still highly interesting specific alternative course was set out in J. Tillotson, 'Anyone for Contract?' (1976) 10 *Journal of the Association of Law Teachers* 135.

144   Collins, *The Law of Contract*, p. xi.

145   Campbell, 'The Undeath of Contract: A Study in the Degeneration of a Research Programme.'

146   A similar conclusion seems to be being reached in Brownsword, 'The Limits of Freedom of Contract and the Limits of Contract Theory' (1995) 22 *Journal of Law and Society* 259 and Brownsword, 'Static and Dynamic Market Individualism', p. 63. A third position, heavily drawing on Weber to develop a theory of business transacting, has been set out in P. Vincent-Jones, 'Contract as Business Transactions: A Socio-legal Analysis' (1989) 16 *Journal of Law and Society* 166. This is undoubtedly the most conceptually clear general theory of business transacting presently available, but, whilst of great general interest, it really is acceptable in detail only to the extent that one can accept ideal-typical methodology and has not as yet generated a sustained discussion. A fourth position is to examine the properties of, as it were, "hybrid" governance structures, for the forms of governance much socio-legal work is revealing are hybrid in that they can be described neither as contracts nor as hierarchies. Hutter and Teubner, 'The Parasitic Role of Hybrids', W.W. Powell, 'Neither Market nor Hierarchy: Network Forms of Organisation' (1990) 295; Stinchcombe, 'Contracts as Hierarchical Documents', G. Teubner, 'Beyond Contract and Organisation? The External Liability of Franchising Systems in German Law', in Joerges, ed, *Franchising and the Law; Theoretical and Comparative Approaches in Europe and the United States*, pp. 105-32I; G. .Teubner, 'The Many-headed Hydra: Networks as Higher

Order Collective Actors,' in J. Mcahaery *et al*, eds, *Corporate Control and Accountability: Changing Structures and the Dynamics of Regulation*, Oxford, Clarendon Press, 1993, ch.3; Teubner, 'Piercing the Contractual Veil: Social Responsibility of Contractual Networks;' H.B. Thorelli, 'Networks; Between Markets and Hierarchies' (1986) 7 *Strategic Management Journal* 37; O.E. Williamson, *Markets and Hierarchies: Analysis and Antitrust Immplications*, New York (USA), Free Press, 1975 and O.E. Williamson, 'Comparative Economic Organisation: The Analysis of Discrete Structural Alternatives' (1991) 36 *Administrative Science Quarterly* 269. I am grateful to Peter Vincent-Jones for assistance in the compilation of this set of references. I have relegated these works to a footnote because, at the moment, the use of "hybridity" in these works seems to me to register serious problems in our understanding of "market" and "hierarchy" rather than to advance what is yet a coherent theory of hybridity itself. Accordingly, the *contractual* implications of these works is at present but vestigially developed.

147   Adams and Brownsword, 'The Ideologies of Contract' (1987) 7 *Legal Studies* 207; Adams and Brownsword, *Understanding Contract Law*, ch. 8; R Brownsword, 'Liberalism and the Law of Contract,' in R. Bellamy, ed, *Liberalism and Recent Legal and Social Philosophy*, Stuttgart (Germany), Franz Steiner, pp.86-100; R. Brownsword, 'The Philosophy of Welfarism and Its Emergence in the Modern English Law of Contract', in R. Brownsword *et al*, eds, *Welfarism in Contract Law*, Aldershot, Dartmouth, 1994, ch. 2; Brownsword, 'Static and Dynamic Market Individualism', Collins, *Law of Contract*, 1st edn and Cooke and Oughton, *The Common Law of Obligations*, chs. 1-4. One should also note the contribution to the welfarist critique made by T. Wilhelmsson of the University of Helsinki, whose own work speaks to the principal concerns of European, including English, critical contract scholarship. T. Wilhemsson, *Critical Studies in Private Law*, Dordrecht (Netherlands) Kluwer, 1992; T. Wilhelmsson, 'Questions for a Critical Contract Law - and a Contradictory Answer: Contract as Social Co-operation', T. Wilhelmsson, 'The Philosophy of Welfarism and Its Emergence in Modern Scandinavian Contract Law,' in Brownsword *et al*, eds, *Welfarism in Contract Law*, ch. 3 and T. Wilhelmsson, *Social Contract Law and European Integration*, Aldershot, Dartmouth, 1995.

148   Adams and Brownsword, *Key Issues in Contract*, p. 299.

149   Campbell, 'The Relational Constitution of the Discrete Contract', in Campbell and Vincent-Jones, eds, *Contract and Economic Organisation*, ch. 3; Collins, 'Contract and Legal Theory', in W. Twining, ed, *Legal Theory and Common Law*, Oxford, Basil Blackwell, 1986, ch 8; Collins, *Law of Contract*, ch. 13; H. Collins, 'Competing Norms of Contractual Behaviour', in Campbell and Vincent-Jones, eds, *Contract and Economic Organisation: Socio-Legal Initiatives*, ch. 4 and Wilhemsson, 'Questions for a Critical Contract Law - and a Contradictory Answer: Contract as Social Co-operation'.

150   D. Campbell, 'Introduction,' in D. Campbell and S. Clay, *Long-term Contracting: A Bibliography and Review of the Litrerature*, Oxford, Centre for

Socio-legal Studies, 1995, pp. 3-38; Campbell and Harris, 'Flexibility in Long-term Contracting: The Role of Co-operation', Deakin *et al*, '"Trust" or Law? Towards an Integrated Theory of Contractual Relations Between Firms', and S. Deakin and F. Wilkinson, 'Contracts, Co-operation and Trust: The Role of the Institutional Framework,' in Campbell and Vincent-Jones, eds, *Contract and Economic Organisation*, ch. 5; C. Lane, 'The Social Constitution of Supplier Relations in Britain and Germany: An Institutionalist Analysis,' in R. Whitley *et al*, eds, *The Changing European Firm*, London, Routledge, forthcoming 1995.

151   D.G. Baird, 'Self-interest and Co-operation in Long-term Contracts' (1990) 19 *Journal of Legal Studies* 583; D.G. Baird *et al*, *Game Theory and the Law*, Cambridge (USA), Harvard University Press, 1994, ch. 3 and M. Hviid, 'Relational Contracts and Repeated Games,' in Campbell and Vincent-Jones, eds, *Contract and Economic Organisation: Socio-legal Initiatives*, ch. 7.

152   Adams and Brownsword, *Key Issues in Contract*, pt 3; R. Brownsword, 'From Co-operative Contracting to a Contract of Co-operation,' in Campbell and Vincent-Jones, eds, *Contract and Economic Organisation: Socio-legal Initiatives*, ch. 2; R. Brownsword, 'Towards a Rational Law of Contract,' in Wilhelmsson, ed, *Perspective of Critical Contract Law*, pp. 241-72 and R. Brownsword, '"Good Faith in Contracts" Revisited' *Current Legal Problems*, forthcoming 1996. I am grateful to Roger Brownsword for letting me see this paper in draft.

153   So F.M.B. Reynolds, 'Review of H Collins' *Law of Contract* (1986) 102 *Law Quarterly Review* 628 does not - despite some cutting remarks - set out to wreck Collins but in effect to argue that the difficulty of introducing a new theory of contract is greater than the difficulty of sophisticatedly refining the classical law to deal with the problems posed by new developments, which he does not deny.

154   M. Cohen, 'The Basis of Contract' (1933) 44 *Harvard Law Review* 553; L.M. Friedman, *Contract Law in America: A Social and Economic Case Study*, Madison (USA), University of Wisconsin Press, 1965; H.C. Havighurst, *The Nature of Private Contract*, Evanston (USA), Northwestern University Press, 1961; M.J. Horwitz, *The Transformation of American Law 19780-1860*, Cambridge (USA), Harvard University Press, 1977; M.J. Horwitz, *The Transformation of American Law 1870-1960*, New York (USA), Oxford University Press, 1992; J.W. Hurst, *Law and the Conditions of Freedom in the Nineteenth Century United States*, Madison (USA), University of Wisconsin Press, 1956; A.A. Leff, 'Contract as Thing' (1970) 19 *American University Law Review* 131; B. Mensch, 'Freedom of Contract as Ideology' (1981) 33 *Stanford Law Review* 753 and M. Rehbinder, 'Status, Contract and the Welfare State' (1971) 23 *Stanford Law Review* 941. The point is even more strongly taken if we regard Wolfgang Friedmann, who was at Columbia when he wrote *Law in a Changing Society*, as in this sense American.

155   I.R. Macneil, *Contracts: Instruments for Social Co-operation. East Africa*, South Hackensack (USA), Fred B Rothman and Co, 1968.

156   Particularly intersting contributions to the, as it were, secondary literature
        based on the work of Goetz and Scott, Goldberg, Macaulay and particularly
        Macneil include J.M. Feinman, 'Critical Approaches to Contract Law' (1983)
        30 *UCLA Law Review* 829; J.M. Feinman, 'The Significance of Contract
        Theory' (1990) 58 *University of Cincinnatti Law Review* 1283; J.M. Feinman,
        'The Last Promissory Estoppel Article' (1992) 61 *Fordham Law Review* 303;
        R.W. Gordon, 'Macaulay, Macneil and the Discovery of Solidarity and Power
        in Contract Law' [1985] *Wisconsin Law Review* 565; G. Gottlieb,
        'Relationism: Legal Theory for a Relational Society' (1983) 50 *University of
        Chicago Law Review* 567; K.A. Strasser, 'Contract's "Many Futures" After
        Death: Unanswered Questions of Scope and Purpose' (1981) 32 *South
        Carolina Law Review* 501; W Whitford, 'Ian Macneil's Contribution to
        Contract Scholarship' [1985] *Wisconsin Law Review* 545 and B. Yngvennson,
        'Re-examining Continuing Relations and the Law' [1985] *Wisconsin Law
        Review* 623. A dissenting view is provided by R.E. Barnett, 'Conflicting
        Visions: A Critique of Ian Macneil's Relational Theory of Contract' (1992) 78
        Virginia Law Review 1175.

157   Ian Macneil has told me that his pathbreaking cases and materials have been
        used in only 4 courses of contract classes anywhere in the US.

13 Company Law

SALLY WHEELER

> Students of company law ......complain that the subject is technical,
> difficult and dull...The reason can.......be found in the fact that
> company law as an academic discipline boasts no long and
> distinguished pedigree.......[C]ompany lawyers lack an intellectual
> tradition which places the particular rules and doctrines of discipline
> within a broader theoretical framework.[1]

Introduction

This chapter examines the possibilities for a socio-legal contribution to a
theoretical framework for company law. In order to assess this possibility
it is necessary to examine the position taken by doctrinal law towards the
corporate form and its ramifications and then to consider the nature of
socio-legal studies and how its interaction with existing extra-legal
influences may help reshape the legal model of the company or at least
formulate a coherent challenge to the doctrinal model. The corporate
structure is the most important forum for economic association offered by
the state and as such it has considerable impact on our daily lives. Its very
existence throws up a number of questions about the nature and scope of
corporate power from within the corporation, such as, who should exercise
control - the capital providers or those who perform management functions
- which groups can be considered to have a stake in the profits made by
the corporation; and should ownership be the primary qualification for a
stake? This in turn leads into questions of a much broader nature: how the
company derives its power from the state and how that power should be
exercised and regulated. There are issues about whether there should be
special responsibilities incumbent upon large transnational companies, the
desirability and effectiveness of states co-operating together to produce
supra-national legal models to facilitate international business and how the

state is reclaiming the corporate form from the private sector to use it for its own political ends.[2] The important contemporary nature of these questions is illustrated by the debates about privatization in the UK[3] and the attempts to create fledging market economies in Central and Eastern Europe following the dismemberment of the old state-trading economies.[4] Some of these issues go beyond what is conventionally defined as company law and shade into questions about the organization and regulation of enterprise. Much is made in this chapter of the failure of the purveyors of company law within the law school to look outside law for analytical inspiration which would yield a wider conception of the "company". However constraints of space limit this chapter to looking at facets of this narrow picture rather than exploring the broader considerations thrown up by "enterprise" as a general term.

As the quotation above indicates, the law school model of the corporate structure largely eschewed these questions as being extra-legal, and instead favoured a micro-legal model which basks in its own technical rigor.[5] The law school's approach to company law and its response to research provides an important background context to the type of socio-legal research that has been conducted and the climate in which it has been carried out. This refusal to acknowledge the connections that need to be made between the legal model and its multifarious background of economic, political, anthropological and social adjuncts is made even more surprising once we take into account the historical development of the corporate structure.[6] Specific contributions which relate the historical evolution of the corporate structure to its present picture are considered below.

Adopting at this stage a generalist perspective, it is possible to see that the corporate form evolved surrounded by contemporary comment focusing on the concerns outlined above, from the perspectives also outlined above. For example, Adam Smith made the point in 1776 that if the corporate form were allowed to develop such that there was a separation between the functions of ownership and management, those with ownership interests may find that they lacked control over management.[7] It is important not to take Smith out of context;[8] his primary concern was the role that corporations would play in the market economy. However that does not make his concern with the role of management any the less relevant. Marshall, who wrote having the benefit of seeing the successful integration of the corporation into a system of market economy, voiced the same concern.[9] This position, as elaborated upon by empirical evidence provided courtesy of Berle and Means[10] in the first instance, has become the *locus classicus* of the mangeralist school, but it appears to have impacted little upon the law school model. The question of shareholder monitoring of management in particular has arrived back on the lawyer's agenda in recent years through the corporate governance debate but, as this contribution will show, law's response has been once again to retreat behind its technical facade and to refuse to deal with the correctness or appropriateness of the assumptions that underpin its model of the corporation.

The Micro-Legal Model: Its Deficiencies And Its Detractors

The legal model is typically set out in the following way. There is the company with its separate legal personality[11] and within the company there are two power blocks comprising the shareholders and the board of directors. The directors' obligations in relation to the company and society in general are regulated by a series of statutory requirements,[12] and the imposition of fiduciary[13] and common law duties.[14] Management power over the company is exercised by the directors,[15] with shareholders able to intervene only in situations where they have expressly reserved the power to do so in the company's constitution or where a special resolution of shareholders is required by statute.[16] Shareholders can either enforce duties owed to the company by directors through use of the mechanisms for minority protection[17] or through the statutory provisions which allow them to appoint[18] and dismiss directors.[19] In both these cases the axiom of power between the management function and the investor function is the company in general meeting at which majority rule prevails.[20] This reflects the focus and approach of the leading company law texts[21] and is reinforced by the findings of a survey carried out by the SPTL Company Law Group.[22] While not pretending to be in any way a comprehensive survey[23] of law school practice, it did indicate that topics such as the function of company law, industrial democracy and social responsibility received sparse attention. The perspective offered in teaching was identified by the respondents as being primarily "black letter".

The model of the company offered here is primarily that of the public company, although the shareholders' meeting and the notion of drawing a distinction between management and shareholders are less relevant for private companies and small businessess.[24] This focus is somewhat unfortunate for two reasons. First, public companies have consistently accounted for around 1 per cent of companies on the Register of Companies.[25] Second, even as a model of the public company it is seriously flawed. If at this point we look simply at the assumptions on which it is built and leave aside for the time being ideas that it should contain, we can see that it is premised on the notion that shareholders want to and indeed can assert control over management in areas such as the development of strategic policy through the forum of the shareholders' meeting and that the meeting backed up by the sanctions of duties is sufficient for monitoring and controlling the activities of management.[26] In fact, the shareholders who are in a position to wield power are likely to be institutional investors and any interventions they make will be as the result of the requirements of their own agenda.[27] We know relatively little about the issues that would help us to build a more coherent model of the company with this as our starting point, such as knowledge of the information flows[28] within the company between both tiers of management,[29] and between management and shareholders, and knowledge about who managers are and the goals of management, assuming those goals are not the same as those of the capital provider ie profit.[30] Such knowledge would help us to assess which organ of the company and which actors were in actual control of strategic policy development.

There are a number of inter-related reasons behind the obsession within the law school with this neat doctrinal model and the exposition of the rules contained within it. The first is that there is a perception that a majority of students who study company law only do so in the belief that it will assist them in a professional career and that this belief should be satisfied and indeed fostered for cohorts of students to come by expounding the 'rules' and information that will be useful in practice.[31] The fallacy of this position is exposed by the findings of empirical studies that have been done on the activities of actors in the corporate sector to the effect that legal rules are unlikely to be of very much more than background use or interest to any successful lawyer.[32] The second reason follows inexorably from the first: given the intellectual luggage that is brought to the study of company law, there are thought to be few texts which can, for teaching purposes, offer an acceptable alternative paradigm to the one outlined above. In the past the most obvious alternative has been offered by Tom Hadden, *Company Law and Capitalism*[33] a contribution to the Law in Context Series. Hadden examines the corporate form as a tool in the organization of capitalism and consequently he eschews placing material in traditional doctrinal categories for an analysis based on the different rules applied by the state to small businesses and quoted companies. Whether or not this type of approach can be seen as assisting the development of a theoretical framework depends on the view taken of contextual work. Hadden's text has been described as atheoretical[34] but if we understand theory as having a more instrumentalist function[35] then there would seem to be no reason why Hadden is not offering a theoretical perspective. Hadden's contribution reflects the concerns that were current in the 1970s and it is in need of updating to include new socio-economic paradigms . A more recent entrant to the market would appear to provide just that - John Parkinson's book *Corporate Power and Responsibility.*[36] Parkinson's book has two themes: the controls offered by company law on the power of management and secondly the reorientation of companies, through legal regulation, away from the traditional maximization of return to shareholders towards assumptions of social responsibility. The following extract from an unnecessarily ungenerous review of Parkinson's book illustrates the contingency of these two reasons given above for the law schools' position.[37]

The book has strengths and weaknesses. The major strength is that it is an excellent ....exposition of much of the theoretical literature relevant to corporate governance and corporate social responsibility and, as such, it should prove invaluable to students who wish to understand the policy arguments underlying much of corporate law......However I think that the book is likely to be less useful to students as a description of existing legal rules......
[there then follows criticism of the way in which the book deals with the *ultra vires* doctrine].......... This brief description is not particularly useful to those ignorant of the history of the *ultra vires* doctrine and ignores some of the problems of interpretation posed by the provisions of the Companies Act 1989.

Writers about company law tend to concentrate their efforts on the law in the books and when they use contextual material it tends to derive from disciplines such as economics or history, rather than from empirical data. Empirical data for academic lawyers often derives only from the facts of cases. Contextual material is valuable for an understanding of many of the policy issues underlying company law and [this book] provides a large amount of useful contextual material *but* [emphasis added] the book would have been improved by the addition of specific concrete examples of the problems raised. ....I would have preferred more detailed fact-stuff about the sort of activities which executives should avoid and which shareholders should not be able to approve.

Essentially this position can be summarized as follows: students of company law need to be taught about legal rules in abstract from their position in a wider sphere; a text which does not do this is unlikely to find itself included on a company law course as anything other than "further reading". This is because material which presents a theoretical model or questions the value of the doctrinal approach is seen as a poor substitute for useful practical rules and examples of applications of those rules. This fate apparently has befallen Hadden's text[38] and will presumably befall Parkinson's thought provoking and powerful analysis.

Defining And Locating Socio-Legal Studies

Both Hadden's model and Parkinson's model are considered too radical for inclusion in the law school curriculum. There is an indivisible link between the profile that a subject is given at undergraduate level and the development of research in that area. It is unlikely that the type of climate in which company law is studied will persuade many students that it is an appropriate subject for study at a theory-orientated academic level as opposed to a practitioner service level. In reality far from undertaking radical reappraisals of the corporation both Hadden and Parkinson are offering contributions from the law in context arm of the socio-legal studies movement.[39] In other words they are providing us with a frame of reference for the legal model from within law itself; they are not drawing on the methodologies and approaches of other disciplines and applying them to the legal model as more theoretical legal studies would. In its desire to impact upon the legal world, socio-legal studies has adopted for itself, it seems, a very wide spectrum of inclusion from law in context work to the sociology of law.[40]   The only common feature of this community is that it is not doctrinal law. The idea of identifying a discipline solely by resort to a negative is not unproblematic. Without stronger identifying features of its own, it remains to be seen how much further socio-legal studies can develop as a recognized and sustainable *modus operandi*.[41] Socio-legal studies allows us, perhaps requires us, to package the legal model as definable in its own terms (in the way that the model of the corporation is set out above) and then to critique that model drawing eclectically on ideas from other disciplines primarily but not exclusively from within the social science and humanities fields.[42] The *socio* in socio-legal studies is there to demonstrate the inter-disciplinary character of the inquiry.

This idea of packaging and digesting law rather than problematising or even rationalising it is not without its critics.[43] It is what seems to lie behind the charge that socio-legal studies has been too reactive to a policy audience[44] and has accepted without question conventional legal categories.[45] However as long as any inquiry offers a critique to those categories by means of ideas imported from outside it would appear to escape this charge. Those areas that are caught squarely within it are what can be termed "legal impact studies"[46] which assess for example the effectiveness of a particular piece of law or legal practice and in doing so have focused on empirical inquiry at the expense of also situating impact within a theoretical frame.[47] However there has to be some confrontation with doctrine on its own terms, some reference to what Cotterrell describes as "categories established in lawyers' law"[48] in order to create a new model through which socio-legal studies can have some impact. To avoid confrontation with doctrine is to cede primacy to it.[49] A lack of engagement with doctrine allows the law school gatekeepers to exclude socio-legal studies because it is not asking questions in a language which law identifies as its language.

Influences For Socio-Legal Work
Law and Economics

The quotation from the book review set out above indicated that the ideas of history and economics were inappropriate forces for the law school consumer to be exposed to. This section examines briefly some of the 'pump-priming' work that has been undertaken in relation to the corporate structure exclusively in disciplines complementary to law. What is meant by this is scholarship which can be built upon in order to examine the corporate form from a socio-legal perspective but which of itself does not engage with legal doctrine or structures in a way which can be considered socio-legal. The primary field in which this has occurred is economics and in particular economic analysis of the reasons why some transactions are organized within firms. Firm in this context is not simply shorthand for company but is being used to denote the fact that economic activity is being conducted at a level above that of an individual entrepreneur. This would bring workers co-operatives and partnerships within the matrix of a firm.[50] However the discussion here of the economic approaches to the firm is confined to their impact on company law. Whereas company law conventionally takes as its starting point entrepreneurial activity, and the desire to support this activity through the structures of limited liability, economists begin with the transaction or exchange as their unit of analysis.[51] The starting point for this type of analysis is the work of Coase[52] who explained the existence of the firm as a way of reducing transaction costs that parties would otherwise incur if they organized the same transactions discretely through the market. By transaction costs Coase meant the costs of bargaining such as those that occur in the sale and purchase of commodities and the recruitment and subsequent employment of specialized labour.[53]

Coase's explanation of the firm has spawned two related schools of thought - institutional and neoclassical approaches. A detailed examination of the coherence of these approaches in terms of their underlying economics and the differences between them would be out of place here and is in any event available elsewhere.[54] What is significant is the challenge that these theories present to the legal model of the firm and the way in which socio-legal work through law and economics and other approaches has answered or can answer the challenge. The major point of these economic theories of the firm for the legal model of the company is that they have no interest in the company as a separate entity or in the idea that duties are owed to the company by directors. For them the central issue is the relationship between the actors involved in the firm. These relationships are relationships of contract, only some of which take the form of private law contract, eg employer and employee.The remainder are exchange relationships only in the very broad sense of actors entering voluntarily into a relationship which has expectations of co-operation on both sides. The firm viewed in this way is nothing more than a web or nexus of contracts. The relationship between management and shareholders is one of principal and agent in which shareholders are the principal. Management behaviour results in agency costs[55] (the cost to shareholders of management decisions which do not enhance their welfare and the cost of imposing controls on management to deal with any divergence from the principal of maximization of profit for shareholder welfare) which shareholders seek to minimize by negotiating the most efficient package they can from the controls available ie the various legal rules and other internal checks on management. The market price for shares in any particular company reflects the agency costs current in that firm and the efficiency of its governance structures. External to the controls that shareholders impose are the controls imposed by the market. Management inefficiency, that is, the failure to maximize return to shareholders, results in a low share price compared to asset value and this should attract takeover bids which will result in the replacement of management.[56] This process is otherwise known as the market for corporate control.[57]

This model of the firm contains as many assumptions that are open to criticism as the law school model. For example it assumes that all shareholders have equal access to information, that they have invested for a commonality of reasons and that their ultimate remedy - the resort to the market - is a feasible one. In other words their shares are assumed to be alienable in the event of obvious management inefficiency. The market for corporate control itself can be criticized for encouraging managers to indulge in short-termism (the taking of profits now rather than investing for future development) possibly to the detriment of shareholder interests in the long run. This having been said, the position taken by the economic theories of the firm demands a re-appraisal by lawyers of the reasons why legal rules exist and whether there is any need for mandatory rules if the focus of rules is not the welfare of the company as an abstract entity but the position adopted by shareholders to control management.[58] It provides the background for a study of takeover practice, both bids and defences.[59] In the USA the economic theories of the firm have generated a considerable amount of activity within the law school,[60] from a variety of perspectives.[61] Interestingly the effect of the economic theories of the firm on law school scholarship is vilified in some quarters for curtailing debate on alternative models of the corporation, notably those which favour a wider conception of those interested in the corporation over and above shareholders.[62] However in the UK the challenge of economic theory to the law school model of the corporation has scarcely been recognized let alone accused of restricting the agenda of debate.[63]

Managerialism

The economic theories of the firm and the law school model of the company make the same assumption about the characteristics of shareholders: that they are in a position to influence or bargain with management. This runs counter to the findings of Berle and Means who by examining the top 200 USA companies in 1929 and finding that the power to select the board of directors was increasingly the province of management not shareholders concluded that there was a separation of ownership on the one hand and control through management on the other. The answer to the apparent supervision of management problem which arises from this situation was according to Berle and Means control through fiduciary duties owed by management which company law currently constitutes as mediated through the company. It is a matter of debate whether Berle and Means embraced the concept of the market for corporate control as an alternative means of control for shareholders.[64] As has already pointed out, the law school model is in a pre-Berle and Means state. The one engagement with their work that has been generated by the law school is the empirical work undertaken by Farrar[65] who examined the control position in the top ten UK companies and 60 New Zealand companies using the categories of control defined by Berle and Means. Farrar's findings were that there was a high incidence of institutional investment with individual holdings rarely exceeding 5 per cent, that directors had low personal holdings and that more companies were in minority control than management control.

Farrar's testing of the Berle and Means model does provide something of a contextual challenge to the law school model but as a matter of theoretical development it raises more questions than it answers. First as a simple matter of mechanics its application of the Berle and Means model rather than a reappraisal leaves unanswered questions of the accuracy of the numerical thresholds used by Berle and Means to indicate control.[66] Second it presupposes that control is something that can be tested numerically against the ability to perform certain functions within the corporation and that the assessment of an economic relationship through the matrix of legal phenomena like the pattern of share ownership is unproblematic.[67] In some ways this criticism is a natural consequence of the existence of the share as evidence of ownership with the share being defined as an interest in profits and the company as a separate entity consisting of an aggregation of all the assets. The significance of the share is something which has not been ignored by marxist analyses of the corporation. For some this involves a retreat into history to explain the development of the share as personalty rather than as realty as marking the beginning of the conception of the company as a separate legal space from its members.[68] For others the separateness of the corporate entity is explained by asserting the appropriation of employee labour to it. This has also been explained by a feminist critique of the corporation namely that through the corporation's insistence that management accept the corporation's practices both moral and political produces an effect on the lives of management's families who offer support to them in pursuit of their personal goals as mediated through the goals of the corporation. The lives of these family members become reflections of the corporations' moral and political order.[69]Other empirical analyses of corporate ownership have suggested that the organizational forum[70] in which the firm exists, by which is meant the position of firm in relation to the activities and structures of competitors in the field, are just as significant for determining structures of control as the ownership of shares.[71] Third, Farrar's research recognized that there was a considerable presence of institutional shareholders. Once we recognize the reality of institutional investment we need to re-examine the Berle and Means model. It proceeds on the assumption that the separation of ownership and control can be justified on the basis of specialization of management and the existence of duties owed by management. Once there is within the corporation a body of shareholders with considerable knowledge of the market and appropriate experience of corporate performance indicators, even if their individual shareholdings fall below that required for control, it is the case that their presence may allow for control through a "constellation of interests":[72] shareholders who can identify each other and who, taken collectively, are too powerful for the board to ignore. This leads into questions about the level of involvement of institutional investors within the governance of the corporation that actually occurs and what level it is reasonable to expect and what type of governance structures could best give effect to their involvement.

Corporate Governance

The growth of institutional investment with the demands it is perceived to make on management leading to allegations of short-termism and the spectacular corporate collapses of the late 1980s have been the impetus behind the interest in the 1990s in corporate governance. In fact there has been a general interest in issues of governance and accountability in relation to a wide variety of organizational forms. The constraints of space dictate that only the UK response to this in relation to companies can be looked at, although the 'corporate governance problem' is by no means confined to the UK.[73] In the UK this interest culminated in the Cadbury Report[74] published in 1992. The Report was commissioned by the private sector - the Financial Reporting Council, the London Stock Exchange and the accounting profession. The Report has two main concerns:[75] the provision of information to shareholders and checks on the activities of directors through the more extensive use of non-executive directors. It consists of a combination of suggestions, exhortations and recommendations which are in the form of a voluntary code of best practice. The report recommends that all listed companies comply with its recommendations and non-listed companies are encouraged to comply.

Interaction between the voluntary nature of the code and the discipline of the market occurs through the London Stock Exchange requirement that as a condition of continued listing, companies provide an annual statement indicating the level of compliance with the code and reasons for any non-compliance.[76] This disclosure will allow the market to decide whether in the context of each company the level of compliance is appropriate and to reflect this in the market price.[77] Presumably a pure managerialist approach would support this type of corporate governance structure as appropriate to control management but would question whether they should be mandatory in nature.[78] The non-mandatory nature of the controls and the involvement of the market makes this form of corporate governance more acceptable within the confines of the economic theories of the firm because at least it assumes that shareholders can select their own package of controls. However it is still a long way from the classical agency picture presented by Fama and Jenson[79] of the board monitoring management and shareholders resorting to the market as a last resort alternative to the break down of internal controls.

Reflected in the recommendations of the Code is the assumption that major shareholders want and will use greater information; for example the inclusion of balance sheet information in interim reports and an assessment by boards of directors of the company's financial position in the annual report[80] are recommended and the idea that company strategies should be communicated to major shareholders is endorsed. Active ownership of shares is encouraged through the use of voting rights at shareholder meetings, positive interest in the composition of boards and regular contact with senior executives to exchange views and information on company performance. It is by no means clear that institutional investors have in place the co-ordinating strategies to use this information.[81] There is evidence from the USA to support the idea that shareholder activism is on the increase[82] but this picture has not yet emerged in the UK where the prevailing culture has been, until now, one of non-participation.[83] It may be that the Cadbury Code will provide the impetus for co-ordination. Alternatively it may be that this strategy for corporate governance does not provide sufficient financial incentives to be attractive.[84] These are issues still to be explored. The existence of these governance measures changes the primacy accorded within the doctrinal model to fiduciary duties as a control mechanism and alters the presentation of the power balance between shareholders and directors. Although the provision of information to *all* shareholders is one of the main planks of the Cadbury Report what has hitherto received little comment is the privileged access to information it suggests for "major" (ie institutional) shareholders. The shareholders' meeting and annual reports are it seems no longer going to be the sole vehicles for conveying information to all shareholders. Some by virtue of the size of their stake will be allowed access to greater knowledge about strategic planning. This alters radically the idea that all shareholders, outside of any extra rights attached to shares or otherwise conferred by the company's constitution, are equal.

Boards of directors in the UK are often made up of executive directors which as representatives of management are unlikely to offer a very effective monitoring in relation to the activities of that group. To combat this the Cadbury Report suggests that every listed company should have on its board at least three non-executives directors[85] whose "calibre .... should be such that their views will carry significant weight in the board's decisions".[86] At least two of these directors should also be "free from any business and other relationships which would inevitably interfere with the exercise of their independent judgment".[87] It is envisaged that non-executive directors will be appointed to sub-board structures such as the audit committee and the remuneration committee. The report assumes that a distinction can be made between the role of management and the monitoring of management in the form of internal structure and that there is sufficient skill and talent available to supply every listed company with three non-executive directors without the system becoming so worn down with inter-locking and reciprocal appointments as to render it nonsensical. Non-executive directors have been seen in some quarters as an ineffective monitoring device because of the difficulties of freeing themselves from loyalties felt to the chairman who appointed them and of conceiving of monitoring as anything more stringent than they would wish to endure themselves in their own management roles.[88] This raises the question of how little we know not only about the activities of non-executive directors but the operation of boards of directors in general; for example, we have no idea of the frameworks and the decision-making culture within which these people operate, of the values that are put upon consensus and consultation. There is a literature which is beginning to develop, inspired

293

both by the requirements of legal doctrine[89] and the perspectives of management and sociology,[90] on conceptions of organizations and power which examines empirically the effectiveness of the current arrangements for corporate governance. These are small scale studies and there is much further work to be done.

(Re)Inventing Paradigms For The Company

The approach to corporate governance set out above is evidence that a very particular model of the company is currently being employed and perpetuated through structures such as the Cadbury Report, namely a property rights approach. Those who commissioned the Cadbury report, the recommendations of the report and the beneficiaries of the report either reflect or stand to gain from promoting the rights of property owners within the corporation. As Charkham[91] points out "corporate governance is set within the framework of its political and social history and attitudes". The current political climate[92] is one which does not recognize interests in corporations beyond that of property rights through share ownership.[93] The Cadbury Committee saw its remit as being one which was confined to the relationship between shareholders and management in the context of a unitary board structure[94] and hence there was no question that disclosure of a wider range of the company's activities (eg environmental impact assessment) should be made to a wider class of stakeholders such as employers and the public in general.[95] Governance is seen as an issue relating only to profit maximization. In the main, the law school approach has been to acquiesce in this, by offering comment which builds on the values expressed in the report,[96] and to leave aside what is meant by the whole concept of governance. It is of course possible to put a wider framework on corporate governance to reflect the presence of other interested parties and wider concerns outside the matrix of property rights. To the extent that this has been done within the law school it has generally been at the level of a plea for corporate governance to reflect "wider public interest" without necessarily suggesting a specific agenda.[97] There are a number of directions in which company law can move to provide this agenda. One is to consider the position of other stakeholders in the corporation such as employees and creditors. Another is to assess the company as being too economically powerful and socially intrusive for regulation to be left largely as a matter of property rights,[98] and thus we have to offer alternative strategies for corporate control and accountability. This may involve creating models of corporate social responsibility or considering what would constitute ethical behaviour by a company. Recent years have seen the emergence of business ethics as a field of study in its own right[99] but the majority of published research in the area ranging from the practical to the theoretical has been produced by philosophers and business sociologists. Whereas corporate social responsibility calls upon companies to address specific problems, business ethics looks more generally towards the adoption of a value framework[100] for the making of decisions[101] often from a Utilitarian standpoint. This type of approach offers a new way of evaluating and analysing the prescriptions of statutory and voluntary codes and judicial decisions about behaviour within and by the company. Alternatively it may involve reconceiving the type of institution a company is and bringing about a consequent reorientation of the explanation of corporate power in terms of, for example, bureaucracy. The divorce from a property rights driven conception of the company and a move towards a wider public interest model fits neatly with the idea of the separate personality of the company as distinct from a share in its profits.[102] To illustrate and to explain what adopting this wider framework of corporate governance would mean for company law this essay will look at just two areas: worker participation and the construction of the company as a bureaucracy. The link between these two areas is drawn by the considerable literature which construes the company as a private government and then goes on to question the company's approach to issues of social justice.[103]

The legislative history of worker participation in the UK is well documented[104] and to this should be added the developments in the European context which have pushed it back onto the agenda. Having successfully resisted[105] moves to force it to adopt a more European style of governance[106] for companies the UK now faces indirect introduction of worker participation through works councils.[107] The question of worker participation involves issues that are outside the definition given to company law in this essay. For example the whole approach to harmonisation within the EC, and issues that might more appropriately be situated within industrial relations such as whether participation in the corporate policy formulation process enhances or detracts from collective bargaining are beyond the scope of this essay. However some questions impinge directly on the model of corporate governance adopted for the company. One of the difficulties of considering employees as stakeholders in the company and entitled to rights of participation alongside the holders of property rights is that within the disciplinary remit of law there is relatively little knowledge about how this impacts on decision-making even in jurisdictions where it has been common for some time. Teubner[108] asserts that the distribution of power within the company, its 'goal structure' and the relationship between capital and labour will all be changed, but this is based upon studies which, in the main, describe the potentiality of the various models rather than offer assessments of their effectiveness. Outside law there is a developing literature which is increasingly critical of the benefits that occur to employees and indeed to society at large through wider governance structures. For example participation structures can be used to enable better communication of management problems to workers, problems which then become problems of the "enterprise" because management power is diffused and participation structures can impose or presume a false community of interests among different groups of workers who in actuality have little in common.[109] Socio-legal studies can offer an empirically informed assessment of the impact of different legal structures and its links with policy formulators can put the whole issue of wider governance more firmly on the agenda in the age of accountability, which until now, in the context of company law in the UK, has centred on accountability to a relatively small and privileged group.

The idea of companies as bureaucratic structures can be pursued at two different levels. On one level it provides a critique of corporate power and as such it appears to be a static model. The seminal work in this area is that of Frug[110] who argues that there has been a failure of the models that are supposed to control management discretion; in his terms formalism (agency theory and managerialism), expertise of management, judicial review (ie corporate litigation in the form of derivative actions) and the market. In this sense Frug is the classic anti-managerialist.[111] What separates him from the anti-managerialists is that he then goes on to suggest at the level of ideology that a failure to realise the inadequacy of the controls on bureaucracy is a serious limit on the power of democracy. This invites us to consider both the justifications of and the demands for regulation of corporate power. By constructing the company as a bureaucracy Frug can place corporations and corporate power on the same level in society as public organisations and government and demand from them all the same level of control and accountability.

What Frug does not provide us with is any indication of how we can call the company a bureaucracy or as encompassing bureaucratic processes; in other words, what common features do the two structures display? It is a consideration of this which moves us to another level within the bureaucracy paradigm. According to Weber[112] bureaucratisation achieves the rationalisation of activities through introducing predictability of actions, the control of arbitrary behaviour (which is Frug's concern) and makes possible cost and benefit analysis. This fits with the goal structure of a corporate organisation. What is more debateable is how organisations achieve this structure. One view is that they do so by resorting to a discourse of power and control which separates and isolates participants and allows the producers of administrative discourse to claim for their utterances the status of "serious speech acts" and institutional justification for their claims to truth.[113] On another it is driven forward by a series of voluntary agreements amongst individuals which reflect a process of negotiation to accommodate interests.[114] Contained within this second view with its dependency on contract is the approach of institutional economists to the theory of the firm. For both of these approaches to bureaucracy, and more broadly, organisations hierarchy is crucial, their divergence occurs when considering how that hierarchy is produced and maintained.

The beginning of a socio-legal inquiry in this area is once again current governance structures and their contribution to the production and maintainence of hierarchy. This could be expanded to look at the extent that horizontal structures with the values of co-operation also exist within the company.[115] An important facet of organisation studies literature is the idenification and impact of what is called imprinting.[116] This looks at how the characteristics of each organisation in areas such as identity of workforce imprints onto its founding structure. The issues arising from the adoption of works councils after company formation would provide an interesting comparison to this. On a more micro-level this could be extended to look at the historic position of particular groups within the organisation and whether changes in the governance structure would alter their position.[117]

Conclusions

What this chapter has attempted to show is the bankruptcy of the legal model ringfenced as it is by the supposed requirements of the practice community. It ignores a wide range of influences which would, if taken into account, give it a radically different shape. It has also shown that to date there is relatively little socio-legal scholarship to fill this void but through identifying some of these influences and considering what questions result it is possible to construct a research agenda for socio-legal studies scholars.

Notes

1   M.Stokes "Company Law and Legal Theory" in *Legal Theory and Common Law* (ed) W Twining (1986) Basil Blackwell p155.

2   See I Thynne "The Incorporated Company as an Instrument of Governance: A Quest for Comparative Understanding" (1994) 7 *Governance: An International J of Policy and Admin* 59.

3   See D Marsh "Privatisation under Mrs Thatcher: A Review of the Literature" (1991) 69 *Public Admin* 549 and D Swann "Privatisation, deregulation and the New Right" in G Jordan and N Ashford (eds) *Public Policy and the Impact of the New Right* 1993 Pinter London 120.

4   There is now a vast amount of literature available on this; for a review see S Wheeler (ed) *The Law of the Business Enterprise* 1994 OUP Oxford 44-47.

5   See for example the comments of D Kelly on the desire of lawyers to construct their inquiry as an exclusively narrow legal one, D Kelly "Review of a Sourcebook of Company Law by Harry Rajak", *The Law Teacher* 24 (1990) 329 at 331.

6   The origins of the corporate form can be traced back to the middle ages (see Scott *The Constitution and Finance of English, Scottish and Irish Joint Stock Companies to 1720,* Cambridge 1909-12) although incorporation was not generally available until the Companies Registration and Regulation Act 1844 and limited liability was not available until the Limited Liability Act of 1856. Interestingly limited liability arrived rather earlier in the United States, see *Spear* v *Grant* (1819) 16 Mass 9, 12 and Livermore "Unlimited Liability in Early American Corporations" (1935) 43 *J of Pol Econ* 674. Nineteenth century supporters of the corporate structure spent considerable time in the shadows of the effects of the South Sea Bubble, see Patterson and Reiffen "The Effect of the Bubble Act on the Market for Joint Stock Shares" (1990) 50 *J of Econ Hist* 163 and Neal *The Rise of Financial Capitalism* Cambridge 1990.

7   See A Smith *The Wealth of Nations* Book V (Everyman Library edn) and Williams *The Emergence of the Theory of the Firm* 1978 London chapter 2

8   On the dangers of doing this see D Campbell "Adam Smith, Farrar on Company Law and the Economics of the Corporation" *Anglo-American Law Review* 19 (1990) 185.

9   See Marshall *Principles of Economics* (8th ed) Macmillan London 1920 and D Schrader *The Corporation as Anomaly* CUP Cambridge 1993.

10   *The Modern Corporation and Private Property* New York 1933.

11   See note 15 infra.

12   See for example CA 1985 sec 234 which dictates that a directors' report must be appended to the annual accounts of a company and CA 1985 sec 317 which requires directors to disclose interests in contracts to the board of directors.

13   For example directors owe a fiduciary duty to the company not to make a profit from their office, see for example *Regal Hastings* v *Gulliver* [1967] 2 AC 134.

14   This is generally referred to as the duty of skill and care, for a precise judicial formulation see *Re City Equitable Fire Ins* [1925] Ch 407 as refined by the judgement of Hoffmann LJ in *Re D'Jan* [1993] BCC 646.

15   Authorities such as *Automatic Self-Cleansing Filter Syndicate Co Ltd* v *Cunningham* [1906] 2 Ch 34 and *Shaw* v *Shaw* [1935] 2 KB 113 make it clear that a company is a separate entity from its shareholders and that directors owe their duties to the company and not to shareholders.

16   See Art 70 of Table A of the CA 1985 which describes the business of the company as being managed by the directors subject to the provisions of the Companies Act, the company's constitution and any special resolution passed by the shareholders. The adoption of Table A is not obligatory but in the absence of any specially drafted articles CA 1985 sec 8(2) would invoke Table A as the company's articles of association.

17   These mechanisms are found in the so-called rule in *Foss* v *Harbottle* (1843) 2 Hare 461, CA 1985 459 and IA 1986 sec 122(1)(g).

18   CA 1985 sec 292.

19   CA 1985 sec 303 deals with removal. See also CA 1985 sec 318 and sec 319 on the regulation the contracts of service of directors.

20   The break on the principle that the decisions of shareholders are governed by majority rule is that they must act '*bona fide* in the best interests of the company', see *Greenhalgh* v *Arderne Cinemas* [1951] Ch 286 per Evershed MR at 291.

21   These are taken to be Sealey, *Cases and Materials in Company Law* (1992) 5th Ed Butterworths London, Gower, *Principles of Modern Company Law* (1992) 5th Ed Sweet and Maxwell, London and Farrar, Furey and Hannigan, *Farrar's Company Law* (1991) 3rd Ed Butterworths London. Some may question the inclusion of Farrar as a conventional text but while it does contain some background material drawn principally from economics it presents a mainly doctrinal legal picture while not giving that material a new organisational slant or perspective.

22   This is written up as I Snaith "Company Law on Degree Courses: Survey Report" (1990) 11 *Company Lawyer* 177.

23   The survey received 27 responses which was calculated to be a response rate of 38.1 per cent.

24   Despite the huge amount of literature available on small businesses from both sociology and economics much of it empirically informed, see for example *Deciphering the Enterprise Culture: Entrepreneurship, Petty Capitalism and the Restructuring of Britain* ed R Burrows 1991 Routledge London and *Entrepreneurship and the New Firm* D Storey 1982 Croom Helm London, it has made little impact on the law school. The two exceptions to this are the now rather dated text by Chesterman; M Chesterman *Small Businesses* 1982 Sweet and Maxwell London and the work done by Freedman as a result of an ESRC Grant supported by the DTI amongst others; J Freedman "Small Businesses and the Corporate Form: Burden or Privilege (1994) 57 *MLR* 555.

25   This information is taken from the DTI publication *Companies In* which shows that for the years 1983-93 1% was the average figure.

26   Or at least if the weakness of the meeting as an event where interaction above the level of rhetoric is unlikely to take place is recognised then there is little interest in putting forward ideas for reform and development, see Gower *Principles* p514-516. A populist agenda for reform is the subject of Butcher's contribution "Reform of the General Meetings" to *Corporate Governance Corporate Control* (eds Sheikh and Rees (eds) Cavendish London 1995.

27   See P Davies "Institutional Investors: A UK View" (1991) 57 *Brooklyn Law Rev* 129 and *Creative Tensions* NAPF London 1990. *Creative Tensions* in particular is an informative and interesting perspective on the positions taken by institutional investors.

28   See the judgement of Turner J in *R* v *P&O European Ferries (Dover) Ltd* (1991) 93 Crim App R 73. A knowledge of the process by which information could and should be transmitted in corporations is essential for a finding of corporate manslaughter. The only work of real depth that has been carried out in this area has been done from primarily a criminal law perpective, see C Wells *Corporations and Criminal Responsibility* OUP Oxford 1993.

29   See however M Parker "Working Together, Working Apart: management culture in a manufacturing firm" (1995) *Soc Rev* 518.

30   As to whether the assumption that a capital provider has as his sole goal profit when that capital provider is a firm owner in the form of an owner-controlled small business see A Gibb and L Davies "In Pursuit of Frameworks for the Development of Growth of the Small Business" (1990-91) 9 *Int Small Bus J* 15 at p20.

31   See A Hicks "Introducing Modern Company Law The Life of a Company" (1994) 28 *The Law Teacher* 138 at 139 where the need to illustrate the "realities of practice" is stressed. Here Hicks expressly disavows that he is advocating a link between teaching which "illustrates the realities of practice" and vocational training for practising lawyers but that instead he sees the "realities of practice" as necessary to assisting the "*theoretical* [emphasis added] study of company law". The differences between our positions centres around the use of the word *theory*. In my view the type of theory that Hicks and others who operate at this level are offering is not legal theory or socio-legal theory but mere technical rigour which the extract from Stokes which begins this chapter so rightly criticises. Hicks' disavowal of the link between this sort of approach and vocational training for lawyers is thrown somewhat into doubt by his contribution to the SPTL Reporter, "Legal Practice is an Academic Matter" (1995) 10 *SPTL Reporter* 6 where he bemoans what he sees as the denigration of the production of practice-orientated material. Hicks' position in this respect is admirably critiqued by T Bradney in "They Teach You Nothing Useful ...." (1995) 11 *SPTL Reporter* 17.

32   There are a wide variety of sources that can be drawn upon for accounts of what lawyers do, see for example D McBarnet, "Law and Capital: The Role of Legal Form and Legal Actors" *IJSl* 12 (1984) 223, S Wheeler "Lawyers and Commercial Disputes" (1991) 18 *JLS* 241, C Campbell "Lawyers and their Public" in N MacCormick (ed) *Lawyers and their Social Setting* (1976) Green Edinburgh p209, and R Goode "The Teaching and Application of Fundamental Concepts of Commercial Law" *The Law Teacher* 25 (1991) 200 at 202. A general overview of the type of functions that lawyers fulfil as opposed to specific examples of lawyers' work is provided by I Ramsey "What do lawyers do? Reflections on the Market for Lawyers" *IJSL* 21 (1993) 355, esp p359-363.

33   (1977) Weidenfeld and Nicolson, London.

34   See "Changing Company Law" C Bradley and J Freedman (1990) 53 *MLR* 397 at 399.

35   The following is a comment by Teubner on the role of theory, "For all Savigny's and Gierke's grandiose schemes for the autonomy and reality of the legal person, for all the novelty value of the 'enterprise *per/se*, separation of property and control and 'private government', theory has always had to leave the 'invention' of regulatory patterns to legal practice. The real business of theory is not to come up with specific proposals for regulation but to construct legal reality in another way. The challenge which confronts theory and which also imposes its limitations on it, is to develop a new perspective on what constitutes a corporation." G Teubner *Law as an Autopoietic System* (1993) Basil Blackwell Oxford at p126.

36   OUP Oxford 1993.

37   C Bradley, "Corporate Power and Control in the 1990's: The Transnational Dimension" *OJLS* 15 (1995) 269 at p272-3. For a more appreciative review see C Riley in *NILQ* 45 (1994) 228.

38   See SPTL survey supra n22 where Hadden's text was mentioned as being course material, recommended or additional reading on only 3.7% of the questionaire responses.

39   Movement is my own choice of an "umbrella " term because it emphasisies for me the idea of ongoing progression and development. For others socio-legal studies is an approach, see H Genn and M Partington *Socio-legal Studies: A Review by the ESRC* an unpublished paper delivered at the ESRC conference in April 1993 or a discipline see P Thomas "Socio-Legal Studies in the UK" in F Bruinsma (ed) *Precaire Waarden, Liber Amicorum Voor Por. Mr A A G Peters* 1994 Gouda Quint Netherlands.

40   Indeed this broad inclusive categorisation is now given quasi-institutional force in the ESRC Review of Socio-Legal Studies of May 1994.

41   See for example the pessimistic view of the future for the American Critical Legal Studies movement put forward by Goodrich. British socio-legal studies would appear to share one if not two of the characteristics he identifies. The first is that it is defined by negation - "the most that can be said is that the strategy of self-identification pursued by the movement ......is predicted upon a species of negation or denial: the critics cluster around a series of portenteous negations: they do not believe in objectivity, (semantic) determinancy or neutrality as attributes of legal judgement" (p310) and the second is the marginality that American Critical Studies has experienced in relation to (p304) whole areas of the law school curriculam This is true of socio-legal studies vis the impact in areas such as property law, European Law in addition to company law to give but a few examples, P Goodrich "Sleeping with the Enemy: An Essay on the Politics of Critical Legal Studies in America" in J Leonard (ed) *Legal Studies as Cultural Studies* (1995) State Univ of New York Press, Albany 299.

42   Scott classifies socio-legal studies, along with interestingly enough biotechnology, as inter-disciplinary and then defines this as the "[presupposition of] the existence of conventional disciplines shaped by scientific affinities and policed by scientific communities......[which] uses components of these disciplines as pre-fabricated elements within larger or more novel scientific structures." Scott *The Meanings of Mass Higher Education* Open Univ Press, Milton Keynes 1995 p149.

43   See for example M Salter "On the idea of a legal world" (1994) 1 *International Journal of the Legal Profession* 283 at 289f.

44   The proximity of socio-legal studies to the policy audience is the basis of the criticisms that are levelled at it as a methodology by R Cotterrell in *Law's Community* OUP 1995 esp chap 14. With respect it appears from the type of literature that Cotterrell makes reference to in other work (see n48 below) and his reference in *Community* to "social studies of law" which are apparently distinct from socio-legal studies (p300) that his paradigm of socio-legal work is atheoretical law in context work which while forming part of the field that is embraced by socio-legal studies should not be taken as definitive of it. It is interesting that in this chapter of *Community* no real reference is made to or review undertaken of the huge volume of socio-legal work that has been conducted in the UK in the last 25 years or so (with the exception of a few references given on p311) to support the assertion that socio-legal studies looks at what "legal agencies do" rather than considering what "legal doctrine and practices *should be* [original emphasis]. If this charge is going to be made then the socio-legal community deserves it to be at least substantiated .

45   See N Lacey "Conceiving Socio-Legal Studies" *Socio-Legal Studies Newsletter* Summer (1994) 2 .

46   See R Lempert "Strategies of Research Design in the Legal Impact Study: The Control of Plausible Rival Hypothesis" (1966) 1 L&S Rev 111.

47   A recurring theme in the texts cited in notes 44-45 and 48-49 is that a separation between the demands of the policy audience and the ability to theoretically ground socio-legal work is something that has been recognised only recently, however see V Gessner and J Thomas "Socio-Legal Research and Policy Studies: A Review of the Issues" (1988) 10 *Law and Policy* 85 at p92 where exactly this point is made. This paper was based on a presentation given at a workshop organised by the IRCSL in 1985.

48   See R Cotterrell *The Sociology of Law* 1992 Butterworths p34 where he places in this category work such as that done by Macaulay and Beale and Dugdale. See S Macaulay "Non-Contractual Relations in Business: A Preliminary Study" (1963) 28 *Am Soc Rev* 55 and H Beale and T Dugdale "Contracts Between Businessmen: Planning and the Use of Contractual Remedies" (1975) 2 *Brit J of Law & Soc* 45.

49   See P Fizpatrick *The Mythology of Modern Law* (1992) Routledge London chap1.

50   Some would exclude from the category of 'firm' those organisations that were not 'for profit' eg charities to the extent that this also excludes co-operatives.

This is unfortunate because much of what is said about the minimisation of transaction costs is relevant to them and the fact that they do not adopt a hierarchical structure in the way that some of the followers of Coase (eg Williamson, see below) deem necessary should not be a matter for exclusion, see for example R Langlois and P Robertson *Firms Markets and Economic Change* (1995) Routledge London p7.

51   This is not to say that there is not a literature which examines, from the standpoint of economics, limited liability, there is and indeed there is a literature which critics its assumptions, see Easterbrook and Fischel *The Economic Structure of Corporate Law* 1991 Harvard Univ Press Cambride Mass ch 2, Ekelund and Tollison "Mercantilist Origins of the Corporation" (1980) *Bell Journal of Economics* 715 and T Gabaldon "The Lemonade Stand: Feminist and Other Reflections on the Limited Liability of Corporate Shareholders" (1992) 42 *Vand Law Rev* 1387 at 1405-1413. However it is not possible to use the differences between lawyers' assumptions about limited liability and the observations of economists to question wholesale the lawyers' approach to the company in the way that it is possible if there is a concentration upon economic theories of the firm and their consequences.

52   "The Nature of the Firm" (1937) NS 4 *Economica* 386, see also Williamson and Ouchim "Market Hierarchies and Visible Hand Perspectives" in Van de Ven and Joyce (eds) *Perspectives on Organisation Design and Behaviour* (1981) Wiley New York 347 at 352.

53   For an extended example of transacion costs within the firm see O Hart *Firms Contracts and Financial Structure* OUP Oxford 1995 p23-28.

54   See for example C Perrow "Market, Hierarchies and Hegomony" in Van de Ven and Joyce op cit n52 and C Perrow "Economic Theories of Organisation" (1986) 15 *Theory and Society*, O Hart "An Economist's Perspective on the Theory of the Firm" (1989) 89 *Col Law Rev* 1757 and Glasberg and Schwartz "Ownership and Control of Corporations" (1983) 9 *Annual Re of Soc* 311 all of which contain accounts accessible to the non-economist from the viewpoint of organisation theory, economics and sociology.

55   Jensen and Meckling "Theory of the Firm: Managerial Behaviour, Agency Costs and Ownership Structure" (1976) 3 *J of Fin Econ* 305.

56   On whether the costs inherent in making a takeover bid are so high that only extreme management failure is disciplined by the market see Coffee "Regulating the Market for Corporate Control: a Critical Assessment of the Tender Offer's Role in Corporate Governance" (1984) 84 *Col L Rev* 1145. See also the work of Roe and Romano who both make the point that restrictive anti-takeover legislation may come about as a result of managerial lobbying, Roe "A Political Theory of American Corporate Finance" (1991) 91 *Col L R* 10 and Romano "The Political Economy of Takeover Statutes" (1987) 73 *Virginia L R* 111.

57   There is a huge literature on the merits and demerits of the market for corporate control. For reviews of the literature see Bradley "Corporate Control:

Markets and Rules" (1990) 53 *MLR* 170 and Brudney "Corporate Governance, Agency Costs and the Rhetoric of Contract" (1985) 85 *Col L R* 1403.

58   See the inquiry as to the status of legal rules in the corporate context by Eisenberg "The Structure of Corporate Law" (1989) 89 *Col L R* 1461.

59   Again in a US context see Powell "Professional Innovation: Corporate Lawyers and Private Lawmaking" (1993) 18 *Law and Social Inquiry* 423.

60   There are critics who assert that despite discussion of the implications of economic theory for the law school model in law reviews the law school corporations course still has a narrow doctrinal focus, presumably similar to the UK position, see Simon "Contract versus Politics in Corparation Doctrine" in Kairys (ed) *The Politics of Law* 1990 Pantheon Books New York 387 at 399.

61   See Gordon "The Mandatory Structure of Corporate Law" (1989) 89 *Col L Rev* 1549, and Bratton "The "Nexus of Contracts" Corporation: A Critical Appraisal" (1989) 74 *Cornell L Rev* 407.

62   See Millon "New Directions in Corporate Law Communitarians, Contractarians and the Crisis in Corporate Law" (1993) 50 *Washington and Lee L R* 1373 at 1388 n43 where he charges Romano with offering as an alternative to the law school curriculum a selection of articles "by neoclassically-orientated economists and more or less doctrinaire contractarian law professors employed at elite law schools" and ignoring other issues.

63   Exceptions include Campbell "Why Regulate the Modern Corporation? The Failure of 'Market Failure" and Bradley "Contracts Trusts and Companies" both contained in McCahery, Picciotto and Scott (eds) *Corporate Control and Accountability* OUP 1993 at p103 and 217 respectively.

64   See Bradley "Corporate Control: Markets and Rules" (1990) 53 *MLR* 170 who attributes this to Berle and Means and cf Farrar "Ownership and Control of Listed Public Companies: Revising or Rejecting the Concept of Control" in Pettet (ed) *Company Law in Change* (1987) Stevens London 39 at 46 who attributes the idea to Manne "Mergers and the Market for Corporate Control" (1965) 73 *J Pol Econ* 110.

65   Op cit n64

66   Leech "Corporate Ownership and Control: A New Look at the Evidence of Berle and Means" (1987) 39 *Oxford Econ Papers* 534 applies a probalistic voting model to the data collected by Berle and Means and suggests that their designation of companies in the sample as management controlled should have been considerably lower. Others for example Francis "Families, Firms and Finance Capital: The Development of UK Industrial Firms with Particular Reference to their Ownership and Control" (1980) 4 *Soc 1* have rejected the 20% shareholding figure of Berle and Means as necessary for control and put it as low as 5%.

67   This is particularly a criticism levelled by Marxists or those who adopt a similar position towards the company, see Thompson "The firm as a dispersed social agency" (1982) *Economy and Society* 241 and Zeitlin "Corporate Control and Ownership: The Large Corporation and the Capitalist Class"

(1974) 79 *Am J of Soc* 1073 primarily because a separation of ownership and control may be seen as leading to a denial of the applicability of class theory to the division of capital and labour.

68   See Ireland, Grigg-Spall and Kelly "The Conceptual Foundations of Modern Company Law" in P Fitzpatrick and A Hunt (eds) *Critical Legal Studies* (1987) Blackwell Oxford

69   See Smith "Women, the family and corporate capitalism" in Stephenson (ed) *Women in Canada* General Publishing Co (1977) at p17 and the critique offered by Lahey and Salter "Corporate Law in Legal Theory and Legal Scholarship: From Classicism to Feminism" (1985) 23 *Osgoode Hall LJ* 543.

70   Zeitlin op cit n67 at p1089-93 criticises the failure of current notions of control to consider the position of rivals for control; what assets each group possess to fight for control and the likely result over time.

71   See Fligstein and Brantley "Bank Control, Owner Control or Organisational Dynamics: Who Controls the Large Modern Corporation" (1992) 98 *Am J of Soc* 280.

72   See Scott *Corporation, Classes and Capitalism* Hutchinson London 1985 pp49, 79-83.

73   See Mitchell "Private Law, Public Interest? The ALI Principles of Corporate Governance"(1993) 61 *Univ of Toronto LR*.

74   "The Financial Aspects of Corporate Governance" December 1992 called the Cadbury Report after the Chairman of the Committee, Sir Adrian Cadbury. A detailed review of its provisions is provided by Finch "Board Performance and Cadbury on Corporate Governance" (1992) *JBL* 576.

75   Much of the information that shareholders obtain comes from audit and there is a literature situated primarily in accounting which is too vast to discuss here on the relationship between audit and corporate governance. A special issue of *Accounting and Business Research* (1993) vol 23 provides a starting point.

76   Para 3.7 of the Code.

77   It may be that the need to report a compliance statement may result either in the establishment of "creative compliance" devices as reported by McBarnet and Whelan in other areas of corporate finance see McBarnet and Whelan "The Elusive Spirit of the Law: Formalism and the Struggle for Legal Control" (1991) 54 *MLR* 848 or that management will co-ordinate their behaviour so that compliance statements across companies become a matter of form as opposed to substance. This type of behaviour occured in relation to the development of takeover legislation see Romano and Roe op cit n56.

78   As Bratton and McCahery point out the presence of institutional investors offers for the first time since Berle and Means the prospect of self-regulation enforced by shareholders, "Regulating Competition Regulatory Capture and Corporate Self-Regulation" (1995) 73 *North Carolina Law Rev* 1861 at 1869.

79   Fama and Jenson "Separation of Ownership and Control" (1983) 26 *J of Law and Econ* 301.

80   Para 6.11 of the Code.

81   See Wittington "Corporate Governance and the Regulation of Financial Reporting" (1993) 23 *Accounting and Business Res* 313.

82   Davis and Thompson "A Social Movement Perspective on Corporate Control" (1994) 39 *Admin Sci Quart* 141.

83   For reinforcement of this point see Stapledon "Exercise of Voting Rights by Institutional Shareholders in the UK" (1995) 3 *Corporate Governance* 144.

84   Op cit Bratten and McCahery at n.78.

85   The idea of non-executive directors as a monitoring force has been current for some time, see Pro-Ned (1982) *The Role of Non-Executive Directors*. There is empirical evidence to suggest that in jurisdictions with restrictive takeover statutes boards of directors are larger and comprise more non-executives as an alternative system of governance from the market for corporate control, Arthur and Taylor "Takeover Markets and Corporate Board Composition: Some Further Evidence (1995) 3 *Corp Gov* 218.

86   Para 4.11 of the Code.

87   Para 4.12 of the Code.

88   Gilson and Roe "Understanding the Japanese Keiretsu: Overlaps between Corporate Governance and Industrial Organisation" (1993) 102 *Yale L J* 871 at 874.

89   See Tomasic and Bottomley *Directing the Top 500* 1993 Allen and Unwin St Leonards. This is a text, not widely available in the UK, based on empirical research done in Australia.

90   See Pettigrew and McNulty "Power and Influences in and around the Boardroom" (1995) 48 *Human Relations* 845 which concentrates on the role of non-executive directors and Hill "The Social Organisation of Boards of Directors" (1995) 46 *BJS* 245 which examines boardroom culture more generally.

91   Charkham *Keeping Good Company* OUP (1994) at 249.

92   That the current political construction put upon the company has fundamentally altered from the position taken in the post-war period to the 1970's can be seen from recalling the contents of the Watkinson Report of 1973, commissioned by the CBI which emphasised the responsibilities of the public company towards its customers, trade suppliers and society in general.

93   The best discussion of the meaning of governance in a corporate context as distinct from the whole concept "corporate governance" and one which places it within a Foucaudian framework is provided by Jackson and Carter, "Organisational Chiaroscuro: Throwing Light on the Concept of Corporate Governance" (1995) 8 *Human Relations* 875.

94   See Appendix 1 to the report.

95   However whether companies would be prepared to disclose information which did not correspond with that perceived as relevant by higher management in a property rights model, unless of course that model was considerably dismantled, is open to question, see the findings of Adams et al "Corporate Equal Opportunities (Non-) Disclosure" *Brit Acc Rev* 27 (1995) 87.

96   See for example Dine "The Governance of Governance" (1994) 15 *The Company Lawyer* 73.

97   Griffiths "Shareholding and the Governance of Public Companies" in Sheikh and Rees (eds) op cit n.26.

98   Lipton and Rosenblum "A New System of Corporate Governance: The Quinquennial Election of Directors" (1991) 58 *Univ of Chicago LR* 187 at 189.

99   See Collins and Wortick "Business and Society/Business Ethics Courses: Twenty Years at the Crossroads" (1995) 34 *Business and Society* 51.

100   It is popularly taken to be the case that business ethics as an inquiry assumes the validity of a wide range of stakeholders in the company and so rejects profit maximisation as a goal. This is not necessarily the case, see Sternberg *Just Business* (1994) Little Brown London.

101   See Vallance *Business Ethics at Work* CUP Cambridge 1995.

102   See n67-69 and accompanying text.

103   See for example Eells *The Government of Corporations* 1962 Free Press New York.

104   See Parkinson op cit n.36 at p408-413 and Windolf "Co-determination and the Market for Corporate Control in the European Community" (1993) 22 *Economy and Society* 137.

105   Worker participation proposals were first put forward in the Fifth EC Dirc (OJ 1972 C131/49). They were based on the German position and included suggestions for compulsory co-determination in public companies within a two-tier board structure. It is worth noting that originally the UK's objections were based not on the issue of participation but on two-tier boards, see the Bullock Committee Report 1978 Cmnd 7231. The policy agenda on this point has now changed considerably, see the following discussion.

106   There is no such thing as a Pan-European model of worker participation; for example it is not mandatory in France but it is at its strongest in Germany. For a Europe-wide review see Gold and Hall *Legal Regulation and the Practice of Employee Participation in the European Community* (1990) European Foundation for the Improvement of Living and Working Conditions, Warwick Working Paper and Lansbury "Workplace Europe: new forms of bargaining and Participation" (1995) 10 *New Technology Work and Employment* 47.

107   Works councils were adopted by the EC using the framework of the Social Policy Agreement, see Council Directive 94/45 Sept 22nd 1994 on the Establishment of a European Works Council or other procedure in Community-scale undertakings or Community-scale groups for the purposes of informing and consulting employees, OJ 1994 L254/64. The UK obtained an opt-out from the Social Policy Agreement under the Treaty of Maastricht. However as the Directive applies to undertakings with more than 1000 employees across the member states and more than 150 in any 2 (excluding the UK) companies in the UK with related companies in other member states may find that they have to adopt works councils. The CBI estimates that this will be the case for about 100 firms with others perhaps voluntarily following

suit, see McGlynn "European Works Councils: Towards Industrial Democracy?" (1995) 24 *ILJ* 78.

108   Teubner "Industrial Democracy through Law? Social Functions of Law in Institutional Innovations" in Daintith and Teubner (eds) *Contract and Organisation: Legal Analysis in the Light of Economic and Social Theory* De Gruyter Berlin (1986) 261 at 263.

109   Grenier and Hogler "Labour Law and Managerial Ideology" (1991) 18 *Work and Occupations* 313 at 323.

110   Frug "The Ideology of Bureaucracy in American Law" (1984) 97 *Harv L R* 1277.

111   See notes 64-72 and accompanying text.

112   Weber "Bureaucracy" in Gerth and Mills (eds) *From Max Weber: Essays in Sociology* OUP New York (1946) 214 and Meyer "The Growth of Public and Private Bureaucracies" in Zukin and DiMaggio (eds) *Structures of Capital* CUP New York (1990) 153.

113   Ferguson *The Feminist Case against Bureaucracy* Temple Univ Press Philadelphia (1984) 62.

114   Weyland "The Americanist Bias in Organisation Theory" (1995) 8 *Governance: An International Journal of Policy and Administration* 113.

115   See the description given to these relationships by Scott op cit n 42 of "flat hierarchies". On the basis of Scott's anyalsis of the future managerial structures of universities participating in a mass higher education system there would appear to be many parallels between this and company structures.

116   Stinchcombe "Social Structure and Organisations" in March (ed) *Handbook of Organisations* (1965) Rand McNally Chicago 142.

117   For an agenda on this point see Ferguson "On Bringing More Theory, More Voices and More Politics to the Study of Organisations" (1994) 1 *Organisation* 81.

309

14 Socio-Legal Studies And The European Union

JO SHAW

Introduction

The reasons commonly given for the absence of critical, contextual, theoretical or socio-legal traditions in scholarship on the European Union are generally unflattering to European lawyers. European lawyers tend to be lumped together rather unhelpfully as unreflective and unresponsive to interdisciplinary or alternative approaches and hidebound by an attention to doctrinal detail which is today rarely so consistently echoed in the study of domestic law.[1] While there may be more than a grain of truth in some of the criticisms, it is not the aim of this chapter to rehearse them. One of the primary objectives of this survey and review of the European dimension of socio-legal studies is instead to look beyond the limitations of legal scholarship which emerge whenever the question of going beyond the doctrinal paradigm is raised, in order to examine constraints and restrictions which emerge within a larger canvas of multi-disciplinary studies of European integration processes. Some of these constraints will be seen to be practical, and are therefore capable of resolution with a greater investment of financial and human resources in this field. Others result from a mindset about law as a closed language and discipline displayed not only by lawyers, but by other practitioners of European studies. These constraints apply not only to *socio-legal* work on the European Union, but also, in many cases, to all forms of non-doctrinal work on the EU. However, the argument will be developed with socio-legal studies specifically in mind, focusing on the possibilities of building upon the relatively few existing examples of inter- or cross-disciplinary work examining legal rules, institutions and practices in the EU and its Member States.

For these purposes, without drawing at this stage rigid lines of demarcation between different forms of non-doctrinal work, I am adapting and applying Cotterell's definition of socio-legal studies as scholarship:

> showing through systematic behavioural studies what law as institutionalized doctrine means in the varied local contexts of social life, where its ultimate value and significance must be judged.[2]

This is a useful working definition, but one that perhaps needs some adaptation in the EU context in order to highlight the contribution of socio-legal studies not only to the understanding of law and legal processes, but also to the understanding of the integration process itself. This is highlighted in the next section on the concept of a 'European dimension' of socio-legal studies. Moreover, it needs to be read in the context of Cotterell's warning that socio-legal studies urgently needs functions which are beyond an instrumental relationship to policy-making and the content of policy, and of the need discussed below for an adequately-grounded theoretical construct of 'European law'. Finally, as a definition, it makes no specific reference to what is undoubtedly an essential element of socio-legal studies, at least within the European dimension, namely that socio-legal scholarship should make a self-conscious contribution to the development of *interdisciplinary* studies.

A European Dimension To Socio-Legal Studies?

What do 'Europe' and 'socio-legal studies' offer each other when they are brought together? Or, to put it another way, what is distinctive and interesting about the creation of a European dimension to socio-legal studies?

Taking the UK perspective as a starting point, it can be argued that there are two principal European dimensions to socio-legal studies.[3]

The first involves the application to EC law and legal institutions of the accepted tools and insights of [UK domestic] socio-legal studies. It begins perhaps by identifying recognized subjects of socio-legal study such as the gap between the law in the books and the law in action, the nature of legal rules,[4] the work of [legal] professionals including judges and practitioners,[5] the impact of political processes upon law[6] or of law upon the conduct of private individuals or public institutions, or perhaps the ideological foundations of legal rules. It then develops a research question which uses as its empirical focus (at least in part) the legal norms and institutions of the European Union. In other words, such work is largely shaped by the established divisions (and preoccupations) of domestic socio-legal studies, and like such work may be undertaken by academics from across the social science disciplines. For example, regulation specialists in a number of disciplines, but especially economists, have increasingly turned their attention to European questions. Other good examples of work exploring this dimension of the Europe/socio-legal studies interaction include McBarnet and Whelan on creative compliance by business enterprises with EU legal rules on, for example, accounting requirements,[7] and Picciotto on international taxation.[8] However, with the widespread intervention of the EU legislators in business and employment relations, there are many potential sites for socio-legal research of this type. Indeed, conversely much business or employment socio-legal studies which examine concepts within the micro-legal canon would be incomplete *without* a European dimension.

There is a sense in which the European dimension or element of much of this work could be said to be coincidental. The defining feature is often what it tells us about, for example, business reactions to regulation, business involvement in regulation, or globalization. It may also inform us about the impact or effectiveness of legal rules and institutions established at the EU level. It certainly warns of the poverty of the narrow doctrinal approach which has formed the dominant tradition of EC law scholarship. It is, from any perspective, a wholly necessary complement to descriptions and analyses of the positive law. Impact based studies, for example, challenge over-optimism about the efficacy of the EU's regulatory edifice.

However, it does not have the question of 'Europe' as its central research focus. It is not concerned principally with European integration processes - what they are, why they occur, how they work - with the institutional actors involved in these processes, or with the specific role of law and legal institutions in European integration.

This, rather, is the province of the second European dimension of socio-legal studies. This is work of an interdisciplinary nature specifically focused on integration processes which addresses the 'legal dimension'. Two examples can be given. There is a developing body of work, principally by political scientists, on the Court of Justice as a political institution. This has involved some collaboration with lawyers, principally seen as 'technicians' feeding in a data set of what the Court (objectively) 'does' in order to develop a theory of the role of the Court in integration processes.[9] The second example involves work, principally from either a 'new institutionalist' perspective, which examines the question of the 'governance' of the EU. One of the main preoccupations of this work is the stress it places upon the autonomy of the EU's own institutions in determining the direction of policy-making, seeing the EU as being more than simply the creature of its Member States (the classical 'intergovernmentalist' position). It draws on the institutionalist insight that institutions themselves are important: they are more than "mere arenas in which policy inputs are simply aggregated".[10] Of those institutions, perhaps the Court of Justice has the greatest autonomy of action, and lawyers are beginning to work fruitfully with political scientists and economists in particular to build up a more complete picture of institutional interactions.[11] Armstrong and Bulmer's work on 'governance' of the single market, a project initiated under the ESRC Single European Market Initiative, provides the best example of interdisciplinary work of this nature.[12]

The distinction between two separate dimensions, while useful, is incomplete. There are works falling wholly within one paradigm or the other. Other work, such as Scott's book *Development Dilemmas in the European Community*[13] could be said to straddle the divide. The book is a self-conscious rejection of the dominant notion that the sum of EC law is

313

to be found in the Treaties, the legislation and the cases. It is also an application of development studies *within* the internal European Union context. In that sense, it belongs to the first category defined. However, it also interrogates the role of regional development policy within a transnational entity defined by economic imperatives, and dominant neo-liberal economic logic, and so contributes to the understanding of how law, as she defines and applies it, operates within that logic. The great value of the distinction, as I shall show in the final section of this chapter, is its ability to identify the important dual role of socio-legal studies in the EU context.

The Identification Of 'Europe'

One reason why socio-legal research has been slow to develop in the field of EC law has been the weakness of 'European legal theory'. Conventional positivist jurisprudence has largely passed EC law by,[14] despite the obvious analytical challenges posed by a legal system which transcends state boundaries.[15] As Bankowski puts it, EC law "decouples law and state; it institutes an order which is neither national nor international law".[16] Nor has EC law attracted extensive analysis from a critical legal standpoint. For a long time, the work of Snyder, particularly on the Common Agricultural Policy,[17] stood largely alone as a sustained critique of the ideological basis of EC law which poses questions about its jurisprudential character while providing detailed account of its substance. Meanwhile, from an 'idealist' and, more recently, a 'constitutionalist' standpoint, Weiler has challenged the transformation from 'Community' to 'Union' and questioned the possibilities of legal development within the EU.[18] A gradual increase in the intensity of theoretical scrutiny directed towards the nature of the European Union is demonstrated by Ward's work on the Treaty of Maastricht as a postmodern text[19] and the work of Bergeron applying theories of the mythology of modern law developed particularly by Fitzpatrick[20] to the Court of Justice's constitutionalisation of the EU Treaties.[21]

I would argue that the unique contribution of *European* legal theory must relate to the possibility of identifying 'Europe' (and 'Europeans'). This is a question which other disciplines, and inter-disciplinary scholarship, have actively wrestled with,[22] acknowledging the absence of clear geographical boundaries, and the slipperiness of any geopolitical or cultural construct of Europe. In contrast, the identification of 'Europe' is a seemingly unproblematic enterprise for lawyers.[23] It could be, for example, simply a question of identifying the participants in integration, Union-style. Another possible explanation is that the simplification of the issue of 'Europe' is a product of terminological sloppiness - talking about *European* law[24] when what we mean is *European Community* law. Even those who acknowledge explicitly the plurality of sources of 'European law', and who recognise its frail degree of legitimacy in a conventional constitutional sense offer no real insight into the role of law in European integration processes beyond the visions of liberal constitutionalism as a bulwark against authoritarianism.[25]

In truth, the common terminological 'slippage' is, to a large extent, due to the implicit (or explicit) attachment of most legal commentary to the cultural colonialism of one particular 'idea of Europe'. In the words of Delors: "Democracy, balance between state and society, between collective and the individual, is Europe's model. This fundamental law....unites us all".[26] This is the "European model of society to which the great majority of European are committed...most people want to retain its spirit and political foundations".[27] The assumption made here is that the path of the European Community - and now of the European Union - is the right path for Europe as a whole. It assumes that there are common European models - Western, Christian and 'white' models for the most part. It posits a form of [implicitly national-type[28]] identity based largely on an amalgam of Western European features of national identity.[29] It is the same values which are assumed to have infused the men (sic) who have, over the years, formed the Court of Justice.[30] Lawyers from time to time make reference to questions of 'identity'[31] but without taking proper cognizance of, for example, the resurgence of intense

315

debates about the notion of nationalism which structure in part the notion of 'identity'.[32]

Thus highly contentious and inadequately grounded propositions about identity and proto-nationhood form the intellectual cornerstone of much legal commentary on the EU. A particularly extreme example of what can happen if uncritical concepts of 'European law' and of 'Europe' are applied is offered by the following comment from Slynn in the Preface to a collection of papers on the Treaty of Maastricht:

> The papers in this book....are written by lawyers of considerable experience and standing in the different spheres. They are often highly critical of what has been done - that is the function and joy of the academic lawyer - yet they are written, as I see it, by lawyers who are wholly in favour of the aims of the Community and of developing integration ("union").... [33]

The reason for this assumption, I would argue is because there has been a tendency to see an indissoluble link between the law, and the process and principles of European integration. The strength of that belief is well illustrated by the following comment from Cappelletti:[34]

> the European Court's vision [is]...one of furthering European integration....I am convinced that such a vision, far from being arbitrary, is fully legitimate, for it is rooted in the text, most particularly in the Preamble and first articles of the EC Treaty...

Yet that putative linkage is by no means as simple as it is often portrayed; lawyers have failed to identify the fallacy of linking law and integration so tightly, because they have paid little attention to the *internal* dynamics or dialectics of EC law.[35] While, pragmatically, the Court of Justice must be viewed as a 'motor of integration' over the last forty years, it is nonetheless possible (indeed ever increasingly so) to identify elements of disintegration (or decentralization) in the EU constitutional structure (e.g. variable geometry after the Treaty of Maastricht[36]), in the case law of the

Court of Justice where a tendency in recent years to appease the Member States has emerged,[37] and in the EU's legislative endeavours which are as much a part of EC law as the case law of the Court.[38]

There is a rather one-dimensional vision of EC law, therefore, which has contributed to the retarded development of a European dimension to socio-legal studies. There has been a failure to theorize the complex relationships between law and processes and concepts of integration - whether economic, monetary, political or socio-cultural. Without a developed sense that law in the EU context is a problematic enterprise, socio-legal studies on the EU will provide little more than a contextualised explanation of existing legal models rather than a critical exploration. However, there is cause to believe that change is coming. The importance of theory as the underpinning of empirical research has been recognized by the award of ESRC funding to an interdisciplinary seminar series/working group on European legal theory. A recent special issue of *Social and Legal Studies* on *Legal Culture, Diversity and Globalization*,[39] while directly addressing the problematic of the EU legal order, highlights the growing interest of legal academics in theorising the interfaces of different legal cultures, as well as the process of comparison. The advent of a concept of European Union citizenship is leading to lawyers and political scientists collaborating more closely in assessing its meaning and potential for future development.[40] Weiler has recently pointed to a renewal of interest in an integrated politico-legal reading of European constitutionalism.[41] All of these developments, as well as the more adventurous explorations of the contours of the EU legal order by authors such as Snyder,[42] Bergeron and Ward indicate, overall, that the outlook for the future is more positive.

Socio-Legal Studies: The *Acquis Communautaire*

In view of the comments in the preceding sections, it is now important to review briefly the main areas of European Community law in which there is an emerging tradition of socio-legal studies: what one might call the *acquis communautaire* in the field of socio-legal studies. It does not seek to give either an exhaustive list of authors working in these fields, or a full account of their contributions, but only to provide a snapshot of a slowly evolving body of work. One limiting factor in the approach taken here is that the primary focus is on UK-based and/or English language work. Special attention is paid to areas where there is particular potential for development. While any categorization of the work will obviously be over-simplistic, nonetheless, for ease of reference, the work is organized into four headings:

- the internal market and the study of regulation
- governing beyond the state: the EU as a multilevel governance structure
- new approaches to the study of the Court of Justice: a court without the law?
- the domestic dimension: enforcement, implementation and compliance.

The Internal Market And The Study Of Regulation

The political decision taken in 1985 to make the completion of the internal market the major short and medium term goal of the European Communities has generated a sizeable and significant literature on regulation and regulatory processes which has concentrated on the legislative endeavours of the EU institutions. It constitutes, so far, probably the most concentrated body of socio-legal work on the EU, although the bulk of the work so far has been undertaken by economists. The dominant figure has been Majone, who has led the way in drawing upon the more developed USA literature on regulatory practices and styles, and in building comparisons between the American and European experiences.[43] Neither Majone's work, nor that of others working in the field, are limited, in the 'European' context, to the experiences of the EU itself; the practice of privatization and (de/re)regulation in the countries of

Western and more recently Eastern Europe has also provided ample material for study.[44]

There have been four principal focuses in the work on regulation.[45] The first comprises comparisons between the Anglo-American and 'Latin' 'styles' of capitalism, and the consequences which this has entailed for the management of the economy and the role of the state. The point is made that the heritage of 'regulation' is relatively small in (continental) Europe. When debates began to gather pace from the early 1980s about 'deregulation', there was little intellectual tradition of regulation studies to draw on in order to consider logically prior questions: 'why regulate' and 'what form, if any, should regulation take?'.

The second focus is upon the regulatory strategies adopted by the EU institutions. This research focus has come to the fore in particular since the acceleration of the EU's legislative activities after the adoption of the Single European Act in 1986, and the associated decision to complete the internal market by the end of 1992. In recent years, work focusing on the choices made by the Commission and the other political institutions has referred increasingly to the decisive role played by the Court of Justice. The Court has not only expansively interpreted the guarantees of negative integration in the Treaties (freedom of movement for goods and services, etc.[46]) but has also offered the institutions maximum regulatory competence through its interpretations of the scope of the legal bases under which the institutions must act.[47]

The EU's current approach to the task of harmonization of laws, which is one of the most important expressions of its regulatory competence, is shaped, therefore, not only by the wishes and choices of the Member States and the political institutions, and by the bounds of the politically expedient, but also by the Court and the bounds of the legally possible. Socio-legal research in this field has concentrated on describing and explaining the complex institutional interactions which constitute the expression and exercise of Community competence.[48] Most of the main areas of EU policy have been covered, including in particular the regulation of utilities (especially telecommunications),[49] public procurement,[50] consumer protection generally,[51] and especially food[52] and product safety.[53]

A third area of emphasis is focused on the future and on the role of the regulatory agencies which are proliferating at the EU level.[54] One of the roles of these agencies (e.g. the European Environmental Agency, or Health and Safety Agency) will be to manage particular sectors of the markets and perhaps, to exercise certain delegated powers. Here the problem is one of accountability and democracy, and the absence of an established tradition, at national level, under which regulatory agencies can be regarded as an autonomous 'fourth branch of government', subject to a variety of controls including judicial review, executive accountability, and requirements of openness and transparency.

Finally, an important subject of enquiry, in particular for economists,[55] has been the 'competition between rules' debate.[56] This approach, first advocated in a report by Padoa-Schioppa,[57] argues that regulation is only economically justified if it remedies a market failure, and that competition between regulators may be a superior substitute (on economic grounds) for harmonization in a transnational setting. A principle of regulatory competition can, as Woolcock has shown,[58] be derived from two sources. On the one hand, there are public choice theories developed by economists to show that there can be a market in regulation which is analogous to a market in goods.[59] On the other hand, there are the empirically observable practical endeavours on the part of the EU regulators to establish a single market, where there has been a consistent tension between negative integration (free movement, and the principle of mutual recognition), and positive integration (harmonization, regulation). In political terms, calls have come principally from voices on the right of the political spectrum for the process of building an internal market to be a deregulatory process, involving 'small government'.[60] What regulatory competition means in practice is "the alteration of national regulation in response to the actual or expected impact of internationally mobile goods, services, or factors on national economic activity".[61] According to Siebert:[62]

Firms will migrate, at least with their expansion, to the most favourable location....The arbitrage of consumers and firms will show which national regulatory system is best in the eyes of the consumer or producer: national regulation will pass a litmus test of private agents voting with their purses and their feet.

As Reich concludes:[63]

Such a concept allows for diversity of Member States' regulations, the most efficient of which will, in the long run, be able to compete successfully for investors and consumers alike, and thereby become the rule of the Community.

The potential downside of 'competition between rules' is the so-called 'race for the bottom' or 'social dumping'[64] where the pressures of international competition, combined with a reluctant (or impotent) regulator, leads to a watering down of regulatory protection for consumers (or employees), particularly in those Member States which have previously adopted high standards. Precisely this question has been interrogated by Eichener in an extended case study of health and safety at work.[65] In the field of labour law, the regulatory competition question is played out partly in the context of an ongoing tension between employment protection and flexibilisation of labour markets.[66]

Governing Beyond The State: The EU As A Multilevel Governance Structure

While the work specifically focused on regulation has provided a critical account of the policy outcomes of the internal market programme, and is proving a fruitful field of socio-legal research, it does not provide complete answers to a number of important questions. First, it does not examine in detail how policy choices are made, and in particular the role of institutions (in the widest sense, including not only policy actors but also legal and normative structures, and standard operating procedures) shape the conditions in which decisions are made. Second, it does not help to explain the degree of autonomy or restriction under which the EU institutions operate, and their relationship to the role of the Member States. Thus, it make no real contribution to an understanding of what is commonly termed the 'governance' of the European Union.[67]

Governance is to be distinguished from 'governments':

> by governing we mean all those activities of social, political and administrative actors that can be seen as purposeful efforts to guide, steer, control or manage (sectors or facets of) societies...By 'governance' we mean the patterns that emerge from governing activities of social, political and administrative actors.[68]

Work which focuses on the practices and principles of governance in the European Union - defined as "a collection of overlapping functionally specific arrangements for mutual coordination among varying sets of participating countries",[69] but, one might also add, a multilevel system involving complex interactions between multiple public and private actors - stands outside what became the dominant substratum of integration theory from the 1950s onwards, namely competing theories of international relations.[70] It draws its main methodological and theoretical inspirations instead from the comparative analysis of political systems[71] and the practice of policy analysis.[72] Unlike most earlier international relations theories which have had little space for the law or the Court of Justice, to the extent in some versions of seeing it almost as an aberration from a norm of Member State bargaining,[73] integration theory which focuses on governance processes does acknowledge and engage with the role of the law and of legal processes. Ironically, this is not because such work necessarily operates within a 'statist' paradigm which would permit the identification of the EU with a law-giving government. On the contrary, much multilevel governance work rejects the predominance of statist categories in international relations theory, arguing that:

The real deficit of integration theory consists in its inability to conceptualize political order in different terms than in the common types of "state" and "state system". Patterns of thinking in the social sciences as well as in legal science are marked by these ordering principles of modernity and these disciplines therefore do not possess the necessary notions to conceptualize governance beyond the state.[74]

The challenge for legal and political analysis is to theorize and explain forms of territorially based governance in Europe which are beyond the state, but nonetheless empirically observable. It is not necessarily important to add a 'name' to that *sui generis* form of political organization,[75] although if and when the European Union becomes more stable, this will happen. One of the central questions picked up here is that of legitimacy. Can there be legitimate governance beyond the borders of the state? This provides a fruitful point of connection to work by legal scholars on the concept of legitimacy in the European Community.[76] Similarly, the role of interest groups in governance processes has been an important focus of research.[77] Again a clear link emerges with existing socio-legal research.[78]

Theories of institutional behaviour, in particular the historical branch of new institutionalism, are drawn upon within this body of research to provide coherent, cross-sectoral explanations for how and why the European Union operates.[79] The fundamental insight of institutionalism is that "institutions matter": "political struggles are mediated by prevailing institutional arrangements".[80] Within the paradigm of institutionalism, which "posits a more independent role for political institutions" ... "without denying the importance of both the social context of politics and the motives of individual actors",[81] it is the historical branch of new institutionalism which seems to offer the most fruitful line of enquiry for research which self-consciously seeks to build the constraints and opportunities of legal analysis into a cross-disciplinary examination of governance regimes. Here the focus of research will be on the historical evolution of the governance regimes which give the key to the policy choices made by regulators who are seeking real-world satisfactory solutions to policy problems, rather than optimal outcomes. So far the work of Armstrong and Bulmer in their project on *The Rule-Making Process in the Single Market*, under the auspices of the ESRC's Single Market Initiative, offers the best evidence of the contribution which this line of research can make to the development of a European dimension to socio-legal studies. Conversely, it highlights the role which socio-legal analysis may play in the role in building integration theory. This - if it occurs - will be a 'first' for law within European studies.[82]

The work of Armstrong and Bulmer, like that of others in the field[83] confirms the central role of the Commission in the institutional framework of the EU; in that context, it highlights the role of the legal competences of the Commission in structuring its responses to the contingencies and opportunities of policy-making. Most importantly, from the perspective of socio-legal research, however, it ties the Court of Justice fully into the institutional matrix,[84] depicting its involvement in a series of continuing conversations with other actors: with the Commission, Council and the European Parliament; with the Member States; with subnational authorities; with private interest groups; with individual litigants; and with national courts.

New Approaches To The Study Of The Court Of Justice: A Court Without The Law?

The work on new institutionalism is just part of an increasingly large body of research which starts from the premise that the Court of Justice is a 'political' institution. Much of this research originates in the USA; this is hardly surprising given the importance of analyses of the politics of the Supreme Court. American constitutional scholars have long denounced 'pure legalist' accounts of the work of the Court of Justice.[85] However, for many years the paths of mainstream legal and political analyses of European integration diverged sharply;[86] the dominant international relations paradigm in political analysis saw no place for the Court, while legal analysis pointed vainly to the undoubted 'constitutionalization' of the Treaties by the Court but proved unable to integrate this into an overall reading of the integration process.[87] The revival of forms of neo-functionalist analysis of integration during the heady days of the '1992' programme,[88] and its application in the Court arena by Burley and Mattli,[89] has led to a new interest by political scientists in what the Court does. Neo-functionalism began life as a predictive theory of the transfer of political sovereignty from the Member States to the European Community, as a consequence of the inexorable process of 'spillover' (from the economic into the political, the monetary and the social). Neofunctionalism describes a process:

> whereby political actors in several distinct national settings are persuaded to shift their loyalties, expectations, and political activities towards a new and larger center, whose institutions possess or demand jurisdiction over the pre-existing national states.[90]

Burley and Mattli argued that the Court of Justice was so successful in constructing the Community legal order because it operated behind a 'mask' of law. Thus the Court's judgments, although political in content, were not 'transparently' so, and so largely escaped the censure of attack from within the political domain. The Court largely successfully represented its actions as the embodiment of legal reasoning. If this thesis is correct about the early years, then it would appear that in recent years something has changed to encourage the Member States to be more forthright in their attempts to control the Court of Justice. Examples now abound of politicians' attacks upon the actions of the Court, and attempts by political action to constrain the Court.[91] The so-called 'Barber Protocol' attached to the Treaty of Maastricht purporting to limit the effects of the *Barber*[92] judgment,[93] and the exclusion of the two outer pillars of the European Union (Common Foreign and Security Policy, Cooperation in Justice and Home Affairs) from the jurisdiction of the Court are two important examples.

Of particular interest to Burley and Mattli is 'legal integration', defined as "the gradual penetration of EC law into the domestic law of its member states".[94] They have instrumentalized this concept through comparative research of the reception of EC law by national courts,[95] an analysis mediated through an attempt to construct judicial self-perceptions and identity. The research pathway opened up by Burley and Mattli has also been followed by many, particularly doctoral research students in the USA. Indeed, it might have been anticipated that this type of research might have been a primary launching pad for socio-legal studies in the EU domain.[96] This seems unlikely to occur until the work in this field sheds its attachment to a strangely one-dimensional and formalistic concept of 'law'. [97] It has been suggested that Burley and Mattli are providing a theory-based explanation of the traditional paradigm[98] - that is, precisely the paradigm of law which socio-legal studies would be at pains to debunk. Law and legal institutions appear static and shorn of the dynamism which is acknowledged by both the Court's supporters and critics as being a vital ingredient in its work. One reason for this weakness appears to be that some of the work is not genuinely interdisciplinary: for the most part, although not exclusively, it is work undertaken by political scientists who appear to rely for their sources of (authoritative) information about what the law 'is' upon self-referential and partially self-justificatory accounts of the Court by insiders (judges, Advocates General, past and present) and upon distinguished practitioners of doctrinal legal writing. In so doing, they appear also to buy the assumption that the law 'is' what books of authority say it 'is'.[99] This necessarily limits their contribution to an enhanced understanding of the social reality of law, although it may highlight the political roles of legal institutions.

The Domestic Dimension: Enforcement, Implementation And Compliance

It is a commonplace of European studies that the European Union - in its policy-making guise - suffers from a serious implementation and enforcement deficit.[100] Within a doctrinal paradigm, legal research concentrates on describing the available enforcement mechanisms and points to the novelty of the direct effect of EC law, allowing individuals to enforce their Community rights in national courts, and to seek references on points of interpretation to the Court of Justice. One of the major contributions of socio-legal studies in every domain of legal research has been to point to the gap between legal mechanisms existing on paper and the reality of compliance and enforcement. In the EU field, McBarnet and Whelan have applied the concept of creative compliance to EU rules on accounting requirements imposed on companies.[101] A similar line of research has been pursued by Matthews and Mayes, within the confines of an ESRC Single Market Initiative project.[102] They use a concept of 'soft law' to characterize behavioural responses by firms in response to proposed rule changes. A concept drawn primarily from international law, and with an existing pattern of usage within the EU,[103] Matthews and Mayes use 'soft law' prescriptively to describe self-regulatory arrangements (such as inter-firm agreements on shop opening hours - an example they develop) which allow firms to reach efficient solutions where regulatory change is proposed, while at the same giving them the credibility to intervene effectively in EU level debate on the precise content of changes.

In view of its enormous practical importance it is not surprising that a number of major studies of implementation have been funded by the EU and other funding agencies. Perhaps the most extensive was a study conducted through the European Institute of Public Administration in Maastricht.[104] A number of caveats have to be placed on much large-scale work. There are serious practical and methodological constraints upon the production of quality socio-legal research which makes a claim to comprehensive coverage in such a transnational setting. Moreover, where the research is driven primarily by the policy agenda of a funding agency - i.e. to find ways of making enforcement better or to increase "effectiveness" (to use the Euro-jargon) - then it falls into the instrumentalist trap for socio-legal studies highlighted and criticized by Cotterrell.[105] It is driven by the "pull of the policy-audience".[106] It is not therefore surprising that probably the most incisive contributions to the compliance debate have been made by researchers doing smaller scale work which is independent of the constraints and agendas imposed by the EU institutions.[107]

Conclusion

This review displays a mixed picture of opportunities and achievements. The possibility for socio-legal studies to build interdisciplinary bridges within the European studies field is clear, and that point will be developed further in the final section. However, constraints of funding, access and language have so far limited the work which has been done. The cost of socio-legal research with a European dimension is bound to be higher than the domestic equivalent. While the EU's 'supranational' political institutions (Commission, European Parliament, Economic and Social Committee) may be relatively accessible to researchers, it is much more difficult to undertake research which involves enquiries into the precise role of the Member States. As is well known, the meetings of the Council remain almost completely secret. It may be possible to build up a picture of the position taken by Member States separately; what is excluded from the research process, as yet, is the collective process of bargaining and negotiation. Consequently, it is only possible to judge the gap between the public positions taken by Member States and the compromises they accept in Council from hearsay and from surmise based on the outcomes of an opaque process of decision-making.

Private interest actors play a significant role in EU legal processes, both in terms of policy making and judicial action. They too have formed an important research focus,[108] but again differences in organisational cultures or working practices may make it more difficult for the UK-based researcher to assess the research data which is gathered.

Most of the socio-legal work which has been undertaken has been documentary in nature. Ethnographic work so far is confined to fields of sociology and anthropology.[109] In a field of study where the pace of change is unrelenting, weight is inevitably placed in all forms of research on the availability and presentation of up-to-date and full information. All of the institutions, but especially the Commission, put out a vast quantity of information in documentary form. Interviews conducted with officials, therefore, are largely supplementary (and one-off) means of pursuing the paper chase which defines so much of EC law, rather than mechanisms for

328

evaluating what they do. Empirical work is fact based, rather than being qualitative in nature. A notable exception is an international project funded by the Commission on women's experience of migration under the free movement rules which has documentary, statistical and qualitative elements.[110] In terms of making use of the variety of methods offered by socio-legal studies, therefore, the European dimension still remains significantly retarded.

Some years ago it might have been possible to argue that the absence of publication opportunities represented a serious constraint on the development of the European dimension of socio-legal studies. The dominance of the doctrinal and uncritical tradition represented a vicious circle which helped both to perpetuate the image of European Community law as rather dull and unreflective, and to strangle at birth the possibilities of breaking out by offering a different research perspective. A number of developments have largely broken this circle: the resurgence of the 'European debate' in the late 1980s encouraged all journals to develop a 'European dimension', including those which have in the past indicated a willingness to publish socio-legal work; the new research culture of the universities has had perhaps one positive by-product, namely the widening of publication opportunities, especially for younger academics who might be coming to EC law other than from a doctrinal background; finally in the EU context itself two important publication forums exist for socio-legal research. First, the *Journal of Common Market Studies*, and second, the recently launched *European Law Journal*, a product of the 'European law in context' movement primarily based at the European University Institute in Florence.[111]

The End And The Beginning: Socio-Legal Studies In An Interdisciplinary Tradition Of European Studies

The emergence of a stronger tradition of socio-legal studies in the field of the EU is pushing at an open door, for the research agenda in European studies is developing along increasingly interdisciplinary lines. It is argued that there is a need

> to try to break free from the shackles of viewing the process of integration separately from the viewpoint of each science discipline in turn. The process is inherently complex and multifaceted, and needs to be analysed coherently with the benefit of ideas from all of these disciplines. It requires interaction between economics and politics, social policy and indeed geography and environmental science.[112]

To this one must add law. It is, in fact, revealing that law was not included on that list, and this tends perhaps to reinforce the extent to which European Community law has hitherto constituted a hermetically sealed discipline, with few points of contact with other fields of European studies. This is well illustrated by the consistent failure of lawyers to engage with interdisciplinary debates through the medium of the *Journal of Common Market Studies*. The development of an interdisciplinary tradition which includes law requires shifts in perceptions on both sides. The arrival of increasingly large numbers of younger scholars of EC law interested in (and with an educational background in) non-doctrinal approaches to the study of law, along with the shifting of attention by some well established socio-legal scholars towards the European dimension should undermine any existing perception that lawyers and legal scholars are simply technicians offering value neutral skills and knowledge for consumption, wherever necessary, by other disciplines. The strengthening of the theoretical underpinning of work on law within the EU is also a vital element of an emergent tradition of socio-legal studies. Lawyers, likewise, should not just be consumers of integration theory, but become themselves participants in the research process from which theoretical insights are generated.

I would argue in conclusion that, despite the rather slow start which has been made in this field, the opportunities of socio-legal research in the 'non-state' forum of the EU offer socio-legal studies one of its best chances of becoming a major player in research about law - its impact, its content, its nature - in the next decade. The role of law in the European Union epitomises all the contradictions inherent in the nature and operation of legal rules - as the expression of governmental will and as a means (however flawed) of societal steering, but also as something which emerges and operates in "everyday conditions of social interaction"[113] as an expression of the human condition. Indeed, a small body of work is now beginning to employ a theoretical construct of 'new legal pluralism' to the study of law in the EU.[114] This augurs well for a blending of the two dimensions of socio-legal studies in the EU arena identified at the beginning of this paper. At present, most socio-legal work on the EU tends to offer a sharper perspective *either* 'law' *or* 'integration', but generally not both. Ultimately, a new research question needs to be posed, namely a shift from the *role* of law in integration, to the *meaning* of law in integration.

I am grateful to Kenneth Armstrong and Gráinne de Búrca for a number of very helpful comments on an earlier draft of this chapter. Responsibility for remaining errors or omissions remains mine alone.

Notes

1   There have always existed sceptical traditions in the field of European Community law, but they have emanated more from those international and constitutional lawyers who have tended, for differing reasons, to take a more limited view of the potential effects of the European Community Treaties. Of more recent origin is the 'judicial sceptic' tradition exemplified by H. Rasmussen, who has challenged the Court of Justice's authority to pursue 'political' interpretations of the EU Treaties and EU legislation: *On Law and Policy in the European Court of Justice*, 1986, Dordrecht: Martinus Nijhoff.

2   R. Cotterrell, *Law's Community*, 1995, Oxford: Oxford University Press, p.296.

3   A third dimension, which requires no further comment, involves the incidental consideration of EC law matters in the context of a broader project. Two recent examples are A. Ogus, *Regulation. Legal Form and Economic Theory*, 1995, Oxford: Clarendon Press, esp. pp.174-9 and R. Baldwin, *Rules and Government*, 1995, Oxford: Clarendon Press, Ch. 8 ("Rules and the European Union").

4   N. Passas and D. Nelken, "The thin line between legitimate and criminal enterprises: Subsidy frauds in the European Community", (1993) 18 *Crime, Law and Social Change* 223.

5   E.g. C. Whelan and D. McBarnet, "Lawyers in the Market: Delivering Legal Services in Europe", (1992) 19 *J. Law and Soc.* 49.

6   C. Harlow, "A Community of Interests. Making the Most of European Law", (1992) 55 MLR 331.

7   "The Elusive Spirit of the Law: Formalism and the Struggle for Legal Control", (1991) 54 MLR 848; "International Corporate Finance and the Challenge of Creative Compliance", in Fingleton and Schoenmaker (eds.), *The Internationalisation of Capital Markets and the Regulatory Response*, 1992, London: Graham and Trotman, p.129 *et seq*; reprinted in S. Wheeler (ed.), *The Business Enterprise*, 1994, Oxford: Oxford University Press.

8   *International Business Taxation*, 1992, London: Weidenfeld and Nicolson; "Transfer Pricing and the Antinomies of Corporate Regulation", in J. McCahery *et al* (eds.), *Corporate Control and Accountability*, 1993, Oxford: Oxford University Press.

9   See *infra* the Section on 'New approaches to the study of the Court of Justice: a court without the law?'.

10   K. Armstrong, "Regulating the free movement of goods: institutions and institutional change", in J. Shaw and G. More (eds.), *New Legal Dynamics of European Union*, 1996, Oxford: Oxford University Press at p.166.

11   See *infra* the Section on 'Institutional actors and policy processes: the challenge of 'governance''.

12   K. Armstrong, op. cit. *supra* n.10; S. Bulmer, "Institutions and Policy Change in the European Communities: The Case of Merger Control" (1994) 72 *Public Administration* 423-444; S. Bulmer, "The Governance of the European Union: A New Institutionalist Approach", (1994) 13 *Journal of Public Policy* 351-380; K. Armstrong and S. Bulmer, *The Governance of the European Union*, forthcoming, Manchester: Manchester University Press.

13   1995, Milton Keynes: Open University Press.

14   The most significant recent contribution is J. Bengoetxea, *The Legal Reasoning of the European Court of Justice*, 1993, Oxford: Oxford University Press.

15   N. MacCormick, "Beyond the Sovereign State", (1993) 56 MLR 1; I. Ward, "Making sense of integration: a philosophy of law for the European Community", (1993) 17 *Journal of European Integration* 101-136 (a Kantian analysis).

16   "Comment on Weiler", in S. Bulmer and A. Scott (eds.), *Economic and Political Integration in Europe. Internal Dynamics and Global Context*, 1994, Oxford: Blackwell at 161.

17   *Law of the Common Agricultural Policy*, 1985, London: Sweet and Maxwell; see also more generally *New Dimensions in European Community Law*, 1990, London: Weidenfeld and Nicolson.

18   "Fin-de-Siècle Europe", in R. Dehousse (ed.), *Europe After Maastricht. An Ever Closer Union*, 1994, Munich: Law Books in Europe; "The State *"über Alles"* Demos, Telos and the German Maastricht Decision", Harvard Jean Monnet Working Paper 6/95.

19   I. Ward, "Identity and Difference: The European Union and Postmodernism", in J. Shaw and G. More, op. cit. *supra* n.12; see also Ward, "In Search of a European Identity", (1994) MLR 315.

20   P. Fitzpatrick, *The Mythology of Modern Law*, 1992, London: Routledge.

21   J. Bergeron, "An Ever Whiter Myth: The Colonisation of Modernity in European Community Law", (1996) *Dublin University Law Journal* (forthcoming); ibid, "The Symbolic State: European Law and Symbolic Exchange at the Twilight of Modernity", in J. Bergeron and P. Fitzpatrick (eds.), *Europe's Other: European Law from Modernity to Postmodernity*, 1996, Aldershot: Dartmouth (forthcoming).

22   E.g. anthropology: V. Goddard *et al*, "Introduction: The Anthropology of Europe", in V. Goddard *et al* (eds.), *The Anthrolopology of Europe. Identities and Boundaries in Conflict*, 1994, London: Berg; H. Varenne, "The Question of European Nationalism", in T. Wilson and E. Smith, *Cultural Change and the New Europe. Perspectives on the European Community*, 1993, Boulder, Col: Westview; historical sociology: G. Delanty, *Inventing Europe. Idea, Identity and Reality*, 1995, London: Macmillan; political science: M. Smith and H. Wallace, "The European Union: towards a policy for Europe", (1994) 70 *International Affairs* 429-444; W. Wallace, "Introduction: the dynamics of European integration", in W. Wallace (ed.), *The Dynamics of European Integration*, 1990, London: Pinter/RIIA; S. Garcia (ed.), *European Identity and the Search for Legitimacy*, 1993, London: Pinter sociology: M. Haller, "The challenge for Contemporary Sociology in the Transformation of Europe", (1990) 5 *International Sociology* 183-204; C. Tilly, "The Future of European States", (1992) 59 *Social Research* 705-718; an excellent interdisciplinary collection is S. Zetterholm (ed.), *National Cultures and European Integration*, 1994, Oxford/Providence: Berg.

23   For exceptions see B. de Witte, "Cultural linkages", in W. Wallace, op. cit. *supra* n.22 and the work of J. Weiler generally.

24   There is, strictly speaking, no such entity as 'European' law, as relations between states within Europe other than those falling under EC law, or under any of the other developed forms of international cooperation within Europe (e.g. the European Economic Area) are characterized as 'international' law. However, the Council of Europe has suggested a definition of European law as "the law governing the structure, organs, and functioning of the Council of Europe and other European orgnaizations or institutions; further the law contained in the conventions and agreements of the Council of Europe and the instruments of other European organizations or institutions": quoted by F. Hondius in "The New Architecture of Europe and ius commune europaeum", in B. de Witte and C. Forder (eds.), *The Common Law of Europe and the Future of Legal Education*, 1992, Dordrecht: Kluwer, at p.215.

25	E. Mestmäcker, "On the legitimacy of European Law", (1994) 58 *RabelsZ* 615.
26	J. Delors, *Our Europe*, 1992, London: Verso, p.18.
27	Ibid, p.157.
28	J. Mackenzie-Stuart, "Foreword: Toward a National Identity in the European Economic Community", in M. Tushnet (ed.), *Comparative Constitutional Federalism. Europe and America*, 1990, New York, etc.: Greenwood Press.
29	See A. Smith, "National Identity and the idea of European unity", (1992) 68 *International Affairs* 55-76.
30	E.g. G. Mancini and D. Keeling, "Language, Culture and Politics in the Life of the European Court of Justice," Paper delivered to the annual meeting of the American Law Schools Association, New Orleans, January 1995.
31	E.g. K. Lenaerts, "The Question of Democratic Representation", Conference Reader for the TMC Asser Conference on *The Treaty on European Union. Suggestions for Revision*, The Hague, September 1995.
32	The different positions on the origins of nationalism and national identity are ethnically based or socially constructed are exemplified by the debates between Ernest Gellner and Anthony Smith. See E. Gellner, *Encounters with Nationalism*, 1994, Oxford: Blackwell; A. Smith, *National Identity*, 1991, Harmondsworth: Penguin.
33	Preface to D. O'Keeffe and P. Twomey (eds.), *Legal Issues of the Maastricht Treaty*, 1994, London, etc.: Chancery/Wiley, at p*vii*.
34	*The Judicial Process in Comparative Perspective*, 1989, Oxford: Clarendon Press, at p.391.
35	I have attempted to provide a sustained critique of the tensions between integration and disintegration in J. Shaw, "European Union legal studies in crisis? Towards a new dynamic", (1996) 16 *OJLS*.
36	R. Harmsen, "A European Union of Variable Geometry: Problems and Perspective", (1994) 45 *Northern Ireland Legal Quarterly* 109-133.
37	E.g. *Opinion 1/94* on the conclusion of the GATT Uruguay Round and the involvement of the EU and its Member States in the World Trade Organisation [1994] ECR I-5267.
38	E.g. the use of minimum harmonization measures allowing Member States to maintain in force stricter requirements; the use of non-binding measures such as Recommendations and Resolutions instead of binding Directives.
39	Vol. 4, No. 4 (1995), ed. D. Nelken.
40	See in particular R. Bellamy *et al* (eds.), *Democracy and Constitutional Culture in the Union of Europe*, 1995, London: Lothian Foundation Press; M. Everson, "The Legacy of the Market Citizen", in J. Shaw and G. More, op. cit. *supra* n.12; A. Rosas and E. Antola (eds.), *A Citizens' Europe*, 1995, London, etc.: Sage.
41	"The Reformation of European Constitutional Law", Plenary Paper delivered to the UACES Research Conference, Birmingham University, September 1995. See also D. Wincott, "Political theory, Law, and European Union", in J. Shaw and G. More, op. cit. *supra* n.12.

42	See in particular F. Snyder, *'Out on the Weekend': Reflections on European Union Law in Context*, EUI Working Paper LAW No. 94/11.
43	Of the work of Majone see in particular *Deregulation or Re-regulation*, 1990, London: Pinter; "Cross-National Sources of Regulatory Policymaking in Europe and the United States", (1991) 11 *Journal of Public Policy* 79; "Market Integration and Regulation: Europe after 1992", (1992) 43 *Metroeconomica* 131; "Regulatory Federalism in the European Community", (1992) *Government and Policy* 299; *Independence vs. Accountability*, EUI Working Paper SPS No. 94/3; *Understanding Regulatory Growth in the European Community*, EUI Working Paper SPS 94/17; "The Rise of the Regulatory State in Europe", (1994) 17 *West European Politics* 77.
44	M. Bishop *et al* (eds.), *The Regulatory Challenge*, 1995, Oxford: Oxford University Press; A. Ogus, op. cit. *supra* n.3.
45	See also R. Dehousse et al, *Europe After 1992. New Regulatory Strategies*, EUI Working Paper LAW No. 92/31; K. Gatsios and P. Seabright, "Regulation in the European Community", (1989) 5 *Oxford Review of Economic Policy* 37; J. Pelkmans, "Regulation and the Single Market: An Economic Perspective", in H. Siebert (ed.), *The Completion of the Internal Market*, 1989, Tübingen: JCB Mohr; J. Kay and J. Vickers, "Regulatory Reform: An Appraisal", in G. Majone, *Deregulation or Re-regulation*, op. cit. *supra* n.43; S. Woolcock, "European and North American Approaches to Regulation," in W. Wallace (ed.), *The end of the West*, forthcoming, 1995; F. McGowan and P. Seabright, "Regulation in the European Community and its impact on the UK", in Bishop, op. cit. *supra* n.44.
46	Case 8/74 *Procureur du Roi* v *Dassonville* [1974] ECR 837; Case 120/78 *Rewe Zentrale* v *Bundesmonopolverwaltung für Branntwein (Cassis de Dijon)* [1979] ECR 649; Case C-159/90 *Society for the Protection of Unborn Children* v *Grogan* [1991] ECR I-4685.
47	Compare the approach of the Court pre-Maastricht in Case C-300/89 *Commission* v *Council (Titanium Dioxide)* [1991] ECR I-2867 where the internal market motive was dominant in the selection of the correct legal basis with its post-Maastricht acknowledgement of the specifities of environmental and other common policies in Case C-155/91 *Commission* v *Council* (17.3.93; unreported) and Case C-187/93 *Parliament* v *Council* [1994] ECR I-2857.
48	E.g. K. Armstrong, op. cit. *supra* n.12.
49	G. Knieps, "Deregulation in Europe: Telecommunications and Transportation", in G. Majone, *Deregulation and Re-regulation*, op. cit. *supra* n.43; see also the contributions of C. Scott and L. Flynn *infra* n.75.
50	E.g. A. Cox and J. Sanderson, "From mobilization of bias to trade wars: the making and implementing of the European Community utilities procurement rules", (1994) 1 *Journal of European Public Policy* 263.
51	J. Falke and C. Joerges, *"Traditional" Harmonisation Policy, European Consumer Protection Progammes and the New Approach*, EUI Working Paper LAW 91/3.

52   E.g. F. Snyder (ed.), *A Regulatory Framework for Foodstuffs in the Internal Market*, EUI Working Paper LAW 94/4.

53   C. Joerges, "Paradoxes of Deregulatory Strategies at Community Level: The Example of Product Safety Policy", in G. Majone, *Deregulation and Re-regulation*, op. cit. *supra* n.43; ibid, *The Juridification of Product Safety*, EUI Working Paper LAW 91/10; ibid, "Product Safety in the European Community: Market Integration, Social regulation and Legal Structures", (1992) 38 *Journal of Behavioural and Social Science* 132.

54   K. Lenaerts, "Regulating the Regulatory Process: "Delegation of Powers" in the European Community", (1993) 18 ELRev. 23; G. Majone, *Independence vs. Accountability*, op. cit. *supra* n.43; M. Everson, "Independent Agencies: Hierarchy Beaters?", (1995) 1 *European Law Journal* 180.

55   But see also a contribution by a lawyer: N. Reich, "Competition between legal orders: a new paradigm of EC law?", (1992) 29 CMLRev. 861.

56   See generally H. Siebert, "The Harmonisation Issue in Europe: Prior Agreement or a Competitive Process?", in H. Siebert, op. cit. *supra* n.45; H. Siebert and M. Koop, "Institutional Competition versus centralization: quo vadis Europe?", (1993) 9 *Oxford Review of Economic Policy* 15; S. Woolcock, *The Single European Market. Centralization or Competition among National rules*, 1994, London: RIAA; J.-M. Sun and J. Pelkmans, "Regulatory Competition in the Single Market", (1994) 33 *Journal of Common Market Studies* 67.

57   *Efficiency, Stability and Equity*, 187, Oxford: Oxford University Press.

58   Op. cit.*supra* n.56 at p.5 *et seq*.

59   Largely derived from C. Tiebout, "A pure theory of local expenditures", (1956) 64 *Journal of Political Economy* 416.

60   E.g. V. Curzon Price, "Three Models of European Integration", in Dahrendorf *et al, Whose Europe? Competing Visions for 1992*, 1989, London: Institute of Economic Affairs.

61   J.-M. Sun and J. Pelkmans, op. cit. *supra* n.56 at pp.68-9.

62   Op. cit. *supra* n.56 at pp.56, 68.

63   Op. cit. *supra* n.55 at p.862.

64   N. Adnett, "Social Dumping and European Economic Integration", (1995) 5 *Journal of European Social Policy* 1.

65   *Social Dumping or Innovative regulation. Processes and Outcomes of European Decision-Making in the Sector of Health and Safety at Work Harmonization*, EUI Working Paper SOS No. 92/28.

66   N. Deakin and F. Wilkinson, "Rights vs. Efficiency? The Economic Case for Transnational Labour Standards", (1994) 23 ILJ 289; G. More, "The Acquired Rights Directive: Frustrating or Facilitating Labour Market Flexibility", in J. Shaw and G. More, op. cit. *supra* n.12.

67   S. Bulmer, "The Governance of the European Union", op. cit. *supra* n.12; M. Jachtenfuchs, "Theoretical Perspectives on European Governance", (1995) 1 *European Law Journal* 115.

68   J. Kooiman, "Social-Political governance: Introduction", in J. Kooiman (ed.), *Modern Governance*, 1993, London etc.: Sage, at p.2.

69   W. Streeck, "Neo-Voluntarism: A New European Social Policy Regime?", (1995) 1 *European Law Journal* 31.

70   Neo-functionalism, and a version of realism focused on intergovernmentalist mechanisms and concepts.

71   S. Hix, "The Study of the European Community: The Challenge of Comparative Politics", (1994) *West European Politics* 1.

72   G. Majone, "Ideas, Interests and Institutions: Explaining the Revival of Policy Analysis in the 1980s", Paper presented to the XVIth World Congress of the International Political Association, Berlin, August 21-25 1994; L. Cram, "Policy-Making and the Integration Process - Implications for Integration Theory". Paper presented to the Fourth Biennial International Conference of the European Community Studies Association, Charleston, SC, May 11-14 1995.

73   A. Moravcsik, "Preferences and Power in the European Community: A Liberal Intergovernmentalist Approach", (1993) 31 *Journal of Common Market Studies* 473.

74   M. Jachtenfuchs and B. Kohler-Koch, "The Transformation of Governance in the European Union". Paper presented at the Fourth Biennial International Conference of the European Community Studies Association, Charleston, SC, May 11-14, 1995 at p.14.

75   See, for example, P. Schmitter, "Representation and the Future Euro-Polity", (1992) 3 *Staatswissenschaft und Staatspraxis* 379.

76   J. Weiler, "Problems of Legitimacy in Post 1992 Europe", (1991) 46 *Aussenwirtschaft* 411-437.

77   E.g. J. Greenwood, J. Gröte and K. Ronit, *Organized Interests and the European Community*, 1992, London/Beverley Hills: Sage.

78   C. Harlow, "A Community of Interests? Making the Most of European Law", (1992) 55 MLR 331-350; ibid, "Towards a Theory of Access for the European Court of Justice", (1992) 12 *Yearbook of European Law* 213; C. Barnard, "A European Litigation Strategy: the Case of the Equal Opportunities Commission", in J. Shaw and G. More, op. cit. *supra* n.10.

79   For a review of much of the recent research see J. Peterson, "Decision-making in the European Union: towards a framework for analysis", (1995) 2 *European Journal of Public Policy* 69-93.

80   S. Bulmer, op. cit. *supra* n.12 at p.355.

81   J. March and J. Olsen, *Rediscovering Institutions*, 1989, New York: Free Press, at p.17

82   Cf. R. Dehousse and J. Weiler, "The legal dimension", in W. Wallace, op. cit. *supra* n.22.

83   From a legal perspective see C. Scott, "Changing Patters of European Community Utilities Law and Policy: An Institutional Hypothesis" and L. Flynn, "Telecommunications and EU Integration", in J. Shaw and G. More, op. cit. *supra* n.10; from a political science perspective: L. Cram, "Calling the

Rune without paying the piper? Social Policy Regulation: The Role of the Commission in European Union Social Policy", (1993) 21 *Policy and Politics* 135-146; ibid, "The European Commission as a Multi-Organization: Social Policy and IT Policy in the EU", (1994) 1 *Journal of European Public Policy* 195-217; S. Bulmer, op. cit. *supra* n.12; G. Peters, "Agenda-Setting in the European Community", (1994) 1 *Journal of European Public Policy* 9-26. See also G. Majone, "The European Community between Social Policy and Social Regulation", (1993) 31 *Journal of Common Market Studies* 153-169. From a rather different perspective of 'leadership' and the interaction between individuals and policy outcomes see H. Drake, "Defining the Commission: the Politics of Legitimacy". Paper presented to the UACES Research Conference, Birmingham, September 18-19, 1995. The central role of the Commission is confirmed by a forthcoming volume: S. George and N. Nugent, *The European Commission*, 1996, London: Macmillan.

84 "The Role of Law or the Rule of the Court of Justice? An 'institutional' account of judicial politics in the European Community", (1995) 2 *Journal of European Public Policy* forthcoming; "The European Court of Justice in Policy Perspective", Paper presented to the Fourth Biennial ECSA Conference, Charleston, SC, USA, May 1995. K. Alter and S. Meunier-Aitsahalia, "Judicial Politics in the European Union: European Integration and the Pathbreaking Cassis de Dijon Decision", (1994) 26 *Comparative Political Studies* 536-561; K. Alter, "Legal Integration in the Euorpean Community and Integration Theory: A Focus on National Judiciaries of the Member States - the Case of Germany". Paper presented to the 2nd ECSA World Conference, Brussels, May 5-6, 1994.

85 E.g. M. Shapiro, "Comparative Law and Comparative Politics", (1981) 53 *Southern California Law Review* 537-42.

86 D. Wincott, op. cit. *supra* n.41.

87 But see an important exception to this bifurcation: J. Weiler, "Community, Member States and European Integration: Is the Law Relevant?", (1982) 21 *Journal of Common Market Studies* 39-56; from the perspective of political analysis, an exception is S. Scheingold, *The Law in Political Integration*, 1971, Cambridge, MA: Barvard University Center for International Affairs and ibid, *The Rule of Law in European Integration*, 1965, New Haven, Conn.: Yale University Press.

88 J. Tranholm-Mikkelsen, "Neo-Functionalism: Obstinate or obsolete? A reappraisal in the light of the new dynamism of the EC", (1991) 20 *Millenium* 1-22.

89 A.-M. Burley and W. Mattli, "Europe before the Court: A Political Theory of Legal Integration", (1993) *International Organization* 41. A note to avoid confusion in the paragraphs which follow: Burley now publishes in the name of Slaughter.

90 E. Haas, "International Integration: The European and the Universal Process", (1961) 15 *International Organization* 366-392; see also Haas' pioneering study *The Uniting of Europe*, 1956, London: Stanford Univ. Press.

91   For their reaction to this see W. Mattli and A.-M. Slaughter, "Law and politics in the European Union: a reply to Garrett", (1995) 49 *International Organization* 183-190 at p.189.

92   Case C-262/88 *Barber* v *Guardian Royal Exchange* [1990] ECR I-1889.

93   See T. Hervey, "Legal Issues concerning the *Barber* Protocol", in O'Keeffe and Twomey, op. cit. *supra* n.33.

94   A.-M. Burley and W. Mattli, op. cit. *supra* n.89 at p.43.

95   As yet unpublished; see W. Mattli and A.-M. Slaughter, *Constructing the European Community Legal System from the Ground up: the Role of Individual Litigants and National Courts*, forthcoming, EUI Working Paper, RSC 1996.

96   See the lines of research suggested by A.-M. Slaughter Burley, "New Directions in Legal Research on the European Community", (1993) 31 *Journal of Common Market Studies* 391-400.

97   I am drawing in this section on my "Introduction" to Shaw and More, op. cit. *supra* n.10 at pp.7-10.

98   D. Wincott, "The European Court of Justice in Policy Perspective". Paper presented to the Fourth Biennial ECSA Conference, Charleston, SC, May 11-15, 1995.

99   There is no space in this paper to consider a further development in studies of the Court of Justice. Based on public awareness and opinion surveys by EUROSTAT, Gibson and Caldeira have been developing models of popular legitimacy for the Court of Justice: J. Gibson and G. Caldeira, "The European Court of Justice: A Question of Legitimacy", (1993) 14 *Zeitschrift für Rechtssoziologie* 204-222; ibid, "The Legitimacy of Transnational Legal Institutions: Compliance, Support, and the European Court of Justice", (1995) 39 *American Journal of Political Science* 459-489; ibid, "The Legitimacy of the Court of Justice in the European Union: Models of Institutional Support", (1995) 89 *American Political Science Review* 356-376.

100   See, for a consideration of implementation questions from a 'governance' perspective: J. From and P. Stava, "Implementation of Community Law: the last stronghold of national control?", in S. Andersen and K. Eliassen (eds.), *Making Policy in Europe. The Europeification of National Policy-making*, 1993, London, etc.: Sage.

101   Op. cit. *supra* n.7.

102   The project is entitled "The Role of the Firm in the Evolution of Rules for the Single European Market"; see D. Matthews and D. Mayes, "The Role of Soft Law in the Evolution of Rules for a Single European Market: the Case of Retailing". Paper presented to the Fourth Biennial International Conference of the European Community Studies Association, Charleston, SC, May 11-15 1995.

103   K. Wellens and G. Borchardt, "Soft Law in European Community Law," (1989) 14 *ELRev.* 267.

104   Research findings published as H. Siedentopf and J. Ziller (eds.), *Making European Policies Work. The Implementation of Community Legislation in the*

Member States 2 vols., 1988, London, etc., Sage. Other examples include the ESRC funded study of the implementation of single market legislation in the UK by Daintith and others published as T. Daintith (ed.), *Implementing EC Law in the United Kingdom: Structures for Indirect Rule* 1995, Chichester, John Wiley & Sons and two notable narrower studies: H.-W. Micklitz et al (eds.), *Federalism and Responsibility* 1994, London, Graham and Trotman (product safety directive) and R. Baldwin and T. Daintith (eds.), *Harmonisation and Hazard: Regulating Health and Safety in the European Workplace*, 1992, London, Graham and Trotman (health and safety directives). A rather different focus - on national judicial behaviour - is to be found in the Hamburg-based study of the application of Articles 85 and 86 EC in national courts: Behrens (ed.), *EEC Competition Rules in National Courts*, Vols. 1 and 2, 1992/1994, Baden-Baden: Nomos.

105   R. Cotterrell, op. cit. *supra* n.2 at pp.296 *et seq.*

106   A. Sarat and S. Silbey, "The Pull of the Policy Audience", (1988) 10 *Law and Policy* 97.

107   See esp.D. McBarnet and C. Whelan, op. cit. *supra* n.7.

108   R. Rawlings, "The Eurolaw Game: Some Deductions from a Saga", (1993) 20 *Journal of Law and Society* 309; C. Barnard, op. cit. *supra* n.78.

109   See G. Ross, *Jacques Delors and European Integration*, 1995, Cambridge: Polity (a masterly and so far unique study based on participant observation of the work of the Delors Cabinet); S. Zabusky, *Launching Europe. An Ethnography of European Cooperation in Space Science*, 1995, Princeton, NJ: Princeton UP; U. Hedetoft, "National Identities and European Integration 'From Below': Bringing People Back In", (1994) 18 *Journal of European Integration* 1. As part of the study of 'European identity', anthropologists C. Shore and A. Black emphasise the importance of work amongst and with the *fonctionnaires* of the European Union: "Citizens' Europe and the Construction of European Identity", in V. Goddard *et al* (eds.) op. cit. *supra* n.22; a similar call for a better understanding of political and cultural integration from Tarrow requires the greater involvement of sociologists and anthropologists in European studies: S. Tarrow, *Rebirth or Stagnation: European Studies after 1989*, 1994, New York.

110   H.L. Ackers, "Women, Citizenship and European Community Law: The Gender Implications of the Free Movement Provisions", [1994] *Journal of Social Welfare and Family Law* 391; ibid, "Research Report: Women, Citizenship and European Community Law: The Gender Implications of the Free Movement Provisions" [1995] *Journal of Social Welfare and Family Law* 498; ibid, "Citizenship, Gender and Dependency in the European Union: The Position of Migrant Women", (1995) *Social Politics* forthcoming.

111   Cf. F. Snyder, op. cit. *supra* n.42.

112   D. Mayes, "The Future Research Agenda", S. Bulmer and A. Scott op. cit. *supra* n.16 at p265.

113   R. Cotterrell, op. cit. *supra* n.2 at p.307.

114   See H. Schepel, "Legal Pluralism in the European Union". Paper presented to the Critical Legal Conference, Edinburgh, September 1995, building particularly on the work of Fitzpatrick, op. cit. *supra* n.20.

15 Family Law

SIMON JOLLY

Introduction

Family law is one of the more successful areas for the socio-legal enterprise. Whilst the laws applicable to the family have changed greatly since the 1960s,[1] socio-legal research has kept pace with these changes, explored the ramifications of the changing nature of the family and, at times, influenced the direction of reform. Major research projects - both empirical and theoretical - have examined divorce, family finance, domestic violence, and the care and protection of children.[2] The rapid development of family law has made the field a constantly stimulating one for the socio-legal researcher, with law reforms generating research, which has itself often encouraged more reform.[3] This development has been fostered and encouraged by the leading role of the Law Commission, which has successfully promoted many of the most significant changes in family law, drawing upon and encouraging socio-legal research in the process.[4] Socio-legal approaches have been integrated into 'mainstream' family law, gaining inclusion in text-books, teaching and journals.[5] There is an acknowledgement of the value of empiricism - and sometimes even of theoretical approaches.[6]

In a more cynical vein, however, it might be said that the wave of law reform has fuelled a multitude of research projects which have sustained the careers of many researchers. Funding for research is limited, but it could be argued that family law has had more than its fair share over the last couple of decades.[7] Socio-legal research is driven by a desire to investigate the workings of the law, and the behaviour of legal actors. The success of such research is often premised upon (a usually tacit) claim that law can be an effective implement of social change, and that therefore research should address legal form and legal practice in order to demonstrate ways of effecting such change. There have been many successes, but these have perhaps sometimes prevented the emergence of a more fully theorised account of law's role in family life, and concealed the extent to which alternative strategies and discourses might better succeed where law, and law reform, have failed.

Socio-legal research does not have to be reformist, and indeed, there have been many significant contributions in of family law which challenge the very notion that law can (or does) act as a force for the benefit of society.[8] The main strength of socio-legal studies has been the wide range of methodological approaches, deriving from many (often opposing) theoretical bases, which can be drawn upon in order to critically consider the relationship between law and society. In that regard, socio-legal studies is less a shared perspective than a common interest. Certainly, within socio-legal work on the family, there has been an emphasis upon empirical projects (not all of which are reformist in orientation), many of which have originated from a few academic centres, in particular the Oxford Centre for Socio-Legal Studies, together with the Bristol Socio-Legal Centre for Family Studies, and latterly the Brunel Centre for the Study of Law, the Child and the Family.[9] Purely theoretical work does, however, form a major part of the canon of socio-legal research which those interested in the field are able to draw upon. Within this chapter I consider the diversity of socio-legal family law,[10] highlighting a few areas in particular, so as to explore those aspects of the socio-legal project upon which I believe attention must be increasingly focused. These future directions for research will be influenced by the rich heritage of past research, but they will also emerge as a consequence of changes in the nature of the family and of family law.

The Ending Of Relationships

Family law has only latterly become established as a coherent sub-discipline of law.[11] Some would argue that it was the reforms of the 1960s which truly signified the birth of modern Family law,[12] but it is certainly true that the divorce law reform of 1969[13] marked a watershed in its history, and that of family law research. The debate, which still continues, over the significance of divorce reform, has proved to be a microcosm of more general arguments as to the usefulness of socio-legal research.[14] What is clear is that the advent of widely available divorce has changed the nature of family relationships, and directed the attention of researchers towards the problems of untangling broken relationships whilst delivering justice (particularly financial justice) to both sides.

Much of the research into post-divorce finances has concentrated upon the legal actors involved in the process: the registrars, judges, barristers and solicitors. Richard Ingleby's 1992 monograph *Solicitors and Divorce* is an obvious example, as is John Eekelaar's study *Regulating Divorce*, (1991).[15] This work has been important in establishing what judges *do* - particularly crucial since the legal process allows so much discretion in the disposition of individual cases. This kind of examination of the *rhetoric* of law (what Eekelaar calls 'the *official version* of what the law seeks to achieve') clearly plays a major role in socio-legal analysis. However, we must not blind ourselves to the very real pragmatic explanations for the large number of socio-legal family research projects which obtain their data by examining legal actors - whether directly, in the context of their performance in court, or indirectly, through interviews in which lawyers/judges are asked to give their views on the way that the law works. Much of this research is carried out by academic lawyers who have often fostered close links with local judges/solicitors.[16] Access is thus easier to obtain, and research can often be conducted on the basis of the existence of shared assumptions and knowledge between interviewer and interviewee. Studying lawyers is also a more efficient way of gathering large amounts of information about how law works, since lawyers are obviously the archetypal 'repeat players' within the legal system, which additionally makes longitudinal, follow-up studies possible.

Some socio-legal research has attempted to evaluate the impact of the law from the perspective of the parties involved. Mervyn Murch, *Justice and Welfare in Divorce*, (1980), considers the process of divorce and child custody from the perspective of the parents involved. More

344

recently, Davis, Cretney & Collins's major study, *Simple Quarrels* (1994), attempted to overcome reliance upon legal actors as the source of information by evaluating the financial battles during divorce from both the solicitors' and litigants' perspective. The research highlighted the prevalence of negotiation over adjudication (a familiar theme in civil justice research), problems of delay in Legal Aid decisions, inaction from solicitors, and difficulty in securing information from recalcitrant spouses, amongst other problems with the system.[17] The most significant study of the longer-term financial impact of divorce is Eekelaar and Maclean's *Maintenance After Divorce*, (1986), which provided a spousal perspective on the economic effects of divorce by surveying the sources of financial support (including maintenance, employment, and welfare benefits) of a representative sample of divorcees. Feminist theory has also had a large influence upon socio-legal research into post-relationship finance. Work such as Carol Smart's *The Ties That Bind* (1984), and Katherine O'Donovan's *Sexual Divisions and the Law* (1985), focused particularly upon the way in which family law sustains patriarchy both practically and ideologically in its management of relationship breakdown. This combination of feminist theory and empirical study has helped move the focus of socio-legal research out of the court-room and into the living-room - or perhaps more accurately, the bedsit.[18]

The 'Diffusion' Of Family Law: Expanding The Socio-Legal Project?

The need for non-courtroom based socio-legal research becomes even more acute in the future as major elements of family law are removed from the courts, and greater power is placed in the hands of administrators, mediators, and non-legal professionals. This process - which could be called the diffusion of family law - has already been emphasised by the introduction of the Child Support Act 1991, and will accelerate rapidly when the long-awaited divorce reforms are introduced. As the role of lawyers in supervising relationship breakdown diminishes,[19] socio-legal researchers must come to terms with the fundamental changes which are being introduced, and find new ways of investigating the hidden power of law in its administrative guise.

The troubled introduction of the Child Support Act 1991 has furthered a move away from formalised legal adjudication,[20] and towards administrative decision-making away from the gaze of the court-room. Much previous research investigating the financial consequences of relationship breakdown has concentrated upon the exercise of discretion, either by judges, or by solicitors. Child support decisions will, however, be made on the basis of a non-discretionary formula, which will be calculated by an employee of the Child Support Agency, so that research which focuses upon the decision-making process itself may reveal little or nothing.[21] Researchers must use diverse methodologies to examine the effect of such decisions upon the lived realities of single parents,[22] and within this research the theoretical focus must shift from the uses of discretion to the uses of power.[23] This move from examining discretion - the traditional focus of socio-legal family law research[24] - to the examination of administrative power seems crucial to the future success of socio-legal research in this area, particularly if further divorce reform reduces the role of the court, and increases the role of mediation. This is not to say, however, that the family justice system will cease to be significant, and in fact it may be that mediation will simply delay, rather than avoid, recourse to the courts. Further analysis, to complement existing studies of legal process and its impact on the family,[25] will continue to be necessary.

Since the 1969 divorce reforms, a considerable amount of socio-legal research has concentrated upon the contradictions and confusions which dominate the current divorce law. The work of Davis and Murch, *The Grounds for Divorce* (1988), is one of the most influential of the recent studies of the divorce process, and has been cited as a factor leading to the pressure for proposed reform in the area, together with John Eekelaar's, *Regulating Divorce* (1991). Assuming that we do see a new, non-fault-based, divorce law,[26] its arrival could have major consequences for socio-legal family law. Divorce will change from being a judicial process to an administrative process, and other professions could take over from lawyers in managing the process.[27] Again, this diffusion of family law will require researchers to respond to the changes by investigating the role of non-legal professionals upon the family.[28] Much socio-legal research has already anticipated this change, and focused upon the role of mediators in the ending of relationships.[29] This research on divorce mediation provides an illustration of the need to adapt to the dispersal of control over the family. In order to respond, socio-legal research must increasingly concentrate not only on the impact of legal professionals within family law, but also on the growing impact of non-legal discourses and professions.

The work of Dingwall and Greatbatch,[30] in particular, illuminates the potential dangers posed by the diffusion of family law, and suggests possible ways ahead for socio-legal research in response. Their research[31] is a deliberately provocative attempt to highlight the weaknesses endemic in some socio-legal research. Socio-legal researchers have become very effective at identifying the ideological bases of family law, but often fail to acknowledge the ideological potential of *non-legal* discourses operating on the family.[32] Dingwall and Greatbatch attempt to come to terms with this by defending the formalism of law, and exposing the concealment of power within the avowedly 'impartial' setting of the mediation process.[33] Ultimately they do not argue for a return to legalism, but rather that we can learn from adverserialism when considering the exercise of power in avowedly 'non-legal' settings. Sociological theories of power are necessary in order for socio-legal scholars to critique less self-evident mechanisms of control than judicial decisions.

Child Law And Socio-legal Research

The rights, welfare, and protection of children have developed into a major concern of socio-legal research - an interest which has burgeoned since the introduction of the Children Act 1989, which codified much of the law governing the upbringing of children. The Children Act itself was influenced by socio-legal research, since it developed from the

347

recommendations of the Report of the Interdepartmental Working Party,[34] which in turn drew heavily upon socio-legal research studies, particularly those examining child protection issues, in order to aid its conclusions.[35] Law reform in this area has also been influenced by the large amount of social policy research which has focused upon the child. Indeed, the links between socio-legal and social policy family research have perhaps been at their most obvious in the areas of child welfare and child protection.[36] Social policy research has examined the relationship between local authority actions and family and child development,[37] and the consequences for children of relationship breakdown,[38] whilst socio-legal research has studied the processes prior to legal intervention, and the nature of that intervention itself, whether in (private) divorce proceedings[39] or in (public) care proceedings.[40] The separation of disciplines, however, has often been more evident in the formation of separate academic cliques than in substantive differences in the nature, and object, of the research undertaken.[41] Social policy research examining the impact of care proceedings upon children and their families, for instance, has considered the regulation of families through administrative processes controlled by local authorities[42] - an area which could easily be characterised as socio-legal, whilst socio-legal research examining the role of the state in supporting children's welfare during divorce[43] could equally be characterised as social policy research. Whatever labels are attached, such work has had considerable success in bringing the issue of children's welfare to the forefront of contemporary concerns in family law.

Socio-legal research on children has often drawn from, and complemented social policy research, whilst giving it a socio-legal 'twist'. Whilst social policy studies on children have developed and critiqued the concepts of children's needs and children's welfare in the context of parental and state care, socio-legal research such as King and Trowell, *Children's Welfare and the Law* (1992), has focused upon the specific (socio-legal) issue of whether the efforts of the legal system to provide 'justice' to all parties in child protection/child abuse cases militate against the welfare of the child to an unacceptable degree.[44] This stream of research draws upon an ongoing debate within social policy about the costs and benefits of state intervention on children's **upbringing, and** focuses upon the processes prior to legal intervention.[45] **King and Trowell** conducted their research by examining a series of cases which are derived from the work of the Tavistock Clinic (where Trowell is a Consultant Psychiatrist). Their conclusion, that the law's intervention frequently harms children's welfare, has again problematised the role of law in the regulation of the family, one of the 'macro-themes' of socio-legal studies in the family law area,[46] and reflects the scepticism which much research on children's welfare has raised about law's ability to mediate between the demands of welfarism and legalism.[47]

Conclusions

Socio-legal family law has produced some excellent research but researchers must adapt and develop new strategies to deal with a wide variety of challenges. Socio-legal studies as a whole must address the challenges posed by the development of critical and postmodern theories which address the roles of law and society. I do not wish to suggest that this is a new phenomenon - Michael Freeman proposed a critical theory of family law in 1985[48]- but it is arguable that socio-legal research on the family has paid too little attention to 'high level' theory. Ruth Deech, in her attack upon socio-legal family law research,[49] claims that empirical evidence - which has often been the primary focus of socio-legal researchers - is liable to misuse and misinterpretation. Whilst this is true,[50] see Law Commission, *The Field of Choice*, (1966), and Wimperis, *The Unmarried Mother and Her Child*, (1960).[51] the answer does not lie in abandoning empirical research, but in making use of theory to problematise, interpret, and *condition* empirical research studies. Eekelaar and Maclean, in their response to Deech, argue that interpretation is always a subjective, value-laden exercise, and that this does not render social science data useless, but focuses attention upon the ideological position adopted by the interpreter (whether the researcher or reader).[52] Whilst acknowledging the inevitability of such values, however, Eekelaar and Maclean do still attempt to 'fire-wall' data itself from the burning of rampant subjectivism. They state that the selection of issues for research within the context of the social construction of social problems, but in stating that 'the researcher moves from findings to evaluation' (p 628), and that 'we cannot see why researchers should be barred from expressing a view about reform provided that these views are differentiated from the presentation of the data' (p 629), they seem to suggest that it is possible to separate data from interpretation[53] - a suggestion which I would reject. It is not possible to 'safely move from the descriptive to the normative' (p 630) because the two states are inseparable. This is, of course, a well-worn, if comparatively recent dispute which impacts upon all areas of socio-legal research. One view is that the 'postmodern' issue is capable of tearing apart socio-legal studies: they are in competition. The strength of socio-legal research, however, is that it does not derive from a single ideology - indeed Eekelaar and Maclean themselves state that socio-legal study, 'needs to draw on broader legal theory', but that it, 'does not stipulate which... theories needs to be used'.[54] 'Background' ideologies must be brought into the foreground if the myth of objectivity (whether in production or interpretation) is to be exploded. Michael King's research may again serve as an illustration of such 'foregrounding' of theory within a socio-legal analysis. King explicitly draws upon legal theory, using the theories of Gunter Teubner and Niklaus Luhmann in particular to explore issues around the treatment of children by the law.[55] If socio-legal research is to explore the *function* of child law, together with the way in which legal actors conceive of children, their rights,[56] and their welfare, then this type of research, drawing upon high-level theory with the traditions of empirical research, seems crucial.[57]

Some of the challenges facing the socio-legal family researcher will undoubtedly come from less intellectual pressures within academia. As research becomes increasingly 'commodified',[58] there is a danger that future projects may become funder-driven rather researcher-driven, with negative consequences.[59] Securing research funding will become more important for many researchers, either to fund their own time, or because of the status which accrues to research fund-holders within academic institutions.[60] Whilst the relationship between funders and researchers can be very productive, and indeed many of the most significant family/law research projects could not have been carried out without support from funding bodies, it may be that the drive for cash will lead to the dominance of user-defined policy-oriented research over other, perhaps more radical projects.[61] This could potentially stifle theoretical work, in particular.

A further pressure comes from the particular characteristics of the research culture which is being created within British academia. Much of the best family/law socio-legal research has been of a longitudinal nature, using a variety of methodologies during the course of the project. Gwynn Davis, *Partisans and Mediators*, (1988), provides an excellent illustration. The project (which contrasted the services offered by solicitors with those of mediators) used open-ended, qualitative interviews with divorcing couples as one of the main methodological tools, together with interviews with solicitors, observation of court hearings, study of court files, observation of mediation appointments, and various other, informal methods. The book was drawn from no less than five separate research studies carried out at the Bristol Centre, which were funded primarily by The Rowntree and Nuffield charitable trusts. This type of approach is often necessary before a fully-rounded socio-legal analysis can be undertaken. However, the combination of the all-pervasive Research Assessment Exercise,[62] and the institutional pressures upon academic staff to produce quick publications (particularly those on fixed term and probationary contracts), encourages a short-termism in research which is an anathema to such an approach.

Whilst the academic environment rapidly alters, the twin subjects of researchers in this area - family and law - will also continue to change. The family is frequently portrayed as a crisis-ridden institution - a tabloid front page headline read, "The End of Family Life in Britain" (*The Daily Express*, August 23 1995), and reported upon record levels of divorce petitions in Britain, suggesting that the decline of the 'traditional' family was linked to falling moral standards, and rising crime rates. Socio-legal research has certainly mapped vast changes in its nature over the past two decades, but talk of the family's decline is merely the manifestation of a nostalgia for a particular, idealised form of the family (in contemporary terms usually the 'nuclear family'). Changing demographics will, however, certainly continue to challenge our conceptions of family.[63] Falling marriage rates, and increasing numbers of 'non-nuclear' families seem likely to be factors, and the growing numbers of elderly family members, living either at home or in care will also influence the future family. Little socio-legal research has so far focused upon the elderly,[64] but the ageing population will make this area increasingly important.[65]

Reports of the family in crisis may prove an exaggeration, but family *law* does seem to be undergoing a crisis of identity. Family law reform has been ceaseless over the last twenty years, and whilst some momentum may dissipate,[66] law reform does not seem likely to stop in the immediate future, but rather to manifest itself in the movement towards dejuridification, which is already apparent in the move from court-room decision-making to administrative decision-making in some areas.[67] Family law may be less recognisable in future as law - in its broadest senses - is imposed upon the family by non-lawyers, in non-legal settings. This increasing influence of non-lawyers upon the family may raise questions about the scope of socio-legal studies itself. Eekelaar and Maclean state that, 'socio-legal study imposes the unifying discipline of observing the way in which law works through those who believe themselves to be acting out the law'.[68] Whilst this offers useful guidance, in future socio-legal family law research may increasingly focus upon the actions of individuals who do *not* 'believe themselves to be acting out the law'. These individuals, whether mediators, child psychologists, social workers, or civil servants, may not characterise their actions as 'legal' - and some observers may agree. Nevertheless, they will be part of the (increasingly broad) technology of control over the family, administrated at arm's length by law, and as such socio-legal researchers should study the nature and consequences of their actions. Socio-legal studies partially developed as a response to the inflexibility and parochial concerns of 'black-letter' approaches to law: it must not itself remain too inflexible to confront the challenges posed by the regulation of future families.

I am grateful to Ralph Sandland and Petra Wilson for commenting on earlier drafts of this chapter.

Notes

1   See B. Hoggett, "Family Law Reform: Where Will It End?", (1992) 3 King's College Law Journal 64, for an overview of developments in family law since the 1960s. It could even be argued that before the 1960s the study of family law did not exist as a separate discipline. Hoggett gives much of the credit to Peter Bromley, who gathered together what is now the commonplace range of interests for those researching the family in his 1957 textbook: P. Bromley, *Family Law*, (1st edition, 1957).

2   *Ibid*, parts II. and III..

3   The Children Act 1989, provides a good illustration of this phenomenon: it has spawned dozens of projects examining the operation of the new law, and the practices of the multiple agencies involved in the protection and support of children. See, *post*, part IV.

4   See, Hoggett - herself a Law Commissioner until recently - *ibid*, (1992), for a review of the Law Commission's key role in the wave of Family Law reform since the 1960s. The Law Commission's first programme of law reform in 1965 was based around family law reform, and by 1992 twenty two out of the thirty Law Commission reports concerning the family had directly generated legislation (p. 66).

5   See, for example, Hoggett and Pearl, *The Family Law and Society: Cases and Materials*, (3rd ed., 1991), Eekelaar, *Family Law and Social Policy*, (2nd ed., 1984).

6   Social policy is certainly easier to promote and recognise within family law than in many other legal areas, although see, R. Deech, "Divorce Law and Empirical Studies", 106 *Law Quarterly Review*, (1990) 229 for a trenchant attack upon the role of socio-legal studies in family law - which is considered *post*.

7   See, Economic and Social Research Council, *Review of Socio-Legal Studies*, (1994) and M. Partington, *Developing the socio-legal research agenda in Civil Law and Civil Justice*, (1994). See P. A. Thomas, Chapter 1 in this book.

8   See, M. D. A. Freeman, "Towards a Critical Family Law" (1985) *Current Legal Problems*, 153, and K. O'Donovan, *Sexual Divisions in the Law*, (1985) and *Family Law Matters*, (1993).

9   See, amongst others, the work of Maclean, Eekelaar, Dingwall, Gibson, Davis, Murch, King, and Piper, who have all been involved with one of the three Centres.

10   Various aspects of socio-legal family/law research will be considered within this paper. It is not intended, however, to serve as a bibliography of socio-legal family law research, but rather to illustrate various approaches to the subject-area, and to suggest possible future directions.

11   I do not mean to imply that family law is always coherent in its form and content, but merely that it is now treated as meriting separate study and research. It could be argued that its relative youth has aided the development

of socio-legal approaches, since there has been no long-established 'black letter' tradition to dominate and define the field of study.

12   See, Hoggett, *ibid*, (1992).

13   Now contained in the Matrimonial Causes Act 1972.

14   See Deech *ibid*, (1990), and the response from Eekelaar and Maclean (1990), "Divorce Law and Empirical Studies - A Reply", 106 *Law Quarterly Review*, 621. See also, *post*, Conclusions.

15   The latter study drew upon earlier work done at the Oxford Centre by Barrington Baker *et al*, *The Matrimonial Jurisdiction of Registrars*, (1977) in order to analyse the attitudes of District Judges towards ancillary relief applications. Again, this work emphasises the longitudinal nature of much family law research, and also the need for continuity. The study, which consisted of a series of semi-structured interviews with District Judges, aimed to replicate the 1977 study, and the interviews were again carried out by Barrington Baker. Eekelaar states that *Regulating Divorce* (1991) looked at the *official* version of what law seeks to achieve, and thus complements Eekelaar and Maclean *Maintenance After Divorce* (1986), which examined the principles under which economic resources should be reallocated in the light of the realities of that reallocation.

16   The importance of such contacts has been emphasised by both Gwynn Davis and John Eekelaar.

17   Even within this study, however, law is placed at the forefront, so that non-litigated outcomes, for example, are not considered. The three year study drew the sample of litigants from the listing of ancillary relief applications. As the authors acknowledged, this led to an underrepresentation of those divorce cases which did *not* end in ancillary relief applications - i.e. negotiated settlements. This may not be a crucial factor, but in their own research, 5 of the 7 cases which *were* taken from divorce stage (the attempt to derive all cases from this stage was abandoned) did *not* end in ancillary relief application - so perhaps the study is unrepresentative of many divorcing couples' experiences? Obviously, methodological problems make identifying the factors involved in early negotiated settlements very difficult (as the authors discovered), but it does seem that room exists for exploring informal settlements.

18   See also M. Maclean, *Surviving Divorce*, (1991) (providing international comparative accounts of post-divorce finances) and C. Smart and S. Sevenhuijsen (eds.), *Child Custody and the Politics of Gender*, (1989).

19   Clearly one of the Government's main intentions in the introduction of the Child Support Act 1991 was to save money by removing child support from the ambit of the courts, hence saving court time as well as Legal Aid fees. See Garnham and Knights, *Putting the Treasury First: The Truth About Child Support*, (1994), Maclean, "The Making of the Child Support Act of 1991: Policy Making at the Intersection of Law and Social Policy" (1994) 21 *Journal of Law and Society*, 4, 505.

20   This trend has been notable for many years in the area of welfare law.

21   There is room for discretion in some parts of the Act, but this is limited. Other aspects of post-divorce finances will still remain within the jurisdiction of the

court, however. These areas primarily comprise spousal support, property transfers, and lump sum payments.

22 Work is already in progress examining the impact of the Child Support Act 1991. Anecdotal evidence, at least, combined with the high non-compliance rates of 'caring parents' under the CSA, seem to suggest that a 'black legal economy' is being created, where cash settlements are made by 'absent parents' in exchange for non-compliance with the CS Agency by the 'caring parent' - the incentive being that any 'caring parent' currently supported by welfare benefits is unlikely to receive any net benefit as a result of the legitimate payment of child support because of the 100% 'clawback' rule.

23 It could be argued that the Child Support Act 1991 represents the materialisation of Foucault's (criminological) 'dispersal of discipline' thesis within family law. See J. Donzelot, *The Policing of Families*, (1980).

24 Much research in the area of child law also concentrates upon the use of discretion: by the court when making decisions based upon the welfare principle, and by local authorities when making decisions about child protection.

25 See, for instance, M. Murch and D. Hooper, *The Family Justice System*, (1992).

26 The White Paper, *Looking to the future: mediation and the ground for divorce*, (1995) (Cm 2799), proposes that the current law will be replaced with a no-fault divorce law which settles the ground for divorce as irretrievable breakdown of the relationship to be demonstrated by a one year period for 'consideration and reflection'. The scope for judicial intervention will be reduced, and it is envisaged that most divorcing couples will negotiate the financial arrangements during the one year period, thus reducing the number of court orders made.

27 As with the Child Support Act 1991, one of the key motivations for change is the desire to save money by reducing the role of legal professionals in the process, thus cutting the growing Legal Aid bill.

28 Further divorce reform will also have ramifications for the teaching of family law: textbooks and courses still usually include a fairly substantial section on the 'five facts' upon which divorce can be based - in practice this law is already mostly irrelevant, but will be entirely superseded in the event of the White Paper becoming law. This will create a 'gap' in syllabus and textbook which should allow space to discuss more socio-legal concerns, in particular heralding a move away from the legal basis of divorce research and teaching, towards a closer exploration of mediation, conciliation, and non-legally regulated power relations within relationships.

29 For research examining and critiquing the claims and work of the mediation movement, see, for instance, Conciliation Project Unit (University of Newcastle), *Report to the Lord Chancellor on the Costs and Effectiveness of Conciliation in England and Wales*, (1989), Gwynn Davis, *Partisans and Mediators*, (1988), Dingwall & Eekelaar (eds), *Divorce Mediation and the Legal Process*, (1988), Christine Piper, *The Responsible Parent*, (1993), and Dingwall & Greatbatch, "The Virtues of Formality", in Eekelaar and Maclean (eds) *A Reader on Family Law* (1994).

30   *Ibid.*

31   Dingwall and Greatbatch have used conversation analysis to analyse the mediation interview in depth.

32   Christine Piper's study, *The Responsible Parent*, (1993) also draws attention to the dangers of 'forced consensus' in the context of mediation involving parents. Socio-legal scholars have long criticised the dissonance between adverserialism and family disputes, but Piper argues that mediation can simply hide dissent and inequality beneath the veneer of coerced consensus, whereby parties are encouraged to see value in their spouse's position, and reach a compromise which may be in no-one's interest.

33   See, further, the exchanges between Marian Roberts and Dingwall and Greatbatch about the role of power, formality, and negotiation in mediation commencing with, M. Roberts "Who is in charge? Reflections on recent research on the role of the mediator" (1992) *Journal of Social Welfare and Family Law* 372, and R. Dingwall and D. Greatbatch, "Who is in charge? Rhetoric and evidence in the study of mediation" (1993) *Journal of Social Welfare and Family Law* 367.

34   D.H.S.S., *Review of Child Care Law* (1985).

35   D.H.S.S., *ibid*, at p 2. See, for example, Dingwall and Eekelaar, *Care or Control?*, (1981), Masson, "The Use of Wardship by Local Authorities", (1989) 52 *Modern Law Review*, 762, and Hilgendorf, *Social Workers and Solicitors in Child Care Cases*, (1981).

36   Domestic violence is another area which links social policy with socio-legal studies, see, for instance, R. E. Dobash and R. P. Dobash, *Women, Violence and Social Change*, (1992).

37   L. Fox Harding, *Perspectives in Child Care Policy*, (1991), S. Millham et al, *Lost in Care*, (1986), J. Thoburn, *Child Placement: principles and practice*, (1988), N. Parton, *The Politics of Child Abuse*, (1985), R. Thorpe, "The Experiences of Children and Parents Living Apart" in J. Triseliotis (ed.) *New Developments in Foster Care and Adoption*, (1980).

38   See A. Mitchell, *Children in the Middle*, (1985), M. Richards, *Post-Divorce Arrangements for Children: A Psychological Perspective*, (1982), Burgoyne and Clark, *Making A Go of It*, (1984).

39   See A. James and W. Hay, *Court Welfare in Action*, (1993), S. Maidment, *Child Custody and Divorce*, (1985), S. Seale, *Children in Divorce: A Study of Information Available to the Scottish Courts on Children Involved in Divorce Actions*, (1984), M. Dodds, "Children and Divorce", (1983), *Journal of Social Welfare and Family Law*, 228, M. Murch, (1980), *ibid*, J. Eekelaar and E. Clive, *Custody After Divorce*, (1977).

40   See, for instance, C. Grace, *Social Workers, Children and the Law*, (1994), Wattam, *Making a Case in Child Protection*, (1991), L. Lambert, M. Buist, Triseliotis, M. Hill, *Freeing Children for Adoption* (1990).

41   Perhaps an explanation for such divisions may be found within the literature on professionalisation, rather than within social policy or socio-legal studies.

42   Millham et al, *ibid*, (1986).

43   M. Richards, "Divorcing Children: Roles for Parents and the State", in J. Eekelaar and M. Maclean, *ibid*, (1994).

44   King and Trowell's research also, however, points to the disciplinary and discursive clashes which are occurring within the area of children's welfare, as psychiatry, law, and sociology compete to define the ideology of children's upbringing. Socio-legal researchers must examine the competing claims of these disciplines, and extend their traditional scepticism about law's claims to those made on behalf of other disciplines.

45   See the trilogy culminating in J. Goldstein, A. Freud, A. Solnit, and S. Goldstein, *In the Best Interests of the Child*, (1986); *cf.* M. Richards, *ibid*, (1982).

46   This issue also touches upon the public/private divide which has been a key issue in feminist socio-legal research.

47   See R. Dingwall, J. Eekelaar, T. Murray, *The Protection of Children: state intervention in family life*, (1983), and C. Grace, *ibid*, (1994).

48   M.D.A. Freeman, *ibid* (1985); *cf*, J. Eekelaar, "What is 'Critical' Family Law?", (1989) 108 *Law Quarterly Review* 244.

49   Deech *ibid*, (1990).

50   Early socio-legal research pre-dating the Divorce Reform Act 1969.

51   Was used to suggest, erroneously, that divorce reform would not lead to a massive increase in the number of divorce petitions. See Law Commission, *The Field of Choice*, (1966) and Wimperis, *The Unmarried Mother and Her Child*, (1960).

52   'Socio-legal researchers need... to make explicit the values which inform their thinking'. *Ibid*, at 627.

53   They also state that, 'exposure of values to critical argument may not entirely eliminate the danger that [the author's] values might distort the collection and presentation of data' (p. 629).

54   Eekelaar and Maclean (eds.) *ibid*, (1994), 2.

55   See, for instance, M. King and C. Piper, *How the Law Thinks About Children* (1990), and M. King, "Law's Healing of Children's Hearings: The Paradox Moves North", (1995) 24 *Jnl Soc. Pol.* 315.

56   There has been a vast amount of research on the issue of children's rights and the law, see, for instance, Eekelaar, "The Emergence of Children's Rights" (1986), 6 *Oxford Journal of Legal Studies* 161.

57   We may, of course, wish to disagree on the theories which King applies to child law, but that very disagreement can encourage a clearer understanding of what researchers are attempting to achieve in this area.

58   See. A. Hunt, "Governing the socio-legal project: or what do research councils do?" (1994) 21 *Journal of Law and Society*, 520.

59   Michael King has persuasively argued that the best socio-legal research has traditionally been produced from researcher-driven, rather than funder-driven work. M. King, letter to Socio-Legal Studies Association Newsletter, Spring 1995.

60   Shifts in the nature and direction of funding are already taking place. The ending of core ESRC funding of the Oxford Centre for Socio-Legal Studies may prove particularly significant for socio-legal family law, since a large amount of research in the family/law field has emanated from the Centre over the past twenty years. The ESRC review of socio-legal research may also

reduce the funding available for family/law research if the consultation paper's suggested move towards civil justice is adopted (see Phil Thomas, Chapter One, *infra*).

61   The long period of ESRC core funding for the Oxford Centre for Socio-Legal Studies has now ended, and it seems unlikely that such support will be offered to another institution in the immediate future. Whilst the concentration by the ESRC upon the Oxford Centre has been criticised (see A. Hunt, *ibid*, (1994)) a shift towards funding for individual research projects may well increase the tendency towards funder-driven research.

62   There is currently a four year period between successive Research Assessment Exercises, in the course of which academics must publish at least four major pieces of research.

63   See R. Collier, *Masculinity, Law and the Family* (1995), on the construction of images of masculinity within the family. Note also, the political scramble for moral highground leading up to the general election in 1997.

64   But see, Maclean, Eaton, & Eekelaar, "Old and at Home: the legal framework, policy imperatives and individual choices which affect the way people manage their property after retirement" (1992) *Journal of Social Welfare and Family Law*, 296, and Finch, Masson, Mason, Haynes & Wallis, *Wills, Inheritance and the Family* (1995).

65   Some of the issues which may need to be addressed are abuse of the elderly by carers, property rights of the elderly (particularly those whose property is sold to pay for their care), and autonomy decisions, including medico-legal issues such as euthanasia, and consent to treatment.

66   The Law Commission's role in promoting family law reform was highlighted at the beginning of this paper (*supra*). It will doubtless continue to be influential, but with the appointment of Brenda Hoggett, previously Family Law Commissioner, to the bench (where she sits as Mrs Justice Hale), there is no longer a Law Commissioner whose primary interests are in the area of family law. It may well also be the case that after the upheaval of the Children Act 1989, the Child Support Act 1991, and of the forthcoming divorce reforms, family law may enjoy a period of comparative legislative calm, but recent history does not suggest that this is likely.

67   See, *supra*, on divorce, child support, and child welfare.

68   Eekelaar and Maclean (eds), *ibid*, (1994), p. 2.